withdrawn

J.B. PRIESTLEY

GARLAND REFERENCE LIBRARY
OF THE HUMANITIES
(VOL. 145)

J.B. PRIESTLEY,
An Annotated Bibliography

Alan Edwin Day
Head, Department of Library and Information Studies,
Manchester Polytechnic

with a foreword by
J.B. Priestley

GARLAND PUBLISHING, INC. • NEW YORK & LONDON
1980

Library of Congress Cataloging in Publication Data

Day, Alan Edwin.
   J. B. Priestley, an annotated bibliography.

   (Garland reference library of the humanities)
   Includes indexes.
    1. Priestley, John Boynton, 1894–   —Bibliography.
I. Title.
Z8713.535.D39 [PR6031.R6]   016.828′912′09
ISBN 0-8240-9798-X   78-68251

Printed on acid-free, 250-year-life paper
Manufactured in the United States of America

CONTENTS

FOREWORD

It is a pleasure to see this carefully prepared and comprehensive bibliography of my work, and Mr. Day has obviously spent a great deal of time and trouble on it. His researches have recalled work that I had even forgotten about myself, and it makes a clear and interesting record which should answer many of the questions I am asked in correspondence from all over the world. I feel that the bibliography will be of considerable value to the serious student, and equally helpful to the casual reader who simply wishes to know something of what I have written.

J.B. PRIESTLEY

PREFACE

John Boynton Priestley was born the son of a Bradford schoolmaster in September 1894. At a very early age his talents as a writer began to emerge: 'I began writing when I was a small boy at school. My greatest enterprise was a magazine entirely written (in every sense of the word) by myself. Only one copy of each number was produced, and the subscription was one halfpenny for a look at two numbers. As a matter of fact I never got any further than the second number, and even that, if I remember rightly, was a rather scrappy affair. I do not think my powers of composition failed me. I was defeated by the labour of copying everything out in a fair round hand. The first number, however, was a prodigious performance, for not only did it contain editorial notes, sporting chat, and a competition, but also the first instalments of no less than four serial stories . . . ' ('How I Began', *Daily News*, 18 June 1927).

Clearly, even then there were unmistakable signs of his abundant versatility and prolific output. At the age of forty he himself noted: 'I suddenly saw that I too had been very versatile, and indeed, in a writing life not a third as long as theirs, had chopped and changed and splashed about just as much as they had. I had written literary criticism, dramatic criticism, and even (God help me!) musical criticism. I had published books of essays, criticism, two biographies, novels both long and short, travel of a kind, and plays. I had made frequent and maddening appearances, in anthologies, collections, volumes of examples for the young, and the like, as an essayist, a novelist, a short-story writer, a dramatist, a sociologist, and even as a poet. I have contributed to encyclopaedias and I have written films. . . . Even the things I had not written—historical dramas in blank verse, thoughts from my garden, impudent accounts of the private lives of fellow authors, lying records of distant and dubious travel—were to my credit' ('Introduction' to *Four-in-Hand*). And, three years later, 'I have a restless nature, easily bored, and so I flit from one kind of work to another, partly sustained by a very genuine interest in the technical problems of all forms of writing. I have always wanted vaguely to be an all-round man of letters on the 18th Century plan, which allowed or commanded a man to write essay or poem, novel or play, just as he pleased' (*Midnight on the Desert*).

In recent years Priestley has acknowledged that he might have done better to have been more ambitious, more prepared to plan his work, less ready to pursue every new idea, no matter how exciting it appeared at the time. He has certainly become disenchanted with the 'all-round man of letters' concept: 'Looking back, I realize now that while I have had a fair number of enemies, I myself have been the worst of them. I have written too much, far too much for my own good. For years I have been standing in my own light, overshadowing my better self ... time after time I have been described—with no malice intended—as a *man of letters*, who has occasionally produced plays and novels, probably mediocre letters-man jobs. Now I declare emphatically that I take no pride whatever in being called a *man of letters*—ugh!—a term applied, especially in my younger days, to any number of book-sodden dreary old hacks' (*Instead of the Trees*). But it may be that his countless thousands of readers, as opposed to a few literary critics, will rest content that he has allowed his fertile imagination full rein and has not restrained his fascination and deep involvement in the mysteries of the literary craft.

My intention in this bibliography is to record the first publication of every piece of Mr. Priestley's writing, in book or serial form, and to indicate its subsequent publication in collected volumes. Rightly, or wrongly, the emphasis is on ephemeral and fugitive items culled from newspapers, journals and magazines of every description rather than on the bibliographical minutiae of different shades of cloth, cancelled leaves or misplaced semicolons. In all truth, Priestley's books do not readily lend themselves to this sort of treatment, and it would be artificial in the extreme to present them in this way. But sufficient collation details, resembling those to be found on library catalogue cards, have been included to identify the size and format of a book and, in the case of Priestley's introductions, prefaces, etc., to other men's books, to indicate the length of his contribution. I have also included significant reprints of his early essays and criticism and all subsequent editions that contain new material, like those in the Everyman Library, for instance, but not straightforward reprints or paperback editions of the novels. Brief annotations have been added whenever appropriate.

I have personally inspected, with very few exceptions, every item in this bibliography. In some instances, reviews in the early issues of *Book Society News* in particular, it has not been possible to include as full a reference as I would have wished.

It is customary to end a preface of this sort by acknowledging one's debts to all manner of people and institutions, but it really would be impossible to name here all those libraries which afforded me the hospitality of their collections, or which patiently answered my letters in full. To Mr. Tony Yablon, a fellow Priestley enthusiast and collector, who has never spared his encouragement and support, I owe a special word of thanks, as I do, of course, to Mr. Priestley, not only for consenting to write a foreword to this bibliography, but also for putting up with my constant interruptions of his time over a period of years.

'His admiring bibliographers would seem to have restored the balance of being incredibly diligent, by laboriously collecting and cataloguing every trifle he wrote. These people seem to me as fantastic as creatures from the moon. . . . The bibliographer so gravely proud of his dates and title-pages, so triumphant when, after years of inquiry, he produces some scrap of writing or other that his author probably wished off the face of the earth, I can vaguely respect because he is at once passionately industrious and selfless, but he seems as strange as an alchemist. . . .

'I have not a word to say in this place or in any other, against this young novelist, but for the life of me I cannot understand why anyone should have gone to the trouble of noting all the details of his books, size and binding and number of pages, and all the rest of it'.

J.B. Priestley
'The Bibliophiles'
Saturday Review, 20 November 1926

A. BOOKS AND PAMPHLETS

A1   THE CHAPMAN OF RHYMES
London, Alexander Moring Ltd., 1918
44p. 19cm. sd.

Note: The circumstances surrounding this publication are
outlined in Frank Hollings' Catalogue No 184 (1933)
quoted in J.T. Winterich's 'Et tu, Priestley?', *Saturday
Review of Literature,* 25 November 1933: 'The author's
first book, suppressed and destroyed by his order before
publication and entirely unrecorded. Written in the
flush of growing manhood whilst serving as a lieutenant
in the Devonshire Regiment during the Great War, the
author's cooler judgement seems to have prevailed when
he saw his effusions in cold print, and in a letter to
the publisher he expressed his dissatisfaction and
ordered that the whole edition should be withdrawn and
destroyed.... The dramatic circumstances of its suppression and the later fame that has come to the author
of 'The Good Companions' combine to make this slim
little volume of verse one of the most desirable and
certainly one of the very rarest of twentieth century
first editions'. Priestley has always been ready to
discuss his work in print but *The Chapman of Rhymes*
never found a mention, not even in his literary reminiscences *Margin Released* (A129), and it was not until
Instead of the Trees (A164) was published in 1977 that
he allowed himself a few brief remarks: 'My very first
book might be said to be without any substance. It was
called *A Chapman of Rhymes*, was a collection of dubious
verse, written in my teens before the First War and sent
to be published, entirely at my own expense, during that
war when I felt, foolishly, I ought to leave something
behind. A little later, still alive and coming to my
senses, I destroyed every copy I could lay hands on, now
well aware of my folly. But only a month or two ago, a
friend sent me a bookseller's catalogue in which this
idiot publication was priced at something over £250.

As an attempt at literature I would value it at well
under 25p but of course there are such men as collectors,
men of means quietly going out of their minds....' It is
interesting to note the discrepancy in the two accounts
of just when exactly *The Chapman of Rhymes* was written
and significant, perhaps, that Priestley himself quotes
its title slightly incorrectly.

A2 BRIEF DIVERSIONS being Tales Travesties and Epigrams
    Cambridge, Bowes & Bowes, 1922.
    60p. 20cm.

'Nearly all these pieces have appeared in the *Cambridge
Review*.... A few travesties and epigrams have been
added, and others have been revised. Many of the tales
were written during the War, many of them while I was in
Flanders...' (Note).

Contents: Note; Tales: The Impossibility of Knowing Every-
one - A Moving Story of Real Life - The True Account of a
Quarrel Between a Man We All Know and a Very Old Family -
At the 'Red Lion,' Rample Street - The Danger of Accepting Gifts While Holding Municipal Office - The Humil-
iating Experience of a Forgotten God - How the Rational
Amusements of the Great Are Limited - The Imprudence of
a Politician in Travelling Further than the Newspapers -
The Wrong World - The Value of a New Point of View - The
Uninvited Guest - How I Met with a Famous Character in
a Cafe - The Mutiny - Death and the Fiddler - The College
of Immortal Fame - The Lonely Soul - The Lost Path - The
Last Glimpse of a Well-Known Figure in Society - Advanced
Thought and the Foolish Idler - The Wonderful View - The
Room of Lost Souls - The Cynicism of Absolute Monarchies -
The Importance of Good Government - The Moral; *Travesties:*
A Dedication for the 'Shropshire Lad' - A Song in the
Manner of Mr Walter de la Mare - AE: The Ineffable Splen-
dour of Thingumbob - Sir Wm Watson: On Receiving an
Edition-de-luxe of Ella Wheeler Wilcox - Professor
Saintsbury: From the History of the Three Blind Mice
(Periods of European Nonsense) - Mr James Stephens:
'Seumas beg again' - A Lecture Not Yet Written or Delivered
by Professor Sir A.T. Quiller-Couch: On the Direct Method
- La Belle Dame Sans Merci: New Style as It Might Possibly
Be Written by Mr Lascelles Abercrombie - The Later Manner
of Mr W.B. Yeats - A Song: Not in the Collected Poems of
Mr Alfred Noyes - From a Great Political Biographical
Drama, 'Bubb Bodington' Not Yet Written by Mr John
Drinkwater; *Epigrams:* The Old Man and the Newspaper - The
Student and His Prelectors; The Operas of Mozart - To an

Indifferent Poet - R.L. Stevenson - To Certain Modern
Theorists - The Author of the Shropshire Lad - The Poetry
of Mr W.B. Yeats - AE - To Professor G.B. Saintsbury -
To the Producer of a Recent Light Musical Entertainment
Who Boasted of Its Cost - The Stout Idealist - Coleridge -
To a Departed Guest - A Very Old Man - The Symphony - Of
a Lady.

A3   PAPERS FROM LILLIPUT
     Cambridge, Bowes & Bowes, 1922.
     vii, 236p.   20cm.

'Some of these essays have appeared in *The London Mercury*,
The Nineteenth Century, *The Outlook*, and *The Cambridge
Review*. Others have been selected from a large number I
contributed (week by week, under the pseudonym of 'Peter
of Pomfret') to the *Yorkshire Observer*. Others again are
the first-fruits of a current series of such things I am
contributing to *The Challenge* under the general title of
'New Papers from Lilliput'....'

Contents: On a Certain Provincial Player - A New Kind of
Fiction - A Mad Shepherd - Audacity in Authorship - In
Praise of the Hyperbole - On Cartomancy - On Being Kind
to the Old - The Dream - On Filling in Forms - Three
Men - The Bogey of Space - A Road to Oneself - The Editor
- On an Old Book of Natural History - On Not Meeting
Authors - The Eternal Cheapjack - Holiday Notes from the
Coast of Bohemia - On a Mouth-Organ - An Apology for Bad
Pianists - A Father's Tragedy - On Getting Off to Sleep -
On Travel by Train - The Peep - On Vulgar Errors - On
Gossip - A Road and Some Moods - On a Certain Contemporary
Essayist - On Life and Lucky Bags - Grigsby: A Record and
an Appreciation - A Paragon of Hosts.

A4   I FOR ONE
     London, John Lane The Bodley Head Limited, 1923.
     viii, 248p.   19cm.

'The following papers, all of which were intended, de-
vised and written for publication in book form, have appeared in the new *Challenge*...' (Note).

Contents: On Beginning - Dixie - On Hating Strangers -
This Unsubstantial Pageant - The Prophets - Haunted - On
Vulgar Optimists - An Ill-Natured Chapter - The Elusive
Letter - An Old Conjurer - In Praise of the Normal Woman -
On Haberdashers - The New Hypocrisy - On Free Speech -
Those Terrible Novelists - Cranks - Song - A Defence of
Dull Company - An Idle Speculation - The Cult of the

Revolver – Toy Balloons – Charles and Emma – All About
Ourselves – A Note on Humpty Dumpty – On Impressing Acquaintances – In the Country – A Coincidence – Charles
Rupert Purvison – A Beetonian Reverie – A Grossly Egotistical Matter.

I FOR ONE
New York, Dodd Mead, 1924.
viii, 248p. 20cm.

I FOR ONE
Freeport (New York), Books for Libraries Press, 1967.
viii, 248p. 22cm.
(Essay Index Reprint Series)

A5   FIGURES IN MODERN LITERATURE
London, John Lane The Bodley Head Limited, 1924.
215p. 22cm.

'All these papers, with the exception of those on Mr
Santayana and Mr Squire, have appeared in the *London Mercury*...' (Note).

Contents: Mr Arnold Bennett – Mr De la Mare – Mr Maurice
Hewlett – Mr A.E. Housman – Mr W.W. Jacobs – Mr Robert
Lynd – Mr George Saintsbury – Mr George Santayana – Mr
J.C. Squire.

FIGURES IN MODERN LITERATURE
New York, Dodd Mead and Company, 1924.
215p. 22½cm.

FIGURES IN MODERN LITERATURE
Freeport (New York), Books for Libraries Press, 1970.
215p. 23cm.
(Essay Index Reprint Series)

FIGURES IN MODERN LITERATURE
St. Clair Shores (Michigan), Scholarly Press, 1970.
215p. 21cm.

A6   THE ENGLISH COMIC CHARACTERS
London, John Lane The Bodley Head, 1925.
276p. 19½cm.

Contents: Bully Bottom – Touchstone – The Illyrians –
Falstaff and His Circle – Parson Adams – The Brothers
Shandy – Mr Collins – Prince Seithenyn – The Two Wellers
– Dick Swiveller – Mr Micawber.

Note: A limited edition of 70 copies was signed by the
author.

THE ENGLISH COMIC CHARACTERS
New York, Dodd Mead, 1925.
276p. 19½cm.

THE ENGLISH COMIC CHARACTERS
London, Bodley Head, 1963.
xiii, 242p. 19cm.
Note: Includes a new introduction by J.B. Priestley,
   pp. viii-xiii.

THE ENGLISH COMIC CHARACTERS
New York, Phaeton Press, 1972.
xiii, 242p. 20cm.

A7 GEORGE MEREDITH
London, Macmillan and Co, Limited, 1926.
vii, 204p. 19cm.
(English Men of Letters Series edited by J.C. Squire)

GEORGE MEREDITH
New York, The Macmillan Company, 1926.
vi, 204p. 18cm.

GEORGE MEREDITH
St. Clair Shores (Michigan), Scholarly Press, 1970.
vi, 204p. 21cm.

A8 ESSAYS OF TO-DAY AND YESTERDAY J.B. PRIESTLEY
London, George G. Harrap & Co. Ltd., 1926.
62p. bibliog. 17cm.

Contents: Introductory Note (initialled F.H.P.) - A Mad
Shepherd - On Cartomancy - On Being Kind to the Old - On
Man's Extravagance - A Curious Grumble - On Doing Nothing
- This Insubstantial Pageant - The Prophets - A Beetonian
Reverie - A Road to Oneself - Bibliography.

Note: A limp cloth cover edition was also published.

A9 TALKING Being One of a Series of Essays Entitled: These
   Diversions
London, Jarrolds Publishers London, 1926.
86p. frontis (port) 17cm.

Note: A limited edition of 75 copies with a bookplate by
Donald Freidl was signed by the author. Priestley was
the general editor of the series - other titles were
Dreaming (Walter de la Mare); *Wandering* (Hilaire Belloc);
Reading (Hugh Walpole); *Playgoing* (James Agate); and
Idling (Robert Lynd).

TALKING   An Essay
New York, Harper & Bros, 1926.
82p. frontis (port)   20cm.
Note: In the United States 'These Diversions' was known
    as 'The Pleasures of Life' series.

A10   ADAM IN MOONSHINE
London, William Heinemann Ltd, 1927.
vii, 293p.   19cm.

Note: 'My first novel, Adam in Moonshine, was all fine
writing and nonsense, a little coloured trial balloon....
It was published in America, where it was an immediate
and complete failure' (*Margin Released*).

ADAM IN MOONSHINE
New York, Harper & Bros, 1927.
303p.   20cm.

ADAM IN MOONSHINE - BENIGHTED
London, William Heinemann Ltd, 1932.
xiv, 352p.   20cm.
(The Works of J.B. Priestley)
Note: pp v-viii 'Introduction' by J.B. Priestley.

A11   OPEN HOUSE   A Book of Essays
London, William Heinemann Ltd, 1927.
viii, 197p.   19cm.

Contents: Home from the Sea - In Crimson Silk - The Berk-
shire Beasts - Dissolution in Haymarket - The Toy Farm -
Doubting It - At a Concert - Not Having the Tourist Mind -
On Overlooking Covent Garden - Ideas in April - Peacock
Pie - Monologue on a Blunderer - A Young Man of Promise -
Having Covered the Card Table - American Notes - My
Revue - Autolycus Again - Sutcliffe and I - Midsummer
Day's Dream - Calling on the Vicar - Different Inside -
The Pessimists - First Nights - A Voluntary Exile -
Parties - The Sacred Bad Temper - The Inn of the Six
Anglers - High, Low, Broad - Youth in Disguise - A Film
Actor - Having Sold the Piano - The Scrap Screen - Open
House.

OPEN HOUSE   A Book of Essays
New York, Harper & Bros, 1927.
201p.   21cm.

A12   THOMAS LOVE PEACOCK
London, Macmillan & Co, Limited, 1927.
viii, 215p.   19cm.
(English Men of Letters Series edited by J.C. Squire)

THOMAS LOVE PEACOCK
New York, The Macmillan Company, 1927.
viii, 215p. 18cm.

THOMAS LOVE PEACOCK Introduced by J.I.M. Stewart
London, Macmillan; New York, St. Martin's Press, 1966.
xxviii, 215p. 19½cm.

THOMAS LOVE PEACOCK
St. Clair Shores (Michigan), Scholarly Press, 1970.
viii, 215p. 22cm.

A13 BENIGHTED
London, William Heinemann Ltd, 1927.
304p. 19½cm.

Note: 'In America it had a very different history. My
American publishers, presumably determined to make a
little money out of one of my books or perish in the
attempt, promptly abandoned my title ... and with the
title any pretensions the book might have had to be a
psychological or philosophical novel. They called it
The Old Dark House and brought it out as a thriller.
So disguised, it had a very good sale indeed, easily
the best that any book of mine had had, either here or
in America, up to that date' (Introduction to *Adam in
Moonshine - Benighted*, 1932).

THE OLD DARK HOUSE
New York, Harper & Bros, 1928.
269p. 19½cm.

Note: The first edition had 'a thin paper seal round
the last few pages, with a message on it informing the
reader that if he could stop reading at that point and
return the book, he would get his money back from the
dealer' (John Tebbel: *A History of Book Publishing in
the United States. Vol. III: The Golden Age Between
Two Wars 1920-1940*, New York, Bowker, 1978).

ADAM IN MOONSHINE - BENIGHTED
London, William Heinemann Ltd, 1932
xiv, 352p. 20cm.
(The Works of J.B. Priestley)
Note: pp v-viii 'Introduction' by J.B. Priestley

A14 THE ENGLISH NOVEL
London, Ernest Benn Limited, 1927.
80p. bibliog. 17cm. Pbk.
(Benn's Sixpenny Library No 87)

THE ENGLISH NOVEL
London, Ernest Benn Limited, 1931.
v, 7-155p. bibliog. 17½cm.
(Benn's Essex Library)

THE ENGLISH NOVEL With 18 Portraits
London, New York, Thomas Nelson and Sons, 1935.
vii, 160p. frontis (port). 16cm.
Note: 'New illustrated edition revised and reset through-
    out'.

THE ENGLISH NOVEL
St. Clair Shores (Michigan), Scholarly Press, 1971.
155p. 22cm.
Note: Reprint of 1931 Essex Library edition.

A15 APES AND ANGELS A Book of Essays
London, Methuen & Co. Ltd, 1928.
viii, 231p. 17½cm.

Contents: The Flower Show - Thick Notebooks - T'Match -
Other People's Accomplishments - The Port - The Two and
Fourpenny Fairyland - First Snow - The New Diary - The
Wicked People - The Dark Hours - Hats - Reminiscences
of Travel - Too Many People - Houses - Stierism - At the
Circus - Servants - Seeing Stratford - Photographs - A
Hostless Visit - Mr Pickwick Returns - Variety - The
Strange Outfitter - Atlantis - The School Magazine -
Insects - A London Hotel - The Artist - Our Theatre -
The Man with the Flare - All the News.

APES AND ANGELS A Book of Essays
London, Library Press, 1972?
viii, 231p. 18cm.
(Minerva Edition of Modern Authors)

Published in the United States as:

TOO MANY PEOPLE and Other Reflections
New York, Harper & Bros, 1928.
224p. 20cm.

TOO MANY PEOPLE and Other Reflections
Freeport (New York), Books for Libraries Press, 1971.
224p. 23cm.
(Essay Index Reprint Series)

A16 FARTHING HALL by Hugh Walpole and J.B. Priestley
London, Macmillan & Co Limited, 1929.
275p. 19½cm.

Note: 'The story was told in letters exchanged between

a middle-aged scholar and an enthusiastic young man. Though I was neither middle-aged nor a scholar, this was the role I preferred, leaving eager youth and ro- mance to Walpole' (*Margin Released*).

FARTHING HALL   by Hugh Walpole and J.B. Priestley Garden City (New York), Doubleday, Doran & Co Inc, 1929. 319p.   20cm.

A17   ENGLISH HUMOUR
London, Longmans Green and Co, 1929.
xii, 180p.   18cm.
(The English Heritage Series edited by Viscount Lee of Fareham and J.C. Squire)
Contains an introduction by Stanley Baldwin.

ENGLISH HUMOUR
Folcroft (Pa), Folcroft Library Editions, 1973.
xi, 180p.   22cm.

A18   THE GOOD COMPANIONS
London, William Heinemann Ltd, 1929.
viii, 640p.   22cm.

Note: 'There are three states of this book. Copies of each state were issued on the day of publication and there is no priority of issue of one over the other. *State* 1. The text on page 66 is perfect. *State* 2. Page 66, line 17, the word "ordinary" is lacking. *State* 3. The word has been replaced, but is slightly out of position' (Percy Muir: *Points 1874-1930 being extracts from a bibliographer's note-book*, Constable, 1931).   The story of how *The Good Companions* came to be written is well told in 'J.B. Priestley and *The Good Companions*', *Strand Magazine*, April 1930; in his introduction to the 'Collected' edition of 1931; and in *Margin Released*.   Alan Day's 'The Golden Gusher', *New Library World*, 80 (950), August 1979: 156-157, may also be of interest.

THE GOOD COMPANIONS
New York, Harper & Bros, 1929.
viii, 640p.   22cm.

THE GOOD COMPANIONS
London, William Heinemann Ltd, 1931.
xvi, 646p.   20½cm.
(The Works of J.B. Priestley)
Note: pp ix-xii 'Introduction' by J.B. Priestley; pp. xiii-xvi contain list of characters not included in any other edition.

A19   THE BALCONINNY and Other Essays
      London, Methuen & Co, Ltd, 1929.
      vi, 214p.   17½cm.

      Contents: The Balconinny – My Debut in Opera – Mr Punch
      – The Disillusioned – Carless at Last – The Skipper – In
      Defence of Kindness – The Tiger – Little Tich – Lectures –
      My Forchern – The Cards – A Fish in Bayswater – Crumpy –
      The Dickens Fayre – Commercial Interlude – Residential –
      At a Dance – Just After Christmas – Code Idder Head – In
      Barsetshire – The Bibliophiles – At the Verdun Film –
      Lord Mayor Unvisited – Among the Cooks – Super Super –
      A New Tobacco – A Vanished Lodging – Modes – On View –
      Out of It.

      THE BALCONINNY
      New York, Harper & Bros, 1930.
      235p.   20cm.
      Note: Lacks the subtitle of Methuen edition.

      THE BALCONINNY
      Freeport (New York), Books for Libraries Press, 1969.
      vi, 235p.   23cm.
      (Essay Index Reprint Series)

A20   THE TOWN MAJOR OF MIRAUCOURT
      London, William Heinemann Ltd, 1930.
      31p.   illus.   22cm.

      Note: Published only in a limited edition of 525
      copies, signed by the author, printed on vellum, and
      presented in a slip-case.   Later included in *Four-in-
      Hand*, 1934 (A34).

A21   ANGEL PAVEMENT
      London, William Heinemann Ltd, 1930.
      xiv, 613p.   22cm.

      Note: A limited edition of 1025 copies, signed by the
      author, and with his portrait facing the title page,
      was also published.

      ANGEL PAVEMENT
      New York, Harper & Bros, 1930.
      494p.   21½cm.

      ANGEL PAVEMENT
      London, William Heinemann Ltd, 1931.
      xiv, 614p.   20½cm.
      (The Works of J.B. Priestley)
      Note: Pp. (ix–xii) Introduction by J.B. Priestley;

pp. (xiii-xiv) include list of characters not included in any other edition. Pages numbered i-xiv comprise Prologue.

ANGEL PAVEMENT
London, J.M. Dent & Sons Ltd, 1937.
xiv, 460p. 17½cm.
(Everymans Library No 938)
Note: Pp ix-xiii Introduction by J.B. Priestley.

ANGEL PAVEMENT With a Foreword by Sinclair Lewis
New York, The Press of the Readers Club, 1942.
v, 409p. 22cm.

A22 THE LOST GENERATION An Armistice Day Article
London, Peace Committee of the Society of Friends, 1932.
2 leaves 21cm.

Note: Reprinted article from the *Evening Standard*, 11 November 1931.

A23 DANGEROUS CORNER A Play in Three Acts
London, William Heinemann Ltd, 1932.
85p. 19cm.

DANGEROUS CORNER A Play in Three Acts
London, Samuel French Limited, 1933.
76p. plates. 21½cm. Pbk.
(French's Acting Edition No 1361)

Note also:

DANGEROUS CORNER A Novel by Ruth Holland from the Play
    by J.B. Priestley with his cooperation, and a Foreword.
London, Hamish Hamilton, 1932.
285p. 19cm. (B20)

A24 FARAWAY
London, William Heinemann Ltd, 1932.
568p. 22cm.

Note: The first 25 copies taken from the press were specially bound in Levant Morocco by Henry T Wood Ltd and were published with a pictorial title page by Kenneth Hobson, a pictorial panel on the upper cover, gilt edges, in a card slip-case.

FARAWAY
New York, Harper & Bros, 1932.
450p. 21½cm.

A25 SELF-SELECTED ESSAYS
London, William Heinemann Ltd, 1932.
vii, 319p. 19cm.

'More than half the essays in this collection have
never appeared in any volume before, and represent what
seems to me the pick of my more recent contributions to
the *Saturday Review* and the *Week-End Review*. The other
essays have been chosen by me from four volumes, *Papers
from Lilliput*, *I for One*, *Open House*, and *Apes and
Angels...*' (Introduction).

Contents: Introduction - Home from the Sea - A London
Hotel - Caledonian Market - The Ring - Petticoat Lane -
The Magic City - The Underworld - In the British Museum
- Among the Glass Jars - At Popular Prices - At
Thurston's - Davis Cup - Man Underground - The Prophets
- Dissolution in Haymarket - Too Many People - Houses -
The Flower Show - The Inn of the Six Anglers - The Toy
Farm - On the Moors - A Road to Oneself - The Pessimists
- These Our Actors - Mad Make-Belief - Before Opening -
A Mad Shepherd - The Eternal Cheapjack - Strange Encoun-
ter - On Cartomancy - On a New Kind of Fiction - A
Beetonian Reverie - An Apology for Bad Pianists - Polish
Interlude - Oberammergau - Lilac in the Rain - Rhine
Legend - The Shining Graces - Our Bad - The Other
Christmas - Seven Gods - Public Dinners - At the Tailor's
- A Musical Party - A Defence of Dull Company - Sutcliffe
and I - Different Inside - In Crimson Silk - The Berk-
shire Beasts - Having Covered the Card Table - Open
House.

SELF-SELECTED ESSAYS
New York, Harper & Bros, 1933.
vii, 319p. 20cm.

SELF-SELECTED ESSAYS
London, William Heinemann Ltd, 1937.
viii, 319p. 20½cm.
(Works of J.B. Priestley)

SELF-SELECTED ESSAYS
Freeport (New York), Books for Libraries Press, 1968.
vi, 319p. 23cm.
(Essay Index Reprint Series)

A26 WONDER HERO
London, William Heinemann Ltd, 1933.
321p. 19cm.

Note: In addition to a limited edition of 175 copies,
signed by the author, six copies were specially bound
in red morocco gilt.

WONDER HERO
New York, Harper & Bros, 1933.
337p.   21½cm.

A27   THE ROUNDABOUT   A Comedy in Three Acts
London, William Heinemann, 1933.
114p.   19cm.

Note: Not collected in *The Plays of J.B. Priestley.*

THE ROUNDABOUT   A Comedy in Three Acts
London, Samuel French Limited, 1933.
77p.   plates.   21½cm.
(French's Acting Edition No 1189).

A28   ALBERT GOES THROUGH   With Illustrations by Edmund
      Blampied
London, William Heinemann Ltd, 1933.
75p.   frontis, illus.   22cm.

Note: Originally published in *Strand Magazine*, November
1933 (C945).

ALBERT GOES THROUGH   With Illustrations by John Alan
      Maxwell
New York, Harper & Bros, 1933.
94p.   frontis, illus, plates.   20cm.

A29   I'LL TELL YOU EVERYTHING by J.B. Priestley and Gerald
      Bullett
New York, The Macmillan Company, 1932.
264p.   19cm.

I'LL TELL YOU EVERYTHING   A Frolic by J.B. Priestley
      and Gerald Bullett
London, William Heinemann Ltd, 1933.
290p.   19cm.

A30   LABURNUM GROVE   An Immoral Comedy in Three Acts
London, William Heinemann Ltd, 1934.
107p.   19cm.

LABURNUM GROVE   An Immoral Comedy in Three Acts
London, Samuel French Limited, 1935.
159p.   plates, diagrs.   19cm.
(French's Acting Edition No 955)

Note also:

LABURNUM GROVE   The Novel of J.B. Priestley's Famous
   Play and Film by Ruth Holland
London, William Heinemann Ltd, 1936.
250p.   18½cm.

A31   ENGLISH JOURNEY Being a Rambling But Truthful Account
       of What One Man Saw and Heard and Felt and Thought
       During a Journey Through England During the Autumn of
       the Year 1933
       London, William Heinemann Ltd in association with
          Victor Gollancz Ltd, 1934.
       422p. 20cm.

       Note: 'Great English Journey Drive', *The Bookseller*, 11
       April 1934, and 'English Journey a Correction Apology
       to Messrs Gollancz', *The Bookseller*, 18 April 1934,
       discuss the publishing agreement between Heinemann and
       Gollancz. Also of interest are Priestley's comments in
       H.C.S.'s 'A Talk with J.B. Priestley', *The Book Window*,
       Spring 1934: 'This is an exception to my rule. Hitherto
       I have always written what I want to write.... But when
       it was suggested to me that the time is ripe for a book
       which shall deal faithfully with English industrial life
       of today, and that I was the man to write such a book,
       it seemed my duty to undertake it.'

       ENGLISH JOURNEY...
       London, William Heinemann Ltd in association with Victor
          Gollancz Ltd, 1934.
       422p. 19cm.
       Note: This is the Gollancz edition in orange-red boards.
          The previous item was in Heinemann's dark blue.

       ENGLISH JOURNEY...
       New York, Harper & Bros, 1934.
       366p. frontis. plates. 21½cm.

       ENGLISH JOURNEY
       London, William Heinemann Ltd, 1949.
       ix, 422p. 20½cm.
       (The Works of J.B. Priestley)
       Note: Pp vii-ix 'Introduction' by J.B. Priestley;
          pp 419-422 comprise an index to names and places,
          not included in previous editions.

A32   THE DUCHESS THEATRE
       London, Duchess Theatre, 1934 (?).
       4-page leaflet by J.P. Mitchelhill and J.B. Priestley.

A33   EDEN END A Play in Three Acts
       London, William Heinemann, 1934.
       108p. 19cm.

       EDEN END A Play in Three Acts
       London, Samuel French, 1935.
       78p. plates. 21½cm. Pbk.
       (French's Acting Edition No 1693)

A34 FOUR-IN-HAND
London, William Heinemann, 1934.
652p. 20cm.

Contents: A Novel: Adam in Moonshine; *Two Plays:* Laburnum
Grove - The Roundabout; *Stories:* The Town Major of Mirau-
court - Mr Strenberry's Tale - The Demon King - Adventure
- Going Up? - What a Life! - Handel and the Racket - An
Arabian Night in Park Lane - The Taxi and the Star;
Comic Characters: Bully Bottom - The Illyrians - Mr
Micawber; *Places and Travel:* Home from the Sea - Polish
Interlude - Oberammergau - Lilac in the Rain - Rhine
Legend - Our Bad - Mr Golspie Arriving in London - Mr
Smeeth in the City - William at Lugmouth - William Goes
to San Francisco; *Essays:* Fiction Made Easy - Man Under-
ground - The Inn of the Six Anglers - The Berkshire
Beasts - Dissolution in Haymarket - At Popular Prices -
The Toy Farm - Among the Glass Jars - At Thurston's -
On the Moors - Open House - The English Character -
Talking.

A35 DUET IN FLOODLIGHT A Comedy
London, William Heinemann Ltd, 1935.
97p. 19cm.

Note: Not included in *The Plays of J.B. Priestley.*

A36 YOU AND ME AND WAR
London, National Peace Council, 1935.
4p. 22 x 14½cm.

Note: Reprinted from *The Star*, 20 March 1935 (C1017).

A37 CORNELIUS A Business Affair in Three Transactions
London, William Heinemann Ltd, 1935.
103p. 19cm.

CORNELIUS A Business Affair in Three Transactions
London, Samuel French Limited, 1936.
76p. plates, diagrs. 21½cm. Pbk.
(French's Acting Edition No 721)

A38 THE GOOD COMPANIONS A Play in Two Acts by J.B. Priestley
and Edward Knoblock (from the novel by J.B. Priestley)
London, Samuel French Limited, 1935.
x, 91p. plates. 22cm. Pbk.
(French's Acting Edition No 1928)

A39 THREE PLAYS AND A PREFACE
London, William Heinemann Ltd, 1935.
xvi, 305p. 20cm.

(The Works of J.B. Priestley)

Contents: Preface - Dangerous Corner - Eden End - Cornelius.

A40   SPRING TIDE   A Comedy in Three Acts by George Billam
         and Peter Goldsmith
      London, William Heinemann Ltd, 1936.
      103p.   19cm.

      Note: Priestley acted as a 'Play Doctor', reconstructing
      the second and third acts, and writing in some new dia-
      logue.   Not included in *The Plays of J.B. Priestley.*

      SPRING TIDE   A Comedy in Three Acts by George Billam
         and J.B. Priestley
      London, Play Rights and Publications, 1936.
      85p.   plates, diagrs.   21cm.   Pbk.

A41   CHARLES DICKENS
      London, Thomas Nelson, 1936.
      24p.   illus.   16cm.

      Note: The title piece (pp. 3-9) is an extract from the
      revised edition of *The English Novel* (A14).   'Enter Mr
      Pickwick' by John Hampden is also included.   Issued for
      the Pickwick Centenary with the compliments of Thomas
      Nelson and W.H. Smith & Sons Ltd.

A42   BEES ON THE BOAT DECK   A Farcical Comedy in Two Acts
      London, William Heinemann, 1936.
      117p.   19cm.

A43   THEY WALK IN THE CITY   The Lovers in the Stone Forest
      London, William Heinemann Ltd, 1936.
      515p.   20cm.

      THEY WALK IN THE CITY   The Lovers in the Stone Forest
      New York, Harper & Bros, 1936.
      392p.   21cm.

      THEY WALK IN THE CITY
      Westport (Connecticut), Greenwood Press, 1972.
      392p.   22cm.

A44   MIDNIGHT ON THE DESERT   A Chapter of Autobiography
      London, William Heinemann Ltd, 1937.
      312p.   22cm.

      MIDNIGHT ON THE DESERT   Being an Excursion into Auto-
         biography During a Winter in America 1935-36.
      New York, Harper & Brothers, 1937.
      310p.   22cm.

A45   TIME AND THE CONWAYS   A Play in Three Acts
      London, William Heinemann, 1937.
      109p.   19cm.

      TIME AND THE CONWAYS   A Play in Three Acts
      New York, Harper & Bros, 1938.
      109p.   21cm.

      TIME AND THE CONWAYS   A Play in Three Acts
      London, Samuel French Limited, 1939.
      84p.   plates.   21½cm.   Pbk.
      (French's Acting Edition No 116)

A46   MYSTERY AT GREENFINGERS   A Comedy of Detection
      London, Samuel French Limited, 1937.
      122p.   18½cm.   Pbk.

      Note: This play was specially written as a test piece
      for amateur dramatic societies competing in the *News
      Chronicle* Drama Contest 1937-38.   (See 'Reply to Drama
      Contest Critic', *News Chronicle*, 12 July 1937).   First
      edition has 'News Chronicle Contest Edition' on front
      cover.   Not included in *The Plays of J.B. Priestley*.

      MYSTERY AT GREENFINGERS   A Comedy of Detection
      London, Samuel French Limited, 1937.
      113p.   plates.   15½cm.   Pbk.
      (French's Acting Edition No 1037)

A47   I HAVE BEEN HERE BEFORE   A Play in Three Acts
      London, William Heinemann Ltd, 1937.
      107p.   19cm.

      I HAVE BEEN HERE BEFORE   A Play in Three Acts
      New York, Harper & Bros, 1938.
      107p.   21cm.

      I HAVE BEEN HERE BEFORE   A Play in Three Acts
      London, Samuel French Limited, 1939.
      77p.   plates.   22cm.   Pbk.
      (French's Acting Edition No 963)

A48   PEOPLE AT SEA   A Play in Three Acts
      London, William Heinemann Ltd, 1937.
      106p.   19cm.

      Note: First produced at the Bradford Civic Playhouse
      September 1937 under the title *I Am a Stranger Here*.

      PEOPLE AT SEA   A Play in Three Acts
      London, Samuel French Limited, 1938.
      75p.   diagrs.   21½cm.   Pbk.
      (French's Acting Edition No 1072)

A49   TWO TIME PLAYS
      London, William Heinemann Ltd, 1937.
      xiii, 221p. plates. 23cm.

      Contents: Introduction – Time and the Conways – I Have
      Been Here Before.

A50   THE DOOMSDAY MEN   An Adventure
      London, William Heinemann Ltd, 1938.
      312p. map on endpapers. 20cm.

      THE DOOMSDAY MEN   An Adventure
      New York, Harper & Bros, 1938.
      287p. 21½cm.

      THE DOOMSDAY MEN   A Thriller of the Atomic Age
      London, Pan Books, 1949.
      256p. 17½cm. Pbk.
      Note: Lacks the dedication in verse to Dorothy Brooke
        included in the original edition.

A51   WHEN WE ARE MARRIED   A Yorkshire Farcical Comedy
      London, William Heinemann, 1938.
      108p. 19cm.

      WHEN WE ARE MARRIED   A Yorkshire Farcical Comedy
      London, Samuel French Limited, 1938.
      76p. plates. 22cm. Pbk.
      (French's Acting Edition No 717)

A52   JOHNSON OVER JORDAN   The Play and All About It (An Essay)
      London, William Heinemann, 1939.
      144p. plates. 23cm.

      JOHNSON OVER JORDAN   The Play and All About It (An Essay)
      New York, Harper & Bros, 1939.
      144p. plates. 21cm.

      JOHNSON OVER JORDAN   A Modern Morality Play in Three
        Acts
      New York, Samuel French, 1941.
      132p. plates, diagrs. 18½cm.
      (French's Standard Library Edition)
      Note: Acting edition.

A53   RAIN UPON GODSHILL   A Further Chapter of Autobiography
      London, William Heinemann Ltd, 1939.
      331p. 22cm.

      RAIN UPON GODSHILL   A Further Chapter of Autobiography
      New York, Harper & Bros, 1939.
      308p. 22½cm.

A54   LET THE PEOPLE SING
      London, William Heinemann Ltd, 1939.
      418p.   20cm.

      Note: This novel was the first to be commissioned for
      broadcasting by the B.B.C.   Priestley himself read the
      first instalment 3 September 1939.   Guy Fletcher's 'The
      BBC and J.B. Priestley Do Something New', *Radio Times*,
      1 September 1939, and 'Mr Priestley at the Microphone',
      The Listener, 31 August 1939 refer.

      LET THE PEOPLE SING   A Novel
      New York, Harper & Bros, 1940.
      v, 351p.   21cm.

A55   IF I RAN THE B.B.C.
      Washington, National Association of Broadcasters, 194(?).
      8p.   23cm.   sd.

A56   POSTSCRIPTS
      London, William Heinemann Ltd, 1940.
      viii, 100p.   19cm.

      Note: Most of these broadcasts were originally published
      in *Answers Magazine*.   Reprinted in 1968 in the United
      States as *All England Listened* (A144).   W.E. Williams'
      'Aces of the Air', *The Listener*, XXIV (604), 8 August
      1940: 212 is informative.

A57   BRITAIN SPEAKS
      New York, Harper & Brothers, 1940.
      viii, 263p.   21½cm.

      Note: The statement 'This story [sic] is published in
      England under the title of POSTSCRIPTS' printed on the
      title page verso is entirely erroneous.   In fact the
      text consists of radio talks transmitted in 1940 on the
      British Broadcasting Corporation's overseas services.
      The autograph signed inscription on The Humanities Re-
      search Center, University of Texas copy reads: 'This is
      a collection of radio talks I gave - usually at 2.30 am -
      during 1940.   As they were recorded they were trans-
      mitted all over the world - to 80 stations in the U.S. -
      Canada, Australia, New Zealand, South Africa, India etc
      etc.   As these talks were addressed to people overseas,
      this book was not published in Britain.   The royalties
      from this book were given to war charities', p. 27
      J.B. Priestley: An Exhibition of Manuscripts and Books
      (H4).   A few of the talks were printed in *The Listener*.

A58   OUT OF THE PEOPLE
      London, Collins in association with William Heinemann
         Limited, 1941.
      127p. 19cm.
      (Vigilant Books)

      Note: Priestley was a member of the Editorial Committee
      for the Series 'dealing with the problems of reconstruc-
      tion after the war'.

      OUT OF THE PEOPLE
      New York, Harper & Bros, 1941.
      xii, 160p. 21½cm.
      Note: A Preface addressed to American readers was in-
         cluded in this edition.

A59   AN OPEN LETTER TO THE NEW WAR CABINET
      London, 1941 Committee, 1942.
      Single sheet folded.

      Note: Although Priestley's name appears in strict alpha-
      betical order as one of 24 signatories, internal evidence
      suggests it was he who composed it. One paragraph is
      lifted word for word from his article 'Postscript to
      1941', *Reynold's News*, 28 December 1941 (C1293).

A60   BLACK-OUT IN GRETLEY A Story of- and for- Wartime
      London, William Heinemann Ltd, 1942.
      215p. 19cm.

      BLACK-OUT IN GRETLEY A Story of- and for- Wartime
      New York, Harper & Bros, 1942.
      273p. 21cm.

A61   BRITAIN AT WAR
      New York, Harper & Brothers, 1942.
      117p. frontis, illus (inc ports), diagrs, maps. 24cm
         x 19cm.

      published in Canada as:

      BRITAIN FIGHTS
      Toronto, Musson Book Co., 1943.
      64p. illus. 20cm.

      Note: The reduced pagination is accounted for by fewer
      illustrations and by the omission of the frontispiece,
      the list of illustrations, and of the map.

A62   DAYLIGHT ON SATURDAY A Novel About an Aircraft Factory
      London, William Heinemann Ltd, 1943.
      306p. 19cm.

DAYLIGHT ON SATURDAY A Novel About an Aircraft Factory
New York, Harper & Bros, 1943.
280p. 21cm.

A63 BRITISH WOMEN GO TO WAR 49 Colour Photographs by P.G.
Hennell
London, Collins Publishers, 1943.
vi, 7-59p. col plates inc frontis port. 25½cm x 19½cm.

A64 THREE PLAYS
London, William Heinemann, 1943.
x, 216p. 19cm.

Contents: Introduction - Music at Night - The Long Mirror - They Came to a City.

Note: The Long Mirror is not included in *The Plays of J.B. Priestley.*

A65 MANPOWER The Story of Britain's Mobilisation for War
London, His Majesty's Stationery Office, 1944.
60p. illus (inc ports on inside covers). 21cm. sd.

Note: Prepared for the Ministry of Labour and National
Service by the Ministry of Information and published
anonymously.

A66 HERE ARE YOUR ANSWERS
London, Common Wealth, 1944.
20p. bibliog. 21cm. sd.
(No 1 Common Wealth Popular Library)

A67 DESERT HIGHWAY A Play in Two Acts and an Interlude
London, William Heinemann Ltd, 1944.
ix, 46p. 22cm.

DESERT HIGHWAY A Play in Two Acts and One Interlude
London, Samuel French Limited, 1944.
66p. diagr. 21½cm. Pbk.
(French's Acting Edition No 684)

A68 THEY CAME TO A CITY
London, Samuel French Limited, 1944.
68p. plates. 21½cm. Pbk.
(French's Acting Edition No 644)

A69 FOUR PLAYS
London, William Heinemann Ltd, 1944.
viii, 226p. 17cm.

Contents: Introduction - Music at Night - The Long Mirror - They Came to a City - Desert Highway.

Note: The Long Mirror is not included in *The Plays of J.B. Priestley.*

FOUR PLAYS
New York, Harper & Bros, 1944.
viii, 289p. 21½cm.

A70   HOW ARE THEY AT HOME? A Topical Comedy in Two Acts
London, Samuel French Limited, 1945.
84p. plates, diagrs. 21½cm. Pbk.
(French's Acting Edition No 1041)

A71   THREE COMEDIES
London, William Heinemann Ltd, 1945.
vii, 240p. 19cm.

Contents: To James Bridie (v-vii) - Good Night Children - The Golden Fleece - How Are They At Home?

Note: The Golden Fleece was written before the Second World War as *Bull Market.*

A72   GENERAL ELECTION - JULY 1945. ADDRESS FROM J.B.
         PRIESTLEY
Cambridge, Published on behalf of J.B. Priestley (B4 Albany, Piccadilly, W1) by his agent, G.C. Morris, 5 Merton Street, Cambridge, 1945.
4p. 26cm x 19cm.

Note: Priestley's manifesto when he stood for Cambridge University as an Independent Progressive candidate.
His address to the voters takes up two and a half pages, brief career details half a page, and a list of eminent men supporting his candidature appears on the fourth.

A73   THREE MEN IN NEW SUITS
London, William Heinemann Ltd, 1945.
170p. 19cm.

THREE MEN IN NEW SUITS
New York, Harper & Bros, 1945.
217p. 20cm.

THREE MEN IN NEW SUITS
London, The Book Club, 1946.
163p. 19cm.
Note: This edition contains a 'Note by the Author'.

A74 LETTER TO A RETURNING SERVICEMAN
London, Home & Van Thal Ltd, 1945.
32p. 19cm.

Note: E.O. Siepmann's 'Letter to Mr. Priestley from a
Returning Serviceman', *Nineteenth Century and After*,
December 1945, is an interesting reply.

A75 THE SECRET DREAM An Essay on Britain, America and
   Russia
London, Turnstile Press, 1946.
38p. 20cm. Pbk.

Note: 'This essay is based upon broadcasts I made on
three Sundays early this year. Those who heard the talks
will notice that there has been considerable expansion
and some revision of the original material' (opening
sentences).

A76 RUSSIAN JOURNEY
London, Writers Group of the Society for Cultural Relations with the U.S.S.R., 1946.
40p. illus. 17½cm. sd.

Note: First published as six articles in the *Sunday Express*, 18 November–23 December 1945 (C1420–C1425).

A77 BRIGHT DAY
London, William Heinemann Ltd, 1946.
368p. 19cm.

BRIGHT DAY
New York, Harper & Bros, 1946.
286p. 21½cm.

BRIGHT DAY With a New Introduction by the Author
London, J.M. Dent & Sons Ltd; New York, E.P. Dutton,
   1966.
iii–xiv, 368p. 18½cm.
Pp ix–xiii 'Introduction' by J.B. Priestley.

A78 THE NEW CITIZEN
London, Council for Education in World Citizenship, 1946.
12p. illus. 12 x 18cm. sd.

A79 H.G. WELLS
London, Chiswick Press, 1946.
Single sheet folded - text on first three pages.

Note: 'Spoken by J.B. Priestley at Golders Green Crema-
torium on Friday, 16th August, 1946'. First printed as

'Goodbye to our Friend', *News Chronicle*, 17 August 1946
(C1440).

A80   EVER SINCE PARADISE   An Entertainment Chiefly Referring
        to Love and Marriage.   With Music by Dennis Arundell
      London, Samuel French Limited, 1946.
      iii, 90p.   22cm.   Pbk.
      (French's Acting Edition No 2164)

A81   THE ARTS UNDER SOCIALISM   Being a Lecture Given to the
        Fabian Society on WHAT THE GOVERNMENT SHOULD DO FOR
        THE ARTS HERE AND NOW
      London, Turnstile Press, 1947.
      32p.   22cm.   sd.

A82   THEATRE OUTLOOK
      London, Nicholson & Watson, 1947.
      76p.   illus (some col.), maps.   23cm.

A83   AN INSPECTOR CALLS   A Play in Three Acts
      London, William Heinemann, 1947.
      viii, 73p.   19cm.

      Note: Includes 'To Michael Macowan' pp v-viii.

      AN INSPECTOR CALLS   A Play in Three Acts
      London, Samuel French Limited, 1948.
      64p.   plates.   22cm.   Pbk.
      (French's Acting Edition No 338)

A84   JENNY VILLIERS   A Story of the Theatre
      London, William Heinemann Ltd, 1947
      190p.   illus.   22cm.

      JENNY VILLIERS   A Story of the Theater
      New York, Harper & Bros, 1947.
      184p.   21cm.

A85   MUSIC AT NIGHT   A Play
      London, Samuel French Limited, 1947.
      75p.   22cm.   Pbk.
      (French's Acting Edition No 1239)

A86   THE ROSE AND CROWN   A Play in One Act
      London, Samuel French Limited, 1947.
      31p.   diagr.   18cm.   sd.
      (French's Acting Edition No 856)

      Note: Not included in *The Plays of J.B. Priestley.*

A87 THREE TIME PLAYS
London, Pan Books, 1947.
x, 270p. 18cm. Pbk.

Contents: Author's Note for This Edition (pp vii-x) -
Dangerous Corner - Time and the Conways - I Have Been
Here Before.

Note: The original edition was Pan Book No 7 and was
reprinted in 1949. It was reissued as Great Pan No 13
in Pan Book's Famous Play Series in 1952. All three
editions have different pictorial covers.

A88 O ZIVOTE, LITERATURE A POLITICE
Praha, Orbis, 1947.
28p. 21cm. sd.

Contents: Nova Britannie - O zivote, literature a
politice - O Britannii a Ceskoslovensku - Vzkaz delnikum
Titovych zavodu.

A89 THE LONG MIRROR A Play in Three Acts
London, Samuel French Limited, 1947.
71p. plate. 22cm. Pbk.
(French's Acting Edition No 327)

Note: This play was printed in *Three Plays* (A64) and
Four Plays (A69). It was not included in *The Plays of
J.B. Priestley.*

A90 THE LINDEN TREE A Play in Two Acts and Four Scenes
London, William Heinemann, 1948.
91p. 19cm.

THE LINDEN TREE A Play in Two Acts
London, Samuel French Limited, 1948.
84p. plates. 22cm. Pbk.
(French's Acting Edition No 714)

THE LINDEN TREE AND AN INSPECTOR CALLS
New York, Harper, 1948.
90p. vi, 73p. 19cm.

A91 THE GOLDEN FLEECE A Comedy in Three Acts
London, Samuel French Limited, 1948.
71p. 22cm. Pbk.
(French's Acting Edition No 934)

Note: 'The next play, *The Golden Fleece*, is your old
friend *Bull Market*, which was first produced at the
Bradford Civic Playhouse and then afterwards, with

considerable success, at your own Glasgow Citizens
Theatre. I changed the title, somewhat reluctantly,
because I was told that *Bull Market* suggested a rural
and agricultural background and not a satire on high
finance' - dedicatory letter to James Bridie in *Three
Comedies* (A71).

A92   THE HIGH TOBY A Play for the Toy Theatre
      Harmondsworth (Middlesex), Penguin Books Ltd In Associa-
        tion With Benjamin Pollock Ltd, 1948.
      16p. coloured scenery and characters by Doris Zinkeisen
        18½ x 22cm. sd.
      (Puffin Cut-Out Book 5)

A93   THE PLAYS OF J.B. PRIESTLEY VOLUME I
      London, William Heinemann Ltd, 1948.
      xi, 477p. 22cm.

      Contents: Introduction (pp vii-xi) - Dangerous Corner -
      Eden End - Time and the Conways - I Have Been Here
      Before - Johnson Over Jordan - Music at Night - The
      Linden Tree.

      published in the United States as:

      SEVEN PLAYS
      New York, Harper, 1950.
      xi, 477p. 23cm.

A94   THE OLYMPIANS Opera in Three Acts Libretto by J.B.
        Priestley Music by Arthur Bliss
      London, Novello and Co Ltd, 1949.
      75p. 19cm. Pbk.

      Note: Correspondence relating to this opera between
      Bliss and Priestley is printed in the former's *As I
      Remember* (B136). Bryan Fairfax's 'Olympians', *The
      Listener*, 17 February 1972, is also valuable for the
      background to this collaboration.

A95   HOME IS TOMORROW A Play in Two Acts
      London, William Heinemann, 1949.
      xi, 68p. 22cm.

      Note: Includes an introduction (pp vii-xi).

      HOME IS TOMORROW A Play in Two Acts
      London, Samuel French Limited, 1950.
      iii, 80p. 22cm. Pbk.
      (French's Acting Edition No 1655)

A96   DELIGHT
      London, William Heinemann Ltd, 1949.
      x, 267p.   21cm.

      Contents: Preface or the Grumbler's Apology - Fountains -
      Shopping in Small Places - Detective Stories in Bed -
      After Finishing Some Work - Meeting a Friend - Decks in
      Early Morning - A Walking Tour - Trying New Blends of
      Tobacco - Gin and Tonic, 1940 - Smoking as Worship -
      Discovering Tomlinson - And the Marx Brothers - Cosy
      Planning - Getting Out of New York - Buying Music to
      Escape Tune Haunting - Moment During Rehearsal - Sound
      of a Football - Romantic Recognition - Old Photograph -
      Coming Home - Smell of Tahiti - Chamber Music at Home -
      Charades - My First Article - Celebrities at Parties -
      Making Writing Simple - Books and Music in Furnished
      Houses - Shakespeare Rediscovered - The Conductors -
      Theatre Curtains - Fantastic Theories - Smoking in Hot
      Bath - A Bit of Writing - Walk in Pine Wood - Answering
      Back - Manly Talk - Frightening Civil Servants - Fiddling
      While Rome Burns - Family Silliness, Domestic Clowning -
      New Box of Matches - Playing with Small Children -
      Mineral Water in Bedrooms of Foreign Hotels - Coming of
      the Idea - Stereoscope - Seeing the Actors - Sunday
      Papers in the Country - Planning Travel - Metaphysics -
      Early Childhood and the Treasure - Reading in Bed about
      Foul Weather - Having One's Fortune Told - Wood - Comic
      Characters - Money for Nothing - Children's Games -
      Suddenly Doing Nothing - Pleasure and Gratitude of
      Children - Atmosphere of Billiards - Knowing a Poet -
      Giving Advice - Delight in Writing - Not Going - Quietly
      Malicious Chairmanship - Secret Brotherhoods - Cosy
      with Work - Other People's Weaknesses - Bragging -
      Plots - Being Solemn about One's Tastes - Dreams - The
      Ironic Principle - Truth and Fiction - Three Lighthouses
      - This Small World - Discovering Vermeer - Lawn Tennis -
      Not Having to Read Books - Homage to Moszkowski - Locusts
      I Have Known - Being Recognized - First Time Abroad -
      Transport in Films - Streets Like Stage Sets - Nature
      as Last Consolation - China and the Chinese - Preparing
      for Old Age - Moments in the Morning - Orchestras Tuning
      Up - Dancing - Escaping from Time - Bass Voices -
      Blossom - Free Passes - Making Stew - No School Report -
      Seeing the North - After a Concert - Buying Books -
      View from My Study - Reading about the *Pink 'Un* Set -
      Orchestras Creeping into Piano - Cooking Picnics - Be-
      ginning to Cast a Play - Waking to Smell Bacon etc. -
      Sketches of C.J. Holmes - Memoranda Self - Van Hoven -

Solemn Antics of Boyhood - Departing Guests - Timeless
Mornings - Women and Clothes - The Delight That Never
Was - But This Is Where We Came In.

Note: A limited edition of 250 copies was signed by the
author.

DELIGHT
New York, Harper, 1949.
xvi, 170p. 20cm.

DELIGHT
Freeport (NY), Books for Libraries Press, 1971.
xvi, 170p. 23cm.

A97   THE PLAYS OF J.B. PRIESTLEY   VOLUME II
London, William Heinemann Ltd, 1949.
xii, 516p. 22cm.

Contents: Introduction (pp vii-xii) - Laburnum Grove -
Bees on the Boat Deck - When We Are Married - Good Night
Children - The Golden Fleece - How Are They At Home? -
Ever Since Paradise.

THE PLAYS OF J.B. PRIESTLEY   VOLUME II
New York, Harper, 1950.
xii, 516p. 23cm.

A98   GOING UP Stories and Sketches
London, Pan Books Ltd, 1950.
219p. 17½cm. Pbk.

'The selection of stories and sketches for this volume
has been made by the present publishers, not by the
author'.

Contents: Stories: Going Up? - Mr Strenberry's Tale -
The Demon King - Adventure - What a Life! - Handel and
the Racket - An Arabian Night in Park Lane - The Taxi
and the Star; *Sketches:* My Debut in Opera - The Tiger -
My Forchern - The Man with the Flare - A London Hotel -
The Inn of the Six Anglers - On the Moors - Mad Make-
Belief - Public Dinners - Different Inside - In Crimson
Silk - Open House - The Berkshire Beasts - Calling on
the Vicar - The Prophets - An Old Conjurer - A Coinci-
dence.

A99   BRIGHT SHADOW A Play of Detection in Three Acts
London, Samuel French Limited, 1950.
70p. diagr. 22cm. Pbk.
(French's Acting Edition No 835)

Note: Not included in *The Plays of J.B. Priestley.*

A100   SUMMER DAY'S DREAM   A Play in Two Acts
London, Samuel French Limited, 1950.
iv, 72p. plates. 22cm. Pbk.
(French's Acting Edition No 1974)

A101   THE PLAYS OF J.B. PRIESTLEY   VOLUME III
London, William Heinemann Ltd, 1950.
xiv, 476p. 22cm.

Contents: Introduction (pp vii-xiv) - Cornelius -
People at Sea - They Came to a City - Desert Highway -
An Inspector Calls - Home Is Tomorrow - Summer Day's
Dream.

THE PLAYS OF J.B. PRIESTLEY   VOLUME III
New York, Harper, 1952.
xiv, 476p. 23cm.

A102   THE PRIESTLEY COMPANION   A Selection from the Writings
of J.B. Priestley with an Introduction by Ivor Brown
Harmondsworth (Middlesex), Penguin Books In Association
With William Heinemann, 1951.
412p. 18cm. Pbk.

'This book is made up of passages I have selected myself from my novels, essays, pieces of autobiography'
(Author's Note).

Contents: Introduction by Ivor Brown (pp 11-21) -
Author's Note (pp 23-24) - Extracts arranged under
subject headings *viz:* Parties; Pastimes and Pleasures;
Peepshows; People; Persons Pleasing or Peculiar;
Places; Polemical; Postscripts; Proceedings; Purely
Personal.

A103   FESTIVAL AT FARBRIDGE
London, William Heinemann, 1951.
593p. 22cm.

published in the United States as:

FESTIVAL
New York, Harper, 1951.
607p. 22cm.

A104   DRAGON'S MOUTH   A Dramatic Quartet in Two Parts by
Jacquetta Hawkes and J.B. Priestley
London, William Heinemann, 1952.
92p. 19cm.

Note: Not included in *The Plays of J.B. Priestley.*

A105   TRY IT AGAIN   A One Act Play
        London, Samuel French Limited, 1953.
        23p.   diagr.   18cm.   sd.
        (French's Acting Edition No 751)

        Note: Not included in *The Plays of J.B. Priestley.*

A106   MOTHER'S DAY   A Comedy in One Act
        London, Samuel French Limited, 1953.
        20p.   diagr.   18cm.   sd.
        (French's Acting Edition No 748)

        Note: Not included in *The Plays of J.B. Priestley.*

A107   PRIVATE ROOMS   A One Act Comedy in the Viennese Style
        London, Samuel French Limited, 1953.
        28p.   diagr.   18cm.   sd.
        (French's Acting Edition No 746)

        Note: Not included in *The Plays of J.B. Priestley.*

A108   THE OTHER PLACE   And Other Stories of the Same Sort
        London, William Heinemann Ltd, 1953.
        265p.   20½cm.

        'The only story here that has been published in a book
        before is 'Mr Strenberry's Tale' (Author's Note).

        Contents: Author's Note - The Other Place - The Grey
        Ones - Uncle Phil on TV - Guest of Honour - Look After
        the Strange Girl - The Statues - The Leadington Inci-
        dent - Mr Strenberry's Tale - Night Sequence.

        Note: 'The Grey Ones' and 'Uncle Phil on TV' were
        printed in *Lilliput*, April-May 1953 (C1741) while
        'Look After the Strange Girl' appeared in *Collier's
        Magazine*, 9 May 1953 (C2309).

        THE OTHER PLACE   And Other Stories of the Same Sort
        New York, Harper, 1953.
        265p.   20cm.

        THE OTHER PLACE   And Other Stories of the Same Sort
        Freeport (New York), Books for Libraries Press, 1971.
        265p.   21cm.
        (Short Story Index Reprint Series)

A109   TREASURE ON PELICAN   A Play in Three Acts
        London, Evans Brothers Limited, 1953.
        90p.   diagr.   21½cm.   Pbk.

        Note: Not included in *The Plays of J.B. Priestley.*

A110　THE MAGICIANS
　　　London, William Heinemann Ltd, 1954.
　　　256p.　20½cm.

　　　THE MAGICIANS
　　　New York, Harper, 1954.
　　　246p.　22cm.

A111　A GLASS OF BITTER　A Play in One Act
　　　London, Samuel French Limited, 1954.
　　　19p.　diagr.　18½cm.　sd.
　　　(French's Acting Edition No 798)

　　　Note: Not included in *The Plays of J.B. Priestley.*

A112　LOW NOTES ON A HIGH LEVEL　A Frolic
　　　London, William Heinemann Ltd, 1954.
　　　160p.　illus.　22½cm.

　　　LOW NOTES ON A HIGH LEVEL
　　　New York, Harper, 1954.
　　　160p.　21cm.

A113　JOURNEY DOWN A RAINBOW by J.B. Priestley and Jacquetta
　　　　Hawkes
　　　London, Heinemann - Cresset, 1955.
　　　xii, 289p.　22½cm.

　　　Note: In 'Dangerous Journey', *Books and Bookmen*, Octo-
　　　ber 1955 (C1816), Priestley tells 'why the trip was
　　　made and writes about the book ... that resulted from
　　　it'.

　　　JOURNEY DOWN A RAINBOW by J.B. Priestley and Jacquetta
　　　　Hawkes
　　　New York, Harper, 1955.
　　　288p.　22cm.

A114　B.B.C. LIGHT PROGRAMME　J.B. PRIESTLEY FESTIVAL
　　　London, British Broadcasting Corporation, 1955.
　　　8p. including covers.　port. on front cover.　25 x
　　　　20cm.　sd.

　　　Contents: An Appreciation by Richard Church (pp 2-3) -
　　　J.B. Priestley introduces the programmes in notes on
　　　*Dangerous Corner, I Have Been Here Before, When We Are
　　　Married, An Inspector Calls, The Linden Tree, The
　　　Golden Entry, Adam in Moonshine, Angel Pavement*, and
　　　Journey Down a Rainbow (pp 4-6).

　　　Note: 'Why I wrote a play about an art dealer', *Radio
　　　Times*, 25 November 1955 (C1824) refers to *The Golden
　　　Entry*, which remains unpublished.

A115   THE WRITER IN A CHANGING SOCIETY
       Aldington (Kent), Hand and Flower Press, 1956.
       29p.   22cm.
       (Herman Ould Memorial Lectures No 3)

       Note: Included in *Thoughts in the Wilderness* (A119).

A116   ALL ABOUT OURSELVES AND OTHER ESSAYS Chosen and Intro-
             duced by Eric Gillett
       London, William Heinemann Ltd, 1956.
       xvi, 286p.   22cm.

       Contents: Introduction (pp ix-xvi) - On Beginning - The
       Grumbler's Apology - Open House - Three Men - Other
       People's Accomplishments - Lectures - On Not Meeting
       Authors - High, Low, Broad - Those Terrible Novelists -
       The Editor - Making Writing Simple - The Artist - The
       Peep - The Man with the Flare - Cranks - On Hating
       Strangers - On Vulgar Optimists - The Pessimists -
       Parties - A Paragon of Hosts - The Inn of the Six
       Anglers - A London Hotel - Commercial Interlude - A
       Vanished Lodging - Out of It - This Insubstantial Pa-
       geant - A Road and Some Moods - Smell of Tahiti - Lilac
       in the Rain - American Notes - The Skipper - On Over-
       looking Covent Garden - At a Concert - The Disillusioned
       - At the Circus - Little Tich - A Film Actor - Ellen
       Terry (Old Photograph) - Seeing Stratford - The
       Illyrians - Midsummer Day's Dream - Bully Bottom - The
       Dickens Fayre - The Two Wellers - Mr Pickwick Returns -
       Prince Seithenyn - Trying New Blends of Tobacco - Auto-
       lycus Again - An Old Conjurer - First Snow - The Dark
       Hours - In Barsetshire - A Beetonian Reverie - A Note
       on Humpty Dumpty - The Berkshire Beasts - Stereoscope -
       Photographs - My Forchern - All About Ourselves - In
       Crimson Silk - A Fish in Bayswater - The Tiger - The
       Sacred Bad Temper - In Praise of the Normal Woman - The
       Balconinny - Strange Encounter - Introduction to "The
       Good Companions" - Our Theatre - Youth in Disguise -
       Having Sold the Piano - At the Tailors - T'Match - The
       Flower Show - The Toy Farm - Peacock Pie - But This Is
       Where We Came In.

       Note: 'Working with Priestley, Eric Gillett, who
       selected the essays for J.B. Priestley's new book,
       gives his reasons for his choice', *Books and Bookmen*,
       May 1956.

A117   THE SCANDALOUS AFFAIR OF MR KETTLE AND MRS MOON   A
             Comedy in Three Acts
       London, Samuel French Limited, 1956.

62p. plate, diagr. 21½cm. sd.
(French's Acting Edition No 45)

Note: Not included in *The Plays of J.B. Priestley* but
collected in *When We Are Married and Other Plays*
(A149).

A118 THE ART OF THE DRAMATIST A Lecture Together with
      Appendices and Discursive Notes
      London, Heinemann, 1957.
      91p. 22½cm.

Note: The Inaugural Lecture, under the Hubert Henry
Davies fund, given at the Old Vic Theatre on 30 September 1956.

A119 THOUGHTS IN THE WILDERNESS
      London, Heinemann, 1957.
      ix, 242p. 22cm.

Contents: Introduction (pp vii-viii) - Thoughts in the
Wilderness - Mass Communications - Block Thinking -
They Come from Inner Space - The Hesperides Conference -
Eros and Logos - Time, Please! - On Education - The
Newest Novels - The Real Clean-Up - Grey Eminences -
Sacred White Elephants - Another Revolution - Something
Else - End of a Party - The New Drolls - Doers and
Seers - A Note on Billy Graham - Our New Society -
Candles Burning Low - A Personal Note - Rough Sketch
of a Lifeboat - Who Is Anti-American? - Bottomley - The
Unicorn - The Staggers and Naggers - The Outsider -
Shaw - The Popular Press - Televiewing - Dr Leavis -
Publishers - The Writer in a Changing Society (A115).

Note: With the exception of the last item all these
essays were first published in *The New Statesman* (5
September 1953 - 10 November 1956).

THOUGHTS IN THE WILDERNESS
New York, Harper, 1957.
ix, 242p. 22cm.

THOUGHTS IN THE WILDERNESS
Port Washington (New York), Kennikat Press, 1971.
viii, 242p. 22cm.
(Essay and General Literature Index Reprint Series)

A120 THE GLASS CAGE A Play in Two Acts
      London, Samuel French Limited, 1958.
      70p. plates, diagr. 21½cm. sd.
      (French's Acting Edition No 992)

Note: Not included in *The Plays of J.B. Priestley*.

A121   TOPSIDE Or the Future of England   A Dialogue
       London, Heinemann, 1958.
       50p.   19cm.

       Note: 'A curious coyness has overcome that distinguished
       publicist, Mr. J.B. Priestley. His latest book, called
       'Topside', which is sitting on our desk, is available
       for sale, but it will not be published. No review
       copies are being sent, it appears in no publisher's
       lists, and booksellers will only get it if they ask
       for it. Mr. Priestley, it seems, is fed up with re-
       viewers and critics, and now prefers to deal straight
       with his public. His publishers, Heinemann's, are
       therefore what they call 'privishing' it...' (*The
       Observer*, 2 November 1958).

A122   THE STORY OF THEATRE
       London, Rathbone Books, 1959.
       69p.   col frontis, col illus (inc ports), col map,
          facsims, col diagrs.   32½cm.

       published in the United States as:

       THE WONDERFUL WORLD OF THE THEATRE
       Garden City (New York), Garden City Books, 1959.
       96p.   col frontis, col illus (inc ports), col map,
          facsims, col diagrs.   28cm.

       Note: A revised edition was published in Great
       Britain in 1969 with title of *The Wonderful World of
       the Theatre* (A147).

A123   LITERATURE AND WESTERN MAN
       London, Heinemann, 1960.
       xiii, 512p.   24cm.

       Note: The first edition included a 21½ x 14cm. leaflet,
       A NOTE BY THE AUTHOR / THE ELIZABETHAN STAGE / SEE PAGE
       31, dated 7 January 1960, referring to Leslie Hobson's
       Shakespeare's Wooden O, then recently published. In
       later editions this was incorporated as a footnote
       to the text.

       Further Note: An extensive report, including quotations
       of Mr Priestley's remarks as guest of honour, of a
       Foyle's Literary Luncheon to mark the publication of
       this book, is to be found in 'Literature and Western
       Man Mr J.B. Priestley's Versatility and Range', *The
       Bookseller*, 27 February 1960.

       LITERATURE AND WESTERN MAN
       New York, Harper, 1960.
       xi, 512p.   25cm.

A124 WILLIAM HAZLITT
      London, Longmans Green & Co for The British Council
         and the National Book League, 1960.
      38p. frontis (port). bibliog. 22cm. sd.
      (Bibliographical Series of Supplements to 'British
         Book News' on Writers and Their Work No 122)

A125 UNSOUND TO THE SUMMIT
      London, Campaign for Nuclear Disarmament (?), 1960.
      4p. folded leaflet. 22cm.

      Note: Reprinted from *The New Statesman*, 7 May 1960
      (C2054).

A126 SATURN OVER THE WATER An Account of His Adventures in
         London, South America and Australia by Tim Bedford,
         Painter; Edited - with Some Preliminary and Con-
         cluding Remarks - by Henry Sulgrave; and Here Pre-
         sented to the Reading Public
      London, Heinemann, 1961.
      xiii, 296p. 20½cm.

      SATURN OVER THE WATER ...
      Garden City (New York), Doubleday, 1961.
      284p. 22cm.

A127 THE THIRTY-FIRST OF JUNE A Tale of True Love, Enter-
         prise and Progress, in the Arthurian and Ad-Atomic
         Ages
      London, Heinemann, 1961.
      168p. illus. 22½cm.

      THE THIRTY-FIRST OF JUNE ...
      Garden City (New York), Doubleday, 1962.
      168p. illus. 22cm.

A128 CHARLES DICKENS A Pictorial Biography
      London, Thames and Hudson, 1961.
      144p. frontis, illus (inc. ports), facsims. 24cm.

      Note: Reissued in 1969 as *Charles Dickens and His
      World* (A151).

      CHARLES DICKENS A Pictorial Biography
      New York, Viking Press, 1961.
      144p. frontis. illus (inc. ports). facsims. 24cm.

A129 THE SHAPES OF SLEEP A Topical Tale
      London, Heinemann, 1962.
      229p. 20½cm.

THE SHAPES OF SLEEP   A Topical Tale
Garden City (New York), Doubleday, 1962.
215p.   22cm.

A130   MARGIN RELEASED   A Writer's Reminiscences and Reflec-
         tions
       London, Heinemann, 1962.
       viii, 236p.   22½cm.

       'I wrote Part Three, *I Had the Time*, after a talk over
       lunch with Mr H.V. Hodson, then editor of the *Sunday
       Times*. We agreed I should write some literary reminis-
       cences that could be serialised in the paper. From
       the first, however, I saw these thirty thousand words
       or so not as Sunday journalism but as part of a
       book.... Passages cut or removed altogether from these
       instalments, to make room for photographs, have been
       restored in this text.... It seemed to me then that
       this Part Three, covering forty years of my professional
       life, would be better understood if I described how I
       began writing, in the years before the First War, and
       then related, in a shorter Part Two, a kind of bridge
       section, what happened to me during that war ...'
       (Preface).

       Contents: The Swan Arcadian (1910-1914) - Carry On,
       Carry On! (1914-1919) - I Had the Time (1920-1960).

       MARGIN RELEASED   A Writer's Reminiscences and Reflec-
         tions
       New York, Harper & Row, 1962.
       236p.   illus.   22cm.

A131   A SEVERED HEAD   A Play in Three Acts by Iris Murdoch
         and J.B. Priestley
       London, Chatto & Windus, 1964.
       108p.   19cm.

       A SEVERED HEAD by Iris Murdoch and J.B. Priestley
         Adapted from the Novel by Iris Murdoch
       London, Samuel French Limited, 1964.
       72p.   illus.   21cm.   Pbk.
       (French's Acting Edition)

A132   SIR MICHAEL AND SIR GEORGE   A Tale of COMSA and DISCUS
         and the New Elizabethans
       London, Heinemann, 1964.
       244p.   20cm.

SIR MICHAEL AND SIR GEORGE   A Comedy of the New Eliza-
   bethans
Boston, Little Brown, 1965.
243p.   21cm.

A133   MAN AND TIME
London, Aldus Books in association with W.H. Allen,
   1964.
316p.   col frontis, illus (some col), facsims, diagrs.
   28cm.

MAN AND TIME
Garden City (New York), Doubleday, 1964.
319p.   col frontis, illus (some col), facsims, diagrs.
   28cm.

A134   TELEVISION.   A POLEMICAL ESSAY AND A STORY / EIN STREIT-
   BARER AUFSATZ UND EINE GESCHICHTE
Ebenhausen (Isartel), Edition Langewiesche - Brandt,
   1965.
100p.   18cm.   Pbk.

Includes 'Televiewing', i.e. 'Thoughts on Televiewing',
New Statesman, 29 September 1956, reprinted *Thoughts in
the Wilderness* (1957); and 'Uncle Phil on TV', *Lilliput*,
April-May 1953, collected in *The Other Place* (1953).
Parallel text in English and German.

A135   LOST EMPIRES   Being Richard Herncastle's Account of
   His Life on the Variety Stage from November 1913 to
   August 1914 Together with a Prologue and Epilogue
London, Heinemann, 1965.
xii, 308p.   22½cm.

LOST EMPIRES...
Boston, Little Brown, 1965.
364p.   24cm.

A136   J.B. PRIESTLEY ON EVERYMAN   Being His Introduction to
   'An Everyman Anthology', Published by Dent on the
   Occasion of the Diamond Jubilee of Everyman's Library.
London, J.M. Dent & Sons Ltd, 1966.
4p.   19cm.   sd.

Note: Also included in *An Everyman Anthology* (B123).

A137   SALT IS LEAVING
London, Pan Books Ltd by arrangement with William
   Heinemann Ltd, 1966.

220p. 18cm. Pbk.
(A Pan Original X560)

SALT IS LEAVING
New York, Harper and Row, 1966.

A138   THE MOMENTS and Other Pieces
London, Heinemann, 1966.
vii, 321p. 19½cm.

Contents: Preface - The Moments - Ambience or Agenda? -
Tobacco - Dark Junction - Conjuring - Wrong 'Ism -
The Mad Sad World - The Blue Yonder Boys - Giving Up
Conferences - Music Halls - Morgan in a Mirror - The
Happy Introvert - Lost Lather - Eroticism, Sex and
Love - Gay with the Arts? - Buzz and Bruit - Writer at
Work - Doubts about Dynamism - Student Mobs - Censor
and Stage - Road to Samarkand - Malaysian Visit -
Hong Kong and Canton - These our Revels - Fifty Years
of the English; *Lectures and Talks:* Life, Literature
and the Classroom - What about the Audience? - Shake-
speare and the Modern World - What Happened to Falstaff.

Note: Of the periodical pieces, 'Giving Up Conferences'
was first printed in *Punch* (C2134); 'The Happy Introvert' in *Review of English Literature* (C2097); 'Eroticism, Sex and Love' in *Saturday Evening Post* (C2101);
'Road to Samarkand' in *Sunday Times* (C2095); 'These
our Revels' in *Sunday Telegraph* (C2116); and 'The
Moments', 'Ambience or Agenda?', 'Tobacco', 'Dark
Junction', 'Conjuring', 'Wrong 'Ism', 'The Mad Sad
World', 'The Blue Yonder Boys', 'Music Hall', 'Morgan
in a Mirror', 'Lost Lather', 'Buzz and Bruit', 'Writer
at Work', 'Doubts about Dynamism', 'Student Mobs',
'Censor and Stage', and 'Fifty Years of the English',
in *New Statesman*.

A139   IT'S AN OLD COUNTRY
London, Heinemann, 1967.
248p. 20cm.

IT'S AN OLD COUNTRY A Novel
Boston, Little Brown, 1967.
276p. 22cm.

A140   THE WORLD OF J.B. PRIESTLEY Chosen and Introduced by
Donald G. MacRae
London, Heinemann Educational Books Ltd, 1967.
xii, 179p. 22½cm.

Contents: Introduction (pp vi-xii) - Youth in Bradford, 1910-1914 (*Margin Released*) - A Saturday Afternoon in Bruddersford (*The Good Companions*) - Bradford Revisited, 1933 (*English Journey*) - In Commercial London (*Angel Pavement*) - Petticoat Lane (*Self-Selected Essays*) - England in the Thirties (*English Journey*) - Moving to the Right (*Rain Upon Godshill*) - Modern America (*Journey Down a Rainbow*) - Literature and Society (*Literature and Western Man*).

A141 OUT OF TOWN Volume One of THE IMAGE MEN
London, Heinemann, 1968.
344p. 22cm.

A142 TRUMPETS OVER THE SEA Being a Rambling and Egotistical Account of the London Symphony Orchestra's Engagement at Daytona Beach, Florida in July-August, 1967.
London, Heinemann, 1968.
160p. 16 plates. illus. ports. 26cm.

A143 LONDON END Volume Two of THE IMAGE MEN
London, Heinemann, 1968.
328p. 22cm.

A144 ALL ENGLAND LISTENED. The Wartime Broadcasts of J.B. Priestley. With an Introduction by Eric Sevareid
New York, Chilmark Press, 1968.
xxv, 146p. 21½cm.

Note: This is the first United States publication of *Postscripts*, 1940 (A56); a new preface by Priestley (pp xii-xxv) is included.

A145 ESSAYS OF FIVE DECADES Selected and with a Preface by Susan Cooper
Boston, Atlantic-Little Brown, 1968.
xxi, 311p. 25cm.

Contents: Preface (pp vii-xv) - I From PAPERS FROM LILLIPUT 1922: Three Men - On a Mouth-Organ - An Apology for Bad Pianists - On Travel by Train. II From I FOR ONE 1923: On Beginning - Haunted - All about Ourselves - A Coincidence. III From FIGURES IN MODERN LITERATURE 1924: Walter de la Mare. IV From THE ENGLISH COMIC CHARACTERS 1925: The Illyrians - Mr Micawber. V From OPEN HOUSE 1927: The Berkshire Beasts - Having Covered the Card Table - The Inn of the Six Anglers - Open House. VI From APES AND ANGELS 1928: The Flower Show - T'Match - First Snow - The Dark

Hours – Seeing Stratford – Mr Pickwick Returns – The
Strange Outfitter – The Man with the Flare. VII From
THE BALCONINNY 1929: The Balconinny – My Debut in
Opera – Carless at Last – Little Tich – My Forchern –
Commercial Interlude – Residential – On View. VIII
From SELF-SELECTED ESSAYS: The Prophets – Dissolution
in Haymarket – On the Moors – These Our Actors –
Strange Encounter – Different Inside. IX From
DELIGHT 1949: Preface, or the Grumbler's Apology –
Fountains – A Walking Tour – Cosy Planning – Moment
During Rehearsal – Old Photograph – Chamber Music at
Home – My First Article – Shakespeare Rediscovered –
Family Silliness, Domestic Clowning – Long Trousers –
Early Childhood and the Treasure – Cosy with Work –
Dreams – Dancing – Blossom – Making Stew – After a
Good Concert – The Delight That Never Was. X From
THOUGHTS IN THE WILDERNESS: Block Thinking – The
Hesperides Conference – Eros and Logos – On Education –
Another Revolution – Who Is Anti-American? – The Uni-
corn – Shaw – Televiewing. XI From the SATURDAY
EVENING POST 12 DEC 1964: Women Don't Run the Country.
XII From THE MOMENTS: The Moments – Tobacco – Wrong
'Ism – The Mad Sad World – Giving Up Conferences – The
Happy Introvert – What Happened to Falstaff. XIII From
the NEW STATESMAN 1966-1967: Dandy Days – Fact or
Fiction? – Disturbing – The Skull Cinema – Off Shore
Island Man – Growing Old.

ESSAYS OF FIVE DECADES   Selected and with a Preface
  by Susan Cooper
London, Heinemann, 1969.
xxi, 311p. 22½cm.

Note: A.E. Day's letter, 'J.B. Priestley's Essays',
Times Literary Supplement, 20 March 1969, notes that
most of the essays included here were already in print
in other collections, and names sources from which
less familiar material might have been culled.

A146   THE PRINCE OF PLEASURE and His Regency 1811-20
       London, Heinemann, 1969.
       304p. illus (some col), coat of arms, facsims, map,
         ports (some col). bibliog. 25cm.

       THE PRINCE OF PLEASURE and His Regency 1811-1820
       New York, Harper & Row, 1969.
       304p. illus (some col), coat of arms, facsims, map,
         ports (some col). bibliog. 26cm.

A147 THE WONDERFUL WORLD OF THE THEATRE
London, Macdonald & Co, 1969.
96p. illus (some col), ports (some col). 28cm.

Note: First published as *The Story of Theatre*, 1959
(A121).

THE WONDERFUL WORLD OF THE THEATRE
Garden City (New York), Doubleday, 1969.
96p. illus (some col), ports (some col). 28cm.

A148 TIME AND THE CONWAYS AND OTHER PLAYS
Harmondsworth (Middlesex), Penguin, 1969.
302p. 18cm. Pbk.

Contents: Time and the Conways - I Have Been Here
Before - An Inspector Calls - The Linden Tree.

A149 WHEN WE ARE MARRIED AND OTHER PLAYS
Harmondsworth (Middlesex), Penguin, 1969.
319p. 18cm. Pbk.

Contents: When We Are Married - Bees on the Boat Deck -
Ever Since Paradise - Mr Kettle and Mrs Moon.

A150 THE IMAGE MEN
Boston, Little Brown, 1969.
xi, 492p. 25cm.

THE IMAGE MEN
London, Heinemann, 1976.
677p. 23cm.

Note: Originally published in 1968 in two volumes:
Out of Town (A141) and *London End* (A143).

A151 CHARLES DICKENS AND HIS WORLD
London, Thames & Hudson, 1969.
144p. illus, ports. facsims. 24cm.

Note: Originally published in 1961 as *Charles Dickens:
A Pictorial Biography* (A128).

CHARLES DICKENS AND HIS WORLD
New York, Viking Press, 1969.
144p. illus. ports. facsims. 24cm.

A152 ANTON CHEKHOV
London, International Textbook Company Limited, 1970.
87p. plates, illus (some col), ports, facsims, map.
bibliog. 22cm.
(International Profiles)

A153   THE EDWARDIANS
        London, Heinemann, 1970.
        302p. illus (some col), ports (some col), facsims.
          bibliog. 26cm.

        THE EDWARDIANS
        New York, Harper & Row, 1970.
        302p. illus (some col), ports (some col), facsims.
          bibliog. 26cm.

A154   SNOGGLE A Story for Anybody Between 9 and 90. Illus-
          trated by Margaret Palmer.
        London, Heinemann, 1971.
        138p. drawings. 22cm.

        SNOGGLE A Story for Anybody Between 9 and 90. Illus-
          trated by Barbara Flynn
        New York, Harcourt Brace Jovanovich, 1972.
        158p. drawings. 21cm.

A155   VICTORIA'S HEYDAY
        London, Heinemann, 1972.
        296p. illus (some col), ports (some col), facsims
          (some col). bibliog. 26cm.

        Note: Some interesting reflections on the background
        to this book and its companion volumes, *The Prince of
        Pleasure* (A146) and *The Edwardians* (A153), may be read
        in John Hadfield's 'The New Priestley', *The Bookseller*,
        22 April 1972.

        VICTORIA'S HEYDAY
        New York, Harper & Row, 1972.
        296p. illus (some col), ports (some col), facsims
          (some col). bibliog. 26cm.

A156   OVER THE LONG HIGH WALL Some Reflections and Specula-
          tions on Life, Death and Time
        London, Heinemann, 1972.
        142p. 23cm.

A157   THE ENGLISH
        London, Heinemann, 1973.
        256p. illus (some col), ports (some col), music,
          facsims. 28cm.

        THE ENGLISH
        New York, Viking Press, 1973.
        256p. illus (some col), ports (some col), music,
          facsims. 28cm.

A158   A VISIT TO NEW ZEALAND
       London, Heinemann, 1974.
       xii, 156p. plates, col. illus. 24cm.

A159   OUTCRIES AND ASIDES
       London, Heinemann, 1974.
       xi, 197p. 20cm.

       'In an earlier period a book of this kind would almost
       certainly have been entitled Table Talk...' (Preface).

       Note: Published in honour of the author's eightieth
       birthday, this book consists of over two hundred short
       informal pieces. 'A few of them, now abridged, were
       taken from a feature, known as *The Uneasy Chair*, that
       ran for some time in *The New Statesman*'.

A160   THE CARFITT CRISIS and Two Other Stories
       London, Heinemann, 1975.
       viii, 195p. 22cm.

       Contents: The Carfitt Crisis or The New Man – Under-
       ground – The Pavilion of Masks A Comedy in a Romantic
       Setting.

       Note: J.B. PRIESTLEY WRITES (inside front dust jacket)
       brief notes on these two romantic novellas sandwiched
       round a short horror story. 'Underground' was first
       published in *Illustrated London News*, Christmas Number
       1974 (C2235), 'The Carfitt Crisis' and 'The Pavilion
       of Masks' (F8) were 'originally conceived in dramatic
       form'; the latter was performed on stage in Germany
       in 1961 and in England in 1963.

A161   PARTICULAR PLEASURES Being a Personal Record of Some
       Varied Arts and Many Different Artists
       London, Heinemann, 1975.
       192p. illus (some col), ports (some col). 26cm.

       Contents: Painting: Pieter Brueghel the Elder: Hunters
       in the Snow; Watteau: Giles; Hogarth: The Graham Chil-
       dren; Highmore: Mr Oldham and His Guests; Gainsborough:
       The Painter's Daughters with a Cat; Constable: Study
       for The Hay Wain and Weymouth Bay; Lawrence: Princess
       de Lieven; Turner: A First Rate Taking in Stores and
       A Tree in a Storm; Cotman: A Dismasted Brig; Corot:
       Avignon from the West; Daumier: Don Quixote; Cézanne:
       Road Near Mont Sainte-Victoire; Elmore: Nude; Gauguin:
       Ala oe Feii? What, Are You Jealous?; Sickert: Café
       Scene; Bonnard: La Table; Vuillard: Indoor Scene with

Children; Nicholson: Begonias; Gore: The Garden, Row-
landson House; Paul Nash: Totes Mer; De Stael: Soccer
Players; Delvaux: Hands; Edna Clarke Hall: Family
Groups. *Music:* Rossini: Overtures; Berlioz: Symphonie
Fantastique, Op 14; Schumann: Symphony No 4 in D minor,
Op 120; Liszt: First Movement of the Faust Symphony;
Verdi: Falstaff; Smetana: Piano Trio in G Minor, Op 15;
Bruckner: Scherzo of Symphony No 7 in E; Brahms:
Clarinet Quintet in B Minor, Op 115; Bizet: Symphony
in C; Tchaikovsky: Symphony No 4 in F Minor, Op 36;
Dvorak: Symphony No 7 in D Minor, Op 70; Faure: Piano
Quartet No 1 in C Minor; Elgar: Symphony No 1 in A
Flat, Op 55; Mahler: Das Lied von der Erde, 'Der
Abscied'; Debussy: Orchestral Suite, La Mer; Richard
Strauss: Tone Poem for Orchestra, Don Juan; Glazunov:
Ballet, The Seasons, Op 67; Sibelius: Finale of Symphony
No 5 in E Flat Major, Op 82; Rachmaninov: Symphony No 3
in A Minor; Holst: Orchestra Suite, The Planets, Op 32;
Ravel: La Valse, Poème Choreographique; Bartok: Music
for Strings, Percussion and Celesta; Bliss: A Cantata
and a Prayer; Walton: Orchestral Suite, Facade. *Acting:*
Peggy Ashcroft; Humphrey Bogart; Gerald du Maurier;
Edith Evans; John Gielgud; Alec Guinness; Edmund Gwenn;
Cedric Hardwicke; Katharine Hepburn; Charles Laughton;
Gertrude Lawrence and Noel Coward; Wilfrid Lawson;
The Lunts; Marilyn Monroe; Laurence Olivier; Jules
Raimu; Claude Rains; Ralph Richardson; Jean Forbes-
Robertson; George C. Scott; Alastair Sim; Arthur Sin-
clair; Sybil Thorndike; Spencer Tracy. *Clowning:* The
Aldwych Comedians; Jack Benny; Charlie Chaplin; Some
Notes at Random; Tommy Cooper; Sid Field; W.C. Fields;
The Fratellini; Grock; Tony Hancock; Leslie Henson;
Sydney Howard; Frankie Howerd; Buster Keaton; Jimmy
Learmouth; The Marx Brothers; Morecambe and Wise;
George Robey and Robb Wilton; Harry Tate; Jacques Tati;
Little Tich.

A162   FOUND, LOST, FOUND Or the English Way of Life
       London, Heinemann, 1976.
       135p.   23cm.

       FOUND, LOST, FOUND
       New York, Stein and Day, 1977.
       134p.   22cm.

A163   ENGLISH HUMOUR
       London, Heinemann, 1976.
       208p.   plates, illus (some col), ports, facsims.   26cm.

'Nearly fifty years ago I was invited to write a book
for the *English Heritage Series* ... a modest volume
called *English Humour*, now long out of print. I am
using the title again because it best describes this
new book on the very same subject. Though I cannot
help sharing some material, what I am not doing is
merely bringing up to date the book I wrote so long
ago..." (Preface).

A164   THE HAPPY DREAM: AN ESSAY
       Manor Farm, Andoversford (Gloucestershire), Whittington
          Press, 1976.
       35p.   21cm.

       Note: Published in a limited edition of 400 copies
       signed by the author. Available either bound in cloth
       or in leather. Reprinted in *Instead of the Trees*
       (A165).

A165   INSTEAD OF THE TREES   A Final Chapter of Autobiography
       London, Heinemann, 1977.
       152p.   23cm.

       Contents: also includes *The Happy Dream* (A164) to which
       is added 'Some afterthoughts'.

       Note: 'The title of this book is not a bit of whimsy....
       In the later 1930s ... I published two books: *Midnight
       on the Desert*, a chapter of autobiography; and *Rain
       upon Godshill*, a further chapter of autobiography. In
       each of them I began by establishing myself in a cer-
       tain place, and then proceeded to recall the events,
       opinions, thoughts, I had known during the previous
       twelve months or so. The first book put me in a hut I
       had used on a ranch in Arizona; the second began in
       my study on the Isle of Wight. But I had roughly
       planned a third chapter of autobiography; and this was
       to have a setting among or near the giant redwood
       trees of California, tranquil ancients to which I had
       taken a great fancy. I never began this third book
       because the war came ... but somewhere at the back of
       my mind I was aware that I had planned a trio of
       volumes and had failed to achieve it. I still didn't
       like that gap. On the other hand, I no longer saw my-
       self finding a lodging somewhere near the giant trees
       or indeed returning to California.... So if there was
       to be a third volume, it would have to be *Instead of
       the Trees*'.
       At one point, however, he had thought in terms of four

books. In a letter to a friend, mentioned in *J.B.
Priestley: An Exhibition of Manuscripts and Books* (H4),
he writes that he has enough material for a sequel to
his two previous autobiographies, which he is consider-
ing calling *Slow Train Through the Blackout*, and adds
that his plan is that there should be four of these
books altogether.

INSTEAD OF THE TREES   A Final Chapter of Autobiography
New York, Stein and Day, 1977.
151p. 22cm.

A166   THREE NOVELS
      London, Heinemann, 1979.
      viii, 759p. 24cm.

      Contents: Introduction (pp vii–viii); *Angel Pavement*;
      Bright Day; and *Sir Michael and Sir George*.

A167   SIX PLAYS
      London, Heinemann, 1979.
      viii, 406p. 24cm.

      Contents: Introduction (pp vii–viii); *Dangerous Corner*;
      Eden End; *Time and the Conways*; *An Inspector Calls*;
      The Linden Tree; and *When We Are Married*.

A168   THE WORKS OF J.B. PRIESTLEY, apparently intended to
      be the definitive collected edition, began publication
      in 1931. Five volumes were issued before the Second
      World War and another appeared in 1947. Since then
      the project seems to have lapsed. All volumes are
      bound in a light blue cloth, have monogrammed endpapers,
      a light blue silk page marker, and the author's name is
      printed in red on the title page.

THE GOOD COMPANIONS
London, William Heinemann Ltd, 1931.
xvi, 646p. 20cm.
Pp ix–xi 'Introduction' by J.B. Priestley; pp xiii–xvi
   Characters.

ANGEL PAVEMENT
London, William Heinemann Ltd, 1931.
xiv, 613p. 20cm.
Four unnumbered pages 'Introduction' by J.B. Priestley;
   Characters on two unnumbered pages.

ADAM IN MOONSHINE. BENIGHTED.
London, William Heinemann Ltd, 1932.

viii, 352p. 20cm.
Pp v-viii 'Introduction by J.B. Priestley'.

THREE PLAYS AND A PREFACE
London, William Heinemann Ltd, 1935.
xvi, 305p. 20cm.
Pp vii-xvi 'Preface' by J.B. Priestley.

SELF-SELECTED ESSAYS
London, William Heinemann Ltd, 1937.
vii, 319p. 20cm.

ENGLISH JOURNEY
London, William Heinemann Ltd, 1949.
ix, 422p. 20cm.
Pp i-ix 'Introduction' by J.B. Priestley; pp 419-422
Index to names and places.

A169   In the late autumn of 1968 Heron Books began advertising 'The Collected Masterpieces of J.B. Priestley'
in their series of collections offered to subscribers
on a monthly basis. A later advertisement remarked:
'It is said that no-one owns a complete collection of
the immense wealth of the work of J.B. Priestley. If
you had the time and money to spare ... if you were
free to browse endlessly in bookshops, you might even-
tually succeed in finding all the works contained in
this series. But what a motley collection it would be!
Some large ... some small ... some bound, some not,
many dog-eared and shabby with age'. This collection
is of course in a uniform edition, 'each precious
volume is bound in deep blue Skivertex with the rich
look of leather. Intricately tooled gold decorations,
silken headbands and elegant typesetting on fine wood-
free paper, complete the distinctive appointments'.
In all twenty-six volumes were issued; each includes
an original head-and-shoulders drawing of Priestley by
Daniel Briffaud as a frontispiece. The first volume,
Angel Pavement, contained an eleven-page General Introduction to Priestley's work by Ivor Brown. Titles:
Angel Pavement; *Bright Day*; *The Good Companions*; *English
Journey*; *Margin Released*; *Plays I*; *Festival at Far-
bridge*; *Literature and Western Man*; *Faraway*; *Adam in
Moonshine / Benighted*; *Journey Down a Rainbow*; *Delight /
Self-Selected Essays*; *The Doomsday Men / The Shapes of
Sleep*; *Low Notes on a High Level / The Thirty First of
June*; *The Moments*; *Plays II*; *The Other Place / The Magi-
cians*; *Daylight on Saturday*; *Wonder Hero*; *They Walk
in the City*; *Blackout in Gretley*; *Midnight on the
Desert / Rain upon Godshill*; *Saturn Over the Water*; *Sir*

Michael and Sir George; *Plays III*; *Lost Empires*; and
Let the People Sing. Early subscribers also received
gratis a bronze medal bearing a none too easily recog-
nizable bust of Priestley. For the collector who
extends his interest to ephemera mention should be made
of a leaflet, *Message to Subscriber's Friend An Invitation from J.B. Priestley Himself*, printed in different colours, and a folded brochure, *Aren't They
Beautiful?*

B. CONTRIBUTIONS TO BOOKS AND PAMPHLETS

B1 ESSAYISTS PAST AND PRESENT A Selection of English Essays,
Edited, with an Introduction and Notes by J.B. Priestley
London, Herbert Jenkins Limited, 1925.
320p. 17½cm.
(The Fireside Library)
Pp 7-32 'Introduction' by J.B. Priestley; pp. 309-320
'Notes' initialled J.B.P.

ESSAYISTS PAST AND PRESENT ...
New York, Lincoln MacVeagh, The Dial Press, 1925.
319p. 17½cm.

ESSAYISTS PAST AND PRESENT
Freeport (New York), Books for Libraries Press, 1967.
319p. 22cm.
(Essay Index Reprint Series)

B2 FOOLS AND PHILOSOPHERS A Gallery of Comic Figures from
English Literature Arranged by J.B. Priestley
London, John Lane The Bodley Head Ltd, 1925.
xii, 299. 17½cm.
Pp v-viii 'Preface' by J.B. Priestley

FOOLS AND PHILOSOPHERS
New York, Dodd Mead, 1925.
xii, 299p. 18cm.

B3 TOM MOORE'S DIARY A Selection Edited, with an Introduction, by J.B. Priestley
Cambridge, at the University Press, 1925.
xv, 218p. frontis (port). 19cm.
Pp v-xv 'Introduction' by J.B. Priestley.

B4 THE DIARY OF THOMAS TURNER OF EAST HOATHLY (1754-1765)
*Edited by Florence Maris Turner (Mrs Charles Lamb)
Great-Great-Granddaughter of the Diarist* with an
Introduction by J.B. Priestley

London, John Lane   The Bodley Head Limited, 1925.
xxx, 112p. 17cm.
Pp v-xxiii 'Introduction' by J.B. Priestley.

B5   THE BOOK OF BODLEY HEAD VERSE Being a Selection of
     Poetry Published at the Bodley Head   Chosen and Edited
     by J.B. Priestley with a Preface by J.C. Squire
     London, John Lane   The Bodley Head Limited, 1926.
     xxi, 218p. 17cm.
     Pp xv-xvi 'Editor's Note' initialled J.B.P.

B6   WONDERFUL LONDON Edited by St. John Adcock
     London, Fleetway House, 3 vols, 1926.
     1152p. illus. 28cm.
     Pp 729-735 (Vol 2) 'How London Strikes a Provincial'
     by J.B. Priestley.

B7   THE LIFE AND OPINIONS OF TRISTRAM SHANDY GENTLEMAN by
     Laurence Sterne with Illustrations and Decorations by
     John Austen and an Introduction by J.B. Priestley.
     London, John Lane   The Bodley Head, 1928.
     xvi, 557p. illus. 26cm.
     Pp v-xvi 'Introduction' by J.B. Priestley.

B8   THE FEMALE SPECTATOR Being Selections from Mrs Eliza
     Heywood's Periodical (1744-1746) Chosen and Edited by
     Mary Priestley with an Introduction by J.B. Priestley
     and Decorations by Constance Rowlands.
     London, John Lane   The Bodley Head Ltd, 1929
     xvii, 112p.
     Pp vii-xv 'Introduction' by J.B. Priestley.

B9   THE HISTORY AND ADVENTURES OF JOSEPH ANDREWS AND HIS
     FRIEND MR ABRAHAM ADAMS by Henry Fielding. Illustrated
     by Norman Tealby with an Introduction by J.B. Priestley
     London, John Lane   The Bodley Head, 1929.
     xxxi, 350p. illus. 26cm.
     Pp vii-xiv 'Introduction' by J.B. Priestley.

B10 SELECTED ESSAYS by Leigh Hunt
     London, J.M. Dent & Sons, Ltd, 1929.
     xvi, 360p. 18cm.
     (Everyman's Library No 829)
     Pp vii-xi 'Introduction' by J.B. Priestley.

B11 THE MERCURY STORY BOOK with an Introduction by J.B.
     Priestley
     London, Longmans Green, 1929.
     xi, 399p. 20cm.
     Pp. ix-xi 'Introduction' by J.B. Priestley.

B12 ENCYCLOPAEDIA BRITANNICA
London and New York, Encyclopaedia Britannica, 14th
edition, 1929.
Vol 7: pp 592-594 'English Literature: VI The Romantic
Period' initialled J.B.Pr.

B13 THE HOUSE WITH THE GREEN SHUTTERS by George Douglas.
With an Introduction by J.B. Priestley.
London, Jonathan Cape, 1929.
288p. 17½cm.
(The Travellers Library No 118)
Pp 5-9 'Introduction' by J.B. Priestley.

B14 THE UNIVERSAL HISTORY OF THE WORLD Written by One
Hundred and Fifty of Our Foremost Living Authorities
in All Branches of Historical Knowledge Edited by
J.A. Hammerton
London, Amalgamated Press, 8 vols, 1927-1930.
Paginated continuously. illus. 22cm.
Vol 7 pp 4535-4552 'The Literature of the Victorian Age'
by J.B. Priestley.

B15 THE BOOK OF FLEET STREET Edited by T. Michael Pope
London, Cassell and Company Limited, 1930.
xii, 306p. plates (inc frontis). 22cm.
Pp 174-182 'An Outpost' by J.B. Priestley.

B16 THE MERCURY BOOK OF VERSE Being a Selection of Poems
Published in The London Mercury 1919-1930. With an
Introduction by Sir Henry Newbolt
London, Macmillan and Co Limited, 1931.
xv, 283p. 20cm.
P 207 'Overheard', 'Consolation for the Unborn',
'At a Night Club' and 'Values' by J.B. Priestley.
Note: First published *The London Mercury*, August 1924
(C345).

B17 THE HISTORICAL PAGEANT OF BRADFORD, PEEL PARK BRADFORD
JULY 13 to 18. THE SOUVENIR BOOK
Bradford, Percy Lund, Humphries & Co Ltd, 1931.
88p. illus, ports. 28 x 22½cm. Lp.
Pp 13-14 'Jess Oakroyd's Homecoming' by J.B. Priestley.

B18 TOM JONES The History of a Foundling by Henry Fielding
with Illustrations by Alexander King and an Introduction by J.B. Priestley
Brattleboro (Vermont), Limited Editions Club, 1931.

870p. illus. 28cm.
Pp 3-8 'Introduction' by J.B. Priestley.
Note: Only 1500 copies were printed for members of the
  Limited Editions Club. Priestley's Introduction was
  reprinted in *A Book of Prefaces* (Limited Editions
  Club, 1941).

B19 MY MAGIC LIFE by David Devant. With an Introduction by
       J.B. Priestley and 20 Illustrations
     London, Hutchinson & Co, 1931.
     xii, 13-287p. plates (inc frontis port). 21cm.
     Pp ix-xi 'Introduction' by J.B. Priestley.

B20 DANGEROUS CORNER a Novel by Ruth Holland from the Play
       by J.B. Priestley with His Cooperation and a Foreword
     London, Hamish Hamilton, 1932.
     285p. 19cm.
     Pp 5-7 'Preface' by J.B. Priestley.

     DANGEROUS CORNER a Novel by Ruth Holland and J.B.
       Priestley
     Garden City (New York), Doubleday Doran & Co, 1933.
     vii, 273p. 20cm.

B21 PETER ARNO'S CIRCUS with an Introduction by J.B.
       Priestley
     London, John Lane The Bodley Head, 1933.
     (50p.) col. frontis. illus. 30 x 22cm.
     (3p.) 'Introduction' by J.B. Priestley.

B22 THE ORIGINAL CLOCK ALMANACK Written in the Yorkshire
       Dialect. 1933
     Idle, Bradford, Watmoughs Ltd, 1933.
     80p. 18cm. sd.
     P 32 'A message from J.B. Priestley: "T'Owd Clock'll
       keep me i toit"'

B23 ESSAYS AND STUDIES by Members of the English Association
       Vol XVIII
     Oxford, The Clarendon Press, 1933.
     159p. 22cm.
     Pp 149-159 'Some Reflections of a Popular Novelist' by
       J.B. Priestley.
     Note: First published in *The London Mercury*, December
       1932 (C905).

B24 CECIL HOUSES Womens Public Lodging House Fund. Fifth
       Report
     London, Cecil Houses, 1933.

40p. plates. 21½cm. sd.
P 20 'What Are You Going to Do?' by J.B. Priestley.
Note: Extract from a speech at the Cambridge Theatre,
18 November 1932.

B25 SEVEN YEARS' HARVEST An Anthology of The Bermondsey
Book 1923-1930 Compiled by Sidney Gutman
London, William Heinemann Ltd, 1934.
xiv, 454p. 21cm.
Pp 380-385 'On a Common Mistake in Criticism' by J.B.
Priestley.
Note: First printed in *The Bermondsey Book*, December
1926 (C486).

B26 CHALLENGE TO DEATH with a Foreword by Viscount Cecil
London, Constable & Co Ltd, 1934.
xv, 343p. 19cm.
Pp 305-321 'The Public and the Idea of Peace' by J.B.
Priestley.

B27 THEATRE AND STAGE. A Modern Encyclopaedic Guide to the
Performance of All Classes of Amateur Dramatic, Oper-
atic and Theatrical Work Edited by Harold Downs Assis-
ted by Well-Known Authorities and Celebrities in the
Theatrical World.
London, Pitman, 2 vols, 1934.
Paginated continuously. illus, ports. 25cm.
Pp 1147-1150 (vol 2) 'Social Significance of the
Theatre' by J.B. Priestley, Novelist, Playwright and
Dramatic Critic.

B28 THE SEDITION BILL EXPLAINED by W. Ivor Jennings. With
a Preface by J.B. Priestley.
London, New Statesman and Nation, 1934.
31p. 21cm. sd.
Pp 5-7 'Preface' by J.B. Priestley.

B29 THE HEART OF ENGLAND by Ivor Brown with a Foreword by
J.B. Priestley
London, B.T. Batsford Ltd, 1935.
viii, 120p. plates. 22cm.
Pp v-vi 'Foreword' by J.B. Priestley.

B30 MAN AND THE MACHINE Edited by Hubert Williams; Preface
by J.B. Priestley
London, George Routledge & Sons Ltd, 1935.
xii, 207p. 19cm.
Pp vii-xii Preface by J.B. Priestley.

B31   THE BEAUTY OF BRITAIN   A Pictorial Survey Introduced by
         J.B. Priestley
      London, B.T. Batsford Ltd, 1935.
      viii, 248p. frontis (col), plates (some col). 20cm.
      Pp 1-10 'The Beauty of Britain' by J.B. Priestley.

B32   TWENTY THOUSAND STREETS UNDER THE SKY A London Trilogy
         by Patrick Hamilton. With an Introduction by J.B.
         Priestley
      London, Constable & Co Ltd, 1935.
      xiii, 301, 164, 286p. 19½cm.
      Pp ix-xiv 'Introduction' by J.B. Priestley.

B33   PORTRAITS AND SELF-PORTRAITS   Collected and Illustrated
         by Georges Schreiber
      Boston, Houghton Mifflin, 1936.
      x, 175p. illus (ports). 26cm.
      P 127 'Self-Portrait' by J.B. Priestley.

B34   SPAIN AND US by J.B. Priestley and Others
      London, Holborn and West Central London Committee for
         Spanish Medical Aid, 1936.
      22p. 21cm. sd.
      Pp 1-2 'The Spanish Revolt and the English Press' by
         J.B. Priestley.

B35   CAMBRIDGE MEMORIES   (The Lighter Side of Long Ago) by
         Thomas Thornely
      London, Hamish Hamilton, 1936.
      191p. 18½cm.
      Pp 7-8 'Foreword' by J.B. Priestley.

B36   PROS AND CONS. A Collection of Recollections Told by
         Celebrated Concert Artistes Edited and Compiled by
         Fred Rome. With a Foreword by J.B. Priestley
      London, Reynolds & Co., 1936.
      v, 7-57p.
      Pp iii-v 'Foreword' by J.B. Priestley.

B37   MANCHESTER ... HEART OF THE INDUSTRIAL NORTH with
         an Introduction by J.B. Priestley
      Manchester, Manchester Chamber of Commerce, 1937.
      48p. 21½cm. sd.
      Pp 4-5 'Foreword' by J.B. Priestley.

B38   THE ADVENTURES OF GIL BLAS OF SANTILLANE by Alain-René
         Le Sage Translated by Tobias Smollett. With an
         Introduction by J.B. Priestley and Illustrations by
         John Austen. 2 vols.

Oxford, Oxford University Press for Limited Editions
Club, 1937.
xix, 329p / x, 330p. illus (some col). 29½cm.
Note: Published in a limited edition of 1500 numbered
copies signed by John Austen.

B39 AN EXCHANGE OF LETTERS by Thomas Mann. With a Foreword
by J.B. Priestley.
London, Friends of Europe, 1937.
14p. 10½cm. sd.
Pp 3-5 'Foreword' by J.B. Priestley.

AN EXCHANGE OF LETTERS by Thomas Mann. With a Foreword
by J.B. Priestley
Stamford (Connecticut), The Overbrook Press, 1938.
Note: Privately printed in a limited edition of 350
copies on the occasion of a dinner given by the Yale
Library Associates in honour of Thomas Mann.

B40 WHAT I BELIEVE by Fourteen Modern Thinkers
London, Frederick Muller, 1937.
64p. 18½cm. sd.
Pp 61-64 J.B. Priestley.
Note: First printed in *News Chronicle*, 9 July 1937
(C1097). Item B124 is an entirely different text.

B41 BRITAIN & THE BEAST
London, J.M. Dent & Sons Ltd, 1937.
xx, 332p. illus. 22½cm.
P viii 'Messages on the Publication of This Book: From
J.B. Priestley'.

B42 PRIVATE LIVES OF FAMOUS FILM STARS
Kingswood (Surrey), World's Work (1913) Ltd, 193?
96p. 24cm. sd.
Pp 3-5 'Gracie Fields.as a Film Star' by J.B. Priestley.

B43 ... A HUNDRED YEARS AGO With a Foreword by J.B.
Priestley
London, School for the Blind, 1938.
39p. illus. 25cm. sd.
Pp 5-9 'Foreword' by J.B. Priestley.

B44 MALVERN FESTIVAL GUIDE 1938
Malvern, 1938.
80p. illus. 24½cm.
Pp 23-24 'A Note from the Workshop' by J.B. Priestley.

B45   WHAT IS HAPPINESS?
      London, John Lane The Bodley Head, 1938.
      124p. 19cm.
      Pp 11-20 J.B. Priestley.

B46   ROSE WINDOW A Tribute Offered to St Bartholomew's
          Hospital by Twenty-Five Authors With a Foreword by
          The Lord Horder
      London, William Heinemann Ltd, 1939.
      xii, 385p. illus. 19½cm.
      Pp 138-179 'Prologue to an Unfinished Novel' by J.B.
          Priestley. From internal evidence this is an early
          draft of the opening chapter of *Let the People Sing*
          (A54).

B47   OUR NATION'S HERITAGE Edited by J.B. Priestley
      London, J.M. Dent and Sons Ltd, 1939.
      xiii, 172p. frontis. plates. 19cm.
      Pp xi-xiii 'Introduction'; pp 81-84 'The Cotswolds'
          (from *English Journey*); and pp 163-169 'Britain Is
          in Danger' by J.B. Priestley.

B48   THE BLACK-OUT BOOK Being One-Hundred-and-One Black-Out
          Nights' Entertainment Compiled by Evelyn August.
          Drawings by Woods Incorporating "Strictly Personal"
          and "A-Zoo" by Muriel and Sydney Box.
      London, George C. Harrap & Co Ltd, 1939.
      216p. illus. 20cm.
      P 13 'Little Things' by J.B. Priestley.

B49   FEDERAL UNION A Symposium Edited by M.S. Chaning-
          Pearce
      London, Jonathan Cape, 1940.
      327p. 20cm.
      Pp 93-99 'Federalism and Culture' by J.B. Priestley
          M.A., LL.D., D.LITT.

B50   HOME FROM DUNKIRK A Photographic Record in Aid of the
          British Red Cross; Introduction by J.B. Priestley
      London, John Murray, 1940.
      32p. 20½cm. sd.
      Pp 2-4 'Excursion to Hell' by J.B. Priestley.
      Note: From a broadcast afterwards reprinted in *Post-
          scripts* (A56).

B51   THE BOOK CRISIS Edited by Gilbert McAllister
      London, Faber for the National Committee for the Defence
          of Books, 1940.

58p. 18cm. sd.
Pp 23-26 'The Tax on Morale' by J.B. Priestley MA,
LL.D., D.LITT.

B52 BRITAIN UNDER FIRE With a Foreword by J.B. Priestley
London, Country Life, 1941.
96p. illus. 25½cm.
Pp 6-7 'The Truth Behind the Pictures' by J.B. Priestley.

B53 PHILHARMONIC by Thomas Russell. With an Introduction by
     J.B. Priestley
London, Hutchinson & Co (Publishers) Ltd, 1942.
180p. illus. 19cm.
Pp 9-14 Introduction by J.B. Priestley.

PHILHARMONIC A Future for the Symphony Orchestra by
     Thomas Russell With an Introduction by J.B. Priestley
Harmondsworth (Middlesex), Penguin Books, 1953.
208p. illus. 18½cm. sd.
Pp 7-12 'Introduction' by J.B. Priestley.
Note: The text of this Introduction shows some changes
from that of the first edition.

B54 TWENTIETH CENTURY AUTHORS A Biographic Dictionary of
     Modern Literature Edited by Stanley J. Kunitz and
     Howard Haycraft
New York, H.W. Wilson, 1942.
vii, 1577p. ports. 26cm.
Pp 1129-1130 'Priestley, John Boynton writes....'

B55 THE ENGLISH SPIRIT Edited with an Introduction by
     Anthony Weymouth
London, George Allen & Unwin Ltd, 1942.
135p. ports. 19cm.
Pp 25-29 'This Land of Ours' by J.B. Priestley. A
talk broadcast in the Empire Service of the British
Broadcasting Corporation.

B56 DEFIANT CITY by Joseph Bato With an Introduction by
     J.B. Priestley
London, Gollancz, 1942.
109p. illus. 29cm.
Pp 7-12 'Introduction' by J.B. Priestley.

B57 WRITERS IN FREEDOM A Symposium Based on the XVII In-
     ternational Congress of the P.E.N. Club Held in Sep-
     tember 1941 Edited by Hermon Ould.
London, Hutchinson & Co., 1942.
152p. 18½cm.
Pp 19-20 'The Duty of the Writer' by J.B. Priestley.

B58   LONDON CALLING   Edited by Storm Jameson
       New York, Harper & Bros, 1942.
       viii, 322p.   20cm.
       Pp 53-58 'The Swan Sings Tirralayo', by J.B. Priestley.
       Note: Also published in *Voices on the Green* (B63) in a
          slightly abridged form and written in the past tense
          and not, as here, in the present.

B59   HOW IT CAN BE DONE   A Careful Examination of the Ways
          in Which We Can, and Cannot, Advance to the Kind of
          Britain for Which Many Hope They Are Fighting by
          Richard Acland. With a Preface by J.B. Priestley
       London, MacDonald & Co (Publishers) Ltd, 1943.
       240p.   19cm.
       Pp 5-13 'Introduction which takes the form of a candid
          open letter to the younger generation in or out of
          the forces' by J.B. Priestley.

B60   THE TOC H GIFT BOOK   Edited and Compiled by Hilda Hughes
          With a Foreword by The Lady Tweedismuir and a Note
          from Tubby Clayton
       London, Frederick Muller, 1944.
       xvi, 253p.   ports.   19cm.
       Pp 250-253 'Out with the Parashots' by J.B. Priestley.
       Note: First published in *Postscripts* (1940).

B61   WRITER'S CONGRESS   The Proceedings of the Conference
          Held in October 1943 under the Sponsorship of the
          Hollywood Writers Mobilization and the University of
          California
       Berkeley and Los Angeles, University of California Press,
          1944.
       xx, 663p.   23cm.
       P 10 'Message from J.B. Priestley'.

B62   C.S. EVANS. Born: June 23rd 1883. Died: November 29th
          1944. Joined William Heinemann in 1944; Became a
          director of the company in 1922; Elected chairman in
          1933.
       London, William Heinemann Ltd, 1945 (Privately printed
          at the Windmill Press for circulation among his
          friends)
       iv, 11p.   frontis 19cm.
       Pp 4-5 'Mr J.B. Priestley's Appreciation Printed in
          The Times of December 2nd 1944' (C1384).

B63   VOICES ON THE GREEN   Edited by A.R.J. Wise and Reginald
          A. Smith
       London, Michael Joseph Ltd, 1945.

224p. illus. 19cm.
Pp 184-189 'The Swan Sings Tirralayo' by J.B. Priestley.
Note: This is a slightly abridged version of the same
essay previously published in *London Calling* (B58).

B64 TEN OF MY FAVOURITE BOOKS
London, National Book League, 1945.
A booklet listing books selected by R.A. Butler, John
Gielgud, W.J. Haley, Augustus John, John Masefield,
J.B. Priestley, Bertrand Russell, Sybil Thorndike,
and G.M. Trevelyan in response to the question: 'Which
ten of your favourite books would you specially
recommend to readers younger than yourself?' Priest-
ley's choice was *Best Stories* by Walter de la Mare
(1942), *An Experiment with Time* by J.W. Dunne (1927),
Diary of a Nobody by George and Weedon Grossmith
(1894), *Far Away and Long Ago* by W.H. Hudson (1918),
Arcadian Adventures with the Idle Rich by Stephen
Leacock (1914), *Moby Dick* by Herman Melville (1851),
The Root and the Flower by L.H. Myers (1935), *The
Wrong Box* by Robert Louis Stevenson and Lloyd Osbourne
(1889), *Tidemarks* by H.M. Tomlinson (1921), and *Life
on the Mississippi* by Mark Twain (1883).
Note: Priestley's list first printed in *Books: News
Sheet of the National Book League*, February 1945
(C1395).

B65 REPRESENTATIVE MAJORITY Twenty-One Years of the B.P.R.A.
by Arthur Thrush
London, The Book Publishers' Representatives' Association, 1945.
x, 150p. plates. 22cm.
Pp 61-62 Letter from Priestley indicating his regret
that illness prevents him from addressing the Association's guest night.

B66 LA CLOCHE DE MINUIT by Patrick Hamilton traduit de
l'Anglais par Henri Thies; introduction de J.B.
Priestley
Paris, Editions du Bateau Ivre, 1946.
318p. 19cm.

B67 G.B.S. 90. Aspects of Bernard Shaw's Life and Work.
Edited by S. Winsten
London, Hutchinson & Co (Publishers) Ltd, 1946.
200p. plates. 23½cm.
Pp 50-54 'G.B.S. - Social Critic' by J.B. Priestley.

B68 SOCIALISM OVER SIXTY YEARS; The life of Jowett of
     Bradford (1864-1944) by Fenner Brockway. Preface by
     J.B. Priestley, Foreword by the Late F.W. Jowett
     London, George Allen and Unwin Ltd for the National
     Labour Press, 1946.
     415p. col frontis, ports, facsims. 22cm.
     Pp 7-12 'Preface' by J.B. Priestley.

B69 SOVIET THEATRE EXHIBITION DORLAND HALL LOWER REGENT ST
     22 JANUARY - 28 FEBRUARY 1946
     London, The Theatre Section Society for Cultural Rela-
     tions with the U.S.S.R., 1946.
     Three-page short untitled introductory statement by
     J.B. Priestley.

B70 SCENES OF LONDON LIFE from Sketches by Boz by Charles
     Dickens. Selected and Introduced by J.B. Priestley.
     With Thirteen Illustrations by George Cruikshank
     London, Pan Books, 1947.
     156p. illus. 17cm. Pbk.
     Pp 11-16 'Introduction' by J.B. Priestley.

B71 VOICES FROM BRITAIN. Broadcast History 1939-45 Com-
     piled and Edited by Henning Krabbe
     London, George Allen & Unwin, 1947.
     304p. frontis, plates. 22cm.
     Pp 48-50 'Dunkirk' and pp 64-67 'The Battle of London'
     by J.B. Priestley.
     Both first published in book form in *Postscripts*,
     1940 (A56).

B72 CURRENT BRITISH THOUGHT NO. 1 With an Introduction by
     Ivor Brown
     London, Nicholas Kaye Ltd, 1947.
     vii, 461p. 23cm.
     Pp 145-147 'Raimu' by J.B. Priestley.
     Note: First published in *The New Statesman*, 28 September
     1946 (C1447).

B73 EGO 8 Continuing the Biography of James Agate
     London, G.G. Harrap, 1946.
     269p. illus (inc ports). 24cm.
     Pp 80-82, 93-95 two letters to the author from J.B.
     Priestley dated 12 April and 25 April 1945.

B74 NIGHTMARE ABBEY AND CROTCHET CASTLE by Thomas Love Pea-
     cock With an Introduction by J.B. Priestley
     London, Hamish Hamilton, 1947.

xi, 228p.   17½cm.
(The Novel Library)
Pp vii-x 'Introduction' by J.B. Priestley.

B75   THE WEB AND THE ROCK by Thomas Wolfe
London, William Heinemann Ltd, 1947.
xii, 642p.   20cm.
Pp ix-xii 'Introduction' by J.B. Priestley.

B76   THE NEGLECTED CHILD AND HIS FAMILY   A Study Made in
1946-7 of the Problem of the Child Neglected in His
Own House Together with Certain Recommendations Made
by a Sub-Committee of the Woman's Group on Public
Welfare with an Introduction by J.B. Priestley
Oxford, Oxford University Press, 1948.
xii, 104p.   21cm.   sd.
Pp ix-xi 'Introduction' by J.B. Priestley.

B77   SOVIET WRITERS REPLY TO ENGLISH WRITER'S QUESTIONS
London, Writers Group of Society for Cultural Relations
with the U.S.S.R., 1948.
68p.   18cm.   sd.
Pp 5-8 'Foreword by J.B. Priestley Who Also Put Some
of the Questions'.

B78   TRIBUTE TO WALTER DE LA MARE   On His Seventy-Fifth
Birthday
London, Faber & Faber, 1948.
195p.   illus.   22cm.
Pp 15-18 'What Lovely Things' by J.B. Priestley.

B79   ADVENTURE IN REPERTORY by Aubrey Dias   with a Foreword
by J.B. Priestley
Northampton, Northampton Repertory Players, 1948.
224p.   illus.   22cm.
Pp 5-6 'Foreword' by J.B. Priestley.

B80   MARGARET McMILLAN   A Memoir by D'Arcy Cresswell   with
a Foreword by J.B. Priestley
London, Hutchinson & Co, 1948.
160p.   frontis (port), plates.   23cm.
Pp 9-10 'Foreword' by J.B. Priestley.

B81   TO ALL WOMEN
London, Labour Party, 1949.
16p.   illus (ports).   32cm.   sd.
P 7 'Family Favourites: J.B. Priestley Author and
Dramatist'.

B82   IN PRAISE OF BERNARD SHAW An Anthology for Old and
        Young Edited by Allen M. Laing
      London, Frederick Muller Ltd, 1949.
      62p. 14 x 11cm.
      P 17 'His Dramatic Achievement' (from the *Daily Herald*);
        p 43 'Mixed Up in Him' by J.B. Priestley.

B83   INTERNATIONAL THEATRE   Edited by John Andrews and Ossia
        Trilling
      London, Sampson Low, 1949.
      xi, 228p. bibliog. 22cm.
      Pp 207-215 'Postscript' by J.B. Priestley.

B84   THE RADIO LISTENER'S WEEK-END BOOK A Selection from
        Notable Broadcasts of the Past Five Years Edited by
        John Pringle
      London, Odhams Press Limited, 1950.
      288p. illus. 21cm.
      Pp 85-91 'Born and Bred in Bradford' by J.B. Priestley.
      First printed in *The Listener*, 27 December 1945 (C1426).

B85   THE OLD WIVES TALE by Arnold Bennett with an Introduction
        by J.B. Priestley
      New York, Harper, 1950.
      xxii, 612p. 21cm.
      Introduction by J.B. Priestley.

B86   TURN OF THE CENTURY 1900-1950 The Story of Fifty Tre-
        mendous Years Edited by Frank Owen
      London, Daily Mail, 1950.
      48p. illus. 38 x 30cm. sd. (i.e., in the form of a
        tabloid newspaper)
      P 16-17 'The Drama' by J.B. Priestley.

B87   THE STORY OF LADY PRECIOUS STREAM A Novel by S.I.
        Hsiung with a Preface by J.B. Priestley. Illustrated
        by A.C. Chang
      London, Hutchinson & Co, 1950.
      176p. illus, col frontis. 21cm.
      Pp 7-9 'Preface' by J.B. Priestley.

B88   OUR FAVOURITE DISH The Theatre Recipe Book. 250 Recipes
        Contributed by Members of the British Theatrical
        Profession. Compiled by Mrs Prince Littler. Edited
        by Naomi Walters
      London, Putnam, 1952.
      xvii, 282p. illus, tables. 19½cm.

P 56 'Sole Marrakesh' by J.B. Priestley.
Note: The same recipe, expressed in different words, was also published in *Celebrity Cooking for You* (B107).

B89 THE YORKSHIRE STORY with an Introduction by J.B. Priestley
York, Yorkshire Insurance Company Limited, 1954.
44p. illus. 19cm. sd.
Pp 3-6 'Introduction' by J.B. Priestley.

B90 THEATRE 1954-55 Edited by Ivor Brown
London, Reinhardt, 1955.
vii, 200p. plates. tables. 22½cm.
Pp 111-114 'The Case Against Shakespeare' by J.B. Priestley.

B91 MEETING AT NIGHT by James Bridie with an Introduction by J.B. Priestley
London, Constable, 1956.
xiv, 85p. 18½cm. Pbk.
Pp vii-xiii 'Introduction' by J.B. Priestley.
Note: 'Much of the above appeared as a *Books in General* article in *The New Statesman & Nation*...' (footnote to Introduction). This was 'Bridie: The Plays and the Man', *New Statesman*, 31 December 1955 (C1827).

B92 OUR MUTUAL FRIEND by Charles Dickens with the Original Illustrations by Marcus Stone and a New Introduction by J.B. Priestley
London, MacDonald & Co, 1957.
xxvi, 881p. illus. 19½cm.
Pp ix-xix 'Introduction' by J.B. Priestley.

B93 COMING TO LONDON Edited by John Lehmann
London, Phoenix House, 1957.
176p. 19cm.
Pp 59-73 'Coming to London' by J.B. Priestley.

B94 THE BODLEY HEAD LEACOCK Edited and Introduced by J.B. Priestley
London, The Bodley Head, 1957.
vii, 9-464p. 19½cm.
Pp 9-13 'Editor's Introduction' by J.B. Priestley.

B95 THE AUTHOR AND THE PUBLIC Problems of Communication. Report of 8th International P.E.N. Congress
London, Hutchinson & Co, 1957.

201p. 22cm.
Pp 27-28 'Statement of the Theme' by J.B. Priestley.

B96   THE BODLEY HEAD SCOTT FITZGERALD Vol. 1 With an
         Introduction by J.B. Priestley
       London, John Lane The Bodley Head, 1958.
       456p. 20cm.
       Pp 7-16 'Introduction' by J.B. Priestley.

B97   NUCLEAR DISARMAMENT
       London, Campaign for Nuclear Disarmament, 1958.
       Single sheet folded. 19 x 11½cm.
       P 2 'Let Britain Lead' by J.B. Priestley, the Vice-
         President.

B98   THE BRYANSTON MISCELLANY Editor Victor Bonham-Carter
       Blandford (Dorset), Bryanston School, 1958.
       144p. 25½cm.
       Pp 48-51 'VERY Short Stories' by J.B. Priestley.
       Note: A limited edition of 350 numbered copies.

B99   THE NEW BOOK OF SNOBS BY VARIOUS HANDS Illustrated
         by Michael Ffolkes and William Makepeace Thackeray
       London, Museum Press, 1959.
       160p. illus. 22cm.
       Pp 99-104 'Literature' by J.B. Priestley.
       Note: First published *Punch*, 21 January 1959 (C2002).

B100   THE COMPLETE IMBIBER 3 Edited by Cyril Ray
       London, Putnam, 1960.
       176p. illus. 23cm.
       Pp 15-19 'Thoughts on Imbibing' by J.B. Priestley.

B101   FOUR ENGLISH NOVELS by J.B. Priestley and O.B. Davis
       New York, Harcourt Brace and Company, 1960.
       789p. illus. 21cm.
       'Prefaces' and 'Afterwords' to *Pride and Prejudice* by
         Jane Austen; *Pickwick Papers* by Charles Dickens;
         The Return of the Native by Thomas Hardy; and *The
         Secret Sharer* by Joseph Conrad; and a 'Final After-
         word' by J.B. Priestley.

B102   JOHN O'LONDON'S ANTHOLOGY
       London, Darwen Finlayson, 1961.
       233p. 22½cm.
       Pp 38-40 'Forty Years On' by J.B. Priestley.
       Note: First published *John O'London's*, 8 October
         1959 (C2039).

B103 THE PROFESSOR'S HOUSE by Willa Cather with an Introduction by J.B. Priestley
London, Hamish Hamilton, 1961.
283p. 19½cm.
Pp 3-7 'Introduction' by J.B. Priestley.

B104 A LOST LADY by Willa Cather with an Introduction by
J.B. Priestley
London, Hamish Hamilton, 1961.
174p. 19½cm.
Pp 3-7 'Introduction' by J.B. Priestley.

B105 AUTHORS TALKING
London, British Broadcasting Corporation, 1961.
48p. ports. 21½ x 14cm. sd.
P 4 'In the Movement' by J.B. Priestley.
Note: Introductory talk which launched the first pro-
grammes of 'Life and Letters', BBC General Overseas
Service.

B106 4 ENGLISH BIOGRAPHIES by J.B. Priestley and O.B. Davis
New York, Harcourt Brace & World Inc., 1961.
767p. illus. 21cm.
'Afterwords' to *Shakespeare of London* by Marchette
Chute; *The Life of Samuel Johnson LL.D.* by James
Boswell; *Queen Victoria* by Lytton Strachey; and
The Edge of Day by Laurie Lee; and a 'Final After-
word' by J.B. Priestley.

B107 CELEBRITY COOKING FOR YOU. Dishes Chosen by the
Famous. Edited by Renee Hellman. Foreword by A.
Dickson Wright
London, Andre Deutsch, 1961.
260p. 21cm.
P 81 'Sole Marrakesh' by J.B. Priestley.

CELEBRITY COOKING Edited by Renee Hellman. Foreword
by A. Dickson Wright. Preface by The Honourable
Angus Ogilvy.
London, Paul Hamlyn, 1967.
239p. illus. 26cm.
P 66 'Sole Marrakesh' by J.B. Priestley.
Note: Priestley's text in the two editions is almost
identical except that the order of the paragraphs
is changed. The same recipe, couched differently,
appeared in *Our Favourite Dish* (B88).

B108 AN AUTOBIOGRAPHY (By Anthony Trollope) With an Introduction by J.B. Priestley

London, Collins, 1962.
286p. 18cm. Pbk.
(The Fontana Library)
Pp 7-16 'Introduction' by J.B. Priestley.

B109 THE BEDPOST: A Miscellany of The Yorkshire Post
       Edited by Kenneth Young
      London, MacDonald & Co, 1962.
      244p. frontis, plates. 20½cm.
      Pp 11-13 'The Friend of Man' by J.B. Priestley.
      Note: Extracts from a speech at the first *Yorkshire
        Post* Literary Luncheon, held at the Hotel Metropole
        in Leeds, Thursday, November 2nd, 1961.

B110 ENCORE THE SUNDAY TIMES BOOK
      London, Michael Joseph, 1962.
      viii, 490p. 23½cm.
      Pp 286-297 'I Had the Time' by J.B. Priestley. First
        printed in *The Sunday Times*, 25 June 1961 (C2066),
        and later incorporated in *Margin Released* (A130).

B111 NEW STATESMANSHIP An Anthology Selected by Edward
       Hyams
      London, Longmans, 1963.
      ix, 290p. illus. 22½cm.
      Pp 236, 238-244 'Britain and the Nuclear Bombs' by
        J.B. Priestley.
      Note: First published *The New Statesman*, 2 November
        1957 (C1919). Later reprinted in *Voices from the
        Crowd* (B117).

B112 THE SUNDAY TIMES BOOK - ENCORE SECOND YEAR Edited
       by Leonard Russell
      London, Michael Joseph Ltd, 1963.
      x, 406p. illus. 24cm.
      Pp 224-225 'The Road to Samarkand' by J.B. Priestley.
      Note: First published in *The Sunday Times*, 2 December
        1962 (C2095).

B113 DAUGHTER OF THE HOUSE by Evelyn Ames With an Intro-
       duction by J.B. Priestley
      London, Hutchinson, 1963.
      (12) 241p. 20½cm.
      Pp (1)-(6) 'Introduction' by J.B. Priestley.

B114 COMPLETE IMBIBER 6 An Entertainment Edited by Cyril
       Ray
      London, Vista Books, 1963.

224p. frontis, illus (some col), facsims. 26cm.
Pp 125-130 'It Isn't Only Peaches Down in Georgia' by
J.B. and Jacquetta Priestley.

B115 ADVENTURES IN ENGLISH LITERATURE by J.B. Priestley and
Josephine Spear
New York, Harcourt Brace and World, Inc., 1963.
848p. illus. 24cm.
P xvi-   'The Land and Its People' by Jacquetta Hawkes
and J.B. Priestley; pp 25-31 'Historical Introduction'
to The Anglo-Saxon Period; pp 49-59 'Historical Introduction, to The Medieval Period; pp 105-115 'Historical Introduction' to The Elizabethan Age; pp 195-
198 'Macbeth: An Afterword'; pp 213-223 'Historical
Introduction' to The Seventeenth Century; pp 273-284
'Historical Introduction' to The Eighteenth Century;
pp 363-372 'The English Novel'; pp 373-383 'Historical Introduction' to The Romantic Age; pp 481-494
'Historical Introduction' to The Victorian Age; pp
603-611 'Historical Introduction' to The Twentieth
Century; pp 661-663 'Introduction' to Modern Poetry;
p 701 'Introduction' to Modern Biography; p 724
'Introduction' to Modern Essays; pp 752-754 'Women
and Clothes', 'No School Report', and 'Cooking
Picnics' (all from *Delight*, A96); and pp 755-758
'Introduction' to Modern Drama, all by J.B. Priestley.

B116 MIGHTIER THAN THE SWORD The P.E.N. Hermon Ould Memorial
Lectures 1953-1961 With a Foreword by C.V. Wedgwood
London, Macmillan & Co Ltd; New York, St Martin's
Press, 1964.
ix, 146p. 22½cm.
Pp 34-54 'The Writer in a Changing Society' by J.B.
Priestley.

B117 VOICES FROM THE CROWD Against the H-Bomb Edited by
David Boulton
London, Peter Owen, 1964.
185p. 22cm.
Pp 38-45 'Britain and the Nuclear Bombs' by J.B.
Priestley.
Note: First published in *The New Statesman*, 2 November
1957 (C1919), and also in *New Statesmanship* (B111).

B118 WAR OF THE WORLDS by H.G. Wells. Introduction by J.B.
Priestley Illustrated by Joe Mugnaini
New York, Heritage Press, 1964.
ix, 188p. illus (some col). 26cm.
Pp v-ix 'Introduction' by J.B. Priestley.

and:

B119   THE TIME MACHINE by H.G. Wells.   Introduction by J.B.
          Priestley   Illustrated by Joe Mugnaini
       New York, Heritage Press, 1964.
       ix, 98p.   illus (some col).   26cm.
       Pp v-ix 'Introduction' by J.B. Priestley.
       Note: B118 and B119 bound back to back in one volume.

B120   STORIES FOR SPEAKERS.   A Wonderful Collection of After-
          Dinner Stories Contributed by a Host of Well-Known
          Personalities.   Compiled by Geoffrey J. Matson
       London, Foulsham, 1965.
       92p.   19cm.
       P 56 'A Bonny Baby' by J.B. Priestley.

B121   STAR CROSSED by Marjorie Tilden.   Introduction by
          J.B. Priestley.   Foreword by John Cowper Powys
       London, Macdonald, 1966.
       72p.   20½cm.
       Pp 9-12 'Introduction' by J.B. Priestley.

B122   NATIONAL FILM ARCHIVE CATALOGUE   Part III   Silent
          Fiction Films 1895-1930.   Foreword by J.B. Priestley
       London, The British Film Institute, 1966.
       (vi), 326p.   plates.   21½cm.   Pbk.
       Pp (iii)-(iv) Foreword by J.B. Priestley.

B123   AN EVERYMAN ANTHOLOGY of Excerpts Grave and Gay from
          Everyman's Library to Celebrate Its Diamond Jubilee
          MCMLXVI
       London, Dent, 1966.
       256p.   18½cm.
       (Everyman's Library No 663)
       Pp 5-8 'Introduction' by J.B. Priestley.   There is also
          an excerpt from *Angel Pavement* (A21) pp 22-24.

B124   WHAT I BELIEVE   Edited and with an Introduction by
          George Unwin
       London, Allen & Unwin, 1966.
       236p.   22½cm.
       Pp 163-171 J.B. Priestley.
       Note: Not to be confused with item B40.

B125   AUTHORS TAKE SIDES ON VIETNAM   Two Questions on the
          War in Vietnam Answered by the Authors of Several
          Nations.   Edited by Cecil Woolf and John Bagguley
       London, Peter Owen, 1967.

xii, 13-232p. 22cm.
Pp 163-165 J.B. Priestley.
Note: First published in *Envoy*, September 1967 (C2163).

B126 THE COLLECTED PLAYS OF HARLEY GRANVILLE-BARKER Volume
      1. Foreword by J.B. Priestley. Introduction by
      Ivor Brown
      London, Sidgwick and Jackson, 1967.
      203p. 20cm. Pbk.
      P 9 'Foreword' by J.B. Priestley.

B127 NOVELS OF THOMAS LOVE PEACOCK *Headlong Hall Night-
      mare Abbey The Misfortunes of Elphin Crotchet Castle*
      Introduction by J.B. Priestley Notes by Barbara
      Lloyd Evans
      London, Pan Books Ltd, 1967.
      xxii, 23-379p. 18cm. Pbk.
      (Pan T31 Bestsellers of Literature Editor: Arthur
      Calder-Marshall)
      Pp v-xv 'Introduction' by J.B. Priestley.

B128 AUTOBIOGRAPHY by John Cowper Powys
      London, Macdonald, 1967.
      xxii, 672p. frontis (port). 22½cm.
      Pp ix-xvii 'Introduction' by J.B. Priestley.

B129 THE SATURDAY BOOK 28 Edited by John Hadfield
      London, Hutchinson & Co, 1968.
      256p. illus (some col), ports. 24cm.
      Pp 97-103 'By Disc to Dream' by J.B. Priestley.

B130 THE SAVING OF SHANDY HALL or HOW TO RAISE £25,000
      in These Hard Times to Banish the Death-Watch
      Beetle, Preserve for Posterity, & Make a Living
      Museum OF THE FORMER HOME OF THE REV. LAURENCE
      STERNE AT COXWOLD IN THE NORTH RIDING OF YORKSHIRE,
      WHERE HE WROTE TRISTRAM SHANDY AND A SENTIMENTAL
      JOURNEY, BOOKS THAT WILL LIVE AS LONG AS THE ENGLISH
      LANGUAGE With a Foreword by J.B. Priestley
      York, The Laurence Sterne Trust, 1968.
      Pp 3-4 'Why Shandy Hall Must Be Saved' by J.B.
      Priestley.
      Note: This appeal brochure was published in a limited
      edition of 750 copies.

B131 PUB A Celebration Edited by Angus McGill
      London, Longmans, 1969.
      243p. illus. 20½cm.
      Pp 106-115 'They Are Called Pobs' by J.B. Priestley.

B132   THE SATURDAY BOOK 29   Edited by John Hadfield
        London, Hutchinson & Co, 1969.
        252p. illus (some col). 23½cm.
        Pp 145-156 'A Holiday Painter' by J.B. Priestley.

B133   CHARLES DICKENS 1812-1870   A Centenary Volume edited
            by E.W.F. Tomlin
        London, Weidenfeld and Nicolson, 1969.
        288p. plates (some col), ports. 25½cm.
        Pp 14-31 'The Great Inimitable' by J.B. Priestley.

B134   E.M. FORSTER A PASSAGE TO INDIA. A CASEBOOK Edited
            by Malcolm Bradbury
        London, Macmillan, 1970.
        252p. bibliog. 20cm.
        Pp 55-58 'A Review' by J.B. Priestley. First printed
            in *London Mercury*, July 1924 (C342).

B135   'THE WINE MINE' A First Anthology Edited by Anthony
            Hogg
        London, Souvenir Press, 1970.
        223p. illus, music, ports. 22cm.
        Includes 'Some Tots and Sips' by J.B. Priestley.
        Note: First published in *The Wine Mine*, Autumn 1962
            (C2088).

B136   AS I REMEMBER by Arthur Bliss
        London, Faber, 1970.
        269p. plates, illus, ports, music. 25cm.
        Pp 171-177 letters by J.B. Priestley to the author
            concerning his opera, *The Olympians* (A94), for
            which Bliss was writing the score. The letters
            are dated 1 August and 20 August 1945, 24 April and
            19 July 1946, and 11 January and 15 January 1947.

B137   THE SHELL GUIDE TO ENGLAND Edited by John Hadfield.
            Preface by J.B. Priestley.
        London, Michael Joseph in association with Rainbird
            Reference Books, 1970.
        921p. plates, illus (some col), col maps. bibliog.
            26cm.
        Pp 9-11 Preface 'On England' by J.B. Priestley.

B138   THE SATURDAY BOOK 31 Edited by John Hadfield
        London, Hutchinson & Co, 1971.
        256p. illus (some col). 23½cm.
        Pp 153-159 'The Art of Smoking' by J.B. Priestley.

B139 UPSTAIRS DOWNSTAIRS A 64-Page Souvenir of the Popular
      London Weekend Television Series. FOREWORD by J.B.
      Priestley.
      London, Independent Television Publications Limited,
      1972.
      64p. (inc. covers). illus, ports, pictorial cover.
      28 x 21cm. sd.
      Pp 2-3 'Foreword' by J.B. Priestley.

B140 HANGOVER SQUARE A Story of Darkest Earls Court by
      Patrick Hamilton. With an Introduction by J.B.
      Priestley.
      London, Constable, 1972.
      xiii, 280p. 20cm.
      Pp ix-xiii 'Introduction' by J.B. Priestley.
      Note: Text identical to 'Introduction' to *Slaves of
      Solitude* by Patrick Hamilton (B141).

B141 SLAVES OF SOLITUDE by Patrick Hamilton. With an Intro-
      duction by J.B. Priestley
      London, Constable, 1972.
      ix, 242p. 20cm.
      Pp v-ix 'Introduction' by J.B. Priestley.
      Note: Text identical to 'Introduction' to *Hangover
      Square* by Patrick Hamilton (B140).

B142 ASPECTS OF ALICE Lewis Carroll's Dreamchild As Seen
      Through the Critics' Looking-Glasses 1865-1971
      Edited by Robert Phillips. Illustrations by Sir
      John Tenniel and Lewis Carroll.
      London, Victor Gollancz Ltd, 1972.
      xxviii, 450p. illus, ports, facsims. 24cm.
      Pp 263-266 'A Note on Humpty Dumpty' by J.B. Priestley.
      Note: First printed in *The Challenge*, 6 April 1923
      (C233) and collected in *I for One* (1923).

B143 OF TIME AND STARS The Worlds of Arthur C. Clarke.
      With an Introduction by J.B. Priestley
      London, Gollancz, 1972.
      208p. 21cm.
      Pp 7-10 'Introduction' by J.B. Priestley.

B144 RADIO TIMES 50TH ANNIVERSARY SOUVENIR 1923-1973
      London, BBC, 1973.
      100p. (inc covers). illus (some col), pictorial covers.
      30 x 23½cm. sd.
      P 50 'I Have No Absolute Proof, But It Was Churchill,
      Not the BBC, WHO STOPPED MY 'POSTSCRIPTS' SAYS J.B.

PRIESTLEY'.
Note: Also includes full-page reproduction of front
cover of *Radio Times*, 18 October 1940, featuring
'Priestley's Postscripts' including a portrait and
long extract from Robert W. Reid's article 'When
Priestley Talks to America' in the same issue.

B145 THE MILITANT SUFFRAGETTES by Antonia Raeburn. Introduction by J.B. Priestley
London, Michael Joseph Ltd, 1973.
xviii, 269p. illus. 22½cm.
Pp xvii-xviii 'Introduction' by J.B. Priestley.

B146 THE BEDSIDE 'GUARDIAN' 24 A Selection from the 'Guar-
dian' 1974-75. Edited by W.L. Webb. With an Intro-
duction by Alastair Hetherington
London, Collins, 1975.
263p. 21cm.
Pp 215-217 'Thanksgiving for Neville Cardus' by J.B.
Priestley.
Note: First published *The Guardian*, 1 March 1975
(C2336).

B147 THE ESSENTIAL WEST RIDING Its Character in Words and
Pictures Foreword by J.B. Priestley
Wakefield (Yorkshire), E.P. Publishing Ltd, 1975.
x, 198p. illus. 22cm.
Pp v-vi 'Foreword' by J.B. Priestley.

B148 PASS THE PORT The Best After-Dinner Stories
Cirencester (Gloucs), Christian Brann Ltd, 1976.
238p. illus. facsim. 23cm.
P 201 J.B. Priestley M.A. Litt.D. LL.D. Author.

B149 CONTEMPORARY NOVELISTS With a Preface by Walter Allen.
Edited by James Vinson.
London, St James Press; New York, St Martin's Press,
2e 1977.
xvii, 1636p. 24½cm.
P 1116 'J.B. Priestley comments' (i.e., on his own
entry).

B150 BOOKS ROUND ABOUT Year Book No 8 1976-77
Bradford (Yorkshire), Federation of Children's Book
Groups, 1977.
60p. illus. 30 x 21cm. sd.
P 1 'Foreword' by J.B. Priestley.

B151   THE ALIENATED   Growing Old Today by Gladys Elder
           Edited by Christine Bernard; Photographs by Mike
           Abrahams; Introduction by J.B. Priestley
       London, Writers and Readers Publishing Cooperative,
           1977.
       144p. illus, ports. bibliog. 21cm.
       Pp 10-11 'Introduction' by J.B. Priestley.

B152   WHAT'S WRONG WITH BRITAIN   Edited by Patrick Hutber.
           Foreword by Lord Home.
       London, Sphere Books in association with the Sunday
           Telegraph, 1978.
       112p. 18cm. Pbk.
       Pp 75-80 'Liberty Not Equality Should Be the U.K.
       Watchword' by J.B. Priestley.
       Note: First published *Sunday Telegraph*, 2 November
       1975 (C2243).

B153   THE GOLDEN AGE OF CRICKET 1890-1914 by David Frith.
           Foreword by J.B. Priestley
       London, Lutterworth Press, 1978.
       192p. illus. 26cm.
       Pp 9-10 'Foreword' by J.B. Priestley. Signed J.B.
           Priestley O.M.

B154   J.B. PRIESTLEY: AN ANNOTATED BIBLIOGRAPHY by
           Alan Edwin Day with a Foreword by J.B. Priestley
       New York, Garland Publishing, 1980.
       xii, 360p. 22cm.
       Foreword by J.B. Priestley p vii.

Addendum:

B155   ILKLEY LITERATURE FESTIVAL April 23rd-28th. SOUVENIR
           PROGRAMME.
       Ilkley (Yorkshire), Ilkley Literature Festival Ltd,
           1973.
       56p. including paper wrapper. illus. 14 x 22cm.
       P 4 'Foreword' by J.B. Priestley.

C. CONTRIBUTIONS TO
NEWSPAPERS, JOURNALS AND MAGAZINES

1912

C1 SECRETS OF THE RAG-TIME KING: A REMARKABLE INTERVIEW.
    London Opinion, XXXV (456), 14 December 1913:442-443.
    Signed J. Boynton Priestley.
    Note: Chapter XXIV 'My First Article', *Delight*, 1949
    (A96) and 'The Swan Arcadian (1910-1914)', *Margin Re-
    leased*, 1962 (A130) refer to the publication of this
    imaginary interview.

1913

C2 ROUND THE HEARTH. *Bradford Pioneer*, 2, 24 January 1913:
    6. Initialled J.B.P.
    Note: 'Now the first regular writing I ever did, as a
    youth in my teens ... was for this same *Bradford
    Pioneer*.... I wrote a weekly feature called *Round the
    Hearth*, in which, as I knew nothing, I wrote about
    everything.... I was not paid anything, but occasionally
    received a free pass to a theatre or music-hall. I
    should like to be able to say that I scribbled away
    every week because I was devoted to the Labour Move-
    ment, but the truth is that, although I shared my
    father's Socialism, I was chiefly influenced by the
    desire to see myself in print'. Preface to A. Fenner
    Brockway: *Socialism Over Sixty Years*, 1946 (B68).
       Norah Fienburgh: 'JB - Meet the Younger Mr Priestley',
    Bradford Pioneer, 18 November 1932, describes the
    'Round the Hearth' series and suggests that they be re-
    printed.

C3   ROUND THE HEARTH. *Bradford Pioneer*, 3, 31 January 1913:
      6.   Initialled J.B.P.

C4   ROUND THE HEARTH. *Bradford Pioneer*, 4, 7 February 1913:
      6.   Initialled J.B.P.

C5   ROUND THE HEARTH. *Bradford Pioneer*, 5, 14 February 1913:
      6.   Initialled J.B.P.

C6   ROUND THE HEARTH. *Bradford Pioneer*, 6, 21 February 1913:
      6.   Initialled J.B.P.

C7   ROUND THE HEARTH. *Bradford Pioneer*, 7, 28 February 1913:
      6.   Initialled J.B.P.

C8   ROUND THE HEARTH. *Bradford Pioneer*, 8, 7 March 1913:6.
      Initialled J.B.P.

C9   ROUND THE HEARTH. *Bradford Pioneer*, 9, 14 March 1913:6.
      Initialled J.B.P.

C10   ROUND THE HEARTH. *Bradford Pioneer*, 10, 21 March 1913:6.
      Initialled J.B.P.

C11   ROUND THE HEARTH. *Bradford Pioneer*, 11, 28 March 1913:6.
      Initialled J.B.P.

C12   ROUND THE HEARTH. *Bradford Pioneer*, 12, 4 April 1913:6.
      Initialled J.B.P.

C13   ROUND THE HEARTH. *Bradford Pioneer*, 13, 11 April 1913:6.
      Initialled J.B.P.

C14   ROUND THE HEARTH. *Bradford Pioneer*, 14, 18 April 1913:6.
      Initialled J.B.P.

C15   ROUND THE HEARTH. *Bradford Pioneer*, 15, 25 April 1913:6.
      Initialled J.B.P.

C16   ROUND THE HEARTH. *Bradford Pioneer*, 16, 2 May 1913:6.
      Initialled J.B.P.

C17   ROUND THE HEARTH. *Bradford Pioneer*, 17, 9 May 1913:6.
      Initialled J.B.P.

C18   ROUND THE HEARTH. *Bradford Pioneer*, 18, 16 May 1913:6.
      Initialled J.B.P.

C19 ROUND THE HEARTH. *Bradford Pioneer*, 19, 23 May 1913:6.
     Initialled J.B.P.

C20 THE MODERN JUGGERNAUT. *Labour Leader*, 22 (10), 29 May
     1913:7. Signed J. Boynton Priestley.

C21 ROUND THE HEARTH. *Bradford Pioneer*, 20, 30 May 1913:
     6. Initialled J.B.P.

C22 ROUND THE HEARTH. *Bradford Pioneer*, 21, 6 June 1913:
     6. Initialled J.B.P.

C23 ROUND THE HEARTH. *Bradford Pioneer*, 22, 13 June 1913:
     6. Initialled J.B.P.

C24 ROUND THE HEARTH. *Bradford Pioneer*, 26, 11 July 1913:
     6. Initialled J.B.P.

C25 ROUND THE HEARTH. *Bradford Pioneer*, 27, 18 July 1913:
     6. Initialled J.B.P.

C26 ROUND THE HEARTH. *Bradford Pioneer*, 28, 25 July 1913:
     6. Initialled J.B.P.

C27 ROUND THE HEARTH. *Bradford Pioneer*, 29, 1 August 1913:
     6. Initialled J.B.P.

C28 ROUND THE HEARTH. *Bradford Pioneer*, 30, 8 August 1913:
     6. Initialled J.B.P.

C29 ROUND THE HEARTH. *Bradford Pioneer*, 31, 15 August 1913:
     6. Initialled J.B.P.

C30 ROUND THE HEARTH. *Bradford Pioneer*, 32, 22 August 1913:
     6. Initialled J.B.P.

C31 ROUND THE HEARTH. *Bradford Pioneer*, 33, 29 August 1913:
     6. Initialled J.B.P.

C32 EDDYING WATERS. *Bradford Pioneer*, 33, 29 August 1913:
     6. Signed J. Boynton Priestley.

C33 EDDYING WATERS. *Bradford Pioneer*, 34, 5 September 1913:
     6. Signed J. Boynton Priestley.

C34 EDDYING WATERS. *Bradford Pioneer*, 35, 12 September
     1913:6. Signed J. Boynton Priestley.

C35   ROUND THE HEARTH. *Bradford Pioneer*, 36, 19 September
      1913:6. Initialled J.B.P.

C36   ROUND THE HEARTH. *Bradford Pioneer*, 37, 26 September
      1913:6. Initialled J.B.P.

C37   ROUND THE HEARTH. *Bradford Pioneer*, 38, 3 October 1913:
      6. Initialled J.B.P.

C38   ROUND THE HEARTH. *Bradford Pioneer*, 39, 10 October
      1913:6. Initialled J.B.P.

C39   A NOCTURNE. *Bradford Pioneer*, 45, 21 November 1913:5.
      Signed J. Boynton Priestley.

                              1919

C40   THE MARKET A REVERIE AMONG THE CITY STALLS. *Yorkshire
      Observer*, 17311, 30 April 1919:12. Initialled J.B.P.

C41   A PAGEANT OF TOWNS. *Yorkshire Observer*, 17329, 21 May
      1919:12. Signed Peter of Pomfret.
      Note: The first twelve of the Peter of Pomfret essays
      appeared under the general title of 'Musings of an
      Idle Fellow'. The last to do so was 'Holidays',
      printed 6 August 1919.

C42   A WAYFARER GOES TO WENSLEYDALE. *Yorkshire Observer*,
      17331, 23 May 1919:12.

C43   TAME DRAGON'S NEST. *Yorkshire Observer*, 17335, 28 May
      1919:12. Signed Peter of Pomfret.

C44   A WAYFARER IN WENSLEYDALE. *Yorkshire Observer*, 17337,
      30 May 1919:12.

C45   THE MOORS. *Yorkshire Observer*, 17341, 4 June 1919:
      14. Signed Peter of Pomfret.

C46   THE TOWN IN JUNE. *Yorkshire Observer*, 17347, 11 June
      1919:10. Signed Peter of Pomfret.

C47   A VINDICATION OF SUBURBIA. *Yorkshire Observer*, 17353,
      18 June 1919:14. Signed Peter of Pomfret.

C48 THE MAGIC FLUTE. *Yorkshire Observer*, 17359, 25 June
1919:13. Initialled JBP.

C49 THE GREAT MAN. *Yorkshire Observer*, 17359, 25 June 1919:
14. Signed Peter of Pomfret.

C50 THREE OPERAS. *Yorkshire Observer*, 17365, 2 July 1919:
12. Signed Peter of Pomfret.

C51 'WALKING ON' AT THE OPERA. *Yorkshire Observer*, 17366,
3 July 1919:16.

C52 WHAT IS WRONG WITH THE 'RED LION'. *Yorkshire Observer*,
17371, 9 July 1919:12. Signed Peter of Pomfret.

C53 MUSIC IN THE PARK. *Yorkshire Observer*, 17377, 16 July
1919:12. Signed Peter of Pomfret.

C54 A RETROSPECT. *Yorkshire Observer*, 17383, 23 July 1919:
12. Signed Peter of Pomfret.

C55 THE GALLEONS OF THE STREET. *Yorkshire Observer*, 17389,
30 July 1919:12. Signed Peter of Pomfret.

C56 HOLIDAYS. *Yorkshire Observer*, 17395, 6 August 1919:12.
Signed Peter of Pomfret.

C57 LIFE AND LUCKY BAGS. *Yorkshire Observer*, 17401, 13
August 1919:12. Signed Peter of Pomfret.
Reprinted: *Papers from Lilliput* (1922).

C58 DECLINE OF CONVERSATION. *Yorkshire Observer*, 17406,
19 August 1919:6. Initialled JBP.

C59 THE YORKSHIRE WOMAN. *Yorkshire Observer*, 17407, 20
August 1919:12. Signed Peter of Pomfret.

C60 THE YORKSHIREMAN. *Yorkshire Observer*, 17413, 27 August
1919:12. Signed Peter of Pomfret.

C61 ON FADDISTS. *Yorkshire Observer*, 17419, 3 September
1919:10. Signed Peter of Pomfret.

C62 ON THE HEROES OF FICTION. *Yorkshire Observer*, 17425,
10 September 1919:12. Signed Peter of Pomfret.

C63 TWO VISIONS. *Yorkshire Observer*, 17431, 17 September
1919:12. Signed Peter of Pomfret.

C64 ON MAD MECHANISTS. *Yorkshire Observer*, 17437, 24 September 1919:12. Signed Peter of Pomfret.

C65 ON THE SENSATIONAL PRESS. *Yorkshire Observer*, 17443, 1 October 1919:12. Signed Peter of Pomfret.

C66 NEW POEMS AND ESSAYS. *Yorkshire Observer*, 17446, 4 October 1919:14. Review of *Sea-Gazer* (Alberta Vickridge), *In Memoriam Edward Thomas*, and *Things Big and Small* (Gilbert Thomas). Initialled J.B.P.

C67 ON GOMBROON. *Yorkshire Observer*, 17449, 8 October 1919:12. Signed Peter of Pomfret.

C68 ON JACKS IN OFFICE. *Yorkshire Observer*, 17455, 15 October 1919:14. Signed Peter of Pomfret.

C69 AT A REVUE. *Yorkshire Observer*, 17461, 22 October 1919:14. Signed Peter of Pomfret.

                                   1920

C70 LATEST REVIEWS: RECENT MINOR VERSE. *Yorkshire Observer*, 17546, 31 January 1920:12. Review of *Skylark and Swallow* (R.L. Gales); *Tween Clyde and Tweed* (Gilbert Rae); *By Tarn and Thames* (Desemea Wilson); and *The Survivors* (Geoffrey Fyson). Initialled JBP.

C71 LATEST REVIEWS. *Yorkshire Observer*, 17552, 7 February 1920:10. Review of *Plays of the Ridings* (F.W. Moorman); *Three Lancashire Plays* (Harold Brighouse); and *Practical Hints on Playwriting* (Agnes Platt). Initialled JBP.

C72 ON A VOLUME OF BURTON. *The Silver Crescent*, 78, Lent 1920:24-26. Initialled J.B.P.

C73 CAMBRIDGE ECLOGUES I. *The Silver Crescent*, 78, Lent 1920:28-29. Initialled J.B.P.

C74 ON A NEW ATLAS. *Yorkshire Observer*, 17619, 27 April 1920:12. Signed Peter of Pomfret.

C75 ON THE FAMILY OF ROGET. *Yorkshire Observer*, 17625, 4 May 1920:12. Signed Peter of Pomfret.

C76 THE MODERN ATTITUDES ON CRITICISM. *Yorkshire Observer*, 17631, 11 May 1920:12. Signed Peter of Pomfret.

C77 RICHES AND POVERTY. *Yorkshire Observer*, 17637, 18 May 1920:14. Signed Peter of Pomfret.

C78 ON SONGS AND SINGERS. *Yorkshire Observer*, 17643, 25 May 1920:12. Signed Peter of Pomfret.

C79 ON GETTING OFF TO SLEEP. *Yorkshire Observer*, 17649, 1 June 1920:12. Signed Peter of Pomfret.
Reprinted: *Papers from Lilliput* (1922).

C80 THE BOHEMIAN COAST: AN ATTRACTIVE HOLIDAY PROGRAMME. *Yorkshire Observer*, 17655, 8 June 1920:12. Signed Peter of Pomfret.
Reprinted slightly amended as 'Holiday Notes from the Coast of Bohemia', *Papers from Lilliput* (1922).

C81 ON AN OLD BOOK OF NATURAL HISTORY. *Yorkshire Observer*, 17661, 15 June 1920:12. Signed Peter of Pomfret.
Reprinted: *Papers from Lilliput* (1922).

C82 FAREWELL TO FAIRIES. *Yorkshire Observer*, 17667, 22 June 1920:12. Signed Peter of Pomfret.

C83 READING IN SUMMER. *Yorkshire Observer*, 17673, 29 June 1920:14. Signed Peter of Pomfret.

C84 ON £10,000 A YEAR. *Yorkshire Observer*, 17679, 6 July 1920:12. Signed Peter of Pomfret.

C85 THE ETERNAL CHEAPJACK. *Yorkshire Observer*, 17685, 13 July 1920:12. Signed Peter of Pomfret.
Reprinted: *Papers from Lilliput* (1922).

C86 ENGLISH LETTERS: SHORT SKETCH OF SIX YEARS' LITERARY OUTPUT 1. POETRY. *Yorkshire Observer*, 17688, 16 July 1920:12.

C87 ENGLISH LETTERS: SHORT SKETCH OF SIX YEARS' LITERARY OUTPUT 2. PROSE. *Yorkshire Observer*, 17690, 19 July 1920:8.

C88 VORTIGERN'S TOWER. *Yorkshire Observer*, 17691, 20 July 1920:10. Signed Peter of Pomfret.

C89 'THE SEA AND THE JUNGLE'. *Yorkshire Observer*, 17697, 27 July 1920:12. Signed Peter of Pomfret.

C90   ARTISTIC LYING. *Yorkshire Observer*, 17703, 3 August
      1920:8. Signed Peter of Pomfret.

C91   OUR CONQUERORS. *Yorkshire Observer*, 17709, 10 August
      1920:12. Signed Peter of Pomfret.

C92   TRAVEL BY TRAIN. *Yorkshire Observer*, 17715, 17 August
      1920:10. Signed Peter of Pomfret.
      Reprinted: *Papers from Lilliput* (1922).

C93   BARBARISM. *Yorkshire Observer*, 17721, 24 August 1920:
      10. Signed Peter of Pomfret.

C94   AT 'POINT RASH JUDGEMENT': HOW WRITERS OF PROSE AND
      POETRY HAVE DENOUNCED EACH OTHERS' WORK. *Yorkshire
      Observer*, 17724, 27 August 1920:6.

C95   THE GLEAM OF THE BLUE BIRD'S WING. *Yorkshire Observer*,
      17727, 31 August 1920:10. Signed Peter of Pomfret.

C96   VULGAR ERRORS. *Yorkshire Observer*, 17733, 7 September
      1920:10. Signed Peter of Pomfret.
      Reprinted: *Papers from Lilliput* (1922).

C97   A READER'S DIARY. *Yorkshire Observer*, 17736, 10 Sep-
      tember 1920:10. Initialled J.B.P.

C98   A READER'S DIARY. *Yorkshire Observer*, 17738, 13 Sep-
      tember 1920:12. Initialled J.B.P.

C99   PRAISE OF TALES. *Yorkshire Observer*, 17739, 14 Sep-
      tember 1920:10. Signed Peter of Pomfret.

C100 A READER'S DIARY. *Yorkshire Observer*, 17740, 15 Sep-
      tember 1920:6. Initialled J.B.P.

C101 A READER'S DIARY. *Yorkshire Observer*, 17744, 20 Sep-
      tember 1920:12. Initialled J.B.P.

C102 A ROAD AND SOME MOODS. *Yorkshire Observer*, 17745, 21
      September 1920:10. Signed Peter of Pomfret.
      Reprinted: *Papers from Lilliput* (1922).

C103 A READER'S DIARY. *Yorkshire Observer*, 17747, 23 Sep-
      tember 1920:8. Initialled J.B.P.

C104 A READER'S DIARY - THE STORIES OF EDGAR ALLAN POE.
      Yorkshire Observer, 17750, 27 September 1920:6.
      Initialled J.B.P.

C105 THE BOGEY OF SPACE. *Yorkshire Observer*, 17751, 28
      September 1920:10. Signed Peter of Pomfret.
      Reprinted: *Papers from Lilliput* (1922).

C106 A READER'S DIARY: A STUDY OF THACKERAY'S REVIEWS.
      Yorkshire Observer, 17753, 30 September 1920:6.

C107 A READER'S DIARY. *Yorkshire Observer*, 17761, 9 Octo-
      ber 1920:10. Initialled JBP.

C108 A ROAD TO ONESELF. *Yorkshire Observer*, 17763, 12 Oc-
      tober 1920:12. Signed Peter of Pomfret.
      Reprinted: *Papers from Lilliput* (1922).

C109 THE WRONG WAY. *Yorkshire Observer*, 17769, 19 October
      1920:10. Signed Peter of Pomfret.

C110 A READER'S DIARY. *Yorkshire Observer*, 17771, 21 Oc-
      tober 1920:12. Initialled J.B.P.

C111 THE SHAM. *Yorkshire Observer*, 17775, 26 October 1920:
      10. Signed Peter of Pomfret.

C112 ON BAD PIANISTS. *Yorkshire Observer*, 17781, 2 Novem-
      ber 1920:10. Signed Peter of Pomfret.
      Reprinted: as 'An Apology for Bad Pianists', *Papers
      from Lilliput* (1922).

C113 A READER'S DIARY. *Yorkshire Observer*, 17786, 8 Novem-
      ber 1920:12. Initialled J.B.P.

C114 THE PEEP. *Yorkshire Observer*, 17787, 9 November 1920:
      10. Signed Peter of Pomfret.
      Reprinted: *Papers from Lilliput* (1922).

C115 A READER'S DIARY. *Yorkshire Observer*, 17787, 9 Novem-
      ber 1920:10. Initialled JBP.

C116 A READER'S DIARY. *Yorkshire Observer*, 17791, 13 No-
      vember 1920:10. Initialled JBP.

C117 ON GOSSIP. *Yorkshire Observer*, 17793, 16 November
      1920:10. Signed Peter of Pomfret.
      Reprinted: *Papers from Lilliput* (1922).

C118 A READER'S DIARY. *Yorkshire Observer*, 17795, 18
      November 1920:14. Initialled JBP.

C119 PROGRESS. *Yorkshire Observer*, 17799, 23 November
      1920:10. Signed Peter of Pomfret.

C120 A READER'S DIARY. *Yorkshire Observer*, 17804, 29 No-
      vember 1920:12. Initialled JBP.

C121 ON I AND ME. *Yorkshire Observer*, 17805, 30 November
      1920:10. Signed Peter of Pomfret.

C122 A READER'S DIARY. *Yorkshire Observer*, 17807, 2 Decem-
      ber 1920:12. Initialled JBP.

C123 A DISAPPOINTMENT. *Yorkshire Observer*, 17811, 7 Decem-.
      ber 1920:14. Signed Peter of Pomfret.

C124 A READER'S DIARY. *Yorkshire Observer*, 17814, 10 Decem-
      ber 1920:10. Initialled JBP.

C125 A MOUTH ORGAN. *Yorkshire Observer*, 17817, 14 December
      1920:10. Signed Peter of Pomfret.
      Reprinted: *Papers from Lilliput* (1922).

C126 THE SANTA CLAUS I KNEW. *Yorkshire Observer*, 17823, 21
      December 1920:10. Signed Peter of Pomfret.

C127 A READER'S DIARY. *Yorkshire Observer*, 17824, 22 Decem-
      ber 1920:10. Initialled JBP.

C128 A READER'S DIARY. *Yorkshire Observer*, 17827, 28 Decem-
      ber 1920:10. Initialled JBP.

                            1921

C129 A READER'S DIARY. *Yorkshire Observer*, 17832, 3 January
      1921:12. Initialled JBP.

C130 STORY OF JENNY A BRADFORD MILL GIRL'S FINE NOVEL.
      Yorkshire Observer, 17833, 4 January 1921:10.
      Review of *The Story of Jenny* (Elizabeth Southwart).

C131 A READER'S DIARY. *Yorkshire Observer*, 17840, 12 Janu-
      ary 1921:10. Initialled JBP.

C132 A MUSE IN MOTLEY: 1. A.E. HOUSMAN: DEDICATION OF THE
      SHROPSHIRE LAD. 2. WALTER DE LA MARE. *Cambridge Re-
      view*, XLII (1042), 25 February 1921:269.
      Reprinted: *Brief Diversions* (1922).

C133 3. AE: THE INEFFABLE SPLENDOUR OF THINGUMBOB 4. A
      SONG: NOT TO BE FOUND IN THE COLLECTED POEMS OF
      ALFRED NOYES. *Cambridge Review*, XLII (1043), 5
      March 1921: 292.
      Reprinted: *Brief Diversions* (1922).

C134 5. SIR WILLIAM WATSON: ON RECEIVING AN EDITION-DE-LUXE
      OF THE COLLECTED WORKS OF ELLA WHEELER WILCOX.
      Cambridge Review, XLII (1044), 22 April 1921:314.
      Reprinted: *Brief Diversions* (1922).

C135 6. PROFESSOR SAINTSBURY: FROM THE HISTORY OF THE
      THREE BLIND MICE. 7. JAMES STEPHENS: 'SEUMAS BEGS
      AGAIN'. *Cambridge Review*, XLII (1045), 29 April
      1921:329.
      Reprinted: *Brief Diversions* (1922).

C136 THREE MEN. *Cambridge Review*, XLII (1047), 13 May 1921:
      361-362.
      Reprinted: *Papers from Lilliput* (1922).

C137 A MUSE IN MOTLEY: 8. LA BELLE DAME SANS MERCI: NEW
      STYLE AS IT MIGHT POSSIBLY BE WRITTEN BY LASCELLES
      ABERCROMBIE. *Cambridge Review*, XLII (1047), 13 May
      1921:360.
      Reprinted: *Brief Diversions* (1922).

C138 9. THE LATER MANNER OF MR. W.B. YEATS. *Cambridge
      Review*, XLII (1048), 20 May 1921:378.
      Reprinted: *Brief Diversions* (1922).

C139 ON CARTOMANCY. *The Silver Crescent*, 82, June 1921:
      20-23. Initialled J.B.P.
      Reprinted: *Papers from Lilliput* (1922).

C140 THE EDITOR. *Cambridge Review*, XLII (1050), 3 June
      1921:408.
      Reprinted: *Papers from Lilliput* (1922).

C141 EIGHT EPIGRAMS. *Cambridge Review*, XLII (1051), 8
      June 1921:423.
      Reprinted: *Brief Diversions* (1922).

C142 THE MORAL TALES OF MODUS THE LACONIC. 1. THE IMPOSSIBIL-
      ITY OF KNOWING EVERYONE. 2. A MOVING STORY OF REAL
      LIFE. 3. THE TRUE ACCOUNT OF A QUARREL BETWEEN A MAN
      WE ALL KNOW AND A VERY OLD FAMILY. 4. AT THE 'RED
      LION' RAMPLE STREET. *Cambridge Review*, XLIII (1052),
      14 October 1921:8.
      Reprinted: *Brief Diversions* (1922).

C143 5. THE DANGER OF ACCEPTING GIFTS WHILE HOLDING MUNICIPAL
      OFFICE. 6. THE HUMILIATING EXPERIENCE OF A FORGOTTEN
      GOD. 7. HOW THE RATIONAL AMUSEMENTS OF THE GREAT ARE
      LIMITED. 8. THE IMPRUDENCE OF A POLITICIAN IN
      TRAVELLING FURTHER THAN THE NEWSPAPERS. *Cambridge
      Review*, XLIII (1053), 21 October 1921:29.
      Reprinted: *Brief Diversions* (1922).

C144 9. THE WRONG WORLD. 10. THE VALUE OF A NEW POINT OF
      VIEW. 11. THE UNINVITED GUEST. 12. HOW I MET WITH
      A FAMOUS CHARACTER IN A CAFE. *Cambridge Review*, XLIII
      (1054), 28 October 1921:43.
      Reprinted: *Brief Diversions* (1922).

C145 13. THE MUTINY. 14. DEATH AND THE FIDDLER. 15. THE
      COLLEGE OF IMMORTAL FAME. 16. THE LONELY SOUL.
      Cambridge Review, XLIII (1055), 4 November 1921:59.
      Reprinted: *Brief Diversions* (1922).

C146 17. THE LOST PATH. 18. THE LAST GLIMPSE OF A WELL
      KNOWN FIGURE IN SOCIETY. 19. ADVANCED THOUGHT AND
      THE FOOLISH IDLER. 20. THE WONDERFUL VIEW. *Cam-
      bridge Review*, XLIII (1056), 11 November 1921:75.
      Reprinted: *Brief Diversions* (1922).

C146a MUSIC. *Cambridge Review*, XLIII (1056), 11 November
      1921:78.

C147 21. THE ROOM OF LOST SOULS. 22. THE CYNICISM OF AB-
      SOLUTE MONARCHIES. 23. THE IMPORTANCE OF GOOD
      GOVERNMENT. 24. THE END PAPER AND MORAL. *Cambridge
      Review*, XLIII (1057), 18 November 1921:94.
      Reprinted: *Brief Diversions* (1922).

C147a MUSIC AND DRAMA. *Cambridge Review*, XLIII (1057), 18
      November 1921:97.

C148 MUSIC. *Cambridge Review*, XLIII (1059), 2 December 1921:
      135.

                              1922

C149 IN PRAISE OF HYPERBOLISM. *Cambridge Review*, XLIII
      (1061), 27 January 1922:171-172.
      Reprinted: *Papers from Lilliput* (1922).

C150   MUSIC. *Cambridge Review*, XLIII (1060), 20 January
       1922:155. Initialled JBP.

C151   MUSIC. *Cambridge Review*, XLIII (1061), 27 January 1922:
       174. Initialled JBP.

C152   MUSIC. *Cambridge Review*, XLIII (1062), 3 February 1922:
       191. Initialled JBP.

C153   MUSIC. *Cambridge Review*, XLIII (1063), 10 February
       1922:209. Initialled JBP.

C154   THE PRODUCTION OF THE 'THREE SISTERS' AT THE NEW THEATRE.
       Cambridge Review, XLIII (1064), 17 February 1922:230.
       Initialled JBP.

C155   GRIGSBY: A RECORD AND AN APPRECIATION. *The Silver
       Crescent*, 84, March 1922:8-14. Initialled J.B.P.
       Reprinted: *Papers from Lilliput* (1922).

C156   MUSIC. *Cambridge Review*, XLIII (1067), 10 March 1922:
       284. Initialled JBP.

C157   ON A NEW KIND OF FICTION. *The Outlook*, XLIX (1259),
       18 March 1922:218-219.
       Reprinted: *Papers from Lilliput* (1922).

C158   THE PROBLEM OF STYLE. *Cambridge Review*, XLIII (1069),
       5 May 1922:318. Review of *The Problem of Style* (J.
       Middleton Murry).

C159   MUSIC. C.U.M.S. CHAMBER CONCERT. *Cambridge Review*,
       XLIII (1070), 12 May 1922:337-338. Initialled J.B.P.

C160   AUTHORSHIP FROM A TO Z. *Cambridge Review*, XLIII
       (1074), 7 June 1922:401-403.

C161   A PARAGON OF HOSTS. *Nineteenth Century*, XCII (DXLV),
       July 1922:99-107.
       Reprinted: *Papers from Lilliput* (1922).

C162   NASTY NOVELS. *The Outlook*, L (1282), 26 August 1922:
       170. Review of *Moral Poison in Modern Fiction* (R.
       Brimley Johnson).

C163   MR GEORGE SAINTSBURY: AN APPRECIATION. *London Mercury*,
       VI (35), September 1922:502-512.
       Reprinted: *Figures in Modern Literature* (1924).

C164   NEW PAPERS FROM LILLIPUT. ON BEING KIND TO THE OLD.
       The Challenge, n.s. 1 (1), 29 September 1922:6-7.
       Reprinted: *Papers from Lilliput* (1922).

C165   BELLES-LETTRES. *London Mercury*, VI (36), October 1922:
       658-660. Reviews of *Soliloquies in England* (George
       Santayana); *My Discovery of England* (Stephen Leacock);
       Lone Swallows (Henry Williamson); *The Call of the Wild
       Flower* (Henry Salt); *Woodland Creatures* (Frances Pitt);
       Translations of Eastern Poetry and Prose (Reynold
       Nicholson); and *The Old Pest* (Carl Ewald).

C166   A MAD SHEPHERD. *The Challenge*, n.s. 1 (2), 6 October
       1922:26-27.
       Reprinted: *Papers from Lilliput* (1922).

C167   ON FILLING IN FORMS. *The Challenge*, n.s. 1 (3), 13 Oc-
       tober 1922:46.
       Reprinted: *Papers from Lilliput* (1922).

C168   THE APOTHEOSIS OF BOSWELL. *The Spectator*, 129 (4920),
       14 October 1922:500-501. Review of *Young Boswell*
       (Chauncey Brewster Tinker). Unsigned.

C169   ON NOT MEETING AUTHORS. *The Challenge*, n.s. 1 (4),
       20 October 1922:66-67.
       Reprinted: *Papers from Lilliput* (1922).

C170   MR HIND AND MORE AUTHORS. *The Spectator*, 129 (4921),
       21 October 1922:559. Review of *More Authors and I*
       (C. Lewis Hind). Unsigned.

C171   HAZLITT AT LAST. *The Spectator* (Literary Supplement),
       129 (4921), 21 October 1922:519-520. Review of *The
       Life of William Hazlitt* (P.P. Howe). Unsigned.

C172   ON HABERDASHERS. *The Challenge*, n.s. 1 (5), 27 Oc-
       tober 1922:86-87.
       Reprinted: *I for One* (1923).

C173   MEMORIES OF YESTERDAY. *The Spectator*, 129 (4922), 28
       October 1922:598-599. Review of *The Nineteen Hundreds*
       (Reginald Auberon). Unsigned.

C174   LITERARY HISTORY AND CRITICISM. *London Mercury*, VII
       (37), November 1922:100-102. Review of *Books and
       Authors* (Robert Lynd); *A Portrait of George Moore*
       (John Freeman); *L'Oeuvre de Swinburne* (Paul de Reul);

By-Ways Round Helicon (Iolo Williams); *Degeneration
in the Great French Masters* (Jean Carrere); and
Essays by Divers Hands.

C175 THE ELUSIVE LETTER. *The Challenge*, n.s. 1 (6), 3
November 1922:106–107.
Reprinted: *I for One* (1923).

C176 ON HATING STRANGERS. *The Challenge*, n.s. 1 (7), 10
November 1922:126–127.
Reprinted: *I for One* (1923).

C177 PAINTERS IN SPAIN. *The Spectator* (Literary Supplement),
129 (4924), 11 November 1922:672, 674. Review of *Poor
Folk in Spain* (Jan and Cora Gordon) and *Through Spain
and Portugal* (Ernest Peixotto). Unsigned.

C178 THOSE TERRIBLE NOVELISTS. *The Challenge*, n.s. 1 (8),
17 November 1922:146–147.
Reprinted: *I for One* (1923).

C179 ON FREE SPEECH. *The Challenge*, n.s. 1 (9), 24 November
1922:166–167.
Reprinted: *I for One* (1923).

C180 O. HENRY IN PRISON. *The Spectator*, 129 (4926), 25
November 1922:706–707. Review of *Through the Shadows
with O. Henry* (A.L. Jennings). Unsigned.

C181 THE POETRY OF MR A.E. HOUSMAN. *London Mercury*, VII
(38), December 1922:171–184.
Reprinted: *Figures in Modern Literature* (1924).

C182 ON A CERTAIN PROVINCIAL PLAYER. *London Mercury*, VII
(38), December 1922:158–163. Signed John Boynton.
Reprinted: *Papers from Lilliput* (1922).

C183 BELLES-LETTRES. *London Mercury*, VII (38), December
1922:213–215. Reviews of *The Legend of Ulenspiegel*
(Charles de Coster); *The Marches of Wessex* (F.J.
Harvey Darton); *George Gissing* (May Yates); *Sketches
from a Library Window* (Basil Anderton); *Odds and Ends
of a Learned Clerk* (Arthur Eckersley); *Will o' the
Wisp* (George Hookham); *Baconian Essays* (E.W. Smith-
son and George Greenwood); and *A Guide to Russian
Literature*.

C184   OF SONG. *The Challenge*, n.s. 1 (10), 1 December 1922:
        186-187.
        Reprinted: *I for One* (1923).

C185   THE NORMAL WOMAN. *The Challenge*, n.s. 1 (11), 8 Decem-
        ber 1922:206-207.
        Reprinted: as 'In Praise of the Normal Woman', *I for
        One* (1923).

C186   TOY BALLOONS. *The Challenge*, n.s. 1 (12), 15 December
        1922:226-227.
        Reprinted: *I for One* (1923).

C187   MR BIRRELL. *The Challenge*, n.s. 1 (12), 15 December
        1922:237. Review of *Collected Essays and Addresses*
        (Augustine Birrell). Initialled JBP.

C188   THE AMBASSADOR OF THE BIRDS AND BEASTS. *The Spectator*,
        129 (4929), 16 December 1922:925-926. Review of
        A Hind in Richmond Park (W.H. Hudson). Unsigned.

C189   DIXIE. *The Challenge*, n.s. 1 (13), 22 December 1922:
        258-259.
        Reprinted: *I for One* (1923).

C190   TRAVELLERS' TALES. *The Spectator*, 129 (4930), 23
        December 1922:971. Review of *Travel Old and New*
        edited by Samuel J. Looker.

C191   THE YEAR'S END. *The Challenge*, n.s. 1 (14), 29 December
        1922:278-279.

1923

C192   LITERARY HISTORY AND CRITICISM. *London Mercury*, VII
        (39), January 1923:324-327. Reviews of *An Essay
        Towards a Theory of Art* (Lascelles Abercrombie); *The
        Poetic Mind* (F.J. Prescott); *Character Problems in
        Shakespeare's Plays* (L.L. Schuking); *Macbeth, King
        Lear and Contemporary History* (L. Winstanley); *The
        Beggar's Opera* (F. Kidson); *A Short History of the
        British Drama* (B. Brawley); *Elizabethan Drama*
        (Janet Spens); and *The Life and Works of John Heywood*
        (R.W. Bolwell).

C193 A DEFENCE OF DULL COMPANY. *The Challenge*, n.s. 1 (15),
      5 January 1923:298–299.
      Reprinted: *I for One* (1923).

C194 PASSIONATE CELIBATES. *Daily News*, 23964, 9 January
      1923:7. Review of *King of the Castle* (Keble Howard);
      The Miracle (E. Temple Thurston); and *Hidden Lives*
      (Leonora Eyles).

C195 A GROSSLY EGOTISTICAL MATTER. *The Challenge*, n.s. 1
      (16), 12 January 1923:318–319.
      Reprinted: *I for One* (1923).

C196 A COINCIDENCE. *The Challenge*, n.s. 1 (17), 19 January
      1923:340–341.
      Reprinted: *I for One* (1923).

C197 ROMANTIC MIDDLE AGE. *Daily News*, 23978, 25 January
      1923:7. Review of *Old Crow* (Alice Brown); *Joseph
      Greer and His Daughter* (Henry Webster); and *Eçho*
      (Margaret Rivers Larminie).

C198 AN OLD CONJUROR. *The Challenge*, n.s. 1 (18), 26
      January 1923:360–361.
      Reprinted: *I for One* (1923).

C199 THE ESSAYIST IN ALL HIS GLORY. *The Challenge*, n.s. 1
      (18), 26 January 1923:367–368. Review of *Solomon in
      All His Glory* (Robert Lynd). Initialled JBP.

C200 BELLES-LETTRES. *London Mercury*, VII (40), February
      1923:435–437. Reviews of *Life of Hazlitt* (P.P. Howe);
      Earlham (Percy Lubbock); *A Hind in Richmond Park*
      (W.H. Hudson); *Lady into Fox* (David Garnett); *Cloud
      Castle* (Edward Thomas); *Austin Dobson Anthology*;
      You Know What People Are (E.V. Lucas); and *A London
      Farrago* (D.B. Wyndham Lewis).

C201 THE CULT OF THE REVOLVER. *The Challenge*, n.s. 1 (19),
      2 February 1923:381–382.
      Reprinted: *I for One* (1923).

C202 A GOOD MARKSMAN AND SOME EASY TARGETS. *The Challenge*,
      n.s. 1 (19), 2 February 1923:390. Review of *These
      Liberties* ('Evoe'). Initialled J.B.P.

C203 ISLANDS. *Daily News*, 23988, 6 February 1923:7. Review
      of *South of the Line* (Ralph Stock); *The Island God*

Forgot (Charles Stilson and Charles Beahan); *The Paper of Mirty Oge* (J.F. McKeon); and *The Fortunate Woman* (Eleanor Reid).

C204 CHARLES AND EMMA. *The Challenge*, n.s. 1 (20), 9 February 1923:400-401.
Reprinted: *I for One* (1923).

C205 TWO DICKENS BOOKS. *The Spectator*, 130 (4937), 10 February 1923:220. Review of *Dickensian Inns and Taverns* (B.W. Matz); and *Mr Dickens Goes to the Play* (Alexander Woolcott). Unsigned.

C206 FIFTY YEARS OF THE AMERICAN STAGE. *The Spectator* (Literary Supplement), 130 (4937), 10 February 1923: 216, 218. Review of *The Print of My Remembrance* (Augustus Thomas). Unsigned.

C207 A NEW CRITIC. *Daily News*, 23994, 13 February 1923:7. Review of *First Essays on Literature* (Edward Shanks).

C208 CRANKS. *The Challenge*, n.s. 1 (21), 16 February 1923: 420-421.
Reprinted: *I for One* (1923).

C209 RALEIGH'S DIVERSIONS. *The Challenge*, n.s. 1 (21), 16 February 1923:429-430. Review of *Laughter from a Cloud* (Sir Walter Raleigh). Initialled JBP.

C210 FOUR POETS. *Daily News*, 23997, 16 February 1923:7. Review of *Poems by Four Authors* (A.Y. Campbell, J.R. Ackerley, E.L. Davison, and F.H. Kendon).

C211 THE COMPLETE BIRRELL. *The Spectator*, 130 (4938), 17 February 1923:292-293. Review of *The Collected Essays of Augustine Birrell*. Unsigned.

C212 ALL ABOUT OURSELVES. *The Challenge*, n.s. 1 (22), 23 February 1923:440-441.
Reprinted: *I for One* (1923). This essay provided the title for *All About Ourselves and Other Essays* (1956).

C213 OPEN COUNTRY. *The Challenge*, n.s. 1 (22), 23 February 1923:448-450. Review of *Extemporary Essays* (Maurice Hewlett). Initialled JBP.

C214 FENIMORE COOPER'S LETTERS. *The Spectator*, 130 (4939), 24 February 1923:332. Review of *Correspondence of James Fenimore Cooper* edited by his grandson. Unsigned.

C215 KEEPING IT UP. *Daily News*, 24005, 26 February 1923:8.
Review of *Chick* (Edgar Wallace); *The Last Discovery*
(Mrs Baille Reynolds); and *Up the Hill of Fleet*
(George Renwick).

C216 MR ROBERT LYND. *London Mercury*, VII (41), March 1923:
598-607.
Reprinted: *Figures in Modern Literature* (1924).

C217 BELLES-LETTRES. *London Mercury*, VII (41), March 1923:
662-663. Reviews of *Collected Essays and Addresses*
(Augustine Birrell); *Outspoken Essays* (W.R. Inge);
The Interpreters (A.E. McMillan); *What the Judge
Thought* (Judge Parry); *Neighbours Henceforth* (Owen
Wister); *As You See It* (V); *Pied Piper's Street*
(V.H. Friedlaender); and *Dr Johnson in Cambridge*
(S.C. Roberts).

C218 THIS INSUBSTANTIAL PAGEANT. *The Challenge*, n.s. 1 (23),
2 March 1923:461-462.
Reprinted: *I for One* (1923).

C219 PATRICIA AND SOME MEN. *Daily News*, 24013, 7 March
1923:7. Review of *The Three Lovers* (Frank Swinnerton).

C220 ON IMPRESSING ACQUAINTANCES. *The Challenge*, n.s. 1
(24), 9 March 1923: 479-480.
Reprinted: *I for One* (1923).

C221 A SOCIAL SATIRE. *The Challenge*, n.s. 1 (24), 9 March
1923:487-488. Review of *Memories of the Future*
(Ronald Knox).

C222 ONE OF OUR CONQUERORS. *The Spectator*, 130 (4941), 10
March 1923:410. Review of *The Real Horatio Bottomley* (Henry J. Houston). Unsigned.

C223 THREE MORE. *Daily News*, 24018, 13 March 1923:7. Review
of *The Scent of the Rose* (Margaret Peterson); *Different Gods* (Violet Quirk); and *The Fountains of Green
Fire* (Percy James Brebner).

C224 AN IDLE SPECULATION. *The Challenge*, n.s. 1 (25), 16
March 1923:500-501.
Reprinted: *I for One* (1923).

C225 AFTERMATH. *The Spectator*, 130 (4942), 17 March 1923:
449-450. Review of *Neighbours Henceforth* (Owen
Wister). Unsigned.

C226 THE NEW HYPOCRISY. *The Challenge*, n.s. 1 (26), 23
        March 1923:520-521.
        Reprinted: *I for One* (1923).

C227 EIGHT WOMEN. *The Challenge*, n.s. 1 (26), 23 March
        1923:530, 532. Review of *Women Writers of the Nine-
        teenth Century* (Marjory A. Bald).

C228 SILAS BRAUNTON. *The Spectator*, 130 (4943), 24 March
        1923:520. Review of *Silas Braunton* by J. Mills
        Whistham. Unsigned.

C229 MR BELLOC. *Daily News*, 24030, 27 March 1923:7. Re-
        view of *On* (Hilaire Belloc).

C230 CHARLES RUPERT PURVISON. *The Challenge*, n.s. ii (1),
        30 March 1923:9-10.
        Reprinted: *I for One* (1923).

C231 MR ERVINE'S ELDERS. *The Challenge*, n.s. ii (1), 30
        March 1923:17. Review of *Some Impressions of My
        Elders* (St John Irvine).

C232 CAN READING BE TAUGHT? *The Bodleian*, XV (1), April
        1923:8-10.

C233 A NOTE ON HUMPTY DUMPTY. *The Challenge*, n.s. ii (2),
        6 April 1923:29-30.
        Reprinted: *I for One* (1923). Also included in *Aspects
        of Alice* (1972) (B142).

C234 THE PROPHETS. *The Challenge*, n.s. ii (3), 13 April
        1923:48-49.
        Reprinted: *I for One* (1923).

C235 A TIDE OF REMEMBRANCE. *The Spectator*, 130 (4946), 14
        April 1923:630. Review of *Memories Wise and Other-
        wise* (Sir Henry Robinson); *Wide Seas and Many Lands*
        (Arthur Mason); and *Recollections of a Rolling Stone*
        (Basil Tozer). Unsigned.

C236 PEOPLE AND BACKGROUNDS. *Daily News*, 24048, 18 April
        1923:7. Review of *The Desert Horizon* (E.L. Grant
        Watson); *The Factory King* (Norman Porrilt); *Anthony
        John* (Jerome K. Jerome); *Sea Ways* (Bartimeus); and
        Sangsue (Ben Ames Williams).

C237 ON BEGINNING. *The Challenge*, n.s. ii (4), 20 April
        1923:68-69.
        Reprinted: *I for One* (1923).

C238 LAUGHTER AND SEX. *The Challenge*, n.s. ii (4), 20
 April 1923:75-76. Review of *The Psychology of Laughter* (J.Y.T. Greig).

C239 THE GLAD EYE MANNER. *Daily News*, 24052, 23 April
 1923:9. Review of *Through the Glad Eyes of a Woman*
 (Jane Doe).

C240 ON VULGAR OPTIMISTS. *The Challenge*, n.s. ii (5), 27
 April 1923:88-89.
 Reprinted: *I for One* (1923).

C241 A NOVEL WITHOUT A MAN. *The Spectator*, 130 (4948), 28
 April 1923:715. Review of *Colleagues* (Geraldine
 Waife). Unsigned.

C242 ANATOLE FRANCE AS A CRITIC. *The Bodleian*, XV (2),
 May 1923:24-25.

C243 FICTION. *London Mercury*, VIII (43), May 1923:97-99.
 Reviews of *Men Like Gods* (H.G. Wells); *The Ladybird*
 (D.H. Lawrence); *The Bright Shawl* (Joseph Hergesheimer);
 and *Speed the Plough* (Mary Butts).

C244 HAUNTED. *The Challenge*, n.s. ii (6), 4 May 1923: 108-
 109.
 Reprinted: *I for One* (1923).

C245 LAST FRUITS. *The Challenge*, n.s. ii (6), 4 May 1923:
 116-117. Review of *De Senectute* (Frederic Harrison).

C246 OUR FAVOURITE WRITERS. *Daily News*, 24062, 4 May 1923:
 7. Review of *Companionable Books* (Henry Van Dyke).

C247 AN ILL-NATURED CHAPTER. *The Challenge*, n.s. ii (7),
 11 May 1923:128-129.
 Reprinted: *I for One* (1923).

C248 AMERICAN SHORT STORIES. *Daily News*, 24068, 11 May
 1923:7. Review of *The Best Short Stories of 1922*.

C249 IN THE COUNTRY. *The Challenge*, n.s. ii (8), 18 May
 1923:148-149.
 Reprinted: *I for One* (1923).

C250 FREDERIC HARRISON'S 'ENVOI'. *The Spectator*, 130 (4951),
 19 May 1923:850-851. Review of *De Senectute*
 (Frederic Harrison). Unsigned.

C251 A BEETONIAN REVERIE. *The Challenge*, n.s. ii (9), 25
 May 1923:168-169.
 Reprinted: *I for One* (1923).

C252 BOOKISH ESSAYS. *Daily News*, 24080, 25 May 1923:7. Review of *On the Margin* (Aldous Huxley) and *End Papers* (Bernard Lintot).

C253 TRAVELLER'S TALES. *The Bodleian*, XV (3), June 1923: 40-42.

C254 FICTION. *London Mercury*, VIII (44), June 1923:208-210. Reviews of *Love's Pilgrim* (J.D. Beresford); *Revolving Lights* (Dorothy M. Richardson); *The Grand Tour* (Romer Wilson); and *The Clockwork Man* (E.V. Odle).

C255 ON THE CHOICE OF A TITLE. *The Challenge*, n.s. ii (10), 1 June 1923:189-190.

C256 MR BENNETT AND THE BEST OF LIFE. *The Spectator*, 130 (4953), 2 June 1923:927-928. Review of *How to Make the Best of Life* (Arnold Bennett). Unsigned.

C257 A NEW STUDY OF CONRAD. *The Spectator*, 130 (4954), 9 June 1923:969-970. Review of *Joseph Conrad: An Appreciation* (Ernst Bendz). Unsigned.

C258 SIR ERNEST SHACKLETON. *The Spectator*, 130 (4955), 16 June 1923:1010-1011. Review of *The Life of Sir Ernest Shackleton* (Hugh R. Mill). Unsigned.

C259 A GUIDE TO ROGUEDOM. *The Spectator*, 130 (4956), 23 June 1923:1046-1047. Review of *The Underworld of London* (Sidney Theodore Felstead). Unsigned.

C260 A MAGISTRATE'S DEBT. *Daily News*, 24106, 25 June 1923: 8. Review of *Pious Opinions* (Sir Charles Biron).

C261 KING COLE ON TOUR. *Daily News*, 24108, 27 June 1923:7. Review of *King Cole and Other Poems* (John Masefield); *Roast Leviathan* (Louis Untermeyer); and *Greek and Latin Anthology* (William Stebbing).

C262 ON DETECTIVE STORIES. *The Bodleian*, XV (4), July 1923:56-58.

C263 FICTION. *London Mercury*, VIII (45), July 1923:317-319. Review of *The Riddle* (Walter de la Mare); *Fantastica* (Robert Nichols); *The Cream of the Jest* (James Branch Cabell); and *The Return of the Hero* (Michael Ireland).

C264 A NEW STUDY OF MR CHESTERTON. *Daily News*, 24124, 16
July 1923:9. Review of *The Innocence of G.K.
Chesterton* (Gerald Bullett).

C265 MEDITATION UPON BORES. *The Challenge*, n.s. ii (17),
20 July 1923:329-330.

C266 THE STORY OF THE QUEST. *The Spectator*, 131 (4960), 21
July 1923:88. Review of *Shackleton's Last Voyage*
(Frank Wild). Unsigned.

C267 PROLEGOMENA. *The Challenge*, n.s. ii (18), 27 July
1923:358. Review of *Scepticism and Faith* (George
Santayana).

C268 MAURICE HEWLETT'S LATER VERSE AND PROSE. *London
Mercury*, VIII (46), August 1923:368-379.
Reprinted: *Figures in Modern Literature* (1924).

C269 BELLES-LETTRES. *London Mercury*, VIII (46), August
1923:444-445. Review of *Modern English Essays 1870-
1920* edited by Ernest Rhys. Signed John Boynton.

C270 FICTION. *London Mercury*, VIII (46), August 1923:438-
440. Review of *The Dove's Rest* (Katherine Mansfield);
The Black Dog (A.E. Coppard); *Grey Weathers* (V.
Sackville-West); and *Our Mr Wrenn* (Sinclair Lewis).

C271 THE WAGNER LEGEND. *The Challenge*, n.s. ii (19), 3
August 1923:375-376. Review of *The Wagnerian Drama*
(H.S. Chamberlain). Initialled JBP.

C272 ON DOING NOTHING. *The Challenge*, n.s. ii (21), 17
August 1923:409-410.

C273 A PERSONALITY: STEPHEN REYNOLDS. *The Spectator*, 131
(4964), 18 August 1923:236. Review of *Letters of
Stephen Reynolds* edited by Harold Wright. Unsigned.

C274 THE FLOOD OF FICTION. *Daily News*, 24161, 28 August
1923:7. Review of *Wild Blood* (Gordon Young); *Out
of the Ages* (Devereux Price); and *Fergus Freeman*
(T.P. Gordon).

C275 FARINGTON AGAIN. *Daily News*, 24164, 31 August 1923:7.
Review of *The Farington Diary 2nd Vol 1802-1804*.

C276   OF CONNY-CATCHING. *The Bodleian*, 15 (6), September
       1923:88-89.

C277   FICTION. *London Mercury*, VIII (47), September 1923:
       544-546. Review of *Star of Earth* (Morris Dallett);
       The Conquered (Naomi Mitchison); *Restoration* (Ethel
       Sidgewick); and *Representative American Short Stories*
       edited by Alexander Jessup.

C278   ARCTIC DAYS. *The Spectator*, 131 (4966), 1 September
       1923:290. Review of *Hunters of the Great North*
       (V. Stefansson). Unsigned.

C279   HALF GENIUS, HALF LUNATIC. *Daily News*, 24167, 4 Sep-
       tember 1923:7. Review of *Tragedies of Sex* (Frank
       Wedekind).

C280   LOOKING ON AT LIFE. *Daily News*, 24169, 6 September
       1923:7. Review of *The Dance of Life* (Havelock Ellis).

C281   EPICUREAN ESSAYS. *The Challenge*, n.s. ii (24), 7
       September 1923:478. Review of *A Guide for the Greedy*
       (Elisabeth Robins Pennell). Initialled JBP.

C282   THE ENEMIES OF LIBERTY. *The Spectator*, 131 (4967), 8
       September 1923:322. Review of *The Enemies of Liberty*
       (E.S.P. Haynes). Unsigned.

C283   SENSE AND SENSIBILITY. *The Challenge*, n.s. ii (26),
       21 September 1923:514-515. Review of *More Prejudice*
       (A.B. Walkley) and *Written in Friendship* (Gerald
       Cumberland).

C284   SIR HALL CAINE'S NEW STORY. *Daily News*, 24187, 27
       September 1923:7. Review of *The Woman of Knockaloe*
       (Hall Caine).

C285   MUSICAL CRITICISM. *The Bodleian*, 15 (7), October
       1923:104-105.

C286   FICTION. *London Mercury*, VIII (48), October 1923:658-
       660. Review of *The End of the House of Allard*
       (Sheila Kaye-Smith); *The Pitiful Wife* (Storm Jameson);
       Many Marriages (Sherwood Anderson); and *Uncanny
       Stories* (May Sinclair).

C287   Q AS A CRITIC. *The Spectator*, 131 (4971), 6 October
       1923:462-463. Review of *The Art of Writing* and
       Studies in Literature (Sir Arthur Quiller-Couch).

C288 CURIOUS GRUMBLE. *The Challenge*, n.s. ii (29), 12
      October 1923:570-571.

C289 AN ITALIAN CRITIC. *The Spectator* (Literary Supple-
      ment), 131 (4972), 13 October 1923:510, 512. Review
      of *Four and Twenty Minds* (Giovanni Papini).

C290 THREE ENGLANDS. *Daily News*, 24202, 15 October 1923:9.
      Review of *A Pedlars Pack* (Rowland Kenney); *Old Man's
      Beard* (J.B. Morton); and *Friends in Solitude* (Percy
      Withers).

C291 STRANGER THAN FICTION. *Daily News*, 24203, 16 October
      1923:9. Review of *The Jewess of Hull* (Reginald
      Glossop); *Film-Struck* (Adolphus Raymond); and
      Ironheart (William McLeod).

C292 MR LUCAS AT EASE. *The Challenge*, n.s. ii (30), 19
      October 1923:596. Review of *Luck of the Year* (E.V.
      Lucas).

C293 THREE ESSAYISTS. *The Spectator*, 131 (4973), 20 Oc-
      tober 1923:559-560. Review of *Fancies v Fads* (G.K.
      Chesterton); *More Prejudice* (A.B. Walkley); and
      Sparks from the Fire (Gilbert Thomas).

C294 MR McKENNA ON HOLIDAY. *Daily News*, 24209, 23 October
      1923:7. Review of *By Intervention of Providence*
      (Stephen McKenna).

C295 ADVENTURES IN CRITICISM. *The Challenge*, n.s. ii (31),
      26 October 1923:616. Review of *Some Authors* (Walter
      Raleigh).

C296 BIG STRONG MEN. *Daily News*, 24214, 29 October 1923:
      10. Review of *Big Strong Man* (Charman Edwards);
      Men's Country (Peter Clark MacFarlane); and *A Year
      at the Outside* (L.G. Moberly).

C297 MR SQUIRE AND MR BAILEY. *Daily News*, 24216, 31 Oc-
      tober 1923:10. Review of *Essays on Poetry* (J.C.
      Squire) and *The Continuity of Letters* (John Bailey).

C298 THE ETHICS AND ECONOMICS OF REPRINTING. *The Bodleian*,
      15 (8), November 1923:120-122.

C299 IN PRAISE OF MR JACOBS. *London Mercury*, IX (49),
      November 1923:26-36.
      Reprinted: *Figures in Modern Literature* (1924).

C300 FICTION. *London Mercury*, IX (49), November 1923:102–
      104. Review of *Kangaroo* (D.H. Lawrence); *A Son at
      the Front* (Edith Wharton); *Deirdre* (James Stephens);
      Captures (John Galsworthy); *Midwinter* (John Buchan);
      and *Narrow Seas* (Neville Brand).

C301 THE HUMOUR OF LONDON. *The Spectator*, 131 (4975), 3
      November 1923:660. Review of *A Story Teller: Forty
      Years in London* (W. Pett Ridge). Unsigned.

C302 DR JOHNSON AND THE MONTHLY REVIEW. *The Spectator*
      (Literary Supplement), 131 (4975), 3 November 1923:
      646, 648. Review of *Contemporary Criticisms of Dr
      Samuel Johnson*.

C303 IN OLD ENGLAND. *The Challenge*, n.s. ii (33), 9 Novem-
      ber 1923:649–650.

C304 ARNOLD BENNETT AT LAST. *The Spectator*, 131 (4976),
      10 November 1923:704. Review of *Riceyman Steps*
      (Arnold Bennett).

C305 TWO SPECTATORS. *Daily News*, 24235, 22 November 1923:
      9. Review of *The World in False Face* (George Jean
      Nathan) and *Fantasies and Impromptus* (James Agate).

C306 'FASHNABLE FAX'. *The Challenge*, n.s. ii (36), 30
      November 1923:709–711.

C307 FICTION. *London Mercury*, IX (50), December 1923:204–
      206. Review of *Riceyman Steps* (Arnold Bennett);
      Peace in Our Time (Oliver Onions); *Told by an Idiot*
      (Rose Macaulay); *Antic Hay* (Aldous Huxley); *The
      Street of the Eye* (Gerald Bullett); and *The Parson's
      Progress* (Compton Mackenzie).

C308 TWO ENTHUSIASTS. *The Spectator* (Literary Supplement),
      131 (4979), 1 December 1923:846–847. Review of
      Fantasies and Impromptus (James Agate) and *Myself
      When Young* (Alec Waugh).

C309 POETRY AND PHILOSOPHY. *Daily News*, 24244, 3 December
      1923:9. Review of *Studies in Idealism* by Hugh
      L'Anson Fausset.

1924

C310 DRAMATIC CRITICISM. *The Bodleian*, 15 (10), January
        1924:152–154.

C311 FICTION. *London Mercury*, IX (51), January 1924:319–
        321. Review of *The Rover* (Joseph Conrad); *Fombombo*
        (T.S. Stribling); *Doomsland* (Shane Leslie); *Black
        Bryony* (T.F. Powys); and *A Perfect Day* (Bohun Lynch).

C312 THE BERKSHIRE MONSTERS. *The Challenge*, n.s. ii (42),
        11 January 1924:844–845.
        Reprinted: as 'The Berkshire Beasts', *Open House* (1927).

C313 THE BEGINNING OF REALISM. *The Challenge*, n.s. ii (42),
        11 January 1924:848–849. Review of *Celestina* (H. Warner
        Allen).

C314 MR JEROME AND SOME DEBATERS. *Daily News*, 24279, 15
        January 1924:7. Review of *A Miscellany of Sense and
        Nonsense* (Jerome K. Jerome); and *Yea and Nay* (C.D.
        Stelling).

C315 MR COPPARD, MR BULLETT AND KATHERINE MANSFIELD – letter.
        The Spectator, 132 (4986), 19 January 1924:86–87.
        Note: This letter concerning A.E. Coppard's review of
        Gerald Bullett's *Street of the Eye* was signed Roger
        Buckworth, but records at *The Spectator* office clearly
        indicate that J.B. Priestley of Wood Close, Chinnor,
        Oxon. was the true correspondent.

C316 THE SPIRIT OF THE ENGLISH. *Daily News*, 24293, 31
        January 1924:7. Review of *The English Secret* (Basil
        de Selincourt).

C317 MR ARNOLD BENNETT. *London Mercury*, IX (52), February
        1924:394–406.
        Reprinted: *Figures in Modern Literature* (1924).

C318 FICTION. *London Mercury*, IX (52), February 1924:
        434–436. Review of *A Poet's Youth* (Margaret Woods);
        Jane – Our Stranger (Mary Borden); and *Herr Arne's
        Hoard* (Selma Lagerlof).

C319 MAN AND NATURE. *Daily News*, 24298, 6 February 1924:7.
        Review of *Nature and Man* (Arthur McDowall).

C320   JANE AUSTEN: A NOTE. *The Spectator*, 132 (4989), 9
       February 1924:205-207. Review of *The Novels of Jane
       Austen* edited by R.W. Chapman.

C321   MR BAILEY'S ADDRESSES. *The Spectator*, 132 (4990), 16
       February 1924:251. Review of *The Continuity of
       Letters* (John Bailey). Unsigned.

C322   A BAD BOOK. *Daily News*, 24310, 20 February 1924:7.
       Review of *Nightcaps* (E.B. Osborn).

C323   A NOTE ON ARIEL. *The Bodleian*, 15 (12), March 1924:
       184-185.

C324   FICTION. *London Mercury*, IX (53), March 1924:546-548.
       Review of *England, My England* (D.H. Lawrence);
       Defeat (Geoffrey Moss); *The Fir and the Palm* (Eliza-
       beth Bibesco); *Capitol Hill* (Harvey Ferguson);
       Marching On (Ray Strachey); and *Wine of Fury* (Leigh
       Rogers).

C325   THE TALES THEY TELL US. *Daily News*, 24334, 19 March
       1924:8. Review of *Inigo Sandys* (E.B.C. Jones);
       Tony (Stephen Hudson); *The Coast of Folly* (Coningsby
       Dawson); *The Swedish Woman* (R.E.C. Long); *Laura of
       the Mist* (Eldon Ward); and *Spanish Love* (Juanita
       Savage).

C326   THE GOODLY FRAME. *The Spectator*, 132 (4996), 29
       March 1924:508. Review of *The Right Place* (C.E.
       Montague).

C327   LOG ROLLING. *The Bodleian*, 16 (1), April 1924:200-202.

C328   FICTION. *London Mercury*, IX (54), April 1924:659-661.
       Review of *Silk - A Legend* (Samuel Merwin); *Anthony
       Dare* (Archibald Marshall); *The Counterplot* (Hope
       Mirlees); *Judgement Eve* (H.C. Harwood); and *The
       Bazaar* (Martin Armstrong).

C329   IN SHORT, EVERYTHING. *Daily News*, 24348, 4 April 1924:
       9. Review of *The Dream* (H.G. Wells).

C330   A ROYAL CHRONICLER. *The Spectator*, 132 (4997), 5
       April 1924:554, 556. Review of *The Letters of Madame
       1661-1708*.

C331   RUSSIAN NIGHTS ENTERTAINMENT. *Daily News*, 24359, 17
       April 1924:6. Review of *My Past and Thoughts*

(Alexander Herzern); *Fifteen Tales* (Ivan Bunin); *The Russian Cook Book* (Princess Alexandre Gagarine); and *Character Revealed by Handwriting* (Princess Anatole Marie Bariatinsky).

C332 STANDING AND STARING. *Daily News*, 24367, 28 April 1924:8. Review of *Secrets* (W.H. Davies).

C333 MR DE LA MARE'S IMAGINATION. *London Mercury*, X (55), May 1924: 33-43.
Reprinted: *Figures in Modern Literature* (1924).

C334 FICTION. *London Mercury*, X (55), May 1924:101-103.
Review of *The Dream* (H.G. Wells); *Woodsmoke* (F. Brett Young); *Sanctions* (Ronald Knox); *Inigo Sandys* (E.B.C. Jones); *The Pentagram* (Huntly Robertson); and *The White Ship* (Aino Kallas).

C335 THREE NOVELS. *Daily News*, 24374, 6 May 1924:8. Review of *Tomorrow and Tomorrow* (Stephen McKenna); *The Shot* (Sibyl Cread); and *Almighty Gold* (J.J. Conington).

C336 AMY MAY. *The Bodleian*, XVI (3), June 1924:232-233.

C337 FICTION. *London Mercury*, X (56), June 1924:212-214.
Review of *Ordeal* (Dale Collins); *The Black Soul* (Liam O'Flaherty); *A Man in the Zoo* (David Garnett); *The Puppet Master* (Robert Nathan); *Gone Native* (Asterisk); *Tomorrow and Tomorrow* (Stephen McKenna); and *Wandering Stars* (Clemence Dane).

C338 MR DE LA MARE'S DARING. *Daily News*, 24403, 9 June 1924:6. Review of *Ding Dong Bell* (Walter de la Mare).

C339 A LADY WHO KNEW TOM MOORE. *Daily News*, 24410, 17 June 1924:6. Review of *Memories of Ninety Years* (Mrs. E.M. Ward).

C340 SIDELIGHTS ON CRITICISM. *Daily News*, 24413, 20 June 1924:9. Review of *The New Vision in German Arts* (H.G. Scheffauer); *Poetic Imagery* (H.W. Wells); *The Ethics of Criticism* (N. Hardy Wallis); and *Greek Literary Criticism* (J.D. Denniston).

C341 DISCOVERING ENGLAND. *The Bodleian*, XVI (4), July 1924: 248-250.

C342 FICTION. *London Mercury*, X (57), July 1924:319-321.
Review of *A Passage to India* (E.M. Forster); *The Voyage* (J. Middleton Murry); *The Heavenly Ladder* (Compton Mackenzie); *The Little Mexican* (Aldous

Huxley); and *Mark Only* (T.F. Powys).
Note: The first of these was reprinted in *E.M. Forster. A Passage to India. A Casebook* edited by Malcolm Bradbury (1970).

C343   MR BIRRELL'S ENCORE. *Daily News*, 24428, 8 July 1924: 8. Review of *More Obiter Dicta* (Augustine Birrell).

C344   PLEA FOR NARRATIVE VERSE. *Daily News*, 24445, 28 July 1924:8. Review of *Essays by Diverse Hands* edited by Edmund Gosse.

C345   FOUR EPIGRAMS. *London Mercury*, X (58), August 1924: 348.
Reprinted: *The Mercury Book of Verse* (1931).

C346   FICTION. *London Mercury*, X (58), August 1924:427-429. Review of *Unity* (J.D. Beresford); *C* (Maurice Baring); *The King of Elfland's Daughter* (Lord Dunsany); *Jennifer Lorn* (Elinor Wylie); and *Night Fears* (L.P. Hartley).

C347   LIVE GIRLS AND DEAD MEN. *Daily News*, 24458, 12 August 1924:6. Review of *The Park Lane Mystery, Tragedy at the Beach Club* (William Johnston); and *Marie Vee* (Douglas Newton).

C348   HAMLET AT LAST. *Daily News*, 24460, 14 August 1924:6. Review of *The Story of Hamlet and Horatio* (Anon).

C349   MYSTERIES AND MARVELS. *Daily News*, 24466, 21 August 1924:6. Review of *The Three Hostages* (John Buchan); *The House of the Arrow* (A.E.W. Mason); *Room 13* (Edgar Wallace); *Seibert of the Island* (Gordon Young); and *The Scented Death* (Anthony Drummond).

C350   FICTION. *London Mercury*, X (59), September 1924: 539-541. Review of *The Natural Man* (Patrick Miller); *The Red Horse* (Christopher Rover); and *After the Verdict* (Robert Hichens).

C351   THE ALL-ROUND MAN OF LETTERS. *Daily News*, 24476, 2 September 1924:6. Review of *Poems* (Collected Works of Arthur Symons Vols 1-3).

C352   BADLY HARNESSED AUTHORS. *Daily News*, 24482, 9 September 1924:8. Review of *The Boy in the Bush* (D.H. Lawrence and M.L. Skinner); *The Triumph of Gallio*

(W.L. George); *Charmeuse* (E. Temple Thurston); and
The Majestic Mystery (Denis Mackail).

C353 SIR JAMES BARRIE. *London Mercury*, X (60), October
1924:624-633.

C354 FICTION. *London Mercury*, X (60), October 1924:658-
660. Review of *Arnold Waterlow* (May Sinclair); *A
Lost Lady* (Willa Cather); *The Little French Girl*
(Anne Douglas Sedgwick); and *Something Childish*
(Katherine Mansfield).

C355 A HAPPY ANGLER. *Daily News*, 24505, 6 October 1924:8.
Review of *Where the Bright Waters Meet* (H. Plunket
Greene).

C356 MR STRACHEY'S TABLE TALK. *Daily News*, 24513, 15
October 1924:8. Review of *The River of Life* (J. St.
Loe Strachey).

C357 AT THE CHAPEL. *Daily News*, 24520, 23 October 1924:8.
Review of *Grey Pastures* (William Haslam Mills).

C358 TWO CRITICS. *Daily News*, 24523, 27 October 1924:8.
Review of *Discoveries* (J. Middleton Murry) and
John Donne (Hugh L'Anson Fausset).

C359 THE FANTASTIC. *The Bodleian*, XVI (8), November 1924:
312-313.

C360 FICTION. *London Mercury*, XI (61), November 1924:98-
100. Review of *The Old Ladies* (Hugh Walpole); *Pipes
and a Dancer* (Stella Benson); *Passion and Pain*
(Stefan Zweig); and *Buddenbrooks* (Thomas Mann).

C361 A POET ON DREAMS. *Daily News*, 24543, 19 November 1924:
8. Review of *The Meaning of Dreams* (Robert Graves).

C362 THE SAINTSBURY PUNCH. *Daily News*, 24549, 26 November
1924:8. Review of *A Last Scrap Book* (George Saintsbury).

C363 PEACOCK'S NOVELS. *Times Literary Supplement*, 1193,
27 November 1924:781-782. Unsigned.

C364 THE ESSAY. *The Bodleian*, XVI (9), December 1924:
328-330.

C365   E. NESBIT: AN APPRECIATION. *The Bookman*, LXVII (399),
       December 1924:157-159.

C366   FICTION. *London Mercury*, XI (62), December 1924:210-
       212. Review of *The White Monkey* (John Galsworthy);
       In the Land of Youth (James Stephens); *Sard Harker*
       (John Masefield); *Elsie and the Child* (Arnold
       Bennett); *Fidelity* (Susan Glaspell); *Schooling* (Paul
       Selver); and *Within a Budding Grove* (Marcel Proust).

                          1925

C367   MODERN ENGLISH NOVELISTS. JOSEPH CONRAD. *English
       Journal*, XIV (1), January 1925:13-21.

C368   FICTION. *London Mercury*, XI (63), January 1925:318-
       320. Review of *Orphan Island* (Rose Macaulay); *Cold
       Harbour* (F. Brett Young); *Mr Godley Beside Himself*
       (Gerald Bullett); *Balisand* (Joseph Hergesheimer);
       The Lovely Lake (Margaret Ashmun); and *The Next
       Corner* (Dudley Carew).

C369   CRITICISM AND CHAT. *Daily News*, 24590, 15 January
       1925:8. Review of *The Critic's Armoury* (Cyril Falls);
       Latitudes (Edwin Muir); and *Aspects of the Modern
       Short Story* (A.C. Ward).

C370   MR SYMONS AS A CRITIC. *Daily News*, 24602, 29 January
       1925:8. Review of *Studies in Two Literatures* and
       Studies in Seven Arts (Collected Works of Arthur
       Symons vols 8-9).

C371   H.G. WELLS. *English Journal*, XIV (2), February 1925:
       89-97. By J.B. Priestly [sic].

C372   CUBWOOD AND CUBHOOD. *The Bodleian*, XVI (11), February
       1925:360-361.

C373   HITS AND MISSES. *Daily News*, 24606, 3 February 1925:
       8. Review of *Bare Souls* (Gameliel Bradford).

C374   TWO WORLDS. *Daily News*, 24614, 12 February 1925:8.
       Review of *Mr Tasker's Gods* (T.F. Powys) and *The
       Little Karoo* (Pauline Smith).

C375 TOLSTOY AND TCHEKOV. *Daily News*, 24625, 25 February
1925:8. Review of *Life and Letters of Anton Tchekov*
and *Tolstoy on Art*.

C376 MR BURDETT'S NINETIES. *The Bodleian*, XIV (12), March
1925:376-377.

C377 CONTEMPORARY CRITICISM: A NOTE. *London Mercury*, XI
(65), March 1925:496-504.

C378 HAZLITT GLEANINGS. *Daily News*, 24650, 26 March 1925:8.
Review of *Hazlitt: New Writings* collected by P.P.
Howe.

C379 ARNOLD BENNETT. *English Journal*, XIV (4), April 1925:
261-268.

C380 VICTORIAN NOVELISTS. *Daily News*, 24665, 14 April 1925:
6. Review of *Charles Dickens and Other Victorians*
('Q').

C381 AFFAIRS OF VENUS. *Daily News*, 24667, 16 April 1925:8.
Review of *The Gay Intrigue* (Jack Kahane); *The Confi-
dence Man* (Laurie York Erskine); and *The Venus Girl*
(Leslie Beresford).

C382 JOHN GALSWORTHY. *English Journal*, XIV (5), May 1925:
347-355.

C383 MILTON AND OTHERS. *Daily News*, 24689, 12 May 1925:4.
Review of *Milton: Man and Thinker* (Denis Saurat);
Common Sense and the Muses (David Graham); and *Notes
on the Authorship of the Shakespeare Plays and Poems*
(Basil E. Lawrence).

C384 THE YOUNGER NOVELISTS. *English Journal*, XIV (6), June
1925:435-443.

C385 JOKES FOR WOMEN. *Saturday Review*, 139 (3632), 6 June
1925:617-618. Extensive letter on Gerald Gould's
notice of *English Comic Characters* (A6) in the previous week's issue.

C386 MR WALKLEY AGAIN. *Daily News*, 24727, 25 June 1925:4.
Review of *Still More Prejudice* (A.B. Walkley).

C387 POETRY AND THE TRAGIC HERO. *Daily News*, 24749, 21 July
1925:4. Review of *The Idea of Great Poetry* (Lascelles

Abercrombie); *The Hero: a Theory of Tragedy* (Albert
Beaumont); and *Between the Old World and the New*
(M.P. Wilkocks).

C388   ON MAN'S EXTRAVAGANCE.   *Saturday Review*, 140 (3640), 1
       August 1925:128-129.

C389   COLERIDGE.   *Daily News*, 24764, 7 August 1925:7.   Review
       of *Coleridge Poetry and Prose* edited by H.W. Garrod.

C390   EDWARD GIBBON.   *Daily News*, 24770, 14 August 1925:4.
       Review of *Selections from Gibbon*.

C391   THE POSITION OF POETRY.   *Daily News*, 24776, 21 August
       1925:4.   Review of *Thamyris: Or Is There a Future
       for Poetry?* (R.C. Trevelyan).

C392   COMIC CHARACTERS IN REAL LIFE.   *Blackwood's Magazine*,
       CCXVIII (MCCXIX), September 1925:344-348.

C393   CHARLES LAMB.   *Daily News*, 24787, 3 September 1925:4.
       Review of *Selected Letters of Charles Lamb* edited
       by G.T. Clapton.

C394   AN ODD FIGURE.   *Daily News*, 24797, 15 September 1925:
       4.   Review of *The Life of Thomas Holcroft* edited by
       Elbridge Colby.

C395   THE LAST CONRAD.   *Daily News*, 24798, 16 September
       1925:4.   Review of *Suspense* (Joseph Conrad).

C396   THE DRAMATIST DRAMATIZED.   *Saturday Review*, 140 (3647),
       19 September 1925:315-316.   Review of *The Collected
       Plays of John Drinkwater*.

C397   JOHN KEATS.   *Daily News*, 24806, 25 September 1925:4.
       Review of *Keats and Shakespeare* (J. Middleton Murry).

C398   THE SECRET OF DICKENS.   *Saturday Review*, 140 (3648),
       26 September 1925:342.   Review of *The Immortal Dickens*
       (George Gissing).

C399   BOOKS AND BROADCASTING.   *The Bodleian*, XVII (7), Oc-
       tober 1925:104-106.

C400   THE FIRST CELT.   *Saturday Review*, 140 (3649), 3 October
       1925:374.   Review of *Early Poems and Stories* (W.B.
       Yeats).

C401 F. ANSTEY: HUMORIS. *The Spectator*, 135 (5075), 3 Oc-
      tober 1925:551-552. Review of *The Last Road* (F.
      Anstey). Unsigned.

C402 RICH AND STRANGE. *Saturday Review*, 140 (3650), 10 Oc-
      tober 1925:404. Review of *Samuel Kelly* (Crosbie
      Garstin) and *Strange Adventures of the Sea* (J.G.
      Lockhart).

C403 CHEKHOV AS CRITIC. *Saturday Review*, 140 (3651), 17 Oc-
      tober 1925:446. Review of *Letters on Literature*
      (Anton Chekhov).

C404 A NOTE ON MR CHESTERTON. *Saturday Review*, 140 (3652),
      24 October 1925:480. Review of *The Everlasting Man*
      (G.K. Chesterton).

C405 STEVENSON. *Daily News*, 24834, 28 October 1925:4. Re-
      view of four volumes of Lothian edition of the works
      of Robert Louis Stevenson.

C406 AN APOLOGY TO GENIUS. *Saturday Review*, 140 (3653), 31
      October 1925:509-510. Review of *Poetry and Criticism*
      (Edith Sitwell).

C407 THREE ESSAYISTS. *Daily News*, 24839, 3 November 1925:
      4. Review of *Essays on Life* (A. Clutton-Brock);
      Safety Pins (Christopher Morley); and *Literary Diver-
      sions* (E. Beresford Chancellor).

C408 THE OTHER OPIUM EATER. *Saturday Review*, 140 (3654),
      7 November 1925:536. Review of *Coleridge at Highgate*
      (Lucy Eleanor Watson).

C409 A PROFESSOR. *Saturday Review*, 140 (3655), 14 November
      1925:571-572. Review of *The Collected Essays of
      W.P. Ker*.

C410 A NEW ANTHOLOGY. *Saturday Review*, 140 (3656), 21
      November 1925:601-602. Review of *The Silver Treasury
      of English Lyrics*.

C411 BACK TO LONDON. *The Spectator*, 135 (5082), 21 November
      1925:922.

C412 THE NOVELIST'S ART. *The Spectator*, 135 (5084), 5 De-
      cember 1925:1047. Review of *The Writing of Fiction*
      (Edith Wharton).

C413 CHANGING FACES. *The Spectator*, 135 (5086), 19 December
        1925:1135-1136.

C414 THREE CRITICS. *Daily News*, 24881, 22 December 1925:4.
        Review of *Collected Essays of W.P. Ker*; *Silhouettes*
        (Edmund Gosse); and *The Background of English Litera-
        ture* (H.J.C. Grierson).

                              1926

C415 CONTEMPORARY AMERICAN FICTION AS AN ENGLISH CRITIC SEES
        IT. *Harper's Monthly Magazine*, 152, January 1926:
        230-234.

C416 HOME FROM THE SEA. *Saturday Review*, 141 (3664), 16
        January 1926:57-58.
        Reprinted: *Open House* (1927).

C417 MONOLOGUE ON A BLUNDERER. *Saturday Review*, 141 (3665),
        23 January 1926:86-87.
        Reprinted: *Open House* (1927).

C418 IN CRIMSON SILK. *Saturday Review*, 141 (3666), 30
        January 1926:116-117.
        Reprinted: *Open House* (1927).

C419 VOLTAIRE AND TWO RUSSIANS. *Daily News*, 24915, 2 Feb-
        ruary 1926:4. Review of *Voltaire* (Richard Aldington);
        Gogol (Janke Lavrin); and *Pushkin* (D.S. Mirsky).

C420 OPEN HOUSE. *Saturday Review*, 141 (3667), 6 February
        1926:154-155.
        Reprinted: *Open House* (1927).

C421 DISSOLUTION IN HAYMARKET. *Saturday Review*, 141 (3668),
        13 February 1926:188-189.
        Reprinted: *Open House* (1927).

C422 THE POETRY OF MR J.C. SQUIRE. *Daily News*, 24927, 16
        February 1926:4. Review of *Poems in One Volume*.

C423 HIGH, LOW, BROAD. *Saturday Review*, 141 (3669), 20
        February 1926:222-223.
        Reprinted: *Open House* (1927).

C424 PARSON YORICK. *Saturday Review of Literature*, II (30), 20 February 1926:569. Review of *The Life and Times of Laurence Sterne* (Wilbur L. Cross).

C425 AT A CONCERT. *Saturday Review*, 141 (3670), 27 February 1926:254-255.
Reprinted: *Open House* (1927).

C426 LAUGHTER AND WORMWOOD. *Daily News*, 24941, 4 March 1926:4. Review of *Rough Justice* (C.E. Montagu).

C427 YOUTH IN DISGUISE. *Saturday Review*, 141 (3671), 6 March 1926:292-293.
Reprinted: *Open House* (1927).

C428 POETS AND A CRITIC. *Daily News*, 24948, 12 March 1926:4. Review of *Authors Dead and Living* (F.L. Lucas).

C429 DOUBTING IT. *Saturday Review*, 141 (3672), 13 March 1926:328-330.
Reprinted: *Open House* (1927).

C430 A SINGLE SEAT. *Saturday Review*, 141 (3673), 20 March 1926:364-365.

C431 LITERARY COMPETITION NO 5. *Saturday Review*, 141 (3673), 20 March 1926:368.

C432 SAKI'S WIT. *Daily News*, 24958, 24 March 1926:4. Review of *Reginald* and *Beasts and Super Beasts* (Saki).

C433 THE TOY FARM. *Saturday Review*, 141 (3674), 27 March 1926:397-398.
Reprinted: *Open House* (1927).

C434 A YOUNG MAN OF PROMISE. *Saturday Review*, 141 (3675), 3 April 1926:444-445.
Reprinted: *Open House* (1927).

C435 RESULT OF COMPETITION NO 5. *Saturday Review*, 141 (3675), 3 April 1926:449.

C436 PEACOCK PIE. *Saturday Review*, 141 (3676), 10 April 1926:471-472.
Reprinted: *Open House* (1927).

C437 THE STATESMAN AS HERO. *Daily News*, 24976, 15 April
        1926:4. Review of *Abraham Lincoln: The Prairie
        Years* (Carl Sandburg).

C438 FIRST NIGHTS. *Saturday Review*, 141 (3677), 17 April
        1926:499-500.
        Reprinted: *Open House* (1927).

C439 BLOOD AND BRAIN. *Daily News*, 24982, 22 April 1926:
        4. Review of *The Art of Thought* (Graham Wallas)
        and *Why We Behave Like Human Beings* (George A.
        Dorsey).

C440 IDEAS IN APRIL. *Saturday Review*, 141 (3678), 24
        April 1926:533-534.
        Reprinted: *Open House* (1927).

C441 SOME CONDITIONS OF GOOD TALK. *Blackwood's Magazine*,
        CCXIX (MCCXXVII), May 1926:609-618. Extract from
        Talking (1926).

C442 JOSEPH HERGESHEIMER AN ENGLISH VIEW. *The Bookman* (NY),
        LXIII (3), May 1926:272-280.

C443 REVOLT AND AMERICAN LITERATURE. *Forum*, LXXV (5), May
        1926:759-770. Signed John Boynton Priestley.

C444 CONTEMPORARY AMERICAN AUTHORS: JOSEPH HERGESHEIMER.
        London Mercury, XIV (79), May 1926:61-70.
        Reprinted: *Contemporary American Authors* edited by
        J.C. Squire (1928).

C445 ON NOT HEARING WHITEMAN'S BAND. *Saturday Review*, 141
        (3679), 1 May 1926:566-567.

C446 ON OVERLOOKING COVENT GARDEN. *Saturday Review*, 141
        (3682), 22 May 1926:613-614.
        Reprinted: *Open House* (1927).

C447 AMERICAN NOTES. *Saturday Review*, 141 (3683), 29 May
        1926:645-646.
        Reprinted: *Open House* (1927).

C448 THOSE NINETIES. *Daily News*, 25005, 1 June 1926:4.
        Review of *The Romantic 90s* (Richard Le Gallienne).

C449 HAVING SOLD THE PIANO. *Saturday Review*, 141 (3684),
        5 June 1926:673-674.
        Reprinted: *Open House* (1927).

C450 MY REVUE. *Saturday Review*, 141 (3685), 12 June 1926: 711-712.
Reprinted: *Open House* (1927).

C451 AUTOLYCUS AGAIN. *Saturday Review*, 141 (3686), 19 June 1926:742-743.
Reprinted: *Open House* (1927).

C452 WHAT IS A NOVEL? *Daily News*, 25025, 22 June 1926:4.
Review of *The Modern Novel* (Elizabeth Drew).

C453 ON AVOIDING A GOOD CRY. *Saturday Review*, 141 (3687), 26 June 1926:774-775.

C454 ENEMIES OF TALK. *Fortnightly Review*, 126, July 1926: 56-57. Also printed in *The Bookman* (NY), LXIV (1), September 1926:6-12. Extract from *Talking* (A9).

C455 ON HOLIDAY WITH THE BODIES. *Saturday Review of Literature*, 142 (3688), 3 July 1926:8-10.

C456 NOT HAVING THE TOURIST MIND. *Saturday Review*, 142 (3689), 10 July 1926:35-37.
Reprinted: *Open House* (1927).

C457 THE DOUBLE LIFE. *Daily News*, 25042, 14 July 1926:4.
Review of *The Undercurrent* (Eric Holland).

C458 MIDSUMMER DAY'S DREAM. *Saturday Review*, 142 (3690), 17 July 1926:64-65.
Reprinted: *Open House* (1927).

C459 SUTCLIFFE AND I. *Saturday Review*, 142 (3691), 24 July 1926:94-95.
Reprinted: *Open House* (1927).

C460 CALLING ON THE VICAR. *Saturday Review*, 142 (3692), 31 July 1926:120-121.
Reprinted: *Open House* (1927).

C461 CHARACTER OF TALK. *English Review*, XLIII (2), August 1926:207-216. Extract from *Talking* (A9).

C462 CHILDREN. *Saturday Review*, 142 (3693), 7 August 1926: 146-147.

C463 THE NATURE OF ROMANCE. *Daily News*, 25066, 11 August 1926:4. Review of *Romanticism* (Lascelles Abercrombie) and *A Call to Order* (Jean Cocteau).

C464   THE SILLY SEASON. *Saturday Review*, 142 (3694), 14
         August 1926:170, 172-173.

C465   DIFFERENT INSIDE. *Saturday Review*, 142 (3695), 21
         August 1926:199-200.
         Reprinted: *Open House* (1927).

C466   THE PESSIMISTS. *Saturday Review*, 142 (3696), 28
         August 1926:223-224.
         Reprinted: *Open House* (1927).

C467   A VOLUNTARY EXILE. *Saturday Review*, 142 (3697), 4
         September 1926:251-252.
         Reprinted: *Open House* (1927).

C468   LITERARY COMPETITION NO 27. *Saturday Review*, 142
         (3697), 4 September 1926:258.

C469   A FILM ACTOR. *Saturday Review*, 142 (3698), 11 Septem-
         ber 1926:281-282.
         Reprinted: *Open House* (1927).

C470   THE BUSY IDLE FELLOW. *Daily News*, 25095, 14 September
         1926:4. Review of *My Life and Times* (Jerome K.
         Jerome).

C471   A HUNDRED YEARS AGO. *Saturday Review*, 142 (3699), 18
         September 1926:309-310.

C472   THE NIGHT-WATCHMAN AGAIN. *Daily News*, 25101, 21 Sep-
         tember 1926:4. Review of *Sea Whispers* (W.W. Jacobs)
         and *A Gleaming Cohort* (G.K. Chesterton).

C473   THE INN OF THE SIX ANGLERS. *Saturday Review*, 142
         (3700), 25 September 1926:331-333.
         Reprinted: *Open House* (1927).

C474   RESULT OF COMPETITION NO 27. *Saturday Review*, 142
         (3700), 25 September 1926:337-338.

C475   THE SACRED BAD TEMPER. *Saturday Review*, 142 (3701),
         2 October 1926:374-375.
         Reprinted: *Open House* (1927).

C476   THE SCRAP SCREEN. *Saturday Review*, 142 (3702), 9 Oc-
         tober 1926:404-405.
         Reprinted: *Open House* (1927).

C477 HAVING COVERED THE CARD TABLE. *Saturday Review*, 142
(3703), 16 October 1926:432-433.
Reprinted: *Open House* (1927).

C478 REAPING THE WHIRLWIND. *Saturday Review*, 142 (3704),
23 October 1926:464-465. Refers to correspondence
he received after his essay 'American Notes' (C447)
was printed.

C479 'CRUMPY'. *Saturday Review*, 142 (3705), 30 October
1926:508-510.
Reprinted: *The Balconinny* (1929).

C480 COLD. *Saturday Review*, 142 (3706), 6 November 1926:
545-546.

C481 MR GOULD AND 'LITTLE CRITICS' - letter. *Saturday Review*, 142 (3706), 6 November 1926:549.

C482 STRANGE AMERICAN. *Daily News*, 25144, 10 November 1926:
4. Review of *The Road to the Temple* (Susan Glaspell).

C483 STIERISM. *Saturday Review*, 142 (3707), 13 November
1926:577-578.
Reprinted: *Apes and Angels* (1928).

C484 THE BIBLIOPHILES. *Saturday Review*, 142 (3708), 20
November 1926:609-611.
Reprinted: *The Balconinny* (1929).

C485 THE DARK HOURS. *Saturday Review*, 142 (3709), 27
November 1926:639-641.
Reprinted: *Apes and Angels* (1928).

C486 ON A COMMON MISTAKE IN CRITICISM. *The Bermondsey
Book*, IV (1), December 1926:8-12.
Reprinted: *Seven Years' Harvest: An Anthology of The
Bermondsey Book 1923-1930* compiled by Sidney Gutman
(1934) (B25).

C487 THE PORT. *Saturday Review*, 142 (3710), 4 December
1926:674-675.
Reprinted: *Apes and Angels* (1928).

C488 A LITERARY GENIUS. *Saturday Review*, 142 (3711), 11
December 1926:722-723.

C489   CODE IDDER HEAD. *Saturday Review*, 142 (3712), 18
         December 1926:762-763.
         Reprinted: *The Balconinny* (1929).

C490   SMELFUNGUS. *Daily News*, 25179, 21 December 1926:4.
         Review of *The Life and Letters of Tobias Smollett*
         (Lewis Melville).

C491   IN DEFENCE OF KINDNESS. *Saturday Review*, 142 (3713),
         25 December 1926:802-803.
         Reprinted: *The Balconinny* (1929).

                          1927

C492   TWENTY SEVEN. *Saturday Review*, 143 (3714), 1 January
         1927:8-9.

C493   H.M. TOMLINSON. *Saturday Review of Literature*, VIII
         (23), 1 January 1927:477-478.

C494   THE NEW DIARY. *Saturday Review*, 143 (3715), 8 January
         1927:42-43.
         Reprinted: *Apes and Angels* (1928).

C495   TOO MANY PEOPLE. *Saturday Review*, 143 (3717), 22
         January 1927:114-116.
         Reprinted: *Apes and Angels* (1928).

C496   FIRST SNOW. *Saturday Review*, 143 (3718), 29 January
         1927:149-150.
         Reprinted: *Apes and Angels* (1928).

C497   HUGH WALPOLE NOVELIST. *The Bookman* (NY), LXIV (6),
         February 1927:687-692.

C498   MARRIAGE AND THE COUNT. *Saturday Review*, 143 (3719),
         5 February 1927:188-190.

C499   THE LOST LAND. *Saturday Review*, 143 (3720), 12 Feb-
         ruary 1927:226-227.

C500   THE CARDS. *Saturday Review*, 143 (3721), 19 February
         1927:265-266.
         Reprinted: *The Balconinny* (1929).

C501 REMINISCENCES OF TRAVEL. *Saturday Review*, 143 (3722),
        26 February 1927:301-302.
        Reprinted: *Apes and Angels* (1928).

C502 THE INIMITABLE. *Daily News*, 25237, 1 March 1927:4.
        Review of *Life of Charles Dickens* (John Forster).

C503 PATISSERIE. *Saturday Review*, 143 (3723), 5 March
        1927:345-347.

C504 AT THE CIRCUS. *Saturday Review*, 143 (3724), 12 March
        1927:386-387.
        Reprinted: *Apes and Angels* (1928).

C505 SERVANTS. *Saturday Review*, 143 (3725), 19 March 1927:
        429-430.
        Reprinted: *Apes and Angels* (1928).

C506 THE WICKED PEOPLE. *Saturday Review*, 143 (3726), 26
        March 1927:465-466.
        Reprinted: *Apes and Angels* (1928).

C507 SERVILITY AND CIVILITY. *Saturday Review*, 143 (3727),
        2 April 1927:514-515.

C508 MR MORLEY'S ESSAYS. *Daily News*, 25268, 6 April 1927:
        4. Review of *The Romany Strain* (Christopher Morley).

C509 HATS. *Saturday Review*, 143 (3728), 9 April 1927:
        554-555.
        Reprinted: *Apes and Angels* (1928).

C510 EASTER CUSTOMS. *Saturday Review*, 143 (3729), 16 April
        1927:594-595.

C511 THE TWO-AND-FOURPENNY FAIRYLAND. *Saturday Review*,
        143 (3730), 23 April 1927:625-627.
        Reprinted: *Apes and Angels* (1928).

C512 LITERARY COMPETITION NO 60. *Saturday Review*, 143
        (3730), 23 April 1927:631.

C513 THE GENIUS OF POE. *Daily News*, 25284, 26 April 1927:
        4. Review of *Tales of Mystery* and *Miscellanies*
        (Edgar Allan Poe).

C514 OTHER PEOPLE'S ACCOMPLISHMENTS. *Saturday Review*, 143
        (3731), 30 April 1927:662-663.
        Reprinted: *Apes and Angels* (1928).

C515   SEEING STRATFORD. *Saturday Review*, 143 (3732), 7 May
         1927:699-700.
         Reprinted: *Apes and Angels* (1928).

C516   RESULT OF COMPETITION NO 60. *Saturday Review*, 143
         (3732), 7 May 1927:704-705.

C517   MR PICKWICK RETURNS. *Saturday Review*, 143 (3733), 14
         May 1927:737-739.
         Reprinted: *Apes and Angels* (1928).

C518   FORTUNE TELLING. *Saturday Review*, 143 (3734), 21 May
         1927:778-779.

C519   INSECTS. *Saturday Review*, 143 (3735), 28 May 1927:
         819-820.
         Reprinted: *Apes and Angels* (1928).

C520   ART AS A MAGIC MIRROR. *Forum*, LXXVII (6), June 1927:
         912-921.

C521   A MISTAKE ABOUT THE FUTURE. *Harper's Magazine*, 155,
         June 1927:114-117.

C522   THE STRANGE OUTFITTER. *Saturday Review*, 143 (3736),
         4 June 1927:862-863.
         Reprinted: *Apes and Angels* (1928).

C523   A TREMENDOUS CHARACTER. *Daily News*, 25321, 8 June
         1927:4. Review of *The Ettrick Shepherd* (Edith C.
         Batho).

C524   HOUSES. *Saturday Review*, 143 (3737), 11 June 1927:
         897-899.
         Reprinted: *Apes and Angels* (1928).

C525   A LIFE LIKE A NIGHTMARE. *Daily News*, 25326, 14 June
         1927:4. Review of *Marcel Proust: His Life and Work*
         (L. Pierre-Quint).

C526   HOW I BEGAN. *Daily News*, 25330, 18 June 1927:4.

C527   A VANISHED LODGING. *Saturday Review*, 143 (3738), 18
         June 1927:933-935.
         Reprinted: *The Balconinny* (1929).

C528   A HOSTLESS VISIT. *Saturday Review*, 143 (3739), 25
         June 1927:971-972.
         Reprinted: *Apes and Angels* (1928).

C529 BAD CRITICS. *Saturday Review*, 144 (3740), 2 July 1927: 10-11.

C530 A FISH IN BAYSWATER. *Saturday Review*, 144 (3741), 9 July 1927:46-48.
Reprinted: *The Balconinny* (1929).

C531 THE LAUGHERS. *Saturday Review*, 144 (3742), 16 July 1927:86-87.

C532 THOMAS LOVE PEACOCK - letter. *Times Literary Supplement*, 1329, 21 July 1927:504.

C533 A NOTE ON CRUMMLES. *Saturday Review*, 144 (3743), 23 July 1927:126-127.

C534 WILLIAM BLAKE. *Daily News*, 25363, 27 July 1927:4.
Review of *Introduction to the Study of Blake* (Max Plowman).

C535 THE SCHOOL MAGAZINE. *Saturday Review*, 144 (3744), 30 July 1927:159-160.
Reprinted: *Apes and Angels* (1928).

C536 THE ARTIST. *Saturday Review*, 144 (3745), 6 August 1927:189-190.
Reprinted: *Apes and Angels* (1928).

C537 MADMAN OR SEER? WILLIAM BLAKE. *John O'London's*, XVII (434), 13 August 1927:560, 562.

C538 A NEW TOBACCO. *Saturday Review*, 144 (3746), 13 August 1927:216-217.
Reprinted: *The Balconinny* (1929).

C539 WILLIAM BLAKE. *Saturday Review of Literature*, IV (3), 13 August 1927:33-34.

C540 A RAKE'S PROGRESS. *Daily News*, 25381, 17 August 1927: 4. Review of *Sir Charles Sedley* (V. de Sola Pinto).

C541 PHOTOGRAPHS. *Saturday Review*, 144 (3747), 20 August 1927:244-245.
Reprinted: *Apes and Angels* (1928).

C542 ATLANTIS. *Saturday Review*, 144 (3748), 27 August 1927:271-272.
Reprinted: *Apes and Angels* (1928).

C543 THE MELANCHOLY OF PROFESSOR FREUD. *Saturday Review*,
      144 (3749), 3 September 1927:299-301.

C544 THE FLOWER SHOW. *Saturday Review*, 144 (3750), 10
      September 1927:328-329.
      Reprinted: *Apes and Angels* (1928).

C545 PARSON YORICK. *Daily News*, 25404, 13 September 1927:
      4. Review of *The Letters of Laurence Sterne* edited
      by R. Brimley Johnson.

C546 WHERE TO LIVE. *Saturday Review*, 144 (3751), 17 Sep-
      tember 1927:360-361.

C547 THE MAN WITH THE FLARE. *Saturday Review*, 144 (3752),
      24 September 1927:390-391.
      Reprinted: *Apes and Angels* (1928).

C548 PESSIMISM AND DEPRESSIMISM. *Forum*, LXXVIII (4), Oc-
      tober 1927:605-612.

C549 T'MATCH. *Saturday Review*, 144 (3753), 1 October 1927:
      422-424.
      Reprinted: *Apes and Angels* (1928).

C550 THE ART OF LETTER WRITING. *Daily News*, 25425, 7 Oc-
      tober 1927:4. Review of *English Letter Writers*
      (R. Brimley Johnson).

C551 ALL THE NEWS. *Saturday Review*, 144 (3754), 8 October
      1927:469-470.
      Reprinted: *Apes and Angels* (1928).

C552 LITERARY COMPETITION NO 84. *Saturday Review*, 144
      (3754), 8 October 1927:475.

C553 GOOD HARVESTING. *Daily News*, 25429, 12 October 1927:
      4. Review of *Leaves and Fruit* (Edmund Gosse).

C554 MODES. *Saturday Review*, 144 (3755), 15 October 1927:
      502-504.
      Reprinted: *Balconinny* (1929).

C555 'DIZZY'. *Daily News*, 25437, 21 October 1927:4. Review
      of *Disraeli: A Picture of the Victorian Age* (Andre
      Maurois).

C556 A NOTE ON NOVELS. *Saturday Review*, 144 (3756), 22 Oc-
      tober 1927:540-541.

C557 RESULT OF COMPETITION NO 84. *Saturday Review*, 144 (3756), 22 October 1927:547.

C558 VARIETY. *Saturday Review*, 144 (3757), 29 October 1927: 578-579.
Reprinted: *Apes and Angels* (1928).

C559 MR FORSTER ON THE NOVEL. *Daily News*, 25445, 31 October 1927:4. Review of *Aspects of the Novel* (E.M. Forster).

C560 AT SCHOOL. *Belle Vue Magazine*, 33, Autumn Term, November 1927:26-27.
Reprinted: *Antiphon*, Autumn 1964.

C561 THE CARRIP. *Punch*, CLXXIII, 2 November 1927:500. Unsigned.

C562 IN A LONDON HOTEL. *Saturday Review*, 144 (3758), 5 November 1927:612-613.
Reprinted: *Apes and Angels* (1928).

C563 IN BARSETSHIRE. *Saturday Review*, 144 (3759), 12 November 1927:658-659.
Reprinted: *The Balconinny* (1929).

C564 OUR THEATRE. *Saturday Review*, 144 (3760), 19 November 1927:694-695.
Reprinted: *Apes and Angels* (1928).

C565 THICK NOTEBOOKS. *Saturday Review*, 144 (3761), 26 November 1927:730-732.
Reprinted: *Apes and Angels* (1928).

C566 LONDON GROUPS AND COTERIES. *The Bookman* (NY), LXVI (4), December 1927:367-370.

C567 THE SPIRIT OF ENGLAND. WHERE ARE OUR MOST TYPICALLY ENGLISH AUTHORS? *John O'London's*, XVIII (450), 3 December 1927:274.

C568 FALSTAFF'S WEDDING. *Saturday Review*, 144 (3762), 3 December 1927:768-769.

C569 G.K.C. on R.L.S. *Daily News*, 25476, 6 December 1927: 4. Review of *Stevenson* (G.K. Chesterton).

C570 A NOTE ON FATHER CHRISTMAS. *Saturday Review*, 144 (3765), 24 December 1927:882-883.

1928

C571   THE HANDSOME DUKE. *Saturday Review*, 145 (3767), 7
       January 1928:6-8.

C572   THE GREAT UNREADABLE. *The Bookman*, LXXIII (438),
       March 1928:310.

C573   THE LOST ART OF NARRATIVE. *Daily News*, 25553, 6
       March 1928:4. Review of *Dead Man's Rock*, *Troy Town*,
       Noughts and Crosses, and *The Splendid Spur* by 'Q'.
       Also printed in *Bookmark*, IV (14), Summer 1928:3-4, 7.

C574   LITTLE TICH. *Saturday Review*, 145 (3776), 10 March
       1928:282-283.
       Reprinted: *The Balconinny* (1929).

C575   COMMERCIAL INTERLUDE. *Saturday Review*, 145 (3778), 24
       March 1928:345-346.

C576   MY FORCHERN. *Saturday Review*, 145 (3780), 7 April
       1928:429-430.
       Reprinted: *The Balconinny* (1929).

C577   SCIENTISTS - AND US. *Saturday Review*, 145 (3782), 21
       April 1928:489-491.

C578   ON AN OLD FAVOURITE. *Saturday Review*, 145 (3784), 5
       May 1928:554-555.

C579   THE ART OF SMOKING. *Daily News*, 25606, 8 May 1928:
       4. Review of *This Smoking World* (A.C. Hamilton).

C580   AN OLD FRIEND. *Daily News*, 25612, 15 May 1928:4.
       Review of *Kai Lung Unrolls His Mat* (Ernest Bramah).

C581   MY DEBUT IN OPERA. *Saturday Review*, 145 (3786), 19
       May 1928:623-624.
       Reprinted: *The Balconinny* (1929).

C582   ON VIEW. *Saturday Review*, 145 (3788), 2 June 1928:
       693-694.
       Reprinted: *The Balconinny* (1929).

C583   AN UNDERPRAISED NOVELIST. *Daily News*, 25624, 29 May
       1928:4. Review of *Anthony Trollope* (Hugh Walpole).

C584 LITERARY COMPETITION NO 119. *Saturday Review*, 145
      (3789), 9 June 1928:730.

C585 THE INTERVIEW. *Saturday Review*, 145 (3790), 16 June
      1928:763-764.

C586 THE SKIPPER. *Saturday Review*, 145 (3791), 23 June
      1928:797-798.
      Reprinted: *The Balconinny* (1929).

C587 RESULT OF COMPETITION NO 119. *Saturday Review*, 145
      (3791), 23 June 1928:803-804.

C588 A COMEDIAN OFF THE STAGE. *Daily News*, 25654, 3 July
      1928:4. Review of *Life and Times of Colley Cibber*
      (Dorothy Senior).

C589 CARLESS AT LAST. *Saturday Review*, 146 (3793), 7 July
      1928:10-11.
      Reprinted: *The Balconinny* (1929).

C590 THE REAL BYRON. *Daily News*, 25672, 24 July 1928:4.
      Review of *Selected Letters of Byron* edited by V.H.
      Collins.

C591 A BALCONY OVER THE SEA. *Saturday Review*, 146 (3796),
      28 July 1928:114-115.
      Reprinted: as 'The Balconinny' in *The Balconinny* (1929).

C592 C.E. MONTAGUE. *London Mercury*, XVIII (106), August
      1928:381-390.

C593 MR PUNCH. *Saturday Review*, 146 (3798), 11 August 1928:
      176-178.
      Reprinted: *The Balconinny* (1929).

C594 THE ROUNDABOUTS. *Daily News*, 25696, 21 August 1928:4.
      Review of *A Selection from the Roundabout Papers*
      edited by W.H. Williams.

C595 DISILLUSIONED. *Saturday Review*, 146 (3800), 25 August
      1928:237-238.
      Reprinted: *The Balconinny* (1929).

C596 A QUEER LIFE. *Daily News*, 25704, 30 August 1928:4.
      Review of *Selections from Swift* edited by W. Tom
      Williams and G.H. Vallins.

C597 HUGH WALPOLE. *English Journal*, XVII (7), September
      1928:529-536.

C598 THE DICKENS FAYRE. *Saturday Review*, 146 (3802), 8
      September 1928:291-293.
      Reprinted: *The Balconinny* (1929).

C599 LECTURES. *Saturday Review*, 146 (3804), 22 September
      1928:354-355.
      Reprinted: *The Balconinny* (1929).

C600 PROSE AND OPIUM. *Daily News*, 25727, 26 September 1928:
      4. Review of *The Ecstasies of Thomas de Quincey*
      edited by Thomas Burke.

C601 THE RETURN. *Saturday Review*, 146 (3806), 6 October
      1928:417-418.

C602 THE OLD PESSIMIST AND THE YOUNG PESSIMIST. *Evening
      News*, 14602, 12 October 1928:8. Review of *Winter
      Words* (Thomas Hardy); *Point Counter Point* (Aldous
      Huxley); *My Brother Jonathan* (Francis Brett Young);
      History of Egg Pandervil (Gerald Bullett); and *Bigger
      and Better Murders* (Charles Merz).

C603 RESIDENTIAL. *Saturday Review*, 146 (3807), 13 October
      1928:465-466.
      Reprinted: *The Balconinny* (1929).

C604 A BATCH OF SHORT STORIES. *Evening News*, 14608, 19
      October 1928:8. Review of *The Silver Thorn* (Hugh
      Walpole); *Silver Circus* (A.E. Coppard); *Quiet Cities*
      (Joseph Hergesheimer); *Action* (C.E. Montague); *Poor
      Women* (Norah Hoult); and *Australian Short Stories*
      edited by George Mackaness.

C605 AT THE VERDUN FILM. *Saturday Review*, 146 (3808), 20
      October 1928:497-498.
      Reprinted: *The Balconinny* (1929).

C606 KATHERINE MANSFIELD AND HER LETTERS. *Evening News*,
      14614, 26 October 1928:11. Review of *Letters*
      (Katherine Mansfield) and *Orlando* (Virginia Woolf).

C607 VARIETY: THE GRAND MANNER. *Saturday Review*, 146 (3809),
      27 October 1928:534-535.

C608 LIGHTWEIGHTS AND MIDDLEWEIGHTS. *Evening News*, 14620,
      2 November 1928:11. Review of *Jerome* (Maurice Bedel);

Show Girl (J.P. McEvoy); *Decline and Fall* (Evelyn
Waugh); *Humdrum* (Harold Acton); *The Pathway* (Henry
Williamson); and *The Partnership* (Phyllis Bentley).

C609   AT POPULAR PRICES. *Saturday Review*, 146 (3810), 3 No-
       vember 1928:570-571.
       Reprinted: *Self-Selected Essays* (1932).

C610   WHAT HAPPENED TO HARDY. *Evening News*, 14626, 9 Novem-
       ber 1928:11. Review of *Early Life of Thomas Hardy*
       (Mrs Hardy); *Heine: The Strange Guest* (Henry Baer-
       lein); and *Houdini* (Harold Kellock).

C611   WITH MODOM. *Saturday Review*, 146 (3811), 10 November
       1928:602-603.

C612   A GREAT GERMAN WAR NOVEL. *Evening News*, 14632, 16
       November 1928:11. Review of *The Magic Mountain*
       (Thomas Mann); *The Case of Sergeant Grischa* (Arnold
       Zweig); *The Cambridge Shorter Bible*; and *An Outline
       History of the Great War*.

C613   LORD MAYOR UNVISITED. *Saturday Review*, 146 (3812), 17
       November 1928:647-648.
       Reprinted: *The Balconinny* (1929).

C614   LYTTON STRACHEY'S NEW BOOK. *Evening News*, 14638, 23
       November 1928:11. Review of *Elizabeth and Essex*
       (Lytton Strachey); *What Is Love* (E.M. Delafield);
       and *The Spacious Adventures of the Man in the Street*
       (Eimar O'Duffy).

C615   MAN UNDERGROUND. *Saturday Review*, 146 (3813), 24 No-
       vember 1928:678-680.
       Reprinted: *Self-Selected Essays* (1932).

C616   A POET IN THE TRENCHES. *Evening News*, 14644, 30
       November 1928:11. Review of *Undertones of War*
       (Edmund Blunden); *The Diary of Dostoyevsky's Wife*;
       and *The Diary of Tolstoy's Wife*.

C617   ESCAPE AND PURSUIT. *Forum*, LXXX (6), December 1928:
       913-919.

C618   AMONG THE COOKS. *Saturday Review*, 146 (3814), 1
       December 1928:719-720.
       Reprinted: *The Balconinny* (1929).

C619 SUPER-SUPER. *Saturday Review*, 146 (3815), 8 December
      1928:757-758.
      Reprinted: *The Balconinny* (1929).

C620 THE OMNIBUS BOOKS. *Evening News*, 14650, 9 December
      1928:11. Review of *Great Short Stories of Detection,
      Mystery and Horror* edited by Dorothy L. Sayers; *Short
      Stories of Thomas Hardy*; *The Stories of Robert L.
      Stevenson*; *Great English Plays*; *Great Poems of the
      English Language*; *Complete Sherlock Holmes Short
      Stories*; and *The Plays of J.M. Barrie*.

C621 THE SLUMP IN POETRY. *Evening News*, 14656, 14 December
      1928:11. Review of *Selected Poems* (Ezra Pound);
      The Collected Poems of W.H. Davies; *Ballads and Poems*
      (Alfred Noyes); *Midsummer Night* (John Masefield);
      The Buck in the Snow (Edna St. Vincent Millay); *An
      Anthology of Nineties Verse* edited by A.J.A. Symons;
      and *Poems* (Mary Webb).

C622 PETTICOAT LANE. *Saturday Review*, 146 (3816), 15
      December 1928:811-812.
      Reprinted: *Self-Selected Essays* (1932).

C623 OUR AUTHORS - AND THE CHRISTMAS SPIRIT. *Evening News*,
      14662, 21 December 1928:8. Review of *A Christmas
      Book* compiled by D.B. Wyndham Lewis and G.C.
      Heseltine.

C624 FLEET STREET BAR. *Saturday Review*, 146 (3817), 22 De-
      cember 1928:844-845.

C625 YORKSHIRE AND CHRISTMAS. WHERE THE FESTIVE SEASON IS
      REALLY FESTIVE. *Yorkshire Post*, 25413, 22 December
      1928:6.

C626 YARNS AND CHARACTERS. *Evening News*, 14666, 28 Decem-
      ber 1928:11. Review of *General Crack* (George Preedy);
      and *Pilgrims of Adversity* (William MacFee).

C627 DOG'S LIFE. *Saturday Review*, 146 (3818), 29 December
      1928:873-874.

1929

C628 ONE THING WE'RE BAD AT IN YORKSHIRE. *Yorkshire Post*,
      25419, 1 January 1929:6.

C629 BOOKS I DON'T LIKE. *Evening News*, 14672, 4 January
      1929:6.

C630 AT A DANCE. *Saturday Review*, 147 (3819), 5 January
      1929:9-10.
      Reprinted: *The Balconinny* (1929).

C631 NOVELS AND PEOPLE A PLEA FOR VARIETY. *Yorkshire Post*,
      25425, 8 January 1929:6.

C632 THE TRAGI-COMEDY OF BALZAC. *Evening News*, 14678, 11
      January 1929:9. Review of *The Life of Honore de
      Balzac* (Rene Benjamin); *Accident* (Arnold Bennett);
      The Studio Crime (Ianthe Jerrold); and *The Death of
      Laurence Vining* (Alan Thomas).

C633 THE TIGER. *Saturday Review*, 147 (3820), 12 January
      1929:39-40.
      Reprinted: *The Balconinny* (1929).

C634 LONDON OR THE PROVINCES. A CANDID COMPARISON. *York-
      shire Post*, 25431, 15 January 1929:6.

C635 A QUIET WRITER. *Evening News*, 14684, 18 January 1929:
      9. Review of *The Garland* and *The Mistress of Husaby*
      (Sigrid Undset); *Boston* (Upton Sinclair); *Ask the
      Young* (W.B. Trites); and *The Prisoner in the Opal*
      (A.E.W. Mason).

C636 AT MADAME TUSSAUDS. *Saturday Review*, 147 (3821), 19
      January 1929:69-70.

C637 DIALECT AND ACCENT. *Yorkshire Post*, 25436, 21 January
      1929:8.

C638 ALL BLURB AND NO PLOT. *Evening News*, 14690, 25 January
      1929:11. Review of *Brown on Resolution* (C.S. Fores-
      ter).

C639 LITERARY LUNCH. *Saturday Review*, 147 (3822), 26
      January 1929:103-104.

C640 WIRELESS WITHOUT TEARS. *Daily Mirror*, 7863, 28 January
      1929:11.

C641 PESSIMISM AND DEPRESSIMISM. *Blackwood's Magazine*,
      CCXXV (MCCLX), February 1929:212-218.

C642 SIR JAMES BARRIE. *English Journal*, XVIII (2), February
      1929:106-119.

C643 THE SENTIMENTAL SEX. *Evening News*, 14696, 1 February
      1929:11. Review of *Portrait in a Mirror* (Charles
      Morgan); *Expiation* (Elizabeth, Countess Russell);
      and *Lily Christine* (Michael Arlen).

C644 AT THE TAILORS. *Saturday Review*, 147 (3823), 2 Feb-
      ruary 1929:139-141.
      Reprinted: *Self-Selected Essays* (1932).

C645 PUBLICITY ACTORS AND AUTHORS. *Yorkshire Post*, 25447,
      2 February 1929:8.

C646 BEFORE RETIRING. *Evening News*, 14702, 8 February 1929:
      11. Review of *The Bride Adorned* (D.L. Murray); *Ex-
      periment with Time* (J.W. Dunne); *The World Does More*
      (Booth Tarkington); *Frederick the Great* (Margaret
      Goldsmith); *Kif* (Gordon Daviot); *Judith Silver* (Hec-
      tor Bolitho); and *Reubens* (Max Brod).

C647 IN THE BRITISH MUSEUM. *Saturday Review*, 147 (3824), 9
      February 1929:174-175.
      Reprinted: *Self-Selected Essays* (1932).

C648 FEATURING MR WELLS. *Evening News*, 14708, 15 February
      1929:11. Review of *The Man Who Was a King* (H.G.
      Wells); *Selections Autobiographical and Imaginative*
      edited by George Gissing; *Sober Feast* (Barbara Black-
      burn); and *Prancing Nigger* (Ronald Firbank).

C649 REDS. *Evening News*, 14714, 22 February 1929:11. Re-
      view of *The Diary of a Communist Undergraduate*
      (N. Ognyov); *The Shepherd and the Child* (John Owen);
      Night Falls on Siva's Hills (Edward Thompson); and
      Three Courtiers (Compton Mackenzie).

C650 CHANGED FACE OF SOHO. *Sunday Dispatch*, 6643, 24
      February 1929:12.

C651 BOOKS I SHALL READ AGAIN. *The Bookman*, LXXV (540),
      March 1929:309-310.

C652 A YOUNG MAN WHO CAN WRITE. *Evening News*, 14720, 1
 March 1929:11. Review of *Paper Houses* (William
 Plomer); *Mamba's Daughters* (Du Bose Heyward); *The
 True Heart* (Sylvia Townsend Warner); *Two Made Their
 Bed* (Louis Marlow); and *The South Polar Trail from
 the Log of Ernest Mills Joyce*.

C653 THE GREAT UGLIFIER. *Evening News*, 14726, 8 March 1929:
 11. Review of *Zola and His Time* (Matthew Josephson);
 Six Mrs Greenes (Lorna Rea); *Footprints* (Kay Strachan);
 Inconsistent Villains (N.A. Templeton-Ellis); *Sails
 and Saddles* (Michael Bruce); and *The Great Trans-
 Pacific Flight* (C.E. Kingsford-Smith).

C654 AT THE DUTCH PICTURES. *Saturday Review*, 147 (3828),
 9 March 1929:315-316.

C655 A SHIEL AMONG US. *Evening News*, 14732, 15 March 1929:
 11. Review of *The Purple Cloud*, *The Lord of the Sea*,
 The Yellow Peril and *Cold Steel* by M.P. Shiel.

C656 AMONG THE GLASS JARS. *Saturday Review*, 147 (3829), 16
 March 1929:350-351.
 Reprinted: *Self-Selected Essays* (1932).

C657 I WANT TO KNOW. *Sunday Dispatch*, 6646, 17 March 1929:1.

C658 MR LEWIS OVER HERE. *Evening News*, 14738, 22 March
 1929:11. Review of *Dodsworth* (Sinclair Lewis); *The
 Diary of Montaigne's Journey to Italy*; and *The Diary
 of a Rum Runner* (Alastair Moray).

C659 BEFORE OPENING. *Saturday Review*, 147 (3830), 23 March
 1929:386-387.
 Reprinted: *Self-Selected Essays* (1932).

C660 LLAN-FAIR-FECHAN LOOK YOU. *Sunday Dispatch*, 6647, 24
 March 1929:1, 9.

C661 CLUES AND CORPSES. *Evening News*, 14743, 28 March 1929:
 11. Review of *The India-Rubber Men* (Edgar Wallace);
 Three Shots (Oscar Gray); *Who Shall Hang?* (Marcus
 Magill); *The Fourth Finger* (Anthony Wynne); *The Crime
 at Tattenham Corner* (Annie Hayes); *Dagworth Combe
 Murder* (Lynn Brock); *Murder of a Mystery Writer* (John
 Hawk); *The Yellow Rock* (David Footman); and *The Per-
 fect Murder Case* (Christopher Bush).

C662   IN HYDE PARK. *Saturday Review*, 147 (3831), 30 March
       1929:429–431.

C663   LANCASHIRE WITH THE LID OFF. *Sunday Dispatch*, 6648,
       31 March 1929:7.

C664   REVIEW of *All Quiet on the Western Front* (Erich Re-
       marque). *Book Society News*, April 1929.

C665   LIVES OF GREAT MEN. *Evening News*, 14749, 5 April 1929:
       11. Review of *Aspects of Biography* (Andre Maurois);
       Great Short Biographies of the World; *Parachute* (Ramon
       Guthrie); and *White Men's Sage* (Eric Linklater).

C666   OUT OF IT. *Saturday Review*, 147 (3832), 6 April 1929:
       468–469.
       Reprinted: *The Balconinny* (1929).

C667   DUBLIN THE SPHINX. *Sunday Dispatch*, 6649, 7 April
       1929:8.

C668   A POET AND THE BIBLE. *Evening News*, 14755, 12 April
       1929:11. Review of *Stories from the Bible* (Walter
       de la Mare); *The Mountain Tavern* (Liam O'Flaherty);
       Costumes by Eros (Conrad Aiken); *Disinherited*
       (Milton Waldman); and *Cousin Matthew* (Watson Dyke).

C669   NOO THOUGHT. *Saturday Review*, 147 (3833), 13 April
       1929:500–501.

C670   NOTTINGHAM – A CITY OF PRETTY GIRLS. *Sunday Dispatch*,
       6650, 14 April 1929:8.

C671   TALES THAT DON'T COME OFF. *Evening News*, 14761, 19
       April 1929:11. Review of *The Love of a Foolish
       Angel* (Helen Beauclerk); *Dark Hester* (Anne Douglas
       Sedgwick); *The Boroughmonger* (Mottram); and *Catherine
       Foster* (H.E. Bates).

C672   AT THURSTON'S. *Saturday Review*, 147 (3834), 20 April
       1929:527–529.
       Reprinted: *Self-Selected Essays* (1932).

C673   ON THE PIER AT WIGAN. *Sunday Dispatch*, 6651, 21 April
       1929:8.

C674   THE GREAT SOLDIER. *Evening News*, 14763, 22 April
       1929:8. Review of *Foch Talks* (Commandant Bugnet).

C675 THE RETURN OF THE WAR. *Evening News*, 14767, 26 April
      1929:8. Review of *All Quiet on the Western Front*
      (Erich Remarque); *Combed Out* (F.A. Voight); and *The
      Path of Glory* (George Blake).

C676 THE RING. *Saturday Review*, 147 (3835), 27 April 1929:
      568-570.
      Reprinted: *Self-Selected Essays* (1932).

C677 LONDON - THE GREATEST SHOW ON EARTH. *Sunday Dispatch*,
      6652, 28 April 1929:18.

C678 REVIEW of *The Wanderer* by Alain-Fournier. *Book Society
      News*, May 1929.

C679 HOW TO BEGIN THINKING OF LITERATURE. *English Journal*,
      XVIII (5), May 1929:365-374.

C680 A YOUNG SINBAD. *Evening News*, 14773, 3 May 1929:11.
      Review of *The Great Horn Spoon* (Eugene Wright);
      Umbala (Harry Dean); *Dancing Catalans* (John Langdon-
      Davies); *That Capri Air* (Signor Cerio); and *Voyage
      of the Annie Marble* (C.S. Forester).

C681 ROBERT AT PLAY. *Saturday Review*, 147 (3836), 4 May
      1929:606-607.

C682 WORLD'S BEST SPA. *Sunday Dispatch*, 6653, 5 May 1929:
      18.

C683 THE DREAM PARTY. *Evening News*, 14779, 10 May 1929:11.
      Review of *The Wanderer* (Alain-Fournier); *Steppenwolf*
      (Herman Hesse); *No Love* (David Garnett); *Roon* (Herbert
      Asquith); and *The Golden Fleece* (John Gunther).

C684 ONE SATURDAY AFTERNOON. *Saturday Review*, 147 (3837),
      11 May 1929:637-638.

C685 OXFORD GOING (MIDDLE) WEST. *Sunday Dispatch*, 6654,
      12 May 1929:18.

C686 A GLIMPSE OF THE ANCIENTS. *Evening News*, 14785, 17
      May 1929. Review of *Private Letters Pagan and
      Christian* (Lady Brooke).

C687 HORTICULTURAL. *Saturday Review*, 147 (3838), 18 May
      1929:670-671.

C688 IN A MAGIC CITY. *Sunday Dispatch*, 6655, 19 May 1929:18.

C689 HUMOUR FROM RUSSIA. *Evening News*, 14791, 24 May 1929:
       9. Review of *The Embezzlers* (Valentine Kataev); *The
       Confusion of Tongues* (Charles Ferguson); and *The
       World Below* (S. Fowler Wright).

C690 BANK HOLIDAY ON THE HEATH. *Saturday Review*, 147 (3839),
       25 May 1929:704-705.

C691 STEVENSON'S GHOST STILL HAUNTS EDINBURGH. *Sunday Dis-
       patch*, 6656, 26 May 1929:18.

C692 TWO HUMOURISTS. *Evening News*, 14797, 31 May 1929:8.
       Review of *Mulliner's Nights* (P.G. Wodehouse) and
       Topsy M.P. (A.P. Herbert).

C693 REVIEW of *The Adventures of Ralph Rashleigh* edited by
       the Earl of Birkenhead. *Book Society News,* June
       1929.

C694 THE APPROACH TO LITERATURE: THE DULL PATCHES. *English
       Journal*, XVIII (6), June 1929:450-455.
       Reprinted: *College English*, November 1960.

C695 THE UNDERWORLD. *Saturday Review*, 147 (3840), 1 June
       1929:733-734.
       Reprinted: *Self-Selected Essays* (1932).

C696 A MIXED BAG OF MEMORIES. *Evening News*, 14803, 7 June
       1929:11. Review of *Child of the Deep* (Joan Lovell);
       Shades of Eton (Percy Lubbock); *Scoundrels and
       Scallywags* (Tom Dival); *Barbarian Stories* (Naomi
       Mitchison); *The Helmers* (Elissa Landi); and *Above
       and Below* (R.D. Dorthy).

C697 PUBLIC DINNERS. *Saturday Review*, 147 (3841), 8 June
       1929:760-761.
       Reprinted: *Self-Selected Essays* (1932).

C698 IN ABERDEEN OF ALL PLACES. *Sunday Dispatch*, 6658, 9
       June 1929:18.

C699 REPLYING TO A CORRESPONDENT. *Evening News*, 14809, 14
       June 1929:11. Review of *The Prince of Somebody*
       (Louis Golding); *Music at Midnight* (Mrs Draper); *Song
       of My Life* (Yvette Guilbert); *The Cleve Family* (Mrs
       Ella Fuller-Maitland); and *A Diet of Crisps* (H.
       Phillips).

C700 THE ALEXANDRA PALACE. *Saturday Review*, 147 (3842), 15
        June 1929:792-793.

C701 DREAM-LIKE WELLS. *Sunday Dispatch*, 6659, 16 June
        1929:8.

C702 THOSE SENTIMENTAL STATES. *Evening News*, 14815, 21
        June 1929:11. Review of *Goodbye Wisconsin* (Glenway
        Westcott); *Little Caesar* (W.R. Burnett); *Banjo*
        (Claude McKay); and *Grimhaven* (Robert Joyce Tasker).

C703 AN AFTERNOON AT LORD'S. *Saturday Review*, 147 (3843),
        22 June 1929:825-826.

C704 OUR DEBT TO THE HEAT WAVE. *Sunday Dispatch*, 6664, 21
        July 1929:12.

C705 THE GRIM CONTINENT. *Evening News*, 14821, 28 June 1929:
        11. Review of *The Adventures of Ralph Rashleigh*;
        A House Is Built (M. Barnard Eldershaw); and *Coonardoo*
        (Katherine Susannah Prichard).

C706 A MUSICAL PARTY. *Saturday Review*, 147 (3844), 29 June
        1929:856-857.

C707 REVIEW of *The Summer Game* (Neville Cardus). *Book
        Society News*, July 1929.

C708 PLOTS THAT DON'T RING TRUE. *Evening News*, 14827, 5
        July 1929:11. Review of *The Sleeping Fury* (Martin
        Armstrong); *The Man Within* (Graham Greene); and
        The Midnight Bell (Patrick Hamilton).

C709 AT THE CALEDONIAN MARKET. *Saturday Review*, 148 (3845),
        6 July 1929:9-10.
        Reprinted: *Self-Selected Essays* (1932).

C710 THESE OUR ACTORS. *Saturday Review*, 148 (3846), 13
        July 1929:40-41.
        Reprinted: *Self-Selected Essays* (1932).

C711 GAMES AND GOOD WRITING. *Evening News*, 14833, 14 July
        1929:11. Review of *The Summer Game* (Neville Cardus)
        and *All Kneeling* (Anne Parish).

C712 WHY WORRY ABOUT FEELING HAMLET'S PULSE. *Evening News*,
        14839, 19 July 1929:11. Review of *Madness in Shake-
        sperian Tragedy* (H. Somerville) and *Another Part of
        the Wood* (Denis Mackail).

C713   MAD MAKE-BELIEVE. *Saturday Review*, 148 (3847), 20 July
         1929:67-69.
         Reprinted: *Self-Selected Essays* (1932).

C714   THE NOVELISTS AND THE HERD. *Evening News*, 14845, 26
         July 1929:11. Reviews of *Three Came Unarmed* (Arnot
         Robinson); *Frolic Wind* (Richard Oke); *In the Long Run*
         (Gladwin Klompers); and *MW-XX3* (Roland Pertwee).

C715   POLISH INTERLUDE 1. *Saturday Review*, 148 (3848), 27
         July 1929:97-98.
         Reprinted: *Self-Selected Essays* (1932).

C716   REVIEW of *Swords and Roses* (Joseph Hergesheimer). *Book
         Society News*, August 1929.

C717   'GIVE US A CHANSE'. *Evening News*, 14851, 2 August
         1929:11. Review of *The Private Opinions of a British
         Blue-Jacket* (Hamish MacLaren); *Henry VIII* (Francis
         Hackett); and *Wolf Solent* (John Cowper Powys).

C718   POLISH INTERLUDE 2. *Saturday Review*, 148 (3849), 3
         August 1929:126-127.

C719   THE MYSTERY OF A MYSTERY STORY. *Evening News*, 14857,
         9 August 1929:11. Review of *The Devil and the Deep
         Sea* (Elizabeth Jordan); *Young Mrs Greeley* (Booth
         Tarkington); *Joining Charles* (Elizabeth Bowen); *The
         Frantic Young Man* (Charles Samuels); *Gathering of
         Eagles* (Val Gielgud); and *Caroline in the Distance*
         (Harold Ohlson).

C720   POLISH INTERLUDE 3. *Saturday Review*, 148 (3850), 10
         August 1929:153-154.

C721   ALL THE FUN OF THE SANDS. *Sunday Dispatch*, 6667, 11
         August 1929:10.

C722   A GREAT STORY-TELLER'S SECRET. *Evening News*, 14863,
         16 August 1929:11. Review of *The Maracot Deep and
         Other Stories* (Conan Doyle).

C723   POLISH INTERLUDE 4. *Saturday Review*, 148 (3851), 17
         August 1929:182-183.

C724   FAREWELL TO FORSYTE. *Evening News*, 14869, 23 August
         1929:9. Review of *A Modern Comedy* (John Galsworthy);
         Mystery of the Roman Hat (Ellery Queen); *Murder at*

the *Keyhole* (R.A.J. Welling); *The 5 Flamboys* (Francis Beeding); and *Tomorrow and Tomorrow* (R.L. Duffus).

C725 DOPED. *Saturday Review*, 148 (3852), 24 August 1929: 209-210.

C726 A SEQUEL THAT IS A SUCCESS. *Evening News*, 14875, 30 August 1929:11. Review of *Nicky, Son of Egg* (Gerald Bullett); *Soldiers of Misfortune* (P.C. Wren); and *The Return of the Scarecrow* (Alfred Noyes).

C727 IN DEFENCE. *Saturday Review*, 148 (3853), 31 August 1929:235-237.

C728 REVIEW of *Life of Sir Edward Marshall Hall* (Edward Marjoribanks) and *Alice Meynell* (Viola Meynell). *Book Society News*, September 1929.

C729 HUMOUR, WIT, SATIRE, IRONY. *English Journal*, XVIII (7), September 1929:542-545.

C730 NEGLECTED LONDON. *Evening News*, 14881, 6 September 1929:11. Review of *Affectionate Regards* (Pett Ridge); *Money* (Karel Capek); *Tales from Shaw* (Gwladys Evan Morris); *Grey Dawn - Red Night* (James Lansdale Hodson); and *The Monkey Tree* (Desmond Coke).

C731 STRANGE ENCOUNTER. *Saturday Review*, 148 (3854), 7 September 1929:264-265.
Reprinted: *Self-Selected Essays* (1932).

C732 TWO GREAT WOMEN. *Evening News*, 14887, 13 September 1929:4. Review of *Alice Meynell* (Viola Meynell); and *Charlotte Bronte* (Rosamund Longbridge).

C733 ANOTHER RETURN. *Saturday Review*, 148 (3855), 14 September 1929:292-293.

C734 HANS AND HARRIET. *Evening News*, 14893, 20 September 1929:11. Review of *Hans Frost* (Hugh Walpole); *Harriet Hume* (Rebecca West); *Petruchio* (G.B. Stern); *The Courts of the Morning* (John Buchan); and *Oliver Elton* (C.E. Montague).

C735 THE MAGIC CITY. *Saturday Review*, 148 (3856), 21 September 1929:316-317.
Reprinted: *Self-Selected Essays* (1932).

C736 THE TRUTH ABOUT JERRY. *Evening News*, 14899, 27 Sep-
        tember 1929:11. Review of *Death of a Hero* (Richard
        Aldington); *Schlump* (anon); *Carr* (Phyllis Bentley);
        and *Death of My Aunt* (C.H.B. Kitchin).

C737 ON AND ON. *Saturday Review*, 148 (3857), 28 September
        1929:344-346.

C738 A NOTE ON WAR BOOKS. *Book Society News*, October 1929.

C739 REVIEW of *A Farewell to Arms* (Ernest Hemingway). *Book
        Society News*, October 1929.

C740 THE TOWN MAJOR OF MIRAUCOURT. *London Mercury*, XX (120),
        October 1929:561-571.
        Reprinted as a slim volume in a limited edition 1930
        (A20). Included in *Four-in-Hand* (1934) (A34).

C741 COME AND SEE THE PAVEMENT SIDE SHOW. *Sunday Dispatch*,
        6675, 6 October 1929:18.

C742 I GO RACING. *Sunday Dispatch*, 6677, 20 October 1929:18.

C743 REVIEW of *Gallipoli Memories* (Compton Mackenzie). *Book
        Society News*, November 1929.

C744 TEST OF A GOOD NOVEL. *English Journal*, XVIII (9), No-
        vember 1929:707-711.

C745 DINING. *Saturday Review*, 148 (3864), 16 November
        1929:574-576.

C746 REVIEW of *The Omnibus Book*. *Book Society News*, De-
        cember 1929.

C747 SHAKESPEARE AS A MAN OF OUR TIME. *English Journal*,
        XVIII (10), December 1929:808-810.

C748 CHRISTMAS AND THE MODERN NOVEL. *John O'London's*, XXII
        (555), 7 December 1929:354.

C749 THE OTHER CHRISTMAS. *Saturday Review*, 148 (3867), 7
        December 1929:670-671.

1930

C750   REVIEW of *Vile Bodies* (Evelyn Waugh). *Book Society News*, January 1930.

C751   THE STUFF OF POETRY. *English Journal*, XIX (1), January 1930:22-24.

C752   RUSSIAN HUMBUG: CRITICS WHO ARE DAZZLED BY 'THE CULT OF THE SAMOVAR': A CHALLENGE TO MR ARNOLD BENNETT. *John O'London's*, XXII (562), 25 January 1930:637-638.

C753   REVIEW of *Adventure* (J.E.B. Seely) and *Courage for Martha* (Barbara Blackburn). *Book Society News*, February 1930.

C754   REVIEW of *White Jade* (Maude Meagher) and *Theatre Street* (Tamara Karsovina). *Book Society News*, March 1930.

C755   DOOMSDAY. *London Magazine*, LXIV (233), March 1930: 255-261.
Reprinted: as 'Mr Strenberry's Tale' in *Four-in-Hand* (1934), *Going Up* (1950), and *The Other Place* (1953).

C756   THE SHINING GRACES. *Week-End Review*, 1 (2), 22 March 1930:54-55.
Reprinted: *Essays of the Year 1929-1930* (1930) and collected in *Self-Selected Essays* (1932).

C757   LIFE ON A HUGE CANVAS. *The Graphic*, CXXVII (3146), 29 March 1930:504. Review of *Rogue Herries* (Hugh Walpole).

C758   REVIEW of *Sir Arthur Nicolson, Bart* (Harold Nicolson) and *High Wages* (Dorothy Whipple). *Book Society News*, April 1930.

C759   ADVENTURE. *London Magazine*, LXIV (234), April 1930: 384-393.
Reprinted: *Four-in-Hand* (1934) and *Going Up* (1950).

C760   J.B. PRIESTLEY AND THE GOOD COMPANIONS. *Strand Magazine*, LXXIX, April 1930:328-333. Ostensibly in the form of an interview but there is a footnote: 'Copyright 1930 by J.B. Priestley'.

C761 SEVEN GODS. *Week-End Review*, 1 (4), 5 April 1930:
      125-126.
      Reprinted: *Self-Selected Essays* (1932).

C762 A LETTER FROM LONDON. *Saturday Review of Literature*,
      VI (39), 19 April 1930:954.

C763 REVIEW of *Desert Islands* (Walter de la Mare). *Book
      Society News*, May 1930.

C764 LONDON'S GIANT TREASURE TROVE. *Travel*, 55, May 1930:
      32-33.

C765 A LONDON LETTER. *Saturday Review of Literature*, VI
      (44), 24 May 1930:1074.

C766 RHINE LEGEND. *Week-End Review*, 1 (12), 31 May 1930:
      411-412.
      Reprinted: *Self-Selected Essays* (1932).

C767 DAVIS CUP. *Week-End Review*, 1 (8), 3 May 1930: 258,
      260.
      Reprinted: *Self-Selected Essays* (1932).

C768 REVIEW of *The Small Years* (Frank Kendon). *Book Society
      News*, June 1930.

C769 OBERAMMERGAU. *Week-End Review*, 1 (13), 7 June 1930:
      445-446.
      Reprinted: *Self-Selected Essays* (1932).

C770 LILAC IN THE RAIN. *Week-End Review*, 1 (15), 21 June
      1930:514-515.
      Reprinted: *Self-Selected Essays* (1932).

C771 WANDERING YOUTH. *John O'London's*, XXIII (584), 28
      June 1930:399.

C772 THE RAG BAG. *Book Society News*, July 1930.

C773 REVIEW of *African Drums* (Fred Puleston). *Book Society
      News*, July 1930.

C774 A LETTER FROM LONDON. *Saturday Review of Literature*,
      VI (50), 5 July 1930:1177.

C775 OUR BAD. *Week-End Review*, 11 (17), 5 July 1930:8-9.
      Reprinted: *Self-Selected Essays* (1932).

C776 ON THE MOORS. *Week-End Review*, ii (19), 19 July 1930: 83–84.
Reprinted: *Self-Selected Essays* (1932).

C777 WHAT THE SOLDIER SAID. *John O'London's*, XXIII (588), 26 July 1930:561–562. Review of *Songs and Slang of the British Soldier 1914–1918*.

C778 REVIEW of *Nor Without Laughter* (Langston Hughes) (initialled J.B.P.) and *War Letters of Fallen Englishmen* edited by Laurence Housman (initialled J.B.P.). *Book Society News*, August 1930.

C779 I LOOK AT THE THEATRE. *Theatre Arts Monthly*, XIV (8), August 1930:655–659. Signed J.B. Priestly [sic].

C780 A LETTER FROM LONDON. *Saturday Review of Literature*, VII (3), 9 August 1930:41.

C781 THEY SAY. *New York Times*, 17 August 1930:ix, 2:2.

C782 REVIEW of *Grand Hotel* (Vicki Baum). *Book Society News*, September 1930.

C783 THESE NOVELS. *Week-End Review*, ii (26), 6 September 1930:313–314.

C784 BEST-SELLERS. *John O'London's*, XXIII (595), 13 September 1930.

C785 REVIEW of *Laments for the Living* (Dorothy Parker) and *Whistler* (James Laver). *Book Society News*, October 1930.

C786 ON BEING MODERN. *Week-End Review*, ii (30), 4 October 1930:446–448.

C787 A LONDON LETTER. *Saturday Review of Literature*, VII (12), 11 October 1930:216.

C788 WHAT WE WANT. *Book Society News*, November 1930.

C789 REVIEW of *A Modern History of the English People 1880–1922* (R.H. Gretton). *Book Society News*, November 1930.

C790 A LETTER FROM ENGLAND. *Saturday Review of Literature*, VII (15), 1 November 1930:299.

C791   LOCAL COLOUR. *John O'London's*, XXIV (603), 8 November
       1930:189-190.

C792   REVIEW of *Last and First Men* (Olaf Stapledon) and *Com-
       plete Short Stories of Saki. Book Society News*,
       December 1930.

C793   THE ENGLISH ROAD. *News Chronicle*, 26405, 3 December
       1930:4. Review of *Canterbury Tales* illustrated by
       Hermann Rosse; *History of Tom Jones* illustrated by
       Spencer Pryse; and *The Pickwick Papers* illustrated
       by C.E. Brook.

C794   THE DREAM OF CHRISTMAS. *John O'London's*, XXIV (607),
       6 December 1930:358.

C795   A CHRISTMAS ENCOUNTER. *Week-End Review*, ii (39), 6
       December 1930:821-822.

C796   A LETTER FROM LONDON. *Saturday Review of Literature*,
       VII (22), 20 December 1930:474.

                              1931

C797   BRADFORD. *Heaton Review*, IV, 1931:7, 9.

C798   REVIEW of *The Heart's Unreason* (Edward Davison). *Book
       Society News*, January 1931.

C799   THE DEMON KING. *Strand Magazine*, LXXXI (1), January
       1931:3-12.
       Reprinted: *Four-in-Hand* (1934) and *Going Up* (1950).

C800   WHAT I EXPECT TO FIND IN AMERICA. *Pictorial Review*,
       32, 2 January 1931:2.

C801   HOME JOHN. *London Opinion*, CVIII (1399), 24 January
       1931:7.

C802   BOOKS. *Book Society News*, February 1931.

C803   TITTLE-TATTLE. *London Opinion*, CVIII (1401), 7 February
       1931:63.

C804   OUR DEBT TO HOLLYWOOD. *London Opinion*, CVIII (1403),
       21 February 1931:119.

C805 REVIEW of *Juan in America* (Eric Linklater). *Book Society News*, March 1931.

C806 ON PARENTS. *London Opinion*, CVIII (1405), 7 March 1931: 175.

C807 Item omitted.

C808 FALSE WHISKERS. *London Opinion*, CVIII (1407), 21 March 1931:231.

C809 ARE AUTHORS HUMAN BEINGS? *The Bookman* (NY), LXXIII, April 1931:137-141.

C810 CHARACTERS. *English Journal*, XX (4), April 1931:325-327.

C811 ARE AUTHORS HUMAN BEINGS? *Nash's - Pall Mall Magazine*, LXXXVII (455), April 1931:26-27, 85-86.

C812 WHAT A LIFE. *Strand Magazine*, LXXXI (4), April 1931: 333-344.
Reprinted: *Four-in-Hand* (1934) and *Going Up* (1950).

C813 THAT QUARTER. *This Quarter*, 3 (4), April-June 1931: 675-680.

C814 LOTTERIES. *London Opinion*, CVIII (1409), 4 April 1931: 289.

C815 BOOKS EVERYWHERE. *Book Society News*, June 1931.

C816 A NOTE ON STYLE. *English Journal*, XX (6), June 1931: 496-498.

C817 REVIEW of *Humour and Fantasy* (Fred Anstey) and *The Hidden Child* (Franz Werfel). *Book Society News*, July 1931.

C818 WHAT HAPPENED IN AMERICA. *John O'London's*, XXV (637), 4 July 1931:449-450.

C819 NEW YORK, THE NIGHTMARE CITY. *Evening Standard*, 33349, 6 July 1931:7.

C820 BURIED IN BABBITT LAND. *Evening Standard*, 33350, 7 July 1931:7.

C821   MARRIAGE AND DIVORCE IN HOLLYWOOD. *Evening Standard*,
       33352, 9 July 1931:7.

C822   YOU CANNOT GO WRONG IF YOU GO TO CANADA. *Evening
       Standard*, 33353, 10 July 1931:7.

C823   THE GLAMOUR OF SAN FRANCISCO. *John O'London's*, XXV
       (639), 18 July 1931:517-518.

C824   THE SOUTH SEAS AND THEIR LITERATURE. *John O'London's*,
       XXV (640), 25 July 1931:549-550.

C825   REVIEW of *Puppets in Yorkshire* (Walter Wilkinson).
       Book Society News, August 1931.

C826   WHAT I SAW IN HOLLYWOOD. *John O'London's*, XXV (641),
       1 August 1931:585-586.

C827   HOME THROUGH CANADA. *John O'London's*, XXV (644), 22
       August 1931:677-678.

C828   REVIEW of *Time Was* (W. Graham Robertson). *Book Society
       News*, September 1931.

C829   BRUTE-CULT. *Book Society News*, October 1931.

C830   REVIEW of *Which Way?* (Theodora Benson). *Book Society
       News*, October 1931.

C831   TRAVEL SNOBS. *Harper's Magazine*, 163, October 1931:
       629-632.

C832   CONTRAST IN COMICS. *Evening Standard*, 33425, 2 October
       1931:7.

C833   MY ELECTION NIGHT. *Evening Standard*, 33447, 28 October
       1931:7.

C834   REVIEW of *A Whip for the Woman* (Ralph Strauss) and
       Return to Yesterday (Ford Madox Ford). *Book Society
       News*, November 1931.

C835   TRAVEL SNOBS. *Strand Magazine*, November 1931.

C836   GIVE US A MERRY ENGLAND FOR MERRY ENGLISHMEN. *Evening
       Standard*, 33454, 5 November 1931:7.

C837   THE LOST GENERATION. *Evening Standard*, 33459, 11
       November 1931:7.

Reprinted as 4p leaflet by Peace Committee of Society of Friends 1932 (A22).

C838 TO DEMOCRACY VIA THE DRESS SUIT. *Evening Standard*, 33465, 18 November 1931:7.

C839 DON'T GOOD COMPANION ME. *Evening Standard*, 33471, 25 November 1931:7.

C840 REVIEW of *A Pier and a Band* (Mary MacCarthy) and *Ellen Terry and Her Secret Self* (Gordon Craig). *Book Society News*, December 1931.

C841 MEN WOMEN AND BOOKS. *Evening Standard*, 33478, 3 December 1931:13. Review of *Bernard Shaw* (Frank Harris); *What I Really Wrote About the War* (Bernard Shaw); *The New Keepsake* (Cobden-Sanderson); and *Gallery Unreserved* (A Galleryite).

C842 BAD-TEMPERED POETS. *Evening Standard*, 33484, 10 December 1931:7. Review of *The Georgiad* (Roy Campbell); *Without My Cloak* (Kate O'Brien); and *Isabella of Spain* (W.T. Walsh).

C843 WHY PEOPLE ARE BUYING MORE BOOKS. *Evening Standard*, 33490, 17 December 1931:7. Review of *Peter Arno's Parade*; *A Persian Journey* (Fred Richards); *Our Fathers* (Alan Bott); *British Artists and the War* (John Rothenstein); *Dinner with James* (Rose Henniker-Heaton); *Puppets in Yorkshire* (Walter Wilkinson); *Wind in the Willows* (Kenneth Grahame); and *The Spider's Palace* (Richard Hughes).

C844 YES, THERE IS A RETURN TO DICKENS. *Evening Standard*, 33496, 24 December 1931:7. Review of *Green Leaves* (J.H. Stonehouse); Dent's Library Edition of Dickens, and Chapman and Hall's Centenary Edition.

C845 NOVELS AND HOW TO SELL THEM. *Evening Standard*, 33500, 31 December 1931:7.

C846 ON PRESENTS. *John O'London's*, XXVI (659), Christmas 1931:334.

C847 THE CHRISTMAS PRESENTS I LIKE. *Yorkshire Weekly Post*, Christmas 1931.

C848 CHEAP BOOKS AND AUTHORS' ROYALTIES. *The Author*, XLI (2), Winter 1931:46.

C849   TOO MANY AUTHORS? *The Author*, XLI (2), Winter 1931:
       57-58.

                              1932

C850   NEW SCHOOL OF DETECTIVE WRITERS. *Evening Standard*,
       33506, 7 January 1932:7. Review of *Sudden Death*
       (Freeman Wills Croft) and *The Polo Ground Mystery*
       (Robin Forsythe). Quoted at length in 'Too Many
       Corpses in Detective Fiction', *The Literary Digest*,
       27 February 1932.

C851   FOUR BOLD YOUNG NOVELISTS. *Evening Standard*, 33512,
       14 January 1932:7. Review of *Facts of Fiction* (Nor-
       man Collins); *The Brothers* (L.A.G. Strong); *Magnolia
       Street* (Louis Golding); and *Chaos Is Come Again*
       (Claude Houghton).

C852   WORK IS AN EXCITING THEME FOR AUTHORS. *Evening Stan-
       dard*, 33518, 21 January 1932:7. Review of *Miner* (F.C.
       Boden); *Evensong* (Beverley Nichols); *Five Hundred
       Points of Good Husbandry* (Thomas Tusser); *City of the
       Red Plague* (George Popoff); *God in the Straw Pen* (John
       Brandane); *Christopher Strong* (Gilbert Frankau); and
       Farmers Glory (A.G. Street).

C853   ROUSSEAU - AND A SLAPDASH BIOGRAPHY. *Evening Standard*,
       33524, 28 January 1932:9. Review of *Jean-Jacques
       Rousseau* (Matthew Josephson); *Shadows on the Rock*
       (Willa Cather); *The Pavilion of Honour* (George Preedy);
       The Puritan (Liam O'Flaherty); *North Wind* (James Lans-
       dale Hodson); and *The Wife* (Sarah Salt).

C854   AN ALDOUS HUXLEY VIEW OF A FANTASTIC WORLD. *Evening
       Standard*, 33530, 4 February 1932:7. Review of
       Brave New World (Aldous Huxley); *Only Yesterday*
       (Frederick Lewis Allen); *Boomerang* (Helen Simpson);
       In England Now (Hans Duffy); *The Crime Conductor*
       (Philip MacDonald); and *The Devil Drives* (Virgil
       Markham).

C855   THIS MAY BE THE NOVEL OF THE YEAR. *Evening Standard*,
       33536, 11 February 1932:7. Review of *The Fountain*
       (Charles Morgan); and *Marine Parade* (Ivor Brown).

C856 EDGAR WALLACE. *Evening Standard*, 33536, 11 February
        1932. Inset in item 855.

C857 FEW WRITERS FIND ELDORADO. *Evening Standard*, 33542,
        18 February 1932:7. Review of *The Rats of Norway*
        (Keith Winter); *The Siege of Pleasure* (Patrick
        Hamilton); *Sale by Auction* (Geoffrey Denis); *Three
        Fevers* (Leo Walmersley); and *Swiss Family Manhattan*
        (Christopher Morley).

C858 A CONTRAST IN TWO GREAT WRITERS. *Evening Standard*,
        33548, 25 February 1932:7. Review of *The Work,
        Wealth and Happiness of Mankind* (H.G. Wells).

C859 NONSENSE ABOUT THE BOOK WORLD. *Evening Standard*, 33554,
        3 March 1932:9. Review of *Three Loves* (A.J. Cronin);
        Ballet for Three Masks (James Cleugh); *Man Made Angry*
        (Hugh Brooke); *Popularity's Wife* (Rachel Ferguson);
        The Black Boxer (H.E. Bates); *Several Occasions* (Mary
        Butts); *Kiss on the Lips* (Katherine Susannah Prichard);
        and *Midsummer Night Madness* (Sean O'Faolain).

C860 THE NEW POETRY. *Evening Standard*, 33560, 10 March
        1932:11. Review of *New Bearings in English Poetry*
        (F.R. Leavis); and *Poets in Brief* edited by F.L.
        Lucas.

C861 A RUSH OF NEW BIOGRAPHIES. *Evening Standard*, 33566,
        17 March 1932:7. Review of *Sir Walter Scott* (John
        Buchan); *The Laird of Abbotsford* (Una Pope-Hennessey);
        Lamb Before Elia (F.V. Morley); *The Last Medici*
        (Harold Acton); *Albert the Good* (Hector Bolitho);
        Robert Emmett (Raymond Postgate); *Sir Otto George
        Trevelyan* (G.M. Trevelyan); *Goethe* (Barker Fairley);
        and *But for the Grace of God* (J.W.N. Sullivan).

C862 THE MOST REMARKABLE WOMAN NOVELIST OF TODAY. *Evening
        Standard*, 33572, 24 March 1932:7. Review of *Secret
        Sentence* (Vicki Baum); *That Was Yesterday* (Storm
        Jameson); *Sons of Singermann* (Myron Brinig); *The
        Great Jasper* (Fulton Oursler); *The Club* (Barbara
        Blackburn); *Death of a Curate* (Kenneth Ashley); and
        Headlines (Janette Cooper).

C863 A YOUNG NOVELIST ARRIVES. *Evening Standard*, 33577, 31
        March 1932:7. Review of *Inheritance* (Phyllis Bent-
        ley); *Fathers of Their People* (H.W. Freeman); *The
        Iron Crown* (Friedrich von Gagern); *Sophka* (Boris

Stankovitch); *Carrying a Gun for Al Capone* (Jack
Bilbo); *From Baltic to Black Sea* (Archibald Forman);
The Girl in a Blue Hat (Johan Fabricius); and *Let's
Pretend* (Cedric Hardwicke).

C864 THE IMMORTAL MEMORY OF DICKENS. *The Dickensian*, XXVIII
(222), Spring 1932:137-140.

C865 TWO KINDS OF TRAVEL. *Evening Standard*, 33583, 7 April
1932:7. Review of *Hindoo Holiday* (J.R. Ackerley);
Limits and Renewals (Rudyard Kipling); *Thirty Years
in the Golden North* (Jan Welzl); *Adventures of an Ob-
scure Victorian* (W.G. Riddell); *Windjammer* (Shaw
Desmond); and *The Needle-Watcher* (Richard Blaker).

C866 WOMEN PUT MEN IN THE PILLORY. *Evening Standard*, 33589,
14 April 1932:9. Review of *Man, Proud Man* (Mabel
Ulrich); *Great Yorkshiremen* (G.C. Heseltine); *Life
and Adventures of Aloysius O'Callaghan* (T. Washington-
Metcalfe); *Barred* (Edouard de Neve); *Soft Answers*
(Richard Aldington); and *Country Air* (Guy Rawlence).

C867 A GOOD LITTLE BOOK FOR SHAKESPEARE WEEK. *Evening Stan-
dard*, 33595, 21 April 1932:7. Review of *The Essential
Shakespeare* (J. Dover Wilson); *The Dinner Knell* (T.
Earle Welby); *Great Love Stories of All Nations*; *How
Things Behave* (J.W.N. Sullivan); *How the World Builds*
(Humphrey Pakington); *The Story of the Wheel* (G.M.
Boumphrey); *Music* (W.J. Turner); *Tales from Two
Pockets* (Karel Capek); and *Hospital* (Norah James).

C868 SOME NEW EXAMPLES OF FANTASTIC FICTION. *Evening Stan-
dard*, 33601, 28 April 1932:7. Review of *Devil's Tor*
(David Lindsay); *The Greater Trumps* (Charles Williams);
Interruption (G.H. Saxon Mills); *Men and Memories*
(William Rothenstein); *All the Daughters of Music*
(Grace Zaring Stone); *Heat Lightning* (Helen Hull);
Grandfather's Steps (Joan Haslip); and *The Wave Breaks*
(Barbara Noble).

C869 THE CONFESSIONS OF MR JOAD. *Evening Standard*, 33607,
5 May 1932:9. Review of *Under the Fifth Rib* (C.E.M.
Joad); *Wild Oats* (Eric Muspratt); *The Soldier and
the Gentlewoman* (Hilda Vaughan); *I'll Never Be Young
Again* (Daphne Du Maurier); *I Was the Man* (Pamela
Frankau); *The Young Vanish* (Francis Everton); and
The Division Bell Mystery (Ellen Wilkinson).

C870 SEX AS A THEME IN NEW NOVELS. *Evening Standard*, 33613,
12 May 1932:7. Review of *New Signatures* (Michael
Roberts); *Maids and Mistresses* (Beatrice Kean Sey-
mour); *A Modern Hero* (Louis Bromfield); *The Store*
(T.S. Stribling); *Home for the Holidays* (R.H. Mottram);
Public Affairs (Barbara Worsley-Gough); *The Moon of
Much Gladness* (Ernest Bramah); and *Phantom Fame*
(Harry Reichenbrach).

C871 A SELF-PORTRAIT BY ARNOLD BENNETT. *Evening Standard*,
33619, 19 May 1932:7. Review of *The Journals of
Arnold Bennett 1896-1910*; *The English Newspaper*
(Stanley Morison); *Enchanted Sand* (D.J. Hall); *Swin-
burne* (Georges Lafourcade); *Lincoln* (Emil Ludwig);
Bath (Edith Sitwell); and *Murder in the Basement*
(Anthony Berkeley).

C872 WRITER WHO WORKED LIKE A HAPPY GOD. *Evening Standard*,
33625, 26 May 1932:7. Review of the Centenary edi-
tion of Tolstoy; *The Volga Flows to the Caspian Sea*
(Boris Pilnyak); *Frank Harris* (Hugh Kingsmill); *Thank
Heaven Fasting* (E.M. Delafield); *Dictator* (George
Slocombe); *Poor Scholars* (A.P. Rossiter); and *The
Orators* (W.H. Auden).

C873 A BOOK ABOUT WOMEN. *Evening Standard*, 33631, 2 June
1932:7. Review of *The True Woman* (C.K. Munro);
Woman (A. Corbett Smith); *Little Red Horses* (G.B.
Stern); *But Wisdom Lingers* (Beatrix Lehmann); *June
Lightning* (Elizabeth Murray); *Sea Green Grocer* (Jasper
Power); *The Greek Coffin Mystery* (Ellery Queen); and
Fanny Kemble (Dorothie de Bear Bobbe).

C874 THE BOOK WORLD. *The Publishers Circular and Book-
sellers Record*, 4 June 1932.
Note: Speech in reply to the toast 'The Book World'.

C875 TWO FINE SPECIMENS OF BOOKS THAT CANNOT BE LABELLED.
Evening Standard, 33637, 9 June 1932:7. Review of
Royal Flush (Margaret Irwin); *Nymph Errant* (James
Laver); *1919* (John Dos Passos); *Candid Reminiscences*
(Upton Sinclair); *Rotunda* (Aldous Huxley); *The Eigh-
teen Sixties* (John Drinkwater); and *Poets of Our Time*
(Eric Gillett).

C876 ARNOLD BENNETT'S LAST STORIES. *Evening Standard*,
33643, 16 June 1932:7. Review of *Dream of Destiny*
and *Venus Rising* by Arnold Bennett; *The Inner Journey*

(Kurt Heuser); *Regiment Reichstag* (Kurt Lamprecht);
The Captain of Kopenick (Carl Zuckmayer); *Cafe Bar*
(Scott Moncrieff); *Mary's Neck* (Booth Tarkington);
English Comedy (John C. Moore); *To the Streets and
Back* (Scott Pearson); *John Clare* (J.W. and A. Tibble);
and *Lady Caroline Lamb* (Elizabeth Jenkins).

C877   MAKING D.H. LAWRENCE A PROPHET SAINT. *Evening Standard*,
       33649, 23 June 1932:7. Review of *The Savage Pil-
       grimage* (Catherine Carswell); *Apocalypse* (D.H. Law-
       rence); *When the Wicked Man* (Ford Madox Ford); *The
       Orchid* (Robert Nathan); *Come, Dreams Are Endless*
       (Sydney Knight); and *Atlantic Murder* (Frank H. Shaw).

C878   HANDEL AND THE RACKET. *Strand Magazine*, LXXXIV (1),
       July 1932:3-11.
       Reprinted: *Four-in-Hand* (1932) and *Going Up* (1950).

C879   AN ARRESTING PIECE OF FICTION. *Evening Standard*, 33656,
       1 July 1932:7. Review of *Two Living and One Dead*
       (Sigurd Christiansen); *Filibusters in Barbary*
       (Wyndham Lewis); *Senor Bun in the Jungle* (Algo Saul);
       Purely for Pleasure (Elinor Mordaunt); and *Sicily*
       (Gabriel Faure).

C880   NOVEL ABOUT A LONDON BOARDING HOUSE. *Evening Standard*,
       33661, 7 July 1932:7. Review of *The Case Is Altered*
       (William Plomer); *Gap in the Curtain* (John Buchan);
       The Discovery of Europe (Paul Cohen Portheim); *Mar-
       riage in Heaven* (Ronald Fraser); *Appius and Virginia*
       (G.E. Trevelyan); and *Doggett's Tours* (Richard Turpin).

C881   THESE WITTY YOUNG NOVELISTS. *Evening Standard*, 33667,
       14 July 1932:1. Review of *Life of Lord Carson* (Ed-
       ward Marjoribanks); *Death Under Sail* (C.P. Snow);
       Country Places (Lady Longford); *The Map of England*
       (Charles Close); *Sheba Visits Solomon* (Helene Eliat);
       and *Sergeant Sir Peter* (Edgar Wallace).

C882   AT THE SIGN OF THE BLACK SOMBRERO. *Evening Standard*,
       33673, 21 July 1932:7. Review of *Doom of Youth*
       (Wyndham Lewis); *All Experience* (Ethel Mannin); *Three
       Lands on Three Wheels* (Jan and Cora Gordon); *A Super-
       ficial Journey through Tokyo and Peking* (Peter
       Quennell); *People in the South* (Alan Pryce-Jones);
       Studies in Sublime Failure (Shane Leslie); *Quartette*
       (Leslie Meller); and *The Case of the Unfortunate
       Village* (Christopher Bush).

C883 FOR YOUR HOLIDAYS - A LITERARY GROCK. *Evening Standard*,
33679, 28 July 1932:7. Review of *The Beachcomber
Pocket Omnibus* (J.B. Morton); *Modern Tales of Horror*
edited by Dashiell Hammett; *The Face of London* (Harold
Clunn); *Secret Loves* (E.F. Benson); *Plummers Cut*
(Basil Maine); *He Fell Among Friends* (Wardle Taylor);
The Captain's Table (Sisley Huddleston); and *The
Weaver's Web* (J. Keighley Snowden).

C884 THE TAXI AND THE STAR. *Strand Magazine*, LXXXIV (2),
August 1932:168-175.
Reprinted: *Four-in-Hand* (1932) and *Going Up* (1950).

C885 LAUGHTER - ITS USE AND ABUSE. *Evening Standard*,
33685, 4 August 1932:7. Review of *The Secret of
Laughter* (A.M. Ludovici); *Carlyle* (Emery Neff); and
Loads of Love (Anne Parish).

C886 A PROBLEM IN LITERARY ETHICS. *Evening Standard*,
33691, 11 August 1932:7. Review of *Golden Horn*
(F. Yeats Brown); and *The Georgian House* (Frank
Swinnerton).

C887 EFFICIENCY THE SECRET OF ETHEL M. DELL'S POPULARITY.
Evening Standard, 33697, 18 August 1932:7. Review
of *The Prison Wall* (Ethel M. Dell); *Hot Water* (P.G.
Wodehouse); *Big Business* (A.S.M. Hutchinson); and
Eye for an Eye (Graham Seton).

C888 A FINE RIPE WALPOLE. *Evening Standard*, 33703, 25
August 1932:7. Review of *The Fortress* (Hugh Walpole);
A Man's Life (Jack Lawson); and *Sticky Fingers*
(Dyke Acland).

C889 AN ARABIAN NIGHT IN PARK LANE. *Strand Magazine*,
LXXXIV (3), September 1932:231-239.
Reprinted: *Four-in-Hand* (1932) and *Going Up* (1950).

C890 ADVICE TO THOSE ABOUT TO WRITE A NOVEL. *Evening Stan-
dard*, 33709, 1 September 1932:7. Review of *The Lost
Generation* (Ruth Holland); *Butler's Gift* (Martin
Hare); *Fanfare for Tin Trumpets* (Margery Sharp);
The Solid Man (O'Reilly Coghlan); *Murder Intended*
(Francis Beeding); *Darkness at Pemberley* (T.H. White);
and *The Murderer of Sleep* (Milward Kennedy).

C891 WHY DO WE NEGLECT SIR WALTER SCOTT. *Evening Standard*,
33715, 8 September 1932:7. Review of *The Waverley*

Pageant (Hugh Walpole); *Greenbanks* (Dorothy Whipple);
Ian and Felicity (Dennis Mackail); *Ebb and Flood*
(James Hanley); *Sea Tangle* (George Blake); and *Truth
Came Out* (E.R. Punshon).

C892   AN AUTHOR WHO IS TOO ORIGINAL. *Evening Standard*,
       33721, 15 September 1932:7. Review of *The Two
       Thieves* (T.F. Powys); *Peking Picnic* (Ann Bridge);
       Inflections 1931 (James Cleugh); *Death to the French*
       (C.S. Forester); and *The Seventh Child* (Romilly John).

C893   SIR WALTER SCOTT: GREAT MAN AND GREAT NOVELIST. *Daily
       Mail*, 11360, 21 September 1932:10.

C894   WANTED MORE CANDOUR AND LESS CHARM. *Evening Standard*,
       33727, 22 September 1932:7. Review of *Reading,
       Writing and Remembering* (E.V. Lucas); *Adventures of
       a Novelist* (Gertrude Atherton); *The Great Victorians*
       (H.J. and Hugh Massingham); *Selected Essays* (T.S.
       Eliot); *Cambridge History of English Literature*;
       Readers Guide to the Everyman Library (R. Farquahar-
       son Sharp); and *Thackeray* (Malcolm Elwin).

C895   LONDON NIGHT CLUB LIFE IN A NOVEL. *Evening Standard*,
       33733, 29 September 1932:11. Review of *Letters of
       D.H. Lawrence* edited by Aldous Huxley; *House Under
       the Water* (Francis Brett Young); *Queer Street* (Edward
       Shanks); *Helen's Lovers* (Gerald Bullett); and
       Kamongo (Homer W. Smith).

C896   THE ODD LITTLE WORLD OF MR EVELYN WAUGH. *Evening
       Standard*, 33739, 6 October 1932:11. Review of
       Black Mischief (Evelyn Waugh); *Venusberg* (Anthony
       Powell); *Cheerful Weather for the Wedding* (Julia
       Strachey); *Invitation to the Waltz* (Rosamond Lehmann);
       and *Discovery* (John Drinkwater).

C897   TELL US MORE ABOUT THESE AUTHORS. *Evening Standard*,
       33745, 13 October 1932:11. Review of *Who Goes Sail-
       ing?* (John Connell); *Public Faces* (Harold Nicolson);
       Family History (V. Sackville-West); *The Common Reader
       Second Series* (Virginia Woolf); *Virginia Woolf* (Wini-
       fred Holtby); *Ramillies* (G.M. Trevelyan); and *Out of
       the Rough* (Bernard Darwin).

C898   ROSE MACAULAY IN CAMBRIDGE MOOD. *Evening Standard*,
       33751, 20 October 1932:11. Review of *They Were De-
       feated* (Rose Macaulay); *Josephus* (Leon Feuchlanger);

Unending Crusade (R. Emmett Sherwood); and *Just the
Other Day* (John Collier and Iain Lang).

C899   A BATCH OF NEW AUTOBIOGRAPHIES. *Evening Standard*,
       33757, 27 October 1932:11. Review of *My World as in
       My Time* (Sir Henry Newbolt); *Memories of a Misspent
       Youth* (Grant Richards); *What a Life* (Doris Arthur
       Jones); *Greek Memories* (Compton Mackenzie); *As We Are*
       (E.F. Benson); *Prairie Trails and Arctic Byways* (H.T.
       Munn); *Deep Water Shoal* (W.A. Robinson); and *Youth
       Looks at the World* (B.A. Fletcher).

C900   W.W. JACOBS AND SOME OTHER HUMOURISTS. *Evening Standard*,
       33763, 3 November 1932:11. Review of *W.W. Jacobs Om-
       nibus*; *The Provincial Lady Goes Further* (E.M. Dela-
       field); *Nymphs and Satires* (Rachel Ferguson); *Honour-
       able and Peculiar Ways* (Peh Der Chen); *Men of Ness*
       (Eric Linklater); *Snow in Harvest* (Joanna Cannan);
       and *First Night* (Lorna Rea).

C901   SOMERSET MAUGHAM'S NOVELS WILL OUTLIVE HIS PLAYS.
       Evening Standard, 33769, 10 November 1932:11. Review
       of *The Plays of Somerset Maugham*; *The Narrow Corner*
       (Somerset Maugham); and *Glenshiels* (Lennox Kerr).

C902   SAHIBS, BARBERS, AND BULLS. *Evening Standard*, 33775,
       17 November 1932:11. Review of *Flowering Wilderness*
       (John Galsworthy); *Journals of Arnold Bennett vol 2*;
       Death in the Afternoon (Ernest Hemingway); and *Fine
       for Silver* (Malachi Whitaker).

C903   OF ACTORS, PLAYS AND PLAYWRIGHTS. *Evening Standard*,
       33781, 24 November 1932:11. Review of *The English
       Dramatic Critics 1660-1932* edited by James Agate;
       Theatre Prospect (Tyrone Guthrie); *The Moon in the
       Yellow River* (Denis Johnston); *Famous Plays of 1932*;
       Wild Decembers (Clemence Dane); *Bernard Shaw* (Archi-
       bald Henderson); *The Inequality of Man* (J.B.S Haldane);
       and *Texts and Pretexts* (Aldous Huxley).

C904   BOOK NOTES 1932. *Book Society Annual*, 2, December 1932.

C905   SOME REFLECTIONS OF A POPULAR NOVELIST. *London Mer-
       cury*, XXVII (158), December 1932:135-142.
       Reprinted: *Essays and Studies XVIII* (B23).

C906   COUPON CONTROVERSY IN THE BOOK WORLD. *Evening Standard*,
       33787, 1 December 1932:11. Review of *The Oxford*

> *Companion to English Literature*; *State Fair* (Phil
> Strong); *Obscure Destinies* (Willa Cather); *Passage
> Through the Present* (George Buchanan); and *Conversa-
> tion Piece* (M.J. Farrell).

C907   TO A HIGHBROW. *John O'London's*, XXVIII (712), 3 Decem-
       ber 1932.

C908   FASCINATING FACTS ABOUT LONDON. *Evening Standard*,
       33793, 8 December 1932:11. Review of *The Adventures
       of a Black Girl in Search of God* (Bernard Shaw); *The
       New Survey of London Life and Labour Vols 3-4*; *Death
       of Felicity Taverner* (Mary Butts); *Our Mothers* (Alan
       Bott); *Purposes and Admiration* (J.E. Barton); *The
       Pre-Raphaelite Comedy* (Francis Bickley); *The Problem
       of Arnold Bennett* (Geoffrey West); and *The Broken
       Men* (Val Gielgud).

C909   FICTION MADE EASY. *Week-End Review*, VI (144), 10
       December 1932:696-697.

C910   TO PEOPLE WHO HAVE NO TIME FOR BOOKS. *Evening Stan-
       dard*, 33799, 15 December 1932:11. Review of *Stam-
       boul Train* (Graham Greene); *Night Flight* (Antoine
       de Saint-Exupery); *A Long Time Ago* (Margaret Kennedy);
       and *Cold Comfort Farm* (Stella Gibbons).

C911   MANY KINDS OF BOOKS. *Evening Standard*, 33805, 22 De-
       cember 1932:7.

C912   SAMUEL BUTLER, A 'MODERN' BEFORE HIS TIME. *Evening
       Standard*, 33810, 29 December 1932:7. Review of
       Butleriana (A.T. Bartholomew); and *Samuel Butler*
       (Clara Stillman).

                              1933

C913   WRITERS START 1933 WELL BY BREAKING THEIR TRADITIONS.
       Evening Standard, 33816, 5 January 1933:9. Review
       of *Pocahontas* (David Garnett) and *Man's Immortality*
       (Michael Arlen).

C914   THE TRUTH ABOUT A TRAMP'S LIFE. *Evening Standard*,
       33822, 12 January 1933:11. Review of *Down and Out in
       Paris and London* (George Orwell) and *The Prodigal
       Father* (Richard Church).

C915 TOO MANY MURDERS IN FICTION. *Evening Standard*, 33828,
19 January 1933:11. Review of *The Egyptian Cross
Mystery* (Ellery Queen); *The Mummy Case* (Dermot
Morrah); *Inspector Frost in Crevanna Cove* (H. Maynard
Smith); *The Murder of Caroline Bundy* (Alice Campbell);
The Frightened Lady (Edgar Wallace); and *The Secret
Enemy* (Elinor O'Duffy).

C916 A MADDENING BUT ENGROSSING BOOK BY H.G. WELLS. *Evening
Standard*, 33834, 26 January 1933:9. Review of *The
Bulpington of Blup* (H.G. Wells); *Try the Sky* (Francis
Stuart); *Jealousy* (Norah James); and *E. Nesbit*
(Dorothy Langley Moore).

C917 HERE AND NOW. *Week-End Review*, VII (157), 11 March
1933:274.

C918 HERE AND NOW. *Week-End Review*, VII (158), 18 March
1933:302-303.

C919 HERE AND NOW. *Week-End Review*, VII (159), 25 March
1933:328-329.

C920 HERE AND NOW. *Week-End Review*, VII (160), 1 April
1933:368-369.

C921 HERE AND NOW. *Week-End Review*, VII (161), 8 April
1933:398-399.

C922 ON BEING AFRAID. *The Listener*, IX (222), 12 April
1933:568.

C923 HERE AND NOW. *Week-End Review*, VII (162), 15 April
1933:427-428.

C924 PEOPLE I DISLIKE. *The Listener*, IX (224), 26 April
1933:651.

C925 HERE AND NOW. *Week-End Review*, VII (164), 29 April
1933:476-477.

C926 MOMENTS OF DELIGHT. *The Listener*, IX (225), 3 May
1933:699.

C927 HERE AND NOW. *Week-End Review*, VII (165), 6 May
1933:504-505.

C928 WHAT THE WORLD NEEDS NOW. *The Listener*, IX (226), 10
May 1933:744.

C929   TRAVEL, GLOOM AND GLAMOUR. *The Listener*, IX (229), 31
       May 1933:851.

C930   ENCHANTMENT. *The Listener*, IX (230), 7 June 1933:894.

C931   IN MY COUNTRY. *The Listener*, IX (231), 14 June 1933:
       941-942.

C932   ABOUT MYSELF. *The Listener*, IX (232), 21 June 1933:
       991.

C933   MY POSTBAG. *The Listener*, IX (233), 28 June 1933:1021.

C934   SECOND POST. *The Listener*, X (234), 5 July 1933:35.

C935   YOUR WORLD AND MINE. *Sunday Chronicle*, 2505, 27 August
       1933:9.

C936   THE BLIGHT THAT IS KILLING SPORT. *Sunday Chronicle*,
       2506, 3 September 1933:9.

C937   THEY MADE IT A SIN TO DRINK. *Sunday Chronicle*, 2507,
       10 September 1933:9.

C938   NOW THAT I AM FORTY - NEARLY. *Sunday Chronicle*, 2508,
       17 September 1933:9.

C939   GET READY FOR PROSPERITY. *Sunday Chronicle*, 2509, 24
       September 1933:9.

C940   THOSE DREADFUL TOWNS. *Sunday Chronicle*, 2510, 1 October
       1933:9.

C941   THEY'VE SLIGHTED BRITAIN. *Sunday Chronicle*, 2511, 8
       October 1933:9.

C942   AND THEY CALL THIS JUSTICE. *Sunday Chronicle*, 2512,
       15 October 1933:9.

C943   BLACKSHIRTS! *Sunday Chronicle*, 2513, 22 October 1933:9.

C944   THEY PLAN TO STEAL YOUR SPARE TIME NOW. *Sunday Chroni-
       cle*, 2514, 29 October 1933:9.

C945   ALBERT GOES THROUGH. *Strand Magazine*, LXXXVI, November
       1933:450-470. Published in book form 1933 (A28).

C946   SUNDAY NIGHT IN OUR WICKED CITIES. *Sunday Chronicle*,
       2515, 5 November 1933:9.

C947 GOOD HONEST VULGARITY. *Sunday Chronicle*, 2516, 12 November 1933:9.

C948 A BAD CLOCK IS A SLOW MURDERER. *Sunday Chronicle*, 2517, 19 November 1933:9.

C949 TURN THE LIMELIGHT OFF THE OXFORD CIRCUS. *Sunday Chronicle*, 2518, 26 November 1933:9.

C950 I WAS A MENACE TO MY FELLOW MEN. *Sunday Chronicle*, 2519, 3 December 1933:9.

C951 THE EVIL THAT LIVES AFTER THEM. *Sunday Chronicle*, 2521, 17 December 1933:9.

C952 MY CHRISTMAS HATE. *Sunday Chronicle*, 2522, 24 December 1933:7.

1934

C953 THE OLD BRITAIN IS DEAD - LONG LIVE THE NEW. *Sunday Chronicle*, 2524, 7 January 1934:9.

C954 ARE THERE NO HONEST MEN LEFT? *Sunday Chronicle*, 2525, 14 January 1934:9.

C955 THE BABIES WHO SHOULD NOT BE BORN. *Sunday Chronicle*, 2526, 21 January 1934:9.

C956 THIS NEW RELIGION. *Sunday Chronicle*, 2527, 28 January 1934:9.

C957 THE HOCUS-POCUS OF THE B.B.C. *Sunday Chronicle*, 2528, 4 February 1934:9.

C958 THE BOXERS, THE BOOERS AND THE BLONDES. *Sunday Chronicle*, 2529, 11 February 1934:9.

C959 Letter to the Editor concerning his article in the next issue (C960). *The Bookseller*, 1474, 23 February 1934:139.

C960 NO MORE 'BEST-SELLER!' *The Bookseller*, 1475, 2 March 1934:146.

C961 BOOKS CHANGE YOUR LIVES. *Clarion*, n.s. 1 (1), 17 March 1934:13.

C962 I FIND THE PERFECT NOVELIST BUT IT IS TWO PEOPLE.
      Clarion, n.s. 1 (2), 24 March 1934:13. Review of *A
      Modern Tragedy* (Phyllis Bentley); *Magnus Merriman*
      (Eric Linklater); *Anthony Adverse* (Hervey Allen);
      Work of Art (Sinclair Lewis); *Winner Take Nothing*
      (Ernest Hemingway); and *Blind Alley* (T. Thompson).

C963 THESE ARE MY ESSENTIAL BOOKS. *Clarion*, 1 (3), 31
      March 1934:11. Review of *I Was a German* (Ernest
      Toller); *Further Extracts from the Novels of Samuel
      Butler*; *Napoleon and His Marshalls* (A.G. MacDonnell);
      and *I Commit to the Flames* (Ivor Brown).

C964 MAN WITH A NOVEL IN HIS KNAPSACK. *Clarion*, 1 (4), 7
      April 1934:11. Review of *Backwaters* (William Holt);
      Bassett (Stella Gibbons); and *After Such Pleasures*
      (Dorothy Parker).

C965 WHY BANISH THE BEST SELLER? *Clarion*, 1 (5), 14 April
      1934:11.

C966 CRUSADER WITH A POP GUN. *Clarion*, 1 (6), 21 April
      1934:11. Review of *Holy Deadlock* (A.P. Herbert);
      and *Experiment with Time* (J.W. Dunne).

C967 THIS BANNED BOOK NONSENSE. *Clarion*, 1 (7), 28 April
      1934:11.

C968 BEHIND THE PLAYBOY'S MASK. *Clarion*, 1 (8), 5 May
      1934:11. Review of *Shame the Devil* (Liam O'Flaherty).

C969 POCKET THESE. *Clarion*, 1 (9), 12 May 1934:10.

C970 FACT IS NOW THE FASHION BUT IT MUST BE DISGUISED AS
      FICTION. *Clarion*, 1 (10), 19 May 1934:11. Review of *I,
      Claudius* (Robert Graves) and *Beyond the Mexique Bay*
      (Aldous Huxley).

C971 THE TRUTH ABOUT THESE MIGHTY ATOMS OF THE BOOK WORLD.
      Clarion, 1 (11), 26 May 1934:11.

C972 LITERARY LEGPULLS. *Clarion*, 1 (12), 2 June 1934:11.
      Review of *Gay Hunter* (J. Leslie Mitchell) and *Last
      and First Men* (Olaf Stapledon).

C973 HERE IS OUR GREATEST LIVING NOVELIST. *Clarion*,
      1 (13), 9 June 1934:11.

C974 CINDERELLA OF FICTION. *Clarion*, 1 (14), 16 June 1934:9.

C975 LITERATURE'S VIRTUOUS FOOL. *Clarion*, 1 (15), 23 June 1934:9. Review of *Fool of Love* (Hesketh Pearson).

C976 LET US NOW FIND FAMOUS NAMES. *Clarion*, 1 (16), 30 June 1934:9.

C977 OLD HIGHGATE VILLAGE - letter. *The Times*, 46830, 11 August 1934:11.

C978 Item omitted.

C979 IT RAINED BUT WHO CARED. *News Chronicle*, 27591, 27 September 1934:1-2.

C980 REVIEW of *Experiment in Autobiography Vol. 1* (H.G. Wells); *Master Sanguine* (Ivor Brown); and *Freedom and Organisation* (Bertrand Russell). *Book Society News*, October 1934.

C981 WRITERS AND WAR. *The Left Review*, 1 (1), October 1934:5.

C982 MR AGATE AT THE PLAY. *Sunday Times*, 5817, 7 October 1934:8. Review of *First Nights* (James Agate).

C983 YOU LONDONERS. *The Star*, 14476, 22 October 1934:4.

C984 REVELATIONS IN SOUTH KENSINGTON. *The Star*, 14478, 24 October 1934:4.

C985 GANG CRAZY. *The Star*, 14484, 31 October 1934:4.

C986 REVIEW of *They Knew Mr Knight* (Dorothy Whipple); *Gerald: A Portrait* (Daphne Du Maurier); and *Railway King* (R.S. Lambert). *Book Society News*, November 1934.

C987 THIS NONSENSE OF PASSPORTS. *The Star*, 14490, 7 November 1934:4.

C988 MY PUB CRAWL. *The Star*, 14496, 14 November 1934:4.

C989 THE STATE AND THE THEATRE. *New Statesman*, VIII (195), n.s., 17 November 1934:717-718.

C990   IMPORTANT PEOPLE. *The Star*, 14502, 21 November 1934:4.

C991   NIGHT LIFE. *The Star*, 14508, 28 November 1934:4.

C992   REVIEW of *Hornet's Nest* (Helen Ashton); *Early Victorian Novelists* (Lord David Cecil); and *Leopold the Unloved* (Ludwig Bauer). *Book Society News*, December 1934.

C993   PRIESTLEY MAKES AMERICAN JOURNEY. *New York Times*, 2 December 1934:IV, 6:2.

C994   THROUGH THE BOX OFFICE WINDOW. *The Star*, 14514, 5 December 1934:4.

C995   BOOKS ON THE RANCH - letter. *Saturday Review of Literature*, XI (22), 15 December 1934:368.

C996   COSY LONDON. *The Star*, 14526, 19 December 1934:4.

C997   YOUNG BARBARIANS. *Saturday Review of Literature*, XI (21), 8 December 1934:339. Review of *O. Henry Memorial Award Prize Studies 1934*.

C998   MORE ON THE CURRENT STATE OF THE THEATRE. *New York Times*, 16 December 1934:XI, 1:3.

C999   J.B. PRIESTLEY ASSUMES THE CRITIC'S MANTLE. *New York Times*, 23 December 1934:IX, 5:3.

C1000   LIFE AND FICTION. *Book Society Annual* No. 3, December 1934.

1935

C1001   SALES BARGAINS. *The Star*, 14536, 2 January 1935:4.

C1002   BARE LEGS. *The Star*, 14542, 9 January 1935:4.

C1003   CASH, COMICS AND CULTURE AT THE B.B.C. *The Star*, 14548, 16 January 1935:4.

C1004   BLACK COATS. *The Star*, 14555, 24 January 1935:4.

C1005   A NEW DEAL FOR ACTORS. *The Star*, 14560, 30 January 1935:4.

C1006   GRAND CANYON. NOTES ON AN AMERICAN JOURNEY PART 1.
        Harper's Magazine, 170, February 1935:269-276.

C1007   £50,000 A YEAR AND HOW TO MAKE IT. *The Star*,
        14566, 6 February 1935:4.

C1008   FUSSING WITH SOLDIERS. *The Star*, 14572, 13 February
        1935:4.

C1009   SHAMATEURS. *The Star*, 14578, 20 February 1935:4.

C1010   I WAS A BAD DRIVER. *The Star*, 14584, 27 February
        1935:4.

C1011   GRAND CANYON. NOTES ON AN AMERICAN JOURNEY PART 2.
        Harper's Magazine, 170, March 1935:399-406.

C1012   ARE THEY REALLY OUR COUSINS? *Sunday Chronicle*, 2584,
        3 March 1935:9.

C1013   A THUNDERING GOOD EXAMPLE. *The Star*, 14590, 6 March
        1935:4.

C1014   THE WOMEN WHO MUST GET THEIR MAN. *Sunday Chronicle*,
        2585, 10 March 1935:4.

C1015   TITLES IN PAWN. *The Star*, 14596, 13 March 1935:4.

C1016   GRAND CANYON. *Sunday Chronicle*, 2586, 17 March
        1935:9.

C1017   YOU AND ME AND WAR. *The Star*, 14602, 20 March 1935:
        4. Reprinted as four-page leaflet by National Peace
        Council, 1935 (A36).

C1018   Item omitted.

C1019   THIS STRANGE COUNTRY SHOWS US OUR FUTURE. *Sunday
        Chronicle*, 2587, 24 March 1935:6.

C1020   GIVE WOMEN A CHANCE. *The Star*, 14608, 27 March 1935:4.

C1021   THEY TAKE MY MONEY. *The Star*, 14614, 3 April 1935:4.

C1022   THE FABLE OF THE TIRED BUSINESS MAN. *The Star*, 14620,
        10 April 1935:4.

C1023   WHOSE HOLIDAY IS IT? *The Star*, 14626, 17 April 1935:4.

C1024 AUDIENCES AND CRITICS. *The Spectator*, 5573, 19 April 1935:649–650.

C1025 I ASK YOU. *The Star*, 14631, 24 April 1935:4.

C1026 OUTSTANDING BOOKS YOU HAVE MISSED. *John O'London's*, XXXIII (837), 27 April 1935:107. Symposium of forty authors, critics, and publishers on books that failed to receive the recognition they deserved. Priestley's choice: *The Wanderer* (Alain-Fournier).

C1027 THIS IS MAY DAY. *The Star*, 14637, 1 May 1935:4.

C1028 ONE MAN'S JUBILEE. *The Star*, 14643, 8 May 1935:4.

C1029 PEOPLE WE DO NOT THANK. *The Star*, 14649, 15 May 1935:4.

C1030 IS THERE ROOM AT THE TOP. *The Star*, 14655, 22 May 1935:4.

C1031 HOKUM. *The Star*, 14661, 29 May 1935:4.

C1032 RISE SIR. *The Star*, 14667, 5 June 1935:4.

C1033 NO COMPLAINT FOR ONCE. *The Star*, 14673, 12 June 1935:4.

C1034 THE RIDDLE OF G.B.S. *The Star*, 14679, 19 June 1935:4.

C1035 THE FOLLY OF HANGING. *The Star*, 14685, 26 June 1935:4.

C1036 TENNIS FOR ALL. *The Star*, 14691, 3 July 1935:4.

C1037 THIS JEW BUSINESS. *The Star*, 14697, 10 July 1935:4.

C1038 WHY ALL THIS NOISE? *The Star*, 14703, 17 July 1935:4.

C1039 HUSH AND YOU PAY. *The Star*, 14709, 24 July 1935:4.

C1040 MASSES, WORKERS, AND THE PEOPLE. *The Star*, 14715, 31 July 1935:4.

C1041 THE B.B.C. AND SEX. *The Star*, 14721, 7 August 1935:2.

C1042 PINTS AND PENCE. *The Star*, 14727, 14 August 1935:4.

C1043 DANCE BAND JOES. *The Star*, 14733, 21 August 1935:4.

C1044   A MOTH AND A MYSTERY. *The Star*, 14739, 28 August
        1935:4.

C1045   MESSAGE FROM J.B. PRIESTLEY. *Sunday Chronicle*,
        2610, 1 September 1935:10. On fiftieth year of the
        newspaper.

C1046   FATHER JELLICOE'S MYSTERY. *The Star*, 14745, 4 Septem-
        ber 1935:4.

C1047   WATCH ALBERTA. *The Star*, 14751, 11 September 1935:4.

C1048   DOCTORS AND US. *The Star*, 14757, 18 September 1935:4.

C1049   FILMS AND THE FUTURE. *The Star*, 14763, 25 September
        1935:4.

C1050   THE TRADE IN FICTION. *The Star*, 14769, 2 October 1935:4.

C1051   PROJECT FOR AN ENGLISH-SPEAKING UNION. *New York
        Times*, 20 October 1935:X, 1:3.

                              1936

C1052   A CROWN BUT NO CORONETS. *The Star*, 14960, 15 May
        1936:4.

C1053   ANOTHER ENGLISH JOURNEY. *The Star*, 14966, 22 May
        1936:4.

C1054   THE FIELD OF GOLD. *The Star*, 14972, 29 May 1936:4.

C1055   MAIDS WANTED. *The Star*, 14978, 5 June 1936:4.

C1056   THE MENACE OF TALKING BOOKS. *The Star*, 14984, 12
        June 1936:4.

C1057   THINGS TO COME AND AS THEY ARE. *The Star*, 14990, 19
        June 1936:4.

C1058   WHY THEY TURN COMMUNIST. *The Star*, 14996, 26 June
        1936:4.

C1059   FILMS AND POLITICS. *The Star*, 15002, 3 July 1936:4.

C1060 SHOULD BOOKS END LIKE THIS? *The Star*, 15008, 10 July
       1936:4.

C1061 COUSINS OR FOREIGNERS. *The Star*, 15014, 17 July
       1936:4.

C1062 FREEDOM - ENGLISH STYLE. *The Star*, 15020, 24 July
       1936:4.

C1063 I GO SHOPPING. *The Star*, 15026, 31 July 1936:4.

C1064 'HOW HAPPY YOU MUST BE'. *Russia Today*, 8 (n.s.),
       August 1936:8-9.

C1065 TWO DANGERS. *World Review of Reviews*, 1 (6), August
       1936:14-16.

C1066 PROTEST. *The Star*, 15032, 7 August 1936:4.

C1067 BOILED CODFISH. *The Star*, 15038, 14 August 1936:4.

C1068 RAISING THE BLAH BLAH BANNER. *The Star*, 15044, 21
       August 1936:4.

C1069 RUSSIA UNVISITED. *The Star*, 15050, 28 August 1936:4.

C1070 TERRIFIC TOPICS. *The Star*, 15056, 4 September 1936:4.

C1071 ARE WE IMMORTAL? *The Star*, 15062, 11 September 1936:4.

C1072 MY ENGLAND. *The Star*, 15068, 18 September 1936:4.

C1073 ENCHANTMENT IN THE STONE FOREST. *The Star*, 15074, 25
       September 1936:4.

C1074 SPRING TIDE: A TALE OF YOUNG LOVE IN LONDON TOWN
       From the Play by J.B. Priestley and George Billam.
       The Star, 15076, 28 September 1936:11; 15077, 29
       September 1936:2; 15078, 30 September 1936:2; 15079,
       1 October 1936:2; 15080, 2 October 1936:2; 15081,
       3 October 1936:2; 15082, 5 October 1936:2; and
       15083, 6 October 1936:12.
       Note: When first published in book form by William
       Heinemann Ltd in 1936 (A40), the authors were given
       as George Billam and Peter Goldsmith; the acting
       edition by Play Rights and Publications presented
       the authors as George Billam and J.B. Priestley.

C1075   LONDON - THEN AND NOW. *The Star*, 15080, 2 October
        1936:4.

C1076   IN THE DEEPS OF LONDON. *The Star*, 15086, 9 October
        1936:4.

C1077   A GOOD PLAY AND A BAD VERDICT. *The Star*, 15092, 16
        October 1936:4.

C1078   AS I SEE IT. *The Star*, 15098, 23 October 1936:4.

C1079   4,464 FAMILIES - letter. *News Chronicle*, 28238, 28
        October 1936:4. Signed by J.B. and Mary Priestley.

C1080   AS I SEE THINGS. *The Star*, 15104, 30 October 1936:4.

C1081   ENGLISH FILMS AND ENGLISH PEOPLE. *World Film News*,
        1 (8), November 1936:3.

C1082   AS I SEE THINGS. *The Star*, 15110, 6 November 1936:4.

C1083   AS I SEE THINGS. *The Star*, 15116, 13 November 1936:4.

C1084   AS I SEE THINGS. *The Star*, 15122, 20 November 1936:4.

C1085   AS I SEE THINGS. *The Star*, 15128, 27 November 1936:4.

C1086   OTHER PROBLEMS OF THE WEEK. *The Star*, 15134, 4 Decem-
        ber 1936:4.

C1087   AS I SEE THINGS. *The Star*, 15142, 14 December 1936:4.

C1088   AS I SEE THINGS. *The Star*, 15146, 18 December 1936:4.

C1089   FINALLY AS I SEE THINGS. *The Star*, 15154, 30 December
        1936:4

                              1937

C1090   ARIZONA DESERT. REFLECTIONS OF A WINTER VISITOR.
        Harper's Magazine, 174, March 1937:358-367.
        Reprinted: *Midnight on the Desert* (1937).

C1091   HOLLYWOOD DEBUNKED. *Sunday Graphic*, 1144, 7 March
        1937:17, 24.

C1092   WOMEN. *Sunday Graphic*, 1145, 14 March 1937:19, 24.

C1093   CRAZY AMERICA. *Sunday Graphic*, 1146, 21 March 1937:
        19, 34.

C1094   AFTER THE CHEERING. *The Star*, 12267, 12 May 1937:4.

C1095   PRINTED MURDER IS VALUED AT $5.000.000 A YEAR. *News-week*, 19 June 1937.

C1096   SIR JAMES BARRIE. *The Listener*, XVII (441), 23 June
        1937:1244.

C1097   WHAT I BELIEVE. *News Chronicle*, 28453, 9 July 1937:10.
        Reprinted: *What I Believe* (1937) (B40).

C1098   REPLY TO DRAMA CONTEST CRITIC. *News Chronicle*, 28456,
        13 July 1937:3.
        Note: This refers to *Mystery at Greenfingers* (A46).

C1099   DO THEY WANT TO KILL THE THEATRE? *News Chronicle*,
        28470, 29 July 1937:10.

C1100   PRIESTLEY ON PUDDINGS. *The Listener*, XVIII (449), 18
        August 1937:333.

C1101   J.B. PRIESTLEY LOOKS BACK. *The Bookman and Everyman*,
        XIII (45), Autumn 1937:1-3.
        Reprinted in the Everyman Library edition of *Angel
        Pavement* (1937) (A21).

C1102   WHAT I BELIEVE. *Sunday Graphic*, 1172, 19 September
        1937:8-9.

C1103   THIS WORLD OF FEAR. *Sunday Graphic*, 1173, 26 Septem-
        ber 1937:8-9.

C1104   THE NEW LONELINESS. *Sunday Graphic*, 1174, 3 October
        1937:8-9.

C1105   THIS EDUCATION BUSINESS. *Sunday Graphic*, 1175, 10
        October 1937:8-9.

C1106   WHAT'S WRONG WITH THE WORLD? *Sunday Graphic*, 1176,
        17 October 1937:8-9.

C1107   THE MYSTERY OF TIME. *Sunday Graphic*, 1177, 24 Oc-
        tober 1937:19.

1938

C1108   VALUE OF A LOCAL PRESS. *Advertisers Aid*, 1938:1-4.

C1109   A COLUMBUS OF TIME. *Saturday Review of Literature*,
        XVII (18), 26 February 1938:6-7. Review of *An*
        Experiment with Time (J.W. Dunne).

C1110   I HAVE BEEN HERE BEFORE From the Play by J.B. Priest-
        ley. *Daily Mail*, 13062, 7 March 1938:18; 13063,
        8 March 1938:22; 13064, 9 March 1938:18; and 13065,
        10 March 1938:22.

C1111   NEW ORLEANS: A FIRST IMPRESSION. *Harper's Magazine*,
        176, May 1938:589-595.

C1112   RAINBOW IN THE DESERT. *Saturday Evening Post*, 210,
        18 June 1938:5-6+.

C1113   IF I RAN THE BBC. *Sunday Dispatch*, 7134, 24 July
        1938:10.
        Reprinted as a pamphlet (A55).

C1114   HAVE YOU EVER CONSIDERED THE YIN AND YANG. *Sunday*
        Dispatch, 7137, 14 August 1938:10.

C1115   I BECAME AN AUTHOR. *The Listener*, XX (497), 21
        August 1938:113-114.

C1116   THIS YOUTH STUNT. *Sunday Dispatch*, 7139, 28 August
        1938:10.

C1117   I WAS HANS KLAUS AND I WAS SHOT DEAD. *Sunday Dis-*
        patch, 7146, 16 October 1938:14.

C1118   WHAT'S WRONG WITH BRITAIN? *Sunday Graphic*, 1230,
        30 October 1938:20-21.

C1119   MEN WOMEN AND MARRIAGE. *Sunday Dispatch*, 7151, 20
        November 1938:12.

C1120   INVITATION TO THE BOMBERS. *Sunday Graphic*, 1233,
        20 November 1938:14-15.

C1121   WHEN I AM DEAD. *Sunday Dispatch*, 7149, 6 November
        1938:12.

C1122 A GRUMBLE ABOUT PANTOMIME. *News Chronicle*, 28908, 27
       December 1938:8.
       Note: This provoked Richard Prentis' 'Pantomime and
       Mr Priestley', *John O'London's*, 6 January 1939
       (H28).

C1123 THE THEATRE AND YOU. *Service in Life and Work*, 7
       (28), Winter 1938:48-54.

                              1939

C1124 IS THERE SUCH THING AS A NEW YEAR? *Daily Mail*,
       13319, 2 January 1939:10.

C1125 BRITAIN WAKE UP. *News Chronicle*, 28920, 10 January
       1939:8.

C1126 Item omitted.

C1127 WHERE IS OUR DEMOCRACY? *News Chronicle*, 28921, 11 Jan-
       uary 1939:8.

C1128 THE BIG SHAM. *News Chronicle*, 28922, 12 January
       1939:14.

C1129 TWO KINDS OF UNEMPLOYED. *News Chronicle*, 28923, 13
       January 1939:17.

C1130 THUNDER ON THE LEFT. *News Chronicle*, 28924, 14
       January 1939:6.

C1131 THE SERIOUS THEATRE AND ITS CRITICS. *New Statesman*,
       XVII (412) n.s., 14 January 1939:52.

C1132 AND IN CONCLUSION. *News Chronicle*, 28926, 17 January
       1939:4.

C1133 MR PRIESTLEY WANTS TO KNOW. *Sunday Graphic*, 1243,
       29 January 1939:22-23.

C1134 OUT OF MY POSTBAG. *News Chronicle*, 28941, 3 February
       1939:10.

C1135 WE NEED RELEASE. *News Chronicle*, 28963, 1 March
       1939:10.

C1136 MY DAY. *Picture Post*, 2 (10), 11 March 1939:15-18.

C1137 Item omitted.

C1138 MR J.B. PRIESTLEY TAKES OVER OUR THEATRE PAGE. *Sunday Pictorial*, 1253, 19 March 1939:24.

C1139 THE ENEMIES OF HAPPINESS. *News Chronicle*, 28982, 23 March 1939:10.

C1140 MR J.B. PRIESTLEY APPEALS FOR UNITY - letter. *Yorkshire Observer*, 23486, 25 March 1939:3.

C1141 I BELIEVE IN TOMORROW. *Sunday Pictorial*, 1254, 26 March 1939:13.

C1142 REFUGEES. *Civil Liberty*, n.s. 4, April 1939:1.

C1143 J.B. PRIESTLEY WISHES SUCCESS TO YORKSHIRE DALESMAN. *Yorkshire Dalesman*, 1 (1), April 1939:2.

C1144 AFTER TEN YEARS. *News Chronicle*, 28996, 10 April 1939:8.

C1145 IS EUROPE FINISHED? *News Chronicle*, 29002, 17 April 1939:10.

C1146 LOST GERMANY. *News Chronicle*, 29008, 24 April 1939:10.

C1147 WHERE ENGLAND STANDS. *Harper's Magazine*, 178, May 1939:580-587.

C1148 HOW TO LIVE IN 1939. *News Chronicle*, 29014, 1 May 1939:10.

C1149 LISTEN YOU WRITERS. *News Chronicle*, 29020, 8 May 1939:10.

C1150 SHOULD A BRITON TELL. *News Chronicle*, 29026, 15 May 1939:10.

C1151 AMERICAN WRITING. *The Listener*, XXI (540), 18 May 1939:1030.

C1152 PROGRESS ON THE GREAT PLAINS. *News Chronicle*, 29032, 22 May 1939:10.

C1153   ALL ABOUT HOLIDAYS. *News Chronicle*, 29038, 29 May
        1939:8.

C1154   WHAT IS FREEDOM? *News Chronicle*, 29044, 5 June 1939:
        10.

C1155   FEDERAL UNION. *News Chronicle*, 29050, 12 June 1939:10.

C1156   WHERE ARE WE GOING? *Picture Post*, 3 (11), 17 June
        1939:67, 69.

C1157   I SPOTTED GRACIE'S GENIUS BUT OTHERS LAUGHED. *Sunday
        Chronicle*, 2808, 18 June 1939:7.

C1158   TO THE NORTH, DWELL THE BARBARIANS. *News Chronicle*,
        29062, 26 June 1939:10.

C1159   A SALUTE TO CHINA. *China News*, July 1939:6. Published
        by the China Campaign Committee, *China News* was out-
        wardly the first number of a new periodical but in
        reality was a once-only publication. Edited by
        Priestley it included articles by both Chiang Kai-
        shek and Mao Tse-tung.

C1160   Item omitted.

C1161   UNEMOTIONAL ENGLAND. *Lilliput Magazine*, 5 (1), July
        1939:75-77.

C1162   AN IDEA FOR BRITISH FILMS. *News Chronicle*, 29068,
        3 July 1939:8.

C1163   WE ARE BEING HELD UP TO RANSOM. *News Chronicle*,
        29074, 10 July 1939:10.

C1164   JEW BAITING. *News Chronicle*, 29080, 17 July 1939:10.

C1165   WE ARE ALL PROPAGANDISTS BUT. *News Chronicle*, 29086,
        24 July 1939:10.

C1166   NOW SMILE. *News Chronicle*, 29092, 31 July 1939:8.

C1167   FAMILY LIFE IS OKAY. *News Chronicle*, 29098, 7 August
        1939:8.

C1168   TRUE, MR WELLS, BUT. *News Chronicle*, 29104, 14 August
        1939:8. Inset J.B. PRIESTLEY AND THE TIMES, amend
        to statement made in 'We Are Being Held Up to
        Ransom' (C1163).

C1169   I CANNOT APPLAUD THE SPORTING LIFE. *News Chronicle*,
        29110, 21 August 1939:8.

C1170   PARADOX OF THE DRAMA. *Daily Telegraph*, 26279, 24
        August 1939:6.

C1171   WE STAND FAST. *News Chronicle*, 29116, 28 August
        1939:8.

C1172   TWO TON ANNIE. *News Chronicle*, 29122, 4 September
        1939:6.

C1173   THE NEW WARTIME. *News Chronicle*, 29128, 11 September
        1939:4.

C1174   YORKSHIRE STANDS WHERE IT DID. *News Chronicle*, 29137,
        21 September 1939:7.

C1175   A VASTLY CHANGED ARMY. *News Chronicle*, 29138, 22 Sep-
        tember 1939:3.

C1176   MEMORY OF A 1916 SHELL HOLE. *News Chronicle*, 29139,
        23 September 1939:3.

C1177   CHIPS WITHOUT FISH WILL NOT DO. *News Chronicle*,
        29140, 26 September 1939:3.

C1178   TWO THINGS ARMY LACK. *News Chronicle*, 29142, 27 Sep-
        tember 1939:3.

C1179   11-HOUR DAY ON SHELLS. *News Chronicle*, 29143, 28
        September 1939:3.

C1180   QUEST FOR GAIETY IN A LAND OF GLOOM. *News Chronicle*,
        29144, 29 September 1939:3.

C1181   DISCIPLINED GIRLS IN KHAKI. *News Chronicle*, 29145,
        30 September 1939:3.

C1182   SUBMARINE IS HEAVEN FOR GADGETEERS. *News Chronicle*,
        29146, 2 October 1939:3.

C1183   SCHUBERT FROM THE SERGEANT'S MESS. *News Chronicle*,
        29147, 3 October 1939:3.

C1184   THE EMPIRE STANDS FAST RIVETED BY THE CLYDE. *News
        Chronicle*, 29148, 4 October 1939:3.

C1185   GAS MASK MAGICIANS. *News Chronicle*, 29149, 5 October
        1939:3.

C1186   AFTER THE FIRST 1,000 MILES. *News Chronicle*, 29150,
        6 October 1939:6.

C1187   HE SEES TINY MACHINES DO BIG WORK. *News Chronicle*,
        29151, 7 October 1939:3.

C1188   BLUE BOOK IS A BEST SELLER, BUT RED BOOKS DRAW NEW
        READERS. *News Chronicle*, 29152, 9 October 1939:3.

C1189   PLANNING PLANES TO 20,000TH OF AN INCH. *News Chronicle*, 29153, 10 October 1939:3.

C1190   JOIN THE CIVIL SERVICE IF YOU WANT BEST HOTELS. *News Chronicle*, 29154, 11 October 1939:3.

C1191   ALL THE FUN OF THE FAIR AT R.A.F. SCHOOL. *News Chronicle*, 29155, 12 October 1939:3.

C1192   A VISIT TO THE B-HUSH B-HUSH C-HUSH. *News Chronicle*,
        29156, 13 October 1939:6.

C1193   DO NOT UNDER-RATE NAZI'S PROPAGANDA. *News Chronicle*,
        29158, 16 October 1939:3.

C1194   THEY PLAY HALMA, BUT IT'S A REAL WAR GAME. *News Chronicle*, 29159, 17 October 1939:3.

C1195   THESE COCKNEY BOYS HAVE MADE A HOME HAPPIER. *News Chronicle*, 29160, 18 October 1939:3.

C1196   FROM TYPEWRITERS TO MILKING PAILS. *News Chronicle*,
        29161, 19 October 1939:3.

C1197   HOW R.A.F. MEN WAIT TO POUNCE ON THE ENEMY. *News Chronicle*, 29164, 23 October 1939:9.

C1198   OUR SAILORS HAVE THE BEST OF EVERYTHING. *News Chronicle*, 29165, 24 October 1939:3.

C1199   WHITE-OUT ALSO WILL BE A BOMBERS' DESPAIR. *News Chronicle*, 29167, 26 October 1939:3.

C1200   WHAT ARE OUR WAR AIMS? *Picture Post*, 5 (5), 4
        November 1939:49.

C1201   OUR CHRISTMAS PROBLEM. *News Chronicle*, 29206, 11
        December 1939:6.

1940

C1202   STRENGTH AND STAY. *The Countryman*, XX (2), January-
        February-March 1940:416, 418. Contributed in re-
        sponse to an invitation which read: 'It would be of
        great help just now to many of your 21,000 fellow
        readers of *The Countryman* if you could very kindly
        say what book or books (old or new), or what study,
        pursuit, recreation, practice or habit of mind you
        have found most efficacious in yielding you refresh-
        ment at this time'.

C1203   THE WAR AND AFTER. *Horizon*, 1 (1), January 1940:15-19.

C1204   THE POSITION OF THE AUTHOR. *The Author*, L (3), Spring
        1940:61-62.

C1205   WHAT I BELIEVE. *Forum and Century*, CIII (5), May 1940:
        248-249.

C1206   COMMONSENSE ABOUT THE WAR. *Reynold's News*, 4682, 26
        May 1940:6.

C1207   LABOUR LEADERS AT THE IVY. *Horizon*, 1 (6), June
        1940:402-405.

C1208   THE FIFTH COLUMN MYSTERY. *Reynold's News*, 4684, 9
        June 1940:6.

C1209   EXCURSION TO HELL. *The Listener*, XXIII (596), 13
        June 1940:1123-1124.
        Reprinted: *Postscripts* (1940) and *Home from Dunkirk*
        (1940).

C1210   BRITAIN SPEAKS. EXTRACTS FROM BROADCASTS TO AMERICA.
        BRITAIN SPEAKS, THE SIGN OF THE DOUBLE CROSS and
        A WORD TO INTELLECTUALS. *The Listener*, XXIV (599),
        4 July 1940:15-16.
        Reprinted: *Britain Speaks* (1940).

C1211   NOW OR NEVER. *Reynold's News*, 4688, 7 July 1940:6.

C1212   THE THREE FACES OF NAZISM AND AMERICAN CRITICISM.
        The Listener, XXIV (600), 11 July 1940:49, 60.
        Reprinted: *Britain Speaks* (1940).

C1213 BOOKS, MUSIC, FILMS - AND WHO CARES. *New Statesman*, XX (490), 13 July 1940:32-33.

C1214 CAMP AND KITCHEN AND NAZI TALES. *The Listener*, XXIV (601), 18 July 1940:88-89.
Reprinted: *Britain Speaks* (1940).

C1215 CENSOR AND THE B.B.C. - letter. *Daily Telegraph*, 26559, 19 July 1940:4.

C1216 THE TIME PROBLEM. *The Spectator*, 5847, 19 July 1940: 55-56.

C1217 THE HOUR OF GREATNESS. *Answers*, CV (2720), 20 July 1940:3.
Reprinted: *Postscripts* (1940).

C1218 AS THE BROADCASTER SEES IT and THE PARENTS' DILEMMA. *The Listener*, XXIV (602), 25 July 1940:121-122.
Reprinted: *Britain Speaks* (1940).

C1219 PRIESTLEY SAYS.... EXTRACTS FROM RECENT TALKS TO NORTH AMERICA. *London Calling*, 45, 18 July 1940:2.

C1220 DARK FACE OF GERMANY. *Answers*, CV (2722), 3 August 1940:3.
Reprinted: *Postscripts* (1940).

C1221 WHAT ENGLAND MEANS TO ME. *Christian Science Monitor*, 3 August 1940:1-2.

C1222 IF WE CANNOT HAVE HOLIDAYS. *Reynold's News*, 4692, 4 August 1940:6.

C1223 TWO-TON ANNIE. *Answers*, CV (2723), 10 August 1940:3.
Reprinted: *Postscripts* (1940).

C1224 A TRIP TO MARGATE. *Answers*, CV (2725), 24 August 1940:3.
Reprinted: *Postscripts* (1940).

C1225 THERE MUST BE NO GOING BACK. *Answers*, CV (2726), 31 August 1940:3.
Reprinted: *Postscripts* (1940).

C1226 THE REAL ENGLISHMAN. *Lilliput Magazine*, 7 (3), No 39, September 1940:177-180.

C1227 POT AND KETTLE CYNICS. *London Calling*, 50, 22 August 1940:2.
    Reprinted: *Britain Speaks* (1940).

C1228 BRITAIN'S ORDINARY FOLK. *London Calling*, 51, 29 August 1940:4.
    Reprinted: *Britain Speaks* (1940).

C1229 THE FIRST YEAR. *Daily Herald*, 7661, 3 September 1940:2.

C1230 'HAPPY LANDINGS' FOR HEROES. *Answers*, CV (2727), 7 September 1940:3.
    Reprinted: *Postscripts* (1940).

C1231 THE TWO MOST DANGEROUS PEOPLE AROUND US. *Sunday Express*, 1132, 8 September 1940:6.

C1232 LONG, LONG TRAIL FROM AUGUST 1914. *Answers*, CV (2728), 14 September 1940:3.
    Reprinted: *Postscripts* (1940).

C1233 WHO ARE THE INDISPENSABLE PEOPLE? *Sunday Express*, 1133, 15 September 1940:6.

C1234 HARD WORK AND HIGH JINKS. *Answers*, CV (2729), 21 September 1940:3.
    Reprinted: *Postscripts* (1940).

C1235 LET US SAY WHAT WE MEAN. *Sunday Express*, 1134, 22 September 1940:6.

C1236 THIS AIR-RAID LIFE OF OURS. *London Calling*, 53, 12 September 1940:6.
    Reprinted: *Britain Speaks* (1940).

C1237 THE DEFIANT CITY. *London Calling*, 54, 19 September 1940:9.

C1238 THE SPIRIT OF LONDON. *London Calling*, 55, 26 September 1940:6.
    Reprinted: *Britain Speaks* (1940).

C1239 J.B. PRIESTLEY'S LUCKY ESCAPE TOLD BY HIMSELF. *London Calling*, 55, 26 September 1940:13.

C1240 WAR ANNIVERSARY. *Answers*, CV (2731), 5 October 1940:3.
    Reprinted: *Postscripts* (1940).

C1241　IS THIS THE END OF THE LURE OF LONDON? *Sunday Express*, 1136, 6 October 1940:9.

C1242　THE BRIGHT FACE OF DANGER. *Answers*, CV (2732), 12 October 1940:3.
　　　　Reprinted: *Postscripts* (1940).

C1243　TATTOO THIS MESSAGE INTO YOUR MIND. *Sunday Express*, 1137, 13 October 1940:9.

C1244　LONDON CAN TAKE IT. *Answers*, CV (2733), 19 October 1940:3.
　　　　Reprinted: *Postscripts* (1940).

C1245　THE-DON'T-ROCK-THE-BOAT-TRICK. *Sunday Express*, 1138, 20 October 1940:4.

C1246　THE DIFFICULTIES I HAD TO FIGHT. *Sunday Express*, 1139, 27 October 1940:6.

C1247　THE TRUTH ABOUT THE POSTSCRIPTS. *News Chronicle*, 29487, 6 November 1940:4.

C1248　WHAT PEOPLE ARE THINKING. *News Chronicle*, 29491, 11 November 1940:4.

C1249　COLD COMFORT FROM THE VICAR. *News Chronicle*, 29497, 18 November 1940:4.

C1250　STAND UP LORD HALIFAX AND TELL THE WORLD. *News Chronicle*, 29503, 25 November 1940:4.

C1251　MR GRAHAM LAIDLER AN APPRECIATION. *The Times*, 48787, 30 November 1940:7.

C1252　GOOD WILL - BAD SENSE. *News Chronicle*, 29509, 2 December 1940:4.

C1253　LETTER TO MR ATTLEE. *News Chronicle*, 29515, 9 December 1940:4.

C1254　THE DILEMMA - AND THE WAY OUT. *News Chronicle*, 29523, 18 December 1940:4.

C1255　THE CHRISTMAS SPIRIT LIVES ON. *New York Times*, 25 December 1940:28:2.

C1256　REMEMBER THE CHILD IN YOUR HEART. *News Chronicle*, 29527, 23 December 1940:4.

1941

C1257   1940 AND 1941. *News Chronicle*, 29533, 1 January 1941:4.

C1258   WHEN WORK IS OVER. *Picture Post*, 10 (1), 4 January
        1941:39-40.
        Note: This issue of *Picture Post* was reprinted by Peter
        Way Ltd in 1974 in their 'Great Newspapers Re-
        printed' series.

C1259   IF YOU HEARD SOMEONE SAY 'GANS' OR 'BATTER' WOULD YOU
        KNOW WHAT HE MEANT? *News Chronicle*, 29541, 10 Jan-
        uary 1941:5.   Initialled J.B.P.

C1260   GOD AND THE WAR. *News Chronicle*, 29555, 27 January
        1941:4.

C1261   PROLOGUE TO PLANNING. *Horizon*, iii (15), March 1941:
        168-170.

C1262   THE BOMB ON THE DANCE FLOOR. *News Chronicle*, 29597,
        17 March 1941:2.

C1263   THE PLAYWRIGHT'S PROBLEM. *The Listener*, XXV (637),
        27 March 1941:445-446.   Discussion between Priestley
        and L.A.G. Strong.

C1264   Item omitted.

C1265   Item omitted.

C1266   THE NEW BRITAIN. *Life Magazine*, 19 May 1941.

C1267   SIR HUGH WALPOLE. *The Times*, 48943, 4 June 1941:7.

C1268   THAT ARMY EDUCATION. *Picture Post*, 11 (10), 7 June
        1941:21-24.

C1269   WELFARE IN THE ARMY. *Picture Post*, 11 (11), 14 June
        1941:25-27, 30.

C1270   I LOOK AT BOURNEMOUTH. *Picture Post*, 11 (12), 21
        June 1941:20-23.

C1271   THE WORK OF E.N.S.A. *Picture Post*, 11 (13), 28 June
        1941:26-27, 30.

C1272   THEY MAKE THE GUNS WE NEED. *Picture Post*, 12 (1), 5
        July 1941:22–25.

C1273   I ASK LORD WOOLTON A FEW QUESTIONS. *Picture Post*,
        12 (2), 12 July 1941:26–27.

C1274   THIS PROBLEM OF COAL. *Picture Post*, 12 (3), 19 July
        1941:21–23.

C1275   THR TRUTH ABOUT THE DOCKERS. *Picture Post*, 12 (4),
        26 July 1941:23–25, 30.

C1276   AN ANCIENT SCHOOL RENEWS ITSELF. *Picture Post*, 12
        (5), 2 August 1941:24–26.

C1277   GETTING TO KNOW ONE ANOTHER. *The Listener*, XXVI (656),
        7 August 1941:183–184.

C1278   AN ARTICLE FOR BRENDAN BRACKEN. *Picture Post*, 12 (6),
        9 August 1941:24–25.

C1279   YOU CANNOT SIGN A PACT WITH LUNACY. *The Listener*,
        XXVI (657), 14 August 1941:220–221.

C1280   REVIEW of *The Bedside Esquire* and *Maigret and M. Labbe*
        (Georges Simenon). *Book Society News*, September
        1941:7–9.

C1281   WAR IS INDIVISIBLE. *The Listener*, XXVI (660), 4 Sep-
        tember 1941:323–324.

C1282   NOW FOR THE THIRD YEAR. *Sunday Dispatch*, 7297, 7
        September 1941:4.

C1283   REVIEW of *The Place of Little Birds* (Michael Home); and
        Berlin Diary (William L. Shirer). *Book Society
        News*, October 1941:7, 9–10.

C1284   ANGLO-SOVIET UNITY. *Anglo-Soviet Journal*, ii (4),
        October 1941:281–282.

C1285   THE DEBITS AND CREDITS OF TWO YEARS OF WAR. *London
        Calling*, 106, 18 September 1941:3.

C1286   WORLD SCIENCE VERSUS NAZI SCIENCE. *The Listener*,
        XXVI (665), 9 October 1941:487–488.

C1287   FASCISM AND NAZISM: THE DIFFERENCE. *The Listener*,
        XXVI (666), 16 October 1941:525.

C1288 WOMEN IN GERMANY AND RUSSIA. *The Listener*, XXVI (667), 23 October 1941:561-562.

C1289 REVIEW of *The Great Within* (Maurice Collis); *Two Survived* (Guy Pearce Jones); and *Measure for Murder* (Clifford Witting). *Book Society News*, November 1941:6, 7, 9.

C1290 BEHIND THE SCENES OF MY BROADCASTS. *London Calling*, 109, 9 October 1941:3-4.

C1291 COMMONERS AND A KING. *The Listener*, XXVI (671), 20 November 1941:682-683.

C1292 AN END TO NUTS AND BALONEY. *The Listener*, XXVI (672), 27 November 1941:717-723.

C1293 POSTSCRIPT TO 1941. *Reynold's News*, 4765, 28 December 1941:4.

C1294 REVIEW of *Above Suspicion* (Helen MacInnes); *This Above All* (Eric Knight); and *When Last I Died* (Gladys Mitchell). *Book Society Annual*, Christmas 1941: 10-11.

C1295 THE MOST FATEFUL PIECES OF EXPLOSIVE OF OUR TIME. *London Calling*, 119, 18 December 1941:3-4.

1942

C1296 REVIEW of *All Change Humanity* (Claude Houghton); *Death and the Dancing Footman* (Ngaio Marsh); *Pattern of Conquest* (Joseph C. Harsch). *Book Society News*, January 1942:4-7.

C1297 THE LINE UP. *The Listener*, XXVII (677), 1 January 1942:3-4.

C1298 BOOK TRADE MUST BE SAVED - letter. *News Chronicle*, 29847, 6 January 1942:2.

C1299 REVIEW of *H.M. Pulham Esq.* (John P. Marquand); *Pied Piper* (Nevil Shute); and *Seeing Is Believing* (Carter Dickson). *Book Society News*, February 1942:1-2, 7-8.

C1300 THE VALUE OF CRITICISM. *The Listener*, XXVII (682), 5 February 1942:163-164.

C1301 MINDING OUR MANNERS. *The Listener*, XXVII (685), 26 February 1942:259-260.

C1302 REVIEW of *Moscow '41* (Alexander Werth); *Strictly Personal* (Somerset Maugham); *Maker of Destruction* (Hermann Rauschning); and *Condition of Peace* (E.H. Carr). *Book Society News*, March 1942:4, 7-8.

C1303 MEN WHO HAVE GIVEN THEMSELVES TO EVIL. *London Calling*, 126, 5 February 1942:3-4.

C1304 THE OUTLINE OF THE NEW CONFEDERATION OF FREE MEN. *London Calling*, 128, 19 February 1942:3-4.

C1305 MINISTERS AND OPINION - letter. *The Times*, 49192, 24 March 1942:5.

C1306 REVIEW of *Musk and Amber* (A.E.W. Mason); and *One Pair of Feet* (Monica Dickens). *Book Society News*, April 1942:1-2, 7.

C1307 ANSWERING YOU. *The Listener*, XXVII (690), 2 April 1942:439. Replies by J.B. Priestley, Leslie Howard, Geoffrey Crowther, and George Strauss, to questions put by American listeners.

C1308 REVIEW of *The Last Enemy* (Richard Hillary); *Roosevelt: World Statesman* (Basil Woon); and *The End Is Not Yet* (Herrymon Maurer). *Book Society News*, May 1942: 5, 9, 11.

C1309 LIFE AND DEATH OF COLONEL BLIMP. *London Calling*, 134, 2 April 1942:3-4.

C1310 LUXURY IN WARTIME SHOULD BE SHARED. *London Calling*, 136, 16 April 1942:8-9.

C1311 DO YOU BELIEVE IN A FUTURE LIFE? *Strand Magazine*, CIII (617), May 1942:15. Answer of four lines by Priestley in response to the question asked by the editor of a number of eminent men.

C1312 THE TIME FOR SOCIAL EXPERIMENTS. *The Listener*, XXVII (698), 28 May 1942:675-676.

C1313 REVIEW of *The Germans* (Emil Ludwig); and *The Book
Revelation in History* (H.S. Bellamy). *Book Society
News*, June 1942:4, 8.

C1314 DEMOCRATIC ENGLAND HAS ARRIVED. *London Calling*, 142,
28 May 1942:3-4.

C1315 OUT WITH THE OLD GANGS. *Sunday Pictorial*, 1421, 7
June 1942:4.

C1316 REVIEW of *Anna* (Norman Collins); and *Nine Lives of
Billy Nelson* (Gerald Kersh). *Book Society News*,
July 1942: 1-2, 7.

C1317 OUR AID TO RUSSIA. *London Calling*, 143, 4 June 1942:
3-4.

C1318 THE MOST EXTRAORDINARY ACHIEVEMENT THAT THIS ISLAND
AND ITS PEOPLE CAN CLAIM. *London Calling*, 145, 18
June 1942:9-10.

C1319 TRAINS AND CLASSES. *New Statesman*, XXIV (596), 25
July 1942:57-58.

C1320 BRITAIN'S SILENT REVOLUTION. *Picture Post*, 15 (13),
27 June 1942:21-22.

C1321 WISHFUL THINKING. *London Calling*, 147, 2 July 1942:
3-4.

C1322 WE HAVE ALLIES AMONG THE GERMAN PEOPLE. *London
Calling*, 149, 16 July 1942:3-4.

C1323 REVIEW of *Death and Tomorrow* (Peter de Polnay); and
House of Shade (Michael Home). *Book Society News*,
September 1942:4, 6-7.

C1324 MR PRIESTLEY REGISTERS FOR NATIONAL SERVICE. *London
Calling*, 152, 6 August 1942:5-6.

C1325 REVIEW of *Enter Three Witches* (D.L. Murray); *Man Who
Watched the Trains Go By* (Georges Simenon); and *A
Narrow Street* (Elliot Paul). *Book Society News*,
October 1942:5-6, 8.

C1326 ZERO HOUR OF THE ENGLISH SPEAKING DEMOCRACIES. *London Calling*, 156, 7 September 1942:7, 9.

C1327 OUR CASE AND OUR CONDUCT. *The Observer*, 7897, 4 October 1942:4.

C1328 VISION NOT HATE WILL WIN THE WAR. *New York Times*, 18 October 1942:VII, 3.

C1329 REVIEW of Centenary edition of Tolstoy's *War and Peace* (initialled J.B.P.) and *Trans-Siberian* (Noel Barber). *Book Society News*, November 1942:1-2, 8.

C1330 REVIEW of *God and Evil* (C.E.M. Joad); and *The Roman Commonwealth* (A.W. Moore). *Book Society Annual*, Christmas 1942:13.

1943

C1331 REVIEW of *West with the Night* (Beryl Markham); *Storm Over the Land* (Carl Sandburg); and *Spain* (Salvador Madariaga) (initialled JBP). *Book Society News*, January/February 1943:5, 9.

C1332 THE GRIM OLD GAME. *London Calling*, 177, 28 January 1943:6-7, 10.

C1333 HANDEL AND THE RACKET. *Musician*, 48, February 1943: 5-8.
       Note: First published in *Strand Magazine*, 1932 (C878).

C1334 REVIEW of *The Two Marshalls* (Philip Guedalla); and *Long Division* (Hester W. Chapman). *Book Society News*, March 1943:1-2, 4-5.

C1335 IN THE WAKE OF THE EIGHTH ARMY. *London Calling*, 180, 16 February 1943:8-9.

C1336 LETTER TO AN AIRCRAFT WORKER. *John O'London's*, XLVIII (1202), 12 March 1943:221-222.

C1337 REVIEW of *Winters' Tales* (Karen Blixon); and *Voices in the Darkness* (Tangye Lean). *Book Society News*, April 1943:7-8.

C1338 WHAT I THINK. *Strand Magazine*, CV (628), April 1943:20-21.

C1339   LESS AND LESS FOR THE CIVILIAN. *London Calling*, 189,
        22 April 1943:3-4.

C1340   REVIEW of *The Mountains Wait* (Theodore Broch); *Fare-
        well My Youth* (Sir Arnold Bax); and *At a Farthing's
        Rate* (Henry Gibbs). *Book Society News*, May/June
        1943:5-6, 9.

C1341   WE MUST BACK RED. *Reynold's News*, 4849, 8 August
        1943:4.

C1342   SPREAD YOURSELVES - letter. *The Observer*, 7933, 13
        June 1943:2.

C1343   URBAN BRITAIN AFTER THE WAR. *Architects Journal*,
        97 (2526), 24 June 1943:418-419.

C1344   MAKE IT MONDAY. *The Listener*, XXIX (754), 24 June
        1943:743.

C1345   REVIEW of *Call No Man Happy* (Andre Maurois); and
        Emperor's Snuff Box (John Dickson Carr). *Book
        Society News*, July 1943:1-2, 5.

C1346   MILLIONS OF US HAVE LOST A FRIEND. AN APPRECIATION
        OF LESLIE HOWARD. *London Calling*, 196, 10 June
        1943:12.

C1347   THE CANADIAN ARMY IN BRITAIN. *London Calling*, 197,
        17 June 1943:3-4.

C1348   ST. JAMES PARK. *The Listener*, XXX (755), 1 July
        1943:7.

C1349   THIS ENGLAND AT ZERO HOUR. *Reynold's News*, 4844,
        4 July 1943:2.

C1350   WHEN THE LIGHTS GO UP IN LONDON. *The Listener*, XXX
        (756), 8 July 1943:35.

C1351   LET US SALUTE.... *The Listener*, XXX (757), 15 July
        1943:69.

C1352   POWER POLITICS WITH THE LID OFF. *The Listener*, XXX
        (758), 22 July 1943:91.

C1353   LET YOUTH TELL US. *The Listener*, XXX (759), 29 July
        1943:119.

C1354   REVIEW of *Reported Safe Arrival* (Michael Harrison);
        Theatre in Soviet Russia (Andre van Gyseghem); *Brief
        Chronicles* (James Agate); and *Constructive Democracy*
        (John Macmurray). *Book Society News*, August 1943:
        6-7, 9, 11.

C1355   FUTURE OF THE THEATRE. *The Author*, LIV (2), Winter
        1943.

C1356   FOUR YEARS HAVE REBUILT BRITISH DEMOCRACY. *New York
        Times*, 5 September 1943:VI, 6 + 28.

C1357   A DRAMATIST'S VIEWS. *New Statesman*, XXVI (657), 25
        September 1943:198-199.

C1358   BEWARE OF THIS WICKED CONSPIRACY. *Reynold's News*,
        4856, 26 September 1943:2.

C1359   REVIEW of *They Were Sisters* (Dorothy Whipple); *One
        World* (Wendell Willkie); *City of the Soul* (Michael
        Home); *Conan Doyle* (Hesketh Pearson); and *U.S.
        Foreign Policy* (Walter Lippmann). *Book Society
        News*, September/October 1943:1-2, 4, 7, 9-10, 13.

C1360   ACTOR AND CRITIC - letter. *New Statesman*, XXVI (659),
        9 October 1943:233.

C1361   NOT CASTLES IN SPAIN - BUT NEW HOMES IN BRITAIN.
        Reynold's News, 4859, 17 October 1943:4.

C1362   REVIEW of *The World of Yesterday* (Stefan Zweig);
        Last Laugh Mr Moto (John P. Marquand) (initialled
        J.B.P.); and *Where Love and Friendship Dwelt* (Mrs
        Belloc Lowndes). *Book Society News*, November
        1943:3, 6-7.

C1363   REVIEW of *So Little Time* (John P. Marquand); *I'm a
        Stranger Here Myself* (Anthony Thorne); *The Fancy*
        (Monica Dickens) (initialled J.B.P.); and *The End
        in Africa* (Alan Moorehead). *Book Society Annual*,
        Christmas 1943:5-6, 8, 10.

C1364   A PLAN FOR THE BBC. *Picture Post*, 21 (13), 24 Decem-
        ber 1943:25-26.

C1365   PLAN FOR MERRIE ENGLAND. *Reynold's News*, 4869, 26
        December 1943:4.

1944

C1366 THE PHILHARMONIC POST AGAIN. *London Philharmonic Post*, January 1944.

C1367 REVIEW of *Burmese Soldier* (Edward Thompson); *Built Before the Flood* (H.S. Bellamy); and *The Great Ship* (Eric Linklater). *Book Society News*, January/February 1944:6-8.

C1368 LET'S HAVE LESS ABOUT THEM, MORE ABOUT US. *Reynold's News*, 4875, 6 February 1944:6.

C1369 NEW JUDGEMENT. *The Dickensian*, XL (270), March 1944: 61-63.

C1370 REVIEW of *A Mingled Chime* (Sir Thomas Beecham); *The Grand Design* (David Pilgrim); *Laura* (Vera Caspary); and *On Native Grounds* (A. Kazin). *Book Society News*, April 1944:4-6, 11.

C1371 HERE ARE YOUR ANSWERS. *Common Wealth Review*, 1 (2), April 1944:9-10.
      Note: 'Two questions from a forthcoming Common Wealth booklet of the same title' (A66).

C1372 THIS FATEFUL DAY. *Reynold's News*, 4887, 30 April 1944:4.

C1373 TWO QUESTIONS - AND THE ANSWERS. *Common Wealth Review*, 1 (3), May 1944:vii-viii.
      Note: From *Here Are Your Answers* (A66).

C1374 REVIEW of *Memories of Happy Days* (Julian Green); *Clues to Christabel* (Mary Fitts); and *He Wouldn't Kill Patience* (Carter Dickson) (initialled JBP). *Book Society News*, May/June 1944:1-2, 5-6.

C1375 REVIEW of *Yeoman's Hospital* (Helen Ashton); and *Berlin Hotel* (Vicki Baum). *Book Society News*, July 1944: 1-2, 5.

C1376 TARGETS FOR TOMORROW. *Reynold's News*, 4896, 2 July 1944:2.

C1377 REVIEW of *English Social History* (G.M. Trevelyan); and *Live Dangerously* (Axel Kielland). *Book Society News*, August 1944:4-5.

C1378   REVIEW of *Pastoral* (Nevil Shute); *The Close Game*
        (Elizabeth Delahautey) (initialled JBP); and *Persons
        and Places* (George Santayana). *Book Society News*,
        September/October 1944:5-6, 9.

C1379   REVIEW of *So Many Loves* (Leo Walmsley); *U.S. War Aims*
        (Walter Lippmann); *Time for Decision* (Sumner Welles);
        and *The Lady in the Lake* (Raymond Chandler) (initialled
        JBP). *Book Society News*, November 1944:9-11.

C1380   A SMASH HIT FARCE. *Lilliput Magazine*, 15 (5), No. 89,
        November 1944:399-401.

C1381   AN OPEN LETTER TO MR LYTTLETON. *Reynold's News*,
        4916, 19 November 1944:2.

C1382   PRIESTLEY ON POLLITT'S 'HOW TO WIN THE PEACE'. *Daily
        Worker*, 4116, 20 November 1944:2.

C1383   BEWARE THIS TORY GRIP ON ENTERTAINMENT. *Daily Herald*,
        8974, 25 November 1944:2.

C1384   MR C.S. EVANS. AN APPRECIATION. *The Times*, 50006, 2
        December 1944:7.
        Reprinted: *C.S. Evans* (B62).

C1385   THE PUBLIC WANT TO KNOW: WERE THOSE JOURNEYS REALLY
        NECESSARY? *Reynold's News*, 4918, 3 December 1944:4.

C1386   AN OLD TOY REDISCOVERED. *Leader Magazine*, 2 (10), 23
        December 1944:7.

C1387   MY XMAS MESSAGE. *Reynold's News*, 4921, 24 December
        1944:4.

C1388   REVIEW of *The Aesthetic Adventure* (William Gaunt);
        The Journey Home (Robert Henriques); *Now I Lay Me Down
        to Sleep* (Ludwig Bemelmans); and *The Next Develop-
        ment in Men* (Lancelot Law Whyte). *Book Society
        Annual*, Christmas 1944:6-7, 9-10, 15.

C1389   AN IDYLLIC SCENE IN THE BAVARIAN ALPS. *Leader Magazine*,
        2 (10), 23 December 1944:7.

1945

C1390 THROUGH THE STEREOSCOPE. *Leader Magazine*, 2 (12), 6
       January 1945:7.

C1391 THROUGH THE STEREOSCOPE. *Leader Magazine*, 2 (13), 13
       January 1945:7.

C1392 GLIMPSES OF THE GIRLS. *Leader Magazine*, 2 (14), 20
       January 1945:7.

C1393 VISION OF HIGH SUMMER. *Leader Magazine*, 2 (15), 27
       January 1945:7.

C1394 SHOW THEM THE REAL BRITAIN IN SHIRTSLEEVES. *News
       Chronicle*, 30797, 29 January 1945:2.

C1395 TEN BOOKS FOR YOUTH: J.B. PRIESTLEY'S CHOICE. *Books
       News Sheet of National Book League*, 186, March 1945:
       22.
       Reprinted: *Ten of My Favourite Books* (B64).

C1396 TRADITION - REAL AND FAKE. *Leader Magazine*, 2 (16),
       3 February 1945:12.

C1397 GOLD RUSH - THE SUPREME IDIOCY. *Leader Magazine*,
       2 (17), 10 February 1945:9.

C1398 REVIEW of *Interim* (R.C. Hutchinson); and *Ten Com-
       posers* (Neville Cardus). *Book Society News*, March
       1945:5-6, 8.

C1399 BROADCASTING TO THE COMMONWEALTH - letter. *The Times*,
       50092, 15 March 1945:5.

C1400 REVIEW of *Beyond the Chindwin* (Bernard Fergusson);
       The Lost Weekend (Charles Jackson); and *Innocent
       Toys* (James Agate). *Book Society News*, April
       1945:4, 8-9.

C1401 CRITICS CONSIDERED. *The Observer*, 8028, 8 April
       1945:2.

C1402 THIS TALK ABOUT LIBERTY. *Reynold's News*, 4938, 22
       April 1945:2.

C1403 A TRIBUTE TO BRITAIN. *Picture Post*, 27 (4), 28
       April 1945:14-17.

C1404   SECOND MUSICAL MANIFESTO. *London Philharmonic Post*,
        May 1945.

C1405   TRIBUTE TO YOU. *Reynold's News*, 4940, 6 May 1945:2.

C1406   JOURNEY INTO DAYLIGHT. *The Listener*, XXXIII (853),
        17 May 1945:543-544.

C1407   REVIEW of *Strange Fruit* (Lillian Smith); *Long Long
        Ago* (Alexander Woollcott); and *A Cockney on Main
        Street* (Herbert Hedge). *Book Society News*, May/
        June 1945:6, 8, 10.

C1408   AUTHORS AND ADVERTISEMENT. *The Author*, LVI (1),
        Autumn 1945:6.

C1409   REVIEW of *I Said the Fly* (Elizabeth Ferrars); *Conan
        Doyle* (Una Pope-Hennessey); *Redbrick and These Vital
        Days* (Bruce Truscott); and *Life of Wagner* (Ernest
        Newman). *Book Society News*, July 1945:6, 8, 10.

C1410   THE FUTURE OF THE THEATRE. *Theatre*, 1, July 1945:4-5.

C1411   IT IS EASY TO PLAY TRICKS WITH WORDS - AS THE TORIES
        ARE DOING. *Reynold's News*, 4948, 1 July 1945:4.

C1412   REVIEW of *Mine Own Executioner* (Nigel Balchin); and
        Most Secret (Nevil Shute). *Book Society News*,
        August 1945:1-2, 6.

C1413   DAWN OF A NEW WORLD. *Reynold's News*, 4954, 12 August
        1945:4.

C1414   U.S. ARMY MATERIAL - letter. *The Times*, 50233, 17
        August 1945:5.

C1415   CULTURAL CAPITAL? *New Statesman*, XXX (758), 1 Septem-
        ber 1945:143.

C1416   I WAS WRONG ABOUT THOSE DEMOB SUITS. *Sunday Express*,
        1394, 16 September 1945:2.

C1417   REVIEW of *Thursday Afternoons* (Monica Dickens); and
        Parm Me (Arthur Kober). *Book Society News*, Sep-
        tember/October 1945:4, 6.

C1418   REVIEW of *Eclipse* (Alan Moorehead); *Assignment with-
        out Glory* (Marcos Spinelli); *Horizon* (Helen MacInnes);

and *The Demon Lover* (Elizabeth Bowen). *Book Society News*, November 1945:4, 6, 8.

C1419 TRAVELLER'S TALE. *The Listener*, XXXIV (879), 15 November 1945:543–544.

C1420 RUSSIAN JOURNEY IN MOSCOW. *Sunday Express*, 1403, 18 November 1945:4.
Reprinted: *Russian Journey* (1946).

C1421 COLLECTIVE FARMS. *Sunday Express*, 1404, 25 November 1945:4.
Reprinted: *Russian Journey* (1946).

C1422 IN THE SOUTHERN REPUBLICS. *Sunday Express*, 1405, 2 December 1945:2.
Reprinted: *Russian Journey* (1946).

C1423 STALINGRAD REBORN. *Sunday Express*, 1406, 9 December 1945:2.
Reprinted: *Russian Journey* (1946).

C1424 THE NOBLE CITY OF LENINGRAD. *Sunday Express*, 1407, 16 December 1945:2.
Reprinted: *Russian Journey* (1946).

C1425 THE RUSSIANS AND OURSELVES. *Sunday Express*, 1408, 23 December 1945:2.
Reprinted: *Russian Journey* (1946).

C1426 BORN AND BRED IN BRADFORD. *The Listener*, XXXIV (885), 27 December 1945:753–754.
Reprinted: *The Radio Listener's Week-End Book* (1950) (B84).

C1427 YOU CANNOT GO HOME AGAIN. *Time*, 46, 31 December 1945: 92.

1946

C1428 REVIEW of *Private Angelo* (Eric Linklater); *China Cycle* (R.T. Dobson); and *Press, Parliament and People* (Francis Williams) (initialled JBP). *Book Society News*, January/February 1946:1-2, 8.

C1429   REVIEW of *Carp Country* (Elizabeth Kyle); and *Looking
         for a Bluebird* (Joseph Wechsberg). *The Bookman*, 1
         (1), March 1946:6, 11.

C1430   J.B. PRIESTLEY WRITES TO THE RUSSIAN SOLDIER. *Soviet
         News*, 1407, 26 March 1946:2. Reprinted from *Krasno-
         armeytz*, 19-20, October 1945:3.

C1431   REVIEW of *The House in Lordship Lane* (A.E.W. Mason);
         and *Death and the Dear Girls* (Jonathan Stagge).
         The Bookman, 1 (2), April 1946:4, 6-7.

C1432   OPEN LETTER TO A THEATRE OWNER. *New Theatre*, 3 (1),
         June 1946:4-5.

C1433   SOME ASPECTS OF THE SOVIET THEATRE. *Drama*, n.s. 1,
         Summer 1946:16, 18-19.

C1434   REVIEW of *Two Solitudes* (Hugh MacLennan); *Three O'Clock
         Dinner* (Josephine Pinckney); *French Personalities
         and Problems* (D.W. Brogan); and *The Trollopes* (L.P.
         and R.P. Stebbins). *The Bookman*, 1 (4), July 1946:
         4-6, 9, 13.

C1435   TABLES IN THE SUN. *The Listener*, XXXVI (912), 4 July
         1946:11-12.

C1436   WE OWE HIM AT LEAST A HUNDRED MILLIONS. *Daily Herald*,
         9487, 27 July 1946:2.

C1437   SHAW AS A SOCIAL CRITIC. *Saturday Review of Litera-
         ture*, XXIX (30), 27 July 1946.
         Reprinted: *GBS 90* (1946) (B67).

C1438   REVIEW of *The River* (Rumer Godden). *The Bookman*, 1
         (5), August 1946:6-7.

C1439   HE SAW THE SHAPE OF THINGS TO COME. *Daily Mail*,
         15682, 14 August 1946:2.

C1440   GOODBYE TO OUR FRIEND. *News Chronicle*, 31276, 17
         August 1946:2. Funeral oration for H.G. Wells
         delivered Golders Green crematorium, 16 August 1946.
         Later printed as *H.G. Wells* (A79).

C1441   WHERE ARE OUR PRODUCERS? *Theatre Newsletter*, 3, 21
         August 1946:4.

C1442   IS THIS THE NEW BRITAIN? *Sunday Pictorial*, 1641, 25
        August 1946:4.

C1443   THEN AND NOW. *The Schoolmaster*, CXLX (n.s. 1942), 29
        August 1946:161, 164.

C1444   THE MOOD OF THE PEOPLE: 1. BAD BEHAVIOUR? *Daily Her-
        ald*, 9537, 23 September 1946:2.

C1445   2. WHAT ABOUT THESE NEW INCENTIVES? *Daily Herald*,
        9538, 24 September 1946:2.

C1446   3. BRITAIN REMADE. *Daily Herald*, 9539, 25 September
        1946:2.

C1447   RAIMU. *New Statesman*, XXXII (814), 28 September 1946:
        227.
        Reprinted: *Film Miscellany*, Winter 1946–47 and *Current
        British Thought No 1* (1947) (B72).

C1448   OURSELVES AND THE RUSSIANS. *Sunday Pictorial*, 1646,
        29 September 1946:5.

C1449   REVIEW of *The Happy Prisoner* (Monica Dickens); *Death
        and the Pleasant Voices* (Mary Fitt); *They Went to
        Portugal* (Rose Macaulay); and *Alexander Woollcott*
        (Samuel Hopkins Adams) (initialled JBP). *The Book-
        man*, 1 (6), September/October 1946:1–2, 7, 10–12.

C1450   WHITHER BRITAIN? – AND WHAT KIND OF COUNTRY DO WE
        WANT? *Daily Mail* (Continental edition), 15 October
        1946.

C1451   REVIEW of *Montgomery* (Alan Moorehead); and *The Orches-
        tra in England* (Reginald Nettel) (initialled JBP).
        The Bookman, 1 (7), November 1946:3–4, 13.

C1452   LETTER TO A YOUNG PRODUCER. *Theatre Today*, 2 July
        1946:13–14.

C1453   WHAT IS THE FREEDOM OF THE PRESS? *Reynold's News*,
        5018, 3 November 1946:4.

C1454   BRITAIN IS MISSING A GREAT OPPORTUNITY. *Daily Herald*,
        9575, 6 November 1946:2.

C1455   PRIESTLEY'S PAGE. *John Bull*, 80 (2109), 16 November
        1946:7–8.

C1456   PRIESTLEY'S PAGE. *John Bull*, 80 (2110), 23 November
        1946:10.

C1457   THE UNESCONIANS AT WORK. *Daily Herald*, 9593, 27
        November 1946:2.

C1458   PRIESTLEY'S PAGE. *John Bull*, 80 (2111), 30 November
        1946:11.

C1459   WHY CAN'T THEY READ ABOUT UNESCO? *Daily Herald*,
        9602, 7 December 1946:2.

C1460   PRIESTLEY'S PAGE. *John Bull*, 80 (2112), 7 December
        1946:11.

C1461   CEMENT FOR WORLD COOPERATION. *Daily Post*, 28507, 12
        December 1946:2.

C1462   PRIESTLEY'S PAGE. *John Bull*, 80 (2113), 14 December
        1946:10.

C1463   TWELVE MEN IN SEARCH OF AN HOLIDAY. *Daily Herald*,
        9611, 18 December 1946:2.

C1464   WHY I BELIEVE IN UNESCO. *The Listener*, XXXVI (936),
        19 December 1946:867-868.

C1465   BRADFORD WHEN I WAS YOUNG. *Yorkshire Observer*,
        25884, 19 December 1946:4. Abridged from Preface
        to *Socialism Over Sixty Years* by A. Fenner Brockway
        (1946) (B68).

C1466   PRIESTLEY'S PAGE. *John Bull*, 80 (2114), 21 December
        1946:7-8.

C1467   A CHRISTMAS LETTER. *New Statesman*, XXXII (826), 21
        December 1946:455-456.

C1468   PRIESTLEY'S PAGE. *John Bull*, 80 (2115), 28 December
        1946:9.

C1468a THE WORLD OF 1947. *Daily Herald*, 9620, 31 December
        1946:2.

                            1947

C1469   PRIESTLEY'S PAGE. *John Bull*, 81 (2116), 4 January
        1947:11.

C1470   LETTER FROM J.B. PRIESTLEY. *Theatre Newsletter*, 13,
        4 January 1947:9.

C1471   W.C. FIELDS. *New Statesman*, XXXIII (828), 4 January
        1947:8.
        Reprinted: *Atlantic Monthly*, March 1947 (C1484).

C1472   PRIESTLEY'S PAGE. *John Bull*, 81 (2117), 11 January
        1947:9.

C1473   PRIESTLEY'S PAGE. *John Bull*, 81 (2118), 18 January
        1947:9.

C1474   PRIESTLEY'S PAGE. *John Bull*, 81 (2119), 25 January
        1947:9.

C1475   HOW CAN WE MAKE THE BEST OF BUREAUCRACY? *Daily Post*,
        28546, 29 January 1947:2.

C1476   REVIEW of *The Last Days of Hitler* (H.R. Trevor-Roper);
        High Bonnet (Idwal Jones); *Ibsen: The Norwegian*
        (M.C. Bradbrook); and *Music on Record* (F.W. Gais-
        berg). *The Bookman*, 1 (9), January/February 1947:
        1-2, 6, 9-10, 15.

C1477   PRIESTLEY'S PAGE. *John Bull*, 81 (2120), 1 February
        1947:13.

C1478   BUREAUCRATS. *Daily Mail* (Continental edition), 6
        February 1947.

C1479   PRIESTLEY'S PAGE. *John Bull*, 81 (2121), 8 February
        1947:13.

C1480   PRIESTLEY'S PAGE. *John Bull*, 81 (2122), 15 February
        1947:11.

C1481   THE GOVERNMENT'S GREATEST BLUNDER. *Daily Post*,
        28563, 18 February 1947:2.

C1482   GO BALD HEADED FOR MORE COAL. *Daily Herald*, 9665,
        21 February 1947:2.

C1483   APATHY? - WELL WHY SHAKE THE VOTERS? *Daily Herald*,
        9671, 28 February 1947:2.

C1484   W.C. FIELDS. *Atlantic Monthly*, 179, March 1947:43-44.
        First published *New Statesman*, 4 January 1947 (C1471).

C1485   PRIESTLEY'S PAGE. *John Bull*, 81 (2123), 8 March
            1947:7.

C1486   ON THE STAIRWAY TO THE STARS. *The Listener*, XXXVII
            (946), 13 March 1947:355-356.

C1487   PRIESTLEY'S PAGE. *John Bull*, 81 (2124), 15 March
            1947:7.

C1488   PRIESTLEY'S PAGE. *John Bull*, 81 (2125), 22 March
            1947:8.

C1489   PRIESTLEY'S PAGE. *John Bull*, 81 (2126), 29 March
            1947:9.

C1490   PRIESTLEY'S PAGE. *John Bull*, 81 (2127), 5 April
            1947:8.

C1491   PRIESTLEY'S PAGE. *John Bull*, 81 (2128), 12 April
            1947:8.

C1492   PRIESTLEY'S PAGE. *John Bull*, 81 (2129), 19 April
            1947:10.

C1493   PRIESTLEY'S PAGE. *John Bull*, 81 (2130), 26 April
            1947:7.

C1494   SOVIET WRITERS ANSWER THEIR QUESTIONS. *Anglo-Soviet
            Journal*, VIII (1), Spring 1947:3-7, 42-43.
            Note: J.B. Priestley printed three questions.
            Reprinted: *Soviet Writers Reply to English Writers'
            Questions* (1948) (B77).

C1495   REVIEW of *The Mountain Village* (Chun-Chan Yeh); *The
            Slaves of Solitude* (Patrick Hamilton); *In the First
            Watch* (William McFee); and *The Other Theatre*
            (Norman Marshall). *The Bookman*, 1 (12), May 1947:
            1-3, 7-8, 10-11.

C1496   PRIESTLEY'S PAGE. *John Bull*, 81 (2131), 3 May 1947:7.

C1497   PRIESTLEY'S PAGE. *John Bull*, 81 (2132), 10 May 1947:7.

C1498   PRIESTLEY'S PAGE. *John Bull*, 81 (2133), 17 May 1947:7.

C1499   BIG BUSINESS EXPORTS THE WORST U.S. VALUES. *Daily
            Post*, 28639, 19 May 1947:2.

C1500 PRIESTLEY'S PAGE. *John Bull*, 81 (2134), 24 May 1947:7.

C1501 PRIESTLEY'S PAGE. *John Bull*, 81 (2135), 31 May 1947:7.

C1502 A NATIONAL THEATRE AUTHORITY. *New Theatre*, 3 (12),
       June 1947:12-13.
       Reprinted from *Arts Under Socialism* (1947).

C1503 PRIESTLEY'S PAGE. *John Bull*, 81 (2136), 7 June 1947:
       11.

C1504 PRIESTLEY'S PAGE. *John Bull*, 81 (2137), 14 June 1947:
       14.

C1505 JAMES AGATE. *New Statesman*, XXXIII (849), 14 June
       1947:431-432.

C1506 PRIESTLEY'S PAGE. *John Bull*, 81 (2138), 21 June 1947:
       7.

C1507 THE NUISANCE WHO WORKED MIRACLES. *Daily Herald*, 9772,
       27 June 1947:2.

C1508 PRIESTLEY'S PAGE. *John Bull*, 81 (2139), 28 June 1947:
       13.

C1509 REVIEW of *Minute for Murder* (Nicholas Blake); and *A
       Free House* (Walter Richard Sickert). *The Bookman*,
       2 (1), June/July 1947:3, 7-8.

C1510 AUTHORS AND THE B.B.C. *The Author*, LVII (4), Summer
       1947:80-81.

C1511 PRIESTLEY'S PAGE. *John Bull*, 82 (2140), 5 July 1947:
       13.

C1512 PRIESTLEY'S PAGE. *John Bull*, 82 (2141), 12 July 1947:
       11.

C1513 PRIESTLEY'S PAGE. *John Bull*, 82 (2142), 19 July 1947:
       14.

C1514 PRIESTLEY'S PAGE. *John Bull*, 82 (2143), 26 July 1947:
       14.

C1515 REVIEW of *Autobiography* (Neville Cardus); and *Russia
       and the Russians* (Edward Crankshaw). *The Bookman*,
       2 (2), August 1947:1-2, 10-11.

C1516 PRIESTLEY'S PAGE. *John Bull*, 82 (2144), 2 August
       1947:14.

C1517 PRIESTLEY'S PAGE. *John Bull*, 82 (2145), 9 August
       1947:10.

C1518 THEATRE AND WORLD. *The Observer*, 8150, 10 August
       1947:4.

C1519 PRIESTLEY'S PAGE. *John Bull*, 82 (2146), 16 August
       1947:10.

C1520 PRIESTLEY'S PAGE. *John Bull*, 82 (2147), 23 August
       1947:6.

C1521 PRIESTLEY'S PAGE. *John Bull*, 82 (2148), 30 August
       1947:6.

C1522 A BRITON'S FAITH IN BRITAIN'S FUTURE. *New York Times*,
       31 August 1947:VI, 5+29.

C1523 REVIEW of *A View of the Harbour* (Elizabeth Taylor);
       Bad Boy of Music (George Antheil); and *Theme and
       Variations* (Bruno Walter). *The Bookman*, 2 (3),
       September 1947:3-4, 6-7.

C1524 PRIESTLEY'S PAGE. *John Bull*, 82 (2149), 6 September
       1947:14.

C1525 CRISIS JOURNEY: DOES BUTLIN KNOW BETTER THAN BEVIN?
       Daily Herald, 9840, 15 September 1947:2.

C1526 TEXTILE TOWNS. *Daily Herald*, 9843, 18 September 1947:
       2.

C1527 CAN YOU BLAME THE MILL GIRLS? *Daily Herald*, 9846, 22
       September 1947:2.

C1528 A MUCK-MYSTIC AMONG THE PIGS. *Daily Herald*, 9852, 29
       September 1947:2.

C1529 REVIEW of *A Case to Answer* (Edgar Lustgarten); *You
       Can't Go Home Again* (Thomas Wolfe) (initialled JBP);
       and *Season in the Sun* (Wolcott Gibbs). *The Bookman*,
       2 (4), October 1947:7-8, 12.

C1530 LETS LOOK MORE PROSPEROUS. *Daily Herald*, 9855, 2 Oc-
       tober 1947:2.

C1531 MR P. AND THE PRESS - letter. *The Times*, 50883, 4 October 1947:5.

C1532 PREFABS AND CHOCOLATE. *Daily Herald*, 9858, 6 October 1947:2.

C1533 IN SOUTH WALES. *Daily Herald*, 9861, 9 October 1947:2.

C1534 WHAT PRIESTLEY TOLD THE AMERICANS. *Sunday Pictorial*, 1700, 12 October 1947:7.

C1535 MEN OF STEEL. *Daily Herald*, 9864, 13 October 1947:2.

C1536 WITH THE MINERS. *Daily Herald*, 9867, 16 October 1947:2.

C1537 LIVERPOOL'S TWO FACES. *Daily Herald*, 9870, 20 October 1947:2.

C1538 FOUR ARGUMENTS. *Daily Herald*, 9873, 23 October 1947:2.

C1539 THE CHALLENGE OF CHANGE. *The Listener*, XXXVIII (978), 23 October 1947:711-712.

C1540 MR CHURCHILL AND MR PRIESTLEY - letter. *The Times*, 50899, 23 October 1947:5.

C1541 I FEEL BETTER AFTER BIRMINGHAM. *Daily Herald*, 9876, 27 October 1947:2.

C1542 I MEET A LIVE WIRE. *Daily Herald*, 9879, 30 October 1947:2.

C1543 HERE ARE OUR CHANCES. *The Listener*, XXXVIII (979), 30 October 1947:755-756.

C1544 PECKHAM 'EXCITING'. *Daily Herald*, 9882, 3 November 1947:2.

C1545 THE LIFE WE LEAD. *Daily Herald*, 9885, 6 November 1947:2.

C1546 WORK, PLAY - AND LIVE. *The Listener*, XXXVIII (980), 6 November 1947:804-805.

C1547 WE NEED MORE THAN ECONOMICS. *Daily Herald*, 9888, 10 November 1947:2.

C1548   TELEGRAM (to Managers on British Theatre Conference).
        Theatre Newsletter, 2 (35), 29 November 1947:7.

C1549   REVIEW of *One Fine Day* (Mollie Panter-Downes);
        Stranger Than Truth (Vera Caspary); *Rogues Gallery*
        (Ellery Queen); and *Gamesmanship* (Stephen Potter)
        (initialled JBP). *The Bookman Annual*, Christmas
        1947:6-8, 10, 16.

C1550   NEW YORK AFTER NINE YEARS. *The Listener*, XXXVIII (986),
        18 December 1947:1049, 1067.

C1551   Item omitted.

                              1948

C1552   REVIEW of *The Field of the Stranger* (Olivia Robertson).
        The Bookman, 2 (6), January 1948:1-2.

C1553   WHY WE MUST SUPPORT UNESCO. *The Listener*, XXXIX (988),
        1 January 1948:5-6.

C1554   PRIESTLEY APPRAISES NEW YORK. *New York Times*, 4
        January 1948:VI, 2 :3.

C1555   THE UNESCO MEETING - letter. *The Listener*, XXXIX
        (990), 15 January 1948:108.

C1556   THEATRE CONFERENCE MAKES A START - THE OPENING ADDRESS.
        Theatre Newsletter, 2 (40), 7 February 1948:1-2.

C1557   THEATRE CONFERENCE - letter. *The Times*, 50994, 13
        February 1948:5.

C1558   THE THEATRE CONFERENCE. *New Statesman*, XXXV (885),
        21 February 1948:151-152.

C1559   PLAYWRITING Q AND A. *The Author*, LVIII (3), Spring
        1948:45-47.

C1560   REVIEW of *Journey into Spring* (Winston Clewes);
        Wasteland (Jo Sinclair) (initialled JBP); *Heyday of
        a Wizard* (Jean Burton); and *Howe and Hummel* (Richard
        H. Rovere). *The Bookman*, 2 (10), May 1948:3-5, 10.

C1561 CANTANKERY-I. *New Statesman*, XXXV (897), 15 May 1948:
       390.

C1562 CANTANKERY-II. *New Statesman*, XXXV (898), 22 May
       1948:408-409.

C1563 IF I OWNED NEWSREELS. *Daily Herald*, 10069, 11 June
       1948:2.

C1564 ANNIVERSARY GREETINGS RECEIVED FROM. *Theatre News-
       letter*, 2 (50), 26 June 1948:1.

C1565 REVIEW of *The Americans* (Geoffrey Gorer); and *Caroline
       Norton* (Alice Acland). *The Bookman*, 2 (11), June/
       July 1948:1-2, 7.

C1566 AT THE AIRPORT. *New Statesman*, XXXVI (906), 17 July
       1948:47.

C1567 REVIEW of *Gentleman's Agreement* (Laura Z. Hobson); and
       Father (Susan Campion). *The Bookman*, 2 (12), August
       1948:4, 9.

C1568 MORE CANTANKERY. *New Statesman*, XXXVI (912), 28
       August 1948:172.

C1569 REVIEW of *Meredith* (Siegfried Sassoon). *The Bookman*,
       3 (1), September 1948:8-9.

C1570 MORE CANTANKERY - letter. *New Statesman*, XXXVI (916),
       25 September 1948:262.

C1571 REVIEW of *The Nightwalkers* (James Norman); *Boys Will
       Be Boys* (E.S. Turner); and *Light on My Days* (Georges
       Duhamel). *The Bookman*, 3 (2), October 1948:5, 9, 12.

C1572 WHY NOT A WORLD TRUCE? *John Bull*, 84 (2205), 2 Oc-
       tober 1948:5-6.

C1573 PLOTS AND DRIFTS. *New Statesman*, XXXVI (917), 2 Oc-
       tober 1948:279-280.

C1574 REVIEW of *No Highway* (Nevil Shute); and *The Loved
       One* (Evelyn Waugh). *The Bookman*, 3 (3), November
       1948:1-2, 5.

C1575 WHAT I AM AFTER IN MY NEW PLAY. *Picture Post*, 41 (8),
       20 November 1948:28.

C1576   THE L.P.O. COUNCIL. *London Philharmonic Post*, November-December 1948.

C1577   OUR THEATRE AND ITS CRITICS. *Theatre Newsletter*, 3 (61/62), 11 December 1948:10.

C1578   THEATRE LEADERSHIP - letter. *New Statesman*, XXXVI (929), 25 December 1948:570.

1949

C1579   REVIEW of *Inishfallen Fare Thee Well* (Sean O'Casey). *The Bookman*, 3 (5), January 1949:10.

C1580   THE WORLD WE LIVE IN. *Sunday Pictorial*, 1764, 9 January 1949:1, 4.

C1581   THE TRUTH ABOUT DEMOCRACY. *Sunday Pictorial*, 1766, 23 January 1949:5.
        Note: This provoked the anger of Mr Michael Foot who published 'The Futility of Mr Priestley' on the front page of *Tribune*, 28 January 1949 (H43).

C1582   J.B. PRIESTLEY REPLIES TO HIS CRITICS. *Sunday Pictorial*, 1768, 6 February 1949:6.

C1583   PRESS COMMISSION - letter. *The Observer*, 8228, 13 February 1949:6.

C1584   Item omitted.

C1585   WE CAN'T ALL BE CHOOSERS. *Sunday Pictorial*, 1771, 27 February 1949:7.

C1586   REVIEW of *Yours Truly* (Franz Toussaint); and *Virginia Woolf* (Bernard Blackstone). *The Bookman*, 3 (6), February/March 1949:6, 10-11.

C1587   A WRITER REFLECTS. *World Review*, n.s. 1, March 1949: 14-16. Herbert Read's 'A Reply to Mr Priestley' appeared in the April 1949 issue (p. 3).

C1588   BRING OUT THE AXE. *Sunday Pictorial*, 1773, 13 March 1949:5.

C1589   LETTERS FROM TWO ISLANDS. *New Statesman*, XXXVII (944), 9 April 1949:349-350.

C1590   LETTERS FROM TWO ISLANDS. *New Statesman*, XXXVII (945), 16 April 1949:377.

C1591   LETTERS FROM TWO ISLANDS. *New Statesman*, XXXVII (946), 23 April 1949:401-402.

C1592   LETTERS FROM TWO ISLANDS. *New Statesman*, XXXVII (947), 30 April 1949:429-430.

C1593   LETTERS FROM TWO ISLANDS. *New Statesman*, XXXVII (948), 7 May 1949:466.

C1594   LETTERS FROM TWO ISLANDS. *New Statesman*, XXXVII (949), 14 May 1949:496-497.

C1595   LETTERS FROM TWO ISLANDS. *New Statesman*, XXXVII (950), 21 May 1949:525-526.

C1596   LETTERS FROM TWO ISLANDS. *New Statesman*, XXXVII (951), 28 May 1949:553-554.

C1597   LETTERS FROM TWO ISLANDS. *New Statesman*, XXXVII (952), 4 June 1949:582-583.

C1598   LETTERS FROM TWO ISLANDS. *New Statesman*, XXXVII (953), 11 June 1949:610.

C1599   LETTERS FROM TWO ISLANDS. *New Statesman*, XXXVII (954), 18 June 1949:639-640.

C1600   LETTERS FROM TWO ISLANDS. *New Statesman*, XXXVII (955), 25 June 1949:670.

C1601   TIVOLI IS FUN FOR EVERYONE. *News Chronicle*, 32166, 1 July 1949:2.

C1602   LETTERS FROM TWO ISLANDS. *New Statesman*, XXXVIII (956), 2 July 1949:9-10.

C1603   LETTERS FROM TWO ISLANDS. *New Statesman*, XXXVIII (957), 9 July 1949:38.

C1604   LETTERS FROM TWO ISLANDS. *New Statesman*, XXXVIII (958), 16 July 1949:66-67.

C1605   LETTERS FROM TWO ISLANDS. *New Statesman*, XXXVIII (959), 23 July 1949:93-94.

C1606   LETTERS FROM TWO ISLANDS. *New Statesman*, XXXVIII
        (960), 30 July 1949:121-122.

C1607   LETTERS FROM TWO ISLANDS. *New Statesman*, XXXVIII
        (961), 6 August 1949:145-146.

C1608   LETTERS FROM TWO ISLANDS. *New Statesman*, XXXVIII
        (962), 13 August 1949:169.

C1609   LETTERS FROM TWO ISLANDS. *New Statesman*, XXXVIII
        (963), 20 August 1949:192-193.

C1610   LETTERS FROM TWO ISLANDS. *New Statesman*, XXXVIII
        (964), 27 August 1949:216-217.

C1611   LETTERS FROM TWO ISLANDS. *New Statesman*, XXXVIII
        (965), 3 September 1949:242-243.

C1612   FROM BICKER TO BLUE ANCHOR. *The Listener*, XLII (1087),
        24 November 1949:883-884.

C1613   SO WE WENT TO COVENTRY. *The Listener*, XLII (1088),
        1 December 1949:933-934.

C1614   UNCHANGING OXFORD. *The Listener*, XLII (1089), 8
        December 1949:981-982.

C1615   SMILING BATH AND CHEERFUL WELLS. *The Listener*, XLII
        (1090), 15 December 1949:1029-1030.

C1616   THE END OF THE JOURNEY. *The Listener*, XLII (1091),
        22 December 1949:1077-1078.

                              1950

C1617   THE I.T.I. A PERSONAL VIEW. *World Theatre*, Introduc-
        tory issue 1950:43-45.

C1618   A LITTLE BOY FIFTY YEARS AGO. *Picture Post*, 46 (1),
        7 January 1950:12-15.

C1619   I CHALLENGE THOSE TORY FAIRY TALES. *Daily Herald*,
        10564, 16 January 1950:2.

C1620   REPLY TO A.J. CUMMINGS - letter. *News Chronicle*,
        32236, 18 January 1950:4.

C1621 THE LABOUR PLAN WORKS. *The Listener*, XLIII (1095), 19 January 1950:112-113.

C1622 AFTER ME THE DELUGE. *New Statesman*, XXXIX (986), 28 January 1950:91-92.

C1623 SID FIELD. *New Statesman*, XXXIX (988), 11 February 1950:159.

C1624 CHARLES DICKENS' PICKWICK PAPERS. *London Calling*, 549, 30 March 1950:13, 17.

C1625 OPEN LETTER TO A RUSSIAN COLLEAGUE. *New Statesman*, XXXIX (998), 22 April 1950:451.

C1626 LIFE IN THIS WORLD. *News Chronicle*, 32425, 3 May 1950:2.

C1627 THEY CAN'T AGREE WITH ME MORE. *News Chronicle*, 32431, 10 May 1950:2.

C1628 A NEW APPROACH - letter. *New Statesman*, XXXIX (1001), 13 May 1950:546.

C1629 WRONG APPROACH. *News Chronicle*, 32437, 17 May 1950:2.

C1630 JUSTICE FOR FATTIES. *News Chronicle*, 32443, 24 May 1950:2.

C1631 NOT KEEPING UP. *News Chronicle*, 32449, 31 May 1950:2.

C1632 WRITERS AT WORK. *The Author*, LX (4), Summer 1950:102.

C1633 THE WRECKERS. *News Chronicle*, 32455, 7 June 1950:2.

C1634 THE TWO RACES. *News Chronicle*, 32461, 14 June 1950:2.

C1635 WRONG CASTING. *News Chronicle*, 32467, 21 June 1950:2.

C1636 COCKTAIL PARTIES. *News Chronicle*, 32479, 5 July 1950:2.

C1637 GREAT-AUNTS. *News Chronicle*, 32485, 12 July 1950:2.

C1638 CLOWN IN A SNOWSTORM. *News Chronicle*, 32491, 19 July 1950:2.

C1639 WORLD TO WORLD. *News Chronicle*, 32497, 26 July 1950:2.

C1640 BY WHAT'S-HIS-NAME. *News Chronicle*, 32503, 2 August 1950:2.

C1641 PEACE CAMPAIGN - letter. *New Statesman*, XL (1013), 5
       August 1950:148.

C1642 LOST LADIES. *News Chronicle*, 32509, 9 August 1950:2.

C1643 NO THANKS. *News Chronicle*, 32516, 17 August 1950:2.

C1644 THE CASE OF THE APRICOT TART. *News Chronicle*, 32521,
       23 August 1950:2.

C1645 THE POOR DUMB CREATURES. *News Chronicle*, 32527, 30
       August 1950:2.

C1646 MESSAGES FROM DISTINGUISHED AUTHORS. *Library Associa-
       tion Record*, 52 (9), September 1950:346.

C1647 THE LYONS OF MY YOUTH. *News Chronicle*, 32533, 6 Sep-
       tember 1950:2.

C1648 OUR DILEMMA. *News Chronicle*, 32539, 13 September
       1950:2.

C1649 THE LEAK. *News Chronicle*, 32545, 20 September 1950:2.

C1650 WRONG JOB. *News Chronicle*, 32551, 27 September 1950:2.

C1651 CHAMBER MUSIC COMES HOME. *Picture Post*, 48 (14), 30
       September 1950:37-39.

C1652 ABOUT THAT LEAK. *News Chronicle*, 32557, 4 October
       1950:2.

C1653 PARTY MANNERS - letter. *The Times*, 51816, 7 October
       1950:7.

C1654 A VULGARIAN'S VIEW. *News Chronicle*, 32563, 11 October
       1950:2.

C1655 PARTY MANNERS - letter. *The Times*, 51822, 14 October
       1950:7.

C1656 THE VULGARIAN AGAIN. *News Chronicle*, 32570, 19 Oc-
       tober 1950:2.

C1657 MOTIVELESS MALIGNITY. *News Chronicle*, 32575, 25 Oc-
       tober 1950:2.

C1658 TIME MUST BE SHRINKING. *News Chronicle*, 32581, 1
       November 1950:2.

C1659 THE MAN G.B.S. *News Chronicle*, 32583, 3 November 1950:2.

C1660 HARD THINKING. *News Chronicle*, 32587, 8 November 1950:2.

C1661 R.L.S. THE REAL ROMANTIC. *The Observer*, 8319, 12 November 1950:4.

C1662 THE RIGHT TO BE WRONG. *News Chronicle*, 32593, 15 November 1950:2.

C1663 THE SNUB. *News Chronicle*, 32599, 22 November 1950:2.

C1664 THE EVIL EYE. *News Chronicle*, 32605, 29 November 1950:2.

C1665 ONE AT A TIME. *News Chronicle*, 32611, 6 December 1950:2.

C1666 SUCCESS. *News Chronicle*, 32617, 13 December 1950:2.

C1667 WHAT WE ARE DOING. *News Chronicle*, 32623, 20 December 1950:2.

C1668 BETWEEN OURSELVES. *News Chronicle*, 32630, 30 December 1950:2.

1951

C1669 AMERICAN DIARY. *Daily Herald*, 10886, 30 January 1951:4.

C1670 AMERICAN DIARY. *Daily Herald*, 10887, 31 January 1951:4.

C1671 AMERICAN DIARY. *Daily Herald*, 10888, 1 February 1951:4.

C1672 AMERICAN DIARY. *Daily Herald*, 10889, 2 February 1951:4.

C1673 AMERICAN DIARY. *Daily Herald*, 10892, 6 February 1951:4.

C1674 AMERICAN DIARY. *Daily Herald*, 10894, 8 February 1951:4.

C1675 AMERICAN DIARY. *Daily Herald*, 10898, 13 February 1951:4.

C1676 AMERICAN DIARY. *Daily Herald*, 10900, 15 February 1951:4.

C1677 MEXICAN INTERLUDE. *Daily Herald*, 10904, 20 February 1951:4.

C1678 AMERICAN DIARY. *Daily Herald*, 10906, 22 February 1951:4.

C1679 AMERICAN DIARY. *Daily Herald*, 10912, 1 March 1951:4.

C1680 AMERICAN DIARY. *Daily Herald*, 10914, 3 March 1951:4.

C1681 CANADA IS WORTH IT. *Saturday Night*, 66, 27 March 1951:8.

C1682 AN APPEAL TO AMATEURS. *Drama*, n.s. 21, Summer 1951: 15-18.

C1683 THE AUTHOR OF THE MAY BOOK: J.B. PRIESTLEY WRITES (Festival at Farbridge). *The Bookman*, May 1951:13-14.

C1684 ON WITH THE FESTIVALS. SPUR OF THE MOMENT. *The Listener*, XLV (1158), 10 May 1951:739-740.

C1685 SEE YOU ON SATURDAYS. *News Chronicle*, 32743, 12 May 1951:2.

C1686 IT'S A GRAND ALLIANCE. *Colliers Magazine*, 127, 16 May 1951:18-19+.

C1687 LONDON'S FESTIVAL: REWARDS AND DISCOVERIES. *The Listener*, XLV (1159), 17 May 1951:791-792.

C1688 J.B.'S UNCONVERSION. *News Chronicle*, 32749, 19 May 1951:2.

C1689 BRITAIN IN A MOOD OF HIGH ADVENTURE. *The Listener*, XLV (1160), 24 May 1951:833-834.

C1690 J.B. PRIESTLEY AT THE FESTIVAL. *London Calling*, 609, 24 May 1951:13.

C1691 YOUNG WRITERS. *News Chronicle*, 32755, 26 May 1951:2.

C1692 PLEASURES OF THE BATH ASSEMBLY. *The Listener*, XLV (1161), 31 May 1951:871-872.

C1693 BRUDDERSFORD REVISITED. *The Listener*, XLV (1162), 7 June 1951:913-914.

C1694 NEWS. *News Chronicle*, 32767, 9 June 1951:2.

C1695 FROM MALVERN TO ALDEBURGH. *The Listener*, XLV (1163), 14 June 1951:953-954.

C1696 THE RENEWED DREAM OF A MERRIE ENGLAND. *New York Times*, 15 July 1951:VI(10).

C1697 ESCAPISTS. *News Chronicle*, 32773, 16 June 1951:2.

C1698 SMOKING. *News Chronicle*, 32779, 23 June 1951:2.

C1699 L.C.C. GRANT TO L.P.O. - letter. *The Times*, 52036, 25 June 1951:5.

C1700 HOTELS. *News Chronicle*, 32785, 30 June 1951:2.

C1701 INFLATION. *News Chronicle*, 32791, 7 July 1951:2.

C1702 SHOP HOURS. *News Chronicle*, 32797, 14 July 1951:2.

C1703 THE ORCHESTRA SPEAKS - letter. *New Statesman*, XLII (1063), 21 July 1951:71.

C1704 B.B.C. *News Chronicle*, 32803, 21 July 1951:2.

C1705 SATIRICAL REVIEWS. *News Chronicle*, 32809, 28 July 1951:2.

C1706 EDUCATION FOR WHAT. *News Chronicle*, 32815, 4 August 1951:2.

C1707 AUTHORS AND CRITICISMS. *News Chronicle*, 32821, 11 August 1951:2.

C1708 CLOSE SEASON. *News Chronicle*, 32827, 18 August 1951:2.

C1709 WRONG MOVE. *News Chronicle*, 32833, 25 August 1951:2.

C1710 TELEVISION ... THE DANGER. *Radio Times*, 112 (1451), 31 August 1951:7.

C1711 CAN THE CRAFT OF PLAYWRITING BE LEARNED? HOW CAN BE-
       GINNERS BE HELPED? English reactions by Alan Dent
       who submitted Questionnaire to J.B. Priestley,
       Terence Rattigan, Christopher Fry and Roger McDou-
       gall. *World Theatre*, 1 (3), Autumn 1951:28-31.

C1712 LET'S GO TO THE PICTURES. *News Chronicle*, 32839,
       1 September 1951:2.

C1713 J.B. PRIESTLEY, PLAYWRIGHT REPLIES TO HIS T.V. CRITICS.
       News Chronicle, 32845, 8 September 1951:2.

C1714 UNSUNG HEROES. *News Chronicle*, 32851, 15 September
       1951:2.

C1715 MANNERS. *News Chronicle*, 32857, 22 September 1951:2.

C1716 WORLD SOCIETY? *News Chronicle*, 32863, 27 September
       1951:2.

C1717 HIGH SPEED DIPLOMACY. *News Chronicle*, 32869, 6 Octo-
       ber 1951:2.

C1718 BEANS ON TOAST. *News Chronicle*, 32875, 13 October
       1951:2.

C1719 BRUDDERSFORD TAKES IT ALL QUIETLY. *News Chronicle*,
       32877, 16 October 1951:2.

C1720 NEW DANGER. *News Chronicle*, 32881, 20 October 1951:2.

C1721 THE CURTAIN RISES. *Colliers Magazine*, 128, 27 October
       1951:38+.

                              1952

C1722 LET US THINK ANEW. *Daily Mail*, 17351, 2 January 1952:2.

C1723 I BELIEVE. *Yorkshire Observer*, 27469, 31 January
       1952:4.

C1724 WONDER OF THE DESERT. *American Magazine*, 153, Feb-
       ruary 1952:22-23+.

C1725 BUT WHAT OF THE OLDER WRITER? *News Chronicle*, 33017,
       29 March 1952:2.

C1726   MR PRIESTLEY IS ANNOYED: OPEN LETTER TO BRADFORD.
          Yorkshire Observer, 27528, 9 April 1952:1.

C1727   DRAGON'S MOUTH - letter. *Manchester Guardian*, 32916,
          22 April 1952:6.

C1728   'DRAGON'S MOUTH' - letter. *The Times*, 52313, 16 May
          1952:7.

C1729   THE STORY OF DRAGON'S MOUTH. *Everybody's*, 24 May 1952:
          12-13.

C1730   THE UGLIEST TREND. *The Author*, Summer 1952.

C1731   PLATFORM PIECE. *Theatre*, 21 June 1952.

C1732   I COME BACK TO A VERY OLD FRIEND. *Sunday Chronicle*,
          5 October 1952:6.

C1733   LAZY, MAYBE, BUT WE CAN INVENT. *Sunday Chronicle*, 12
          October 1952:4.

C1734   THE FRISCO MAN IN SILK STOCKINGS. *Sunday Chronicle*,
          19 October 1952:4.

C1735   THE MONDAY NIGHT I MIGHT HAVE SAVED MANKIND. *Sunday
          Chronicle*, 26 October 1952:4.

C1736   MY IMPRESSION OF JAPAN. *Contemporary Japan*, XXI (7-9),
          November 1952:433-437.

C1737   ON THE ISLAND WHERE GIRLS MAY NOT GO. *Sunday Chroni-
          cle*, 2 November 1952:4.

C1738   PIN TABLES, BAD WHISKY - IS THIS PROGRESS? *Sunday
          Chronicle*, 9 November 1952:4.

C1739   NOBODY LOVES US MAKING A-BOMBS, NOT EVEN THE JAPS.
          Sunday Chronicle, 16 November 1952:4.

                              1953

C1740   Item omitted.

C1741   TWO NEW STORIES. *Lilliput*, 32 (5), No. 191, April-
          May 1953:65-80 and 83-98.
          Contents: 'Uncle Phil on TV' and 'The Grey Ones', both
          collected in *The Other Place* (1953).

C1742 THOUGHTS IN THE WILDERNESS. *New Statesman*, XLVI
(1174), 5 September 1953:250-251.
Reprinted: *Thoughts in the Wilderness* (1957).

C1743 ON MASS COMMUNICATION. *New Statesman*, XLVI (1177),
26 September 1953:342.
Reprinted: *Thoughts in the Wilderness* (1957).

C1744 MASS COMMUNICATIONS. *New York Times*, 4 October 1953:
II, 15:2.

C1745 BLOCK THINKING. *New Statesman*, XLVI (1182), 31 October 1953:514, 516.
Reprinted: *Thoughts in the Wilderness* (1957).

C1746 I DISAGREE LORD SAMUEL. *News Chronicle*, 33516, 6
November 1953:4.

C1747 THEY COME FROM INNER SPACE. *New Statesman*, XLVI
(1187), 5 December 1953:712, 714.
Reprinted: *Thoughts in the Wilderness* (1957).

C1747a THE FOURTH ACT. *Punch*, CCXXV (5908), 16 December 1953:
718-719.

C1748 BOOKS OF THE YEAR (chosen by eminent contemporaries).
Sunday Times, 6818, 20 December 1953:6.

C1749 THE HESPERIDES CONFERENCE. *New Statesman*, XLVI
(1190), 26 December 1953:815-816.
Reprinted: *Thoughts in the Wilderness* (1957).

1954

C1750 PRIESTLEY'S PRIMER: LESSONS FOR LITTLE ONES. *Punch*,
CCXXVI (5914), 27 January 1954:148-149.

C1751 EROS AND LOGOS. *New Statesman*, XLVII (1195), 30 January 1954:123-124.
Reprinted: *Thoughts in the Wilderness* (1957).

C1752 PRIESTLEY'S PRIMER. *Punch*, CCXXVI (5916), 10 February 1954:206-207.

C1753 PRIESTLEY'S PRIMER. *Punch*, CCXXVI (5918), 24 February 1954:262-263.

C1754 WHO'S MUZZY MR L? - letter. *News Chronicle*, 33610, 26 February 1954:4.

C1755 I'M NOT SOUR - letter. *Daily Mirror*, 15642, 1 March 1954:7.

C1756 TIME PLEASE! *New Statesman*, XLVII (1201), 13 March 1954:307-308.
Reprinted: *Thoughts in the Wilderness* (1957).

C1757 THE AMERICAN NOVEL. *Sunday Times*, 6830, 14 March 1954:5. Review of *Rebels and Ancestors* (Maxwell Geismar); and *The Man from Main Street* (Sinclair Lewis).

C1758 PRIESTLEY'S PRIMER. *Punch*, CCXXVI (5922), 24 March 1954:378-379.

C1759 THE GOOD AMERICAN - letter. *Encounter*, ii (4), April 1954:59.

C1760 ON EDUCATION. *New Statesman*, XLVII (1206), 17 April 1954:495-496.
Reprinted: *Thoughts in the Wilderness* (1957).

C1761 THE RIGHT ACCENT. *New York Times*, 2 May 1954:16.

C1762 PRIESTLEY'S PRIMER. *Punch*, CCXXVI (5928), 5 May 1954: 552-553.

C1763 A NOVEL ON THE HEROIC SCALE. *Sunday Times*, 6838, 9 May 1954:5. Review of *The Adventures of Augie March* (Saul Bellow).

C1764 LIKE IT, OR LUMP IT, COME HELL OR HIGH WATER, I AM A WRITER. *New York Times Book Review*, 30 May 1954: VII, 5.

C1765 THE FUTURE OF THE WRITER. *London Magazine*, 1 (5), June 1954:63-67.

C1766 THE NEWEST NOVELS. *New Statesman*, XLVII (1216), 26 June 1954:824, 826.
Reprinted: *Thoughts in the Wilderness* (1957).

C1767 MILK IN THE COCONUT. *Sunday Times*, 6846, 4 July 1954: 5. Review of *The American Thesaurus of Slang* (L.V. Berney and M. Van Der Bark).

C1768   THE REAL CLEAN-UP. *New Statesman*, XLVIII (1220), 24
        July 1954:95.
        Reprinted: *Thoughts in the Wilderness* (1957).

C1769   JUNG AND THE WRITER. *Times Literary Supplement*, 2740,
        6 August 1954:500 (iii).

C1770   CAMPS OF DEATH. *Sunday Times*, 6851, 8 August 1954:3.
        Review of *Human Behaviour in the Concentration Camps*
        (Elie A. Cohen).

C1771   THE INSANE SPECIALISTS AND THE INDIVIDUAL. *Saturday
        Night*, 69, 28 August 1954:7-8.

C1772   PIGS AT SEA. *Encounter*, iii (3), September 1954:38-
        40.

C1773   GREY EMINENCES. *New Statesman*, XLVIII (1226), 4 Sep-
        tember 1954:256-258.
        Reprinted: *Thoughts in the Wilderness* (1957).
        Note: also appeared as 'Sir Nuclear Fission', *Bulletin
        of the Atomic Scientists*, October 1955 (C1817).

C1774   ONE OF OUR EGOISTS. *Sunday Times*, 6858, 26 September
        1954:5.   Review of *The Ordeal of George Meredith*
        (Lionel Stevenson).

C1775   SACRED WHITE ELEPHANTS. *New Statesman*, XLVIII (1230),
        2 October 1954:384-385.
        Reprinted: *Thoughts in the Wilderness* (1957).

C1776   GREY EMINENCES - letter. *New Statesman*, XLVIII
        (1230), 2 October 1954:392.

C1777   ALIVE AND KICKING. *Sunday Times*, 6860, 10 October
        1954:5.   Review of *Hackenfeller's Ape* (Brigid
        Brophy); *Under the Net* (Iris Murdoch); *Smith* (Kate
        Christie); *Lucky Jim* (Kingsley Amis); *Hurry on Down*
        (John Wain); *The Goodly Seed* (John Wylie); and
        Violins Saint Jacques (Patrick Leigh Fermor).

C1778   HENRY FIELDING: THEN AND NOW. *The Listener*, LII
        (1357), 14 October 1954:609-610.

C1779   HARD AND SOFT CENTRES. *Sunday Times*, 6862, 24 Oc-
        tober 1954:5.   Review of *Sweet Thursday* (John Stein-
        beck); and *Private's Progress* (Alan Hackney).

C1780 BOOKS IN GENERAL. *New Statesman*, XLVIII (1234), 30
       October 1954:541-542. Review of *Collected Works of
       C.G. Jung*.

C1781 EIGHTY AND FORTY. *Sunday Times*, 6864, 7 November
       1954:5. Review of *A Glastonbury Romance* (John Cow-
       per Powys); and *Hester Lily* (Elizabeth Taylor).

C1782 ANOTHER REVOLUTION. *New Statesman*, XLVIII (1236), 13
       November 1954:604, 606.
       Reprinted: *Thoughts in the Wilderness* (1957).

C1783 WHERE EDUCATION FAILS: TODAY'S HARD FACTS. *Saturday
       Night*, 70, 13 November 1954:7-8.

C1784 COPS AND ROBBERS. *Sunday Times*, 6866, 21 November
       1954:5. Review of *Maigret Right and Wrong* (Georges
       Simenon).

C1785 THE GENTLE ANARCHIST: POWER AND PEOPLE. *The Listener*,
       LII (1343), 25 November 1954:897-898.

C1786 THE GENTLE ANARCHIST: MACHINERY AND PERSONALITY. *The
       Listener*, LII (1344), 2 December 1954:951-952.

C1787 SOMETHING ELSE. *New Statesman*, XLVIII (1239), 4
       December 1954:731-732.
       Reprinted: *Thoughts in the Wilderness* (1957).

C1788 IN AMERICA. *Sunday Times*, 6868, 5 December 1954:5.

C1789 THE HISTORICAL METHOD. *Sunday Times*, 6870, 19 Decem-
       ber 1954:4.

C1790 A GREAT AMERICAN SIN. THE SOCIETY OF NOMADMASS. *The
       Nation*, 179 (26), 25 December 1954:547-549.
       Note: similar but not identical in content to chapter
       eleven of *Journey Down a Rainbow* (1955) (A113).

                              1955

C1791 THINGS ARE MAKING SLAVES OF US. *News Chronicle*,
       33872, 1 January 1955:4.

C1792 GEMS CHOICE IN FUCHSIA YAWS. *Sunday Times*, 6872, 2
       January 1955:5. Review of *Dubliners* (James Joyce).

C1793 THE CHARM SCHOOL. *Sunday Times*, 6874, 16 January
        1955:5. Review of *Good Morning Miss Dove* (Frances
        Gray Patton); *Tender Is the Night* (Scott Fitzgerald);
        and *Brother Nap* (Frank Tilsley).

C1794 END OF A PARTY. *New Statesman*, XLIX (1246), 22 Jan-
        uary 1955:96.
        Reprinted: *Thoughts in the Wilderness* (1957).

C1795 WIZARD'S WAY. *Sunday Times*, 6876, 30 January 1955:5.
        Review of *Loser Takes All* (Graham Greene).

C1796 UNHAPPY FAMILIES. *Sunday Times*, 6878, 13 February
        1955:5. Review of *Mother and Son* (Ivy Compton Bur-
        nett); and *The Novels of I. Compton Burnett* (Robert
        Liddell).

C1797 THE NEW DROLLS. *New Statesman*, XLIX (1250), 19 Feb-
        ruary 1955:238, 240.
        Reprinted: *Thoughts in the Wilderness* (1957).

C1798 A CRACK IN THE ICE. *Sunday Times*, 6880, 27 February
        1955:4. Review of *The Thaw* (Ilya Ehrenburg);
        Kongoni (G.R. Fazackerley); and *Cards of Identity*
        (Nigel Dennis).

C1799 HAPPY RETURN. *Sunday Times*, 6881, 6 March 1955:5.
        Review of *A World of Love* (Elizabeth Bowen).

C1800 DOERS AND SEERS. *New Statesman*, XLIX (1253), 12 March
        1955:348, 350.
        Reprinted: *Thoughts in the Wilderness* (1957).

C1801 WE ARE GENTLE ANARCHISTS. *London Calling*, 806, 14
        April 1955:10.

C1802 PERSONALITY IN ECLIPSE. *London Calling*, 807, 21 April
        1955:10.

C1803 A NOTE ON BILLY GRAHAM. *New Statesman*, XLIX (1249),
        23 April 1955:570, 572.
        Reprinted: *Thoughts in the Wilderness* (1957).

C1804 QUINTET. *Sunday Times*, 6884, 24 April 1955:4. Review
        of *Lost Innocence* (Celia Bertin); *The Picnic at
        Sakarra* (P.H. Newby); *Violent Saturday* (W.L. Heath);
        Noble in Reason (Phyllis Bentley); and *Federigo*
        (Howard Nemerov).

C1805 WHAT THIS ELECTION OUGHT TO BE ABOUT. *News Chronicle*, 33596, 5 May 1955:6.

C1806 WHERE PROTEST FAILS. *Sunday Times*, 6887, 15 May 1955:4. Review of *Stranger Come Home* (W.L. Shirer).

C1807 YOU KNOW WHAT PEOPLE ARE. *Radio Times*, 127 (1646), 27 May 1955:5.

C1808 A POET'S LONDON CHILDHOOD. *Sunday Times*, 6892, 19 June 1955:5. Review of *Over the Bridge* (Richard Church).

C1809 WHY I REGRET THE CLOSING OF BRADFORD'S GIANT-PIE SHOP. *Yorkshire Observer*, 28518, 20 June 1955:4.

C1810 OUR NEW SOCIETY. *New Statesman*, L (1271), 16 July 1955:63-64.
Reprinted: *Thoughts in the Wilderness* (1957).

C1811 THE WISE OLD MAN. *Sunday Times*, 6897, 24 July 1955:3.

C1812 SHE LIVED MANFULLY. *News Chronicle*, 34028, 28 July 1955:6. Review of *Elinor Glyn* (Anthony Glyn).

C1813 CANDLES BURNING LOW. *New Statesman*, L (1274), 6 August 1955:155-156.
Reprinted: *Thoughts in the Wilderness* (1957).

C1814 SIX OPINIONS (on article 'Modern Drama and Society' by John Gassner). *World Theatre*, Autumn 1955.

C1815 A PERSONAL NOTE. *New Statesman*, L (1279), 10 September 1955:292-293.
Reprinted: *Thoughts in the Wilderness* (1957).

C1816 DANGEROUS JOURNEY. *Books and Bookmen*, 1 (1), October 1955:7.

C1817 SIR NUCLEAR FISSION. *Bulletin of the Atomic Scientists*, XI (8), October 1955:293-294.
Note: First printed as 'Grey Eminences', *New Statesman*, 4 September 1954 (C1773). F.C. Irion's 'Sir Nuclear Fission: A Realistic Myth', *Bulletin of the Atomic Scientists*, October 1955, replied.

C1818 ROUGH SKETCH OF A LIFEBOAT. *New Statesman*, L (1282), 1 October 1955:388, 390.
Reprinted: *Thoughts in the Wilderness* (1957).

C1819   WHO WILL PASS HIS SCRUTINY? *News Chronicle*, 34088, 6
        October 1955:8. Review of *D.H. Lawrence: Novelist*
        (F.R. Leavis).

C1820   MY WORK AND MYSELF. *Radio Times*, 129 (1667), 21 Oc-
        tober 1955:5.

C1821   TWO FAILURES – letter. *Books and Bookmen*, 1 (2), No-
        vember 1955:25.
        Note: In response to David Millward's 'Magnificent
        Grumbler', *Books and Bookmen*, October 1955 (H56).

C1822   WHO IS ANTI-AMERICAN? *New Statesman*, L (1287), 5
        November 1955:566-567.
        Reprinted: *Thoughts in the Wilderness* (1957).

C1823   THE TWO LIVES OF MR KIPLING. *News Chronicle*, 34124,
        17 November 1955:6. Review of *Rudyard Kipling*
        (Charles Carrington).

C1824   WHY I WROTE A PLAY ABOUT AN ART DEALER. *Radio Times*,
        129 (1672), 25 November 1955:5.

C1825   WHERE ARE WE GOING? *News Chronicle*, 34136, 1 December
        1955:4.

C1826   THOUGHTS ON BOTTOMLEY. *New Statesman*, L (1292), 10
        December 1955:786, 788.
        Reprinted: *Thoughts in the Wilderness* (1957).

C1827   BRIDIE: THE PLAYS AND THE MAN. *New Statesman*, L
        (1295), 31 December 1955:884-885. Review of *James
        Bridie and His Theatre* by Winifred Bannister.
        Note: Much of this was reprinted in Priestley's Intro-
        duction to *Meeting at Night* by James Bridie (1956)
        (B91).

                              1956

C1828   SAMPLE CARLYLE IN ONE VOLUME. *News Chronicle*, 34176,
        19 January 1956:6. Review of *Carlyle: Selected
        Works* edited by Julian Symons.

C1829   OUR BOOKS DESERVE A FAIRER LAW. *News Chronicle*,
        34212, 1 March 1956:6. Review of *Obscenity and the
        Law* (Norman St. John Stevas).

C1830   J.B. PRIESTLEY IN THE ISLE OF WIGHT. *London
        Calling*, 855, 22 March 1956:5-6.

C1831   THOUGHTS ON THE UNICORN. *New Statesman*, LI (1307),
        31 March 1956:300, 302.
        Reprinted: *Thoughts in the Wilderness* (1957).

C1832   I NEARLY MISSED WILL THAT DAY AT STRATFORD. *News
        Chronicle*, 34255, 21 April 1956:4.

C1833   THOUGHTS ON THE STAGGERS AND NAGGERS. *New Statesman*,
        LI (1313), 12 May 1956:524, 526.
        Reprinted: *Thoughts in the Wilderness* (1957).

C1834   CANADA'S BAD MANNERED NEWSPAPERS. *Saturday Night*,
        71, 26 May 1956:7-8.

C1835   CANADIAN NOTES AND IMPRESSIONS. *The Listener*, LV
        (1418), 31 May 1956:713-714.

C1836   CANADA: A FRUSTRATED NATION. *The Listener*, LV (1419),
        7 June 1956:743-744.

C1837   CANADIAN NOTES AND IMPRESSIONS: - letter. *The Lis-
        tener*, LV (1420), 14 June 1956:803.

C1838   BROADWAY AND PLAYWRITING. *New Statesman*, LI (1319),
        23 June 1956:735-736. Review of *How Not to Write
        a Play* (Walter Kerr).

C1839   WHAT TO DO ABOUT THE ARTS. *Saturday Night*, 71, 23
        June 1956:10-11.

C1840   THE REVOLUTION THAT NEVER WAS. *Reynold's News*, 5517,
        1 July 1956:3.

C1841   THOUGHTS ON THE OUTSIDER. *New Statesman*, LII (1321),
        7 July 1956:10-11.
        Reprinted: *Thoughts in the Wilderness* (1957).

C1842   RETREAT TO A BOWLER HAT. *Reynold's News*, 5518, 8
        July 1956:3.

C1843   DON'T SAY GOODBYE TO YOURSELVES. *Reynold's News*,
        5519, 15 July 1956:3.

C1844   THOUGHTS ON SHAW. *New Statesman*, LII (1324), 28
        July 1956:96-97.
        Reprinted: *Thoughts in the Wilderness* (1957).

C1845   THOUGHTS ON THE POPULAR PRESS. *New Statesman*, LII
        (1328), 25 August 1956:208.
        Reprinted: *Thoughts in the Wilderness* (1957).

C1846   AS I SEE IT. *Reynold's News*, 5527, 9 September 1956:7.

C1847   AS I SEE IT. *Reynold's News*, 5528, 16 September 1956:7.

C1848   AS I SEE IT. *Reynold's News*, 5529, 23 September 1956:7.

C1849   JAMES BRIDIE AND THE THEATRE. *The Listener*, LVI
        (1435), 27 September 1956:457-458.

C1850   THOUGHTS ON TELEVIEWING. *New Statesman*, LII (1333),
        29 September 1956:367-368.
        Reprinted: *Thoughts in the Wilderness* (1957).

C1851   AS I SEE IT. *Reynold's News*, 5530, 30 September 1956:9.

C1852   NOTE BY A YOUNG BRADFORDIAN. *Yorkshire Life Illustra-*
        ted, X (10), October 1956:17.

C1853   AS I SEE IT. *Reynold's News*, 5531, 7 October 1956:9.

C1854   THE VERY WORST YEARS OF THEIR LIVES. *News Chronicle*,
        34403, 11 October 1956:8. Review of *Andersonville*
        (MacKinlay Kantor).

C1855   AS I SEE IT. *Reynold's News*, 5532, 14 October 1956:9.

C1856   AS I SEE IT. *Reynold's News*, 5533, 21 October 1956:9.

C1857   THE ENGLISH CLASS SYSTEM. *London Calling*, 886, 25
        October 1956:10.

C1858   AS I SEE IT. *Reynold's News*, 5534, 28 October 1956:7.

C1859   AS I SEE IT. *Reynold's News*, 5535, 4 November 1956:9.

C1860   BOOK OF A HUNDRED MONTHS. *Sunday Times*, 6964, 4
        November 1956:7. Review of *The Lost Steps* (Alejo
        Carpentier).

C1861   THOUGHTS ON DR LEAVIS. *New Statesman*, LII (1339), 10
        November 1956:579-580. Signed by Dr. J.B. Priestley.
        Reprinted: *Thoughts in the Wilderness* (1957).

C1862 AS I SEE IT. *Reynold's News*, 5536, 11 November 1956:9.

C1863 AS I SEE IT. *Reynold's News*, 5537, 18 November 1956:7.

C1864 AS I SEE IT. *Reynold's News*, 5538, 25 November 1956:9.

C1865 AS I SEE IT. *Reynold's News*, 5539, 2 December 1956:9.

C1866 AS I SEE IT. *Reynold's News*, 5540, 9 December 1956:9.

C1867 AS I SEE IT. *Reynold's News*, 5541, 16 December 1956:7.

C1868 AS I SEE IT. *Reynold's News*, 5542, 23 December 1956:7.

C1869 BOOKS OF THE YEAR. *Sunday Times*, 6971, 23 December
       1956:8. Contributions from eminent contemporaries.

C1870 AS I SEE IT. *Reynold's News*, 5543, 30 December 1956:7.

                              1957

C1871 AS I SEE IT. *Reynold's News*, 5544, 6 January 1957:9.

C1872 AS I SEE IT. *Reynold's News*, 5545, 13 January 1957:7.

C1873 AS I SEE IT. *Reynold's News*, 5546, 20 January 1957:9.

C1874 AS I SEE IT. *Reynold's News*, 5547, 27 January 1957:7.

C1875 AS I SEE IT. *Reynold's News*, 5548, 3 February 1957:7.

C1876 AS I SEE IT. *Reynold's News*, 5549, 10 February 1957:9.

C1877 AS I SEE IT. *Reynold's News*, 5550, 17 February 1957:9.

C1878 AS I SEE IT. *Reynold's News*, 5551, 24 February 1957:7.

C1879 AS I SEE IT. *Reynold's News*, 5552, 3 March 1957:9.

C1880 THE GREAT MAGIC. *Kent and Sussex Courier*, 6328, 5
       April 1957:7.

C1881 IS ENGLAND A LAND OF MIDGET MINDS? *Daily Mail*, 18962,
       6 April 1957:4. By Kenneth Allsop (an interview ar-
       ticle).

C1882   I'M NOT SUCH A TESTY OLD CODGER YET.... *Daily Mail*,
        18968, 13 April 1957:4.
        Note: refers to above interview.

C1883   THOUGHTS ON PUBLISHERS. *New Statesman*, LIII (1361),
        13 April 1957:486-488.
        Reprinted: *Thoughts in the Wilderness* (1957).

C1884   MAN IS ONLY A SMALL LINK. *Daily Mail*, 18972, 18
        April 1957:4.

C1885   HOUSMAN: A STRANGER AND AFRAID. *News Chronicle*,
        34591, 22 May 1957:6. Review of *A.E. Housman: A
        Divided Life* (George L. Warner).

C1886   TRAVELLER'S TALE. *Reynold's News*, 5565, 2 June 1957:3.

C1887   BROWN'S REPUBLIC AGAIN. *New Statesman*, LIII (1369),
        8 June 1957:732-733.
        Note: 'The dream did not vanish in daylight ... but
        lingered long enough for me to write a piece on it,
        a piece that was printed as a 'middle' and later
        found its way into a book of such things, though
        I'll be hanged if I can find it now.' This refers
        to 'That Quarter', *This Quarter*, April-June 1931
        (C813).

C1888   TRAVELLER'S TALE. *Reynold's News*, 5566, 9 June 1957:4.

C1889   TRAVELLER'S TALE. *Reynold's News*, 5567, 16 June 1957:3.

C1890   ALL UPPER CRUST IS POOR FARE. *Reynold's News*, 5568,
        23 June 1957:9.

C1891   THE BOOK TRADE. *News Chronicle*, 34621, 25 June 1957:6.

C1892   YOU DON'T EVEN DRINK AND YOU'RE 15. *Reynold's News*,
        5569, 30 June 1957:9.

C1893   ACCENTS. *New Statesman*, LIV (1373), 6 July 1957:7-8.

C1894   CHRISTINE, THE PRESS, AND POKER FACE. *Reynold's News*,
        5570, 7 July 1957:9.

C1895   DICKENS USED TO GROUSE ABOUT THESE BUNS. *Reynold's
        News*, 5571, 14 July 1957:9.

C1896   BUT FAR TOO MANY PEOPLE. *New Statesman*, LIV (1375),
        20 July 1957:76-78.

C1897 WHY OFFICES FLOURISH AND OLD THEATRES DIE. *Reynold's News*, 5572, 21 July 1957:9.

C1898 LET'S HEAR MORE OF MR SMITH & CO. *Reynold's News*, 5573, 28 July 1957:9.

C1899 KING CHARLIE DOES IT AGAIN. *Sunday Dispatch*, 28 July 1957:8.

C1900 TAKE A TIP FROM ME - SMOKE SLOWLY. *Reynold's News*, 5574, 4 August 1957:7.

C1901 THE WALRUS AND THE CARPENTER. *New Statesman*, LIV (1378), 10 August 1957:168.

C1902 THE MYTHS THAT MADE US 'SNOOTY DOOKS'. *Reynold's News*, 5575, 11 August 1957:7.

C1903 DEAR DAME PEGGY DON'T BE DAFT. *Reynold's News*, 5576, 18 August 1957:9.

C1904 MORE NEWS FROM NOWHERE. *Reynold's News*, 5577, 25 August 1957:9.

C1905 WHAT WAS WRONG WITH PINFOLD. *New Statesman*, LIV (1381), 31 August 1957:244.
Note: This notice of Evelyn Waugh's *The Ordeal of Gilbert Pinfold* prompted that writer's 'Anything Wrong with Priestley?', *Spectator*, 13 September 1957 (H61).

C1906 ECONOMICS OF BARBARISM. *Reynold's News*, 5578, 1 September 1957:9.

C1907 EVEN THE ARTS ARE GOING WEST. *Reynold's News*, 5579, 8 September 1957:9.

C1908 POLLS, PASSIONS AND PUBLIC OPINION. *Reynold's News*, 5580, 15 September 1957:5.

C1909 BEAUTY QUEENS DON'T RATE A CIVIC WELCOME. *Reynold's News*, 5581, 22 September 1957:5.

C1910 PORTRAIT OF A POET AS A YOUNGISH MAN. *News Chronicle*, 34699, 25 September 1957:6. Review of *Golden Sovereign* (Richard Church).

C1911 HERE'S A MUSIC HALL TURN FOR THE BETTER. *Reynold's News*, 5582, 29 September 1957:5.

C1912   THIS GIRL IS THE BEST OF THOSE A...Y Y...G M.N.
        Sunday Dispatch, 13 October 1957:6. Review of
        Declaration (Tom Maschler).

C1913   PARTY CONFERENCES AND TV DON'T MIX. *Reynold's News*,
        5583, 6 October 1957:5.

C1914   COMMITTEE GETS HET UP OVER THE HEAT. *Reynold's News*,
        5584, 13 October 1957:5.

C1915   LET'S NOT GET SPACE HAPPY. *News Chronicle*, 34717, 16
        October 1957:4.

C1916   ADVENTURE TOO OFTEN HAS A PHONEY ACCENT. *Reynold's
        News*, 5585, 20 October 1957:5.

C1917   OUR YOUNG WRITERS WON'T USE THEIR TEETH. *Reynold's
        News*, 5586, 27 October 1957:5.

C1918   HAZLITT: A FINE MODEL. *Sunday Times*, 7015, 27 October
        1957:14.

C1919   BRITAIN AND THE NUCLEAR BOMBS. *New Statesman*, LIV
        (1390), 2 November 1957:554-556.
        Reprinted as a pamphlet. Later included in *New States-
        manship* (1963) (B111), and *Voices from the Crowd*
        (1964) (B117).

C1920   JUSTICE IS DEAR TO ME - FAR TOO DEAR. *Reynold's News*,
        5587, 3 November 1957:5.

C1921   OUTLAWS WE SHOULD BRING WITHIN THE LAW. *Reynold's
        News*, 5588, 10 November 1957:5.

C1922   MORPHIA TRAGEDY. *Reynold's News*, 5589, 17 November
        1957:1.

C1923   GOOD LUCK - BUT ARE THEY HAPPY HERE? *Reynold's News*,
        5589, 17 November 1957:5.

C1924   THE DISRESPECT FOR FICTION. *The Listener*, LVIII
        (1495), 21 November 1957:831-832.

C1925   WE HAVE SO MUCH, YET THE GUSTO'S GONE. *Reynold's News*,
        5590, 24 November 1957:5.

C1926   OH GIVE ME A COLD CURE BEFORE A SPUTNIK. *Reynold's
        News*, 5591, 1 December 1957:5.

C1927 THE ART OF THE DRAMATIST. THE NATURE OF THE DRAMA.
       The Listener, LVIII (1497), 5 December 1957:917-919.

C1928 LIFE IS DRABBER WITHOUT THIS MAGIC FOOD. *Reynold's
       News*, 5592, 8 December 1957:5.

C1929 THE DRAMATIST AND HIS WORK. *The Listener*, LVIII (1498),
       12 December 1957:975-977.

C1930 MY TV PLAY – AND HOW THE CRITICS FAILED. *Reynold's
       News*, 5593, 15 December 1957:5.

C1931 THE DRAMATIST AND HIS COLLEAGUES. *The Listener*,
       LVIII (1499), 19 December 1957:1025-1027.

C1932 ANGEL PAVEMENT ON TELEVISION. *Radio Times*, 137 (1780),
       20 December 1957:10.

C1933 NOW FOR THE GOOD CHEER CASH CAN'T BUY. *Reynold's
       News*, 5594, 22 December 1957:5.

C1934 UTOPIAN NIGHT. *New Statesman*, LIV (1398), 28 December
       1957:869-870.

C1935 MY CHALLENGE: LET'S LIGHT UP THIS GLOOM. *Reynold's
       News*, 5595, 29 December 1957:5.

C1936 'CALM' – letter. *The Observer*, 8687, 29 December
       1957:7.

                          1958

C1937 MR ANDERSON AND ADMASS – letter. *Encounter*, X (1),
       January 1958:69.

C1938 THIS IS OUR DUTY. *Reynold's News*, 5596, 5 January
       1958:6.

C1939 NOTHING DEMOCRATIC ABOUT BAD MANNERS. *Reynold's News*,
       5597, 12 January 1958:5.

C1940 THE CINEMA BORES ME. *Reynold's News*, 5598, 19 January
       1958:5.

C1941 MARRIAGE TODAY IS HAPPIER. *Reynold's News*, 5599, 26
       January 1958:5.

C1942 THE FESTIVAL IN THE FOLLY. *High Fidelity Magazine*,
       February 1958:36-37, 123.

C1943 Item omitted.

C1944 LET'S TURN BACK TO BOOKS. *Reynold's News*, 5600, 2
       February 1958:6.

C1945 I'M TIRED OF DEEP SOUTH DECADENCE. *Reynold's News*,
       5601, 9 February 1958:4. Review of *The Town*
       (William Faulkner); *Leave Me Alone* (David Karp);
       The Hills of Beverley (Libbie Block); and *Ladies
       Day* (Chard Powers Smith).

C1946 MR MIFFIN AND THE MONSTER. *Reynold's News*, 5602, 16
       February 1958:6. Review of *The One Eyed Monster*
       (Allan Prior); *Cinderella Nightingale* (Robert Muller);
       A Wilderness of Monkeys (Marshall Pugh); and *Every-
       man's Dictionary of Literary Biography*.

C1947 A GREAT TRAVELLER IN WORDS. *Reynold's News*, 5603, 23
       February 1958:4. Review of *The Last Year: A Memoir
       of Thomas Mann* (Erika Mann); and *H.M. Tomlinson: A
       Selection from His Writings*.

C1948 HOW I WRITE MY PLAYS. *Books and Art*, 1 (6), March
       1958:59.

C1949 A CAT AND DOG FIGHT IN PRINT. *Reynold's News*, 5604,
       2 March 1958:6. Review of *Henry James and H.G. Wells*
       (edited by Leon Edel and Gordon N. Ray); *The Bank
       Audit* (Bruce Marshall); and *Point of Return* (Margaret
       Dick).

C1950 H-BOMB HOTCHPOTCH. *Daily Herald*, 13065, 5 March 1958:4.

C1951 NO MUMBO ABOUT HIS JUMBO. *Reynold's News*, 5605, 9
       March 1958:4. Review of *The Roots of Heaven* (Ro-
       main Gary); and *A Cage for Lovers* (Dawn Powell).

C1952 THIS NUCLEAR MADNESS. *Punch*, CCXXXIV (6134), 12 March
       1958:342-343.

C1953 JOHN WAIN RUNS INTO HIS OWN TRAP. *Reynold's News*,
       5606, 16 March 1958:6. Review of *The Contenders*
       (John Wain); *The Advocate's Devil* (C.P. Harvey);
       At Home (William Plomer); and *Miss Bantling Is
       Missing* (Joseph Meagher).

C1954 HIGH AND DRY ON THE LEFT BANK. *Reynold's News*,
5607, 23 March 1958:6. Review of *Watt* (Samuel
Beckett); *I Hear Voices* (Paul Ableman); *Two by Two*
(Martha Gellhorn); and *The Chinese Bell Murders*
(Robert van Gulik).

C1955 CAMPAIGN REPORT. *New Statesman*, LV (1411), 29 March
1958:402-403.

C1956 Letter. *New Statesman*, LV (1411), 29 March 1958:408.

C1957 THE TORTOISE WHO WILL END AS A LION. *Reynold's News*,
5608, 30 March 1958:6. Review of *The Conscience
of the Rich* (C.P. Snow); and *Big Sur and the Oranges
of Hieronymous Bosch* (Henry Miller).

C1958 THE SECRET OF SUCCESS BY NUMBERS. *Reynold's News*,
5609, 6 April 1958:4. Review of *Parkinson's Law*
(C. Northcote Parkinson); *Second-Class Taxi* (Syl-
vester Stein); *The Dreaming Suburb* (R.F. Delderfield);
and *The Birth of a Grandfather* (May Sarton).

C1959 49 HOURS ADD UP TO A GREAT NOVEL. *Reynold's News*,
5610, 13 April 1958:6. Review of *By Love Possessed*
(James Gould Cozzens); and *As Music and Splendour*
(Kate O'Brien).

C1960 NOW A RELUCTANT BOGEYMAN TELLS ALL. *Reynold's News*,
5611, 20 April 1958:6. Review of *Autobiography of
Charles Darwin*; *Against the Wind* (Geoffrey Household); and *Bid the Soldiers Shoot* (John Lodwick).

C1961 WHAT IS WRONG WITH THE CHILD? *Reynold's News*, 5612,
27 April 1958:6. Review of *The Asphalt Playground*
(John Wiles).

C1962 MAN IS TURNING TO FALSE GODS. *Reynold's News*, 5613,
4 May 1958:6. Review of *The Undiscovered Self*
(C.G. Jung).

C1963 YOU HEAR JOYCE CARY TALKING. *Reynold's News*, 5614,
11 May 1958:6. Review of *Art and Reality* (Joyce
Cary); *Naked under Capricorn* (Olaf Ruhen); and
Young Men in the Sun (Peter Greave).

C1964 THACKERAY'S LOVE LIFE STILL A MYSTERY. *Reynold's
News*, 5615, 18 May 1958:6. Review of *Thackeray:
The Age of Wisdom 1847-1863* (Gordon N. Ray).

C1965 REVOLT OF COMMON SENSE - letter. *New Statesman*, LV
       (1419), 24 May 1958:668.

C1966 THE GLORIOUS DAYS OF THE UPPER CLASS. *Reynold's News*,
       5616, 25 May 1958:6. Review of *The Rainbow Comes
       and Goes* (Diana Cooper); and *The Idiom of the People*
       (James Reeve).

C1967 YOUNG REBELS' ANGER IS MISPLACED. *Reynold's News*,
       5617, 1 June 1958:6. Review of *The Angry Decade*
       (Kenneth Allsop).

C1968 FICTION OWES SO MUCH TO A PARSON. *Reynold's News*,
       5618, 8 June 1958:6. Review of *Laurence Sterne as
       Yorick* (William Connely); *Letters of John Cowper
       Powys to Louis Wilkinson*; *Ten Years After* (Herbert
       Steinhouse); and *Love Among the Cannibals* (Wright
       Morris).

C1969 BELLOC WAS DOGGED BY ILL-LUCK. *Reynold's News*, 5619,
       15 June 1958:6. Review of *Letters from Hilaire
       Belloc* and *The Life of Hilaire Belloc* (Robert
       Speaight).

C1970 HURRAH FOR THIS ANGRY OLD MAN. *Reynold's News*,
       5620, 22 June 1958:6. Review of *Landor* (Malcolm
       Elwin); *England on the Anvil* (John Raymond); and
       Private Life (Alan Hackney).

C1971 IT'S A CRIME TO MURDER SO MANY. *Reynold's News*,
       5621, 29 June 1958:6. Review of *The Finishing
       Stroke* (Ellery Queen); *Someone from the Past*
       (Margot Bennett); *The Bachelors of Broken Hill*
       (Arthur Hopfield); *The Taste of Ashes* (Howard
       Browne); *Some Women Won't Wait* (A.A. Fair); *A Pen-
       knife in My Heart* (Nicholas Blake); *Out of this
       World* (Marten Cumberland); *Murder in Melbourne*
       (Dulcie Gray); and *Murder's Little Sister* (Pamela
       Branch).

C1972 A BOOK THAT THINKS TOO MUCH. *Reynold's News*, 5622,
       6 July 1958:6. Review of *No Down Payment* (John Mc-
       Partland); *Confessions of a European in England*
       (J.H. Huizinga); and *Clerks in Lowly Orders*
       (Stuart Mitchell).

C1973 THIS IS JUST MY KIND OF MEDICINE. *Reynold's News*,
       5623, 13 July 1958:6. Review of *Medicine and Man*
       (Ritchie Calder); and *Casualty* (Robert Romanis).

C1974 THOSE TOUGH GUYS GROW FAMILIAR. *Reynold's News*,
5624, 20 July 1958:6. Review of *Playback* (Raymond
Chandler).

C1975 MA'MSELLES STEP ON MY CORNS! *Reynold's News*, 5625,
27 July 1958:6. Review of *An Age of Fiction*
(Germaine Bree); *The American Novel and Its Tradition* (Richard Chase); and *Granite and Rainbow* (Virginia Woolf).

C1976 PLEASE DON'T ACT LIKE A GENIUS. *Reynold's News*,
5626, 3 August 1958:4. Review of *Crescendo* (Phyllis
Bentley); *Young Mr Keefe* (Stephen Birmingham); and
The Human Situation (Macneile Dixon).

C1977 FAST AND WEST. *Reynold's News*, 5627, 10 August 1958:
4. Review of *The Naked God* (Howard Fast); and
The Court and the Castle (Rebecca West).

C1978 BOOKS ABOUT ART. *Reynold's News*, 5628, 17 August
1958:4. Review of *Impressionist Paintings in the
Louvre*; *Picasso*; *Paul Klee*; *A Concise History of
Art* (Germain Bazin); and *Writers at Work*.

C1979 A NOVELIST WHO COULD GO A LONG WAY. *Reynold's News*,
5629, 24 August 1958:6. Review of *Common People*
(Philip Callow); *Theophile Gautier* (Joanna Richardson); and *Who Goes Hang?* (Stanley Hyland).

C1980 BARTOK'S END: WHAT IS OURS? *Reynold's News*, 31 August
1958:4. Review of *The Naked Face of Genius* (Agatha
Fausset).

C1981 WHO GOES WHERE? *New Statesman*, LVI (1434), 6 September 1958:268, 270.

C1982 A RUSSIAN EPIC. *Reynold's News*, 5631, 7 September
1958:6. Review of *Dr. Zhivago* (Boris Pasternak).

C1983 LET MYTHS KEEP THEIR MAGIC. *Reynold's News*, 5632,
14 September 1958:6. Review of *The King Must Die*
(Mary Renault); *The Skinner* (Jay Gilbert); *The
Threshold* (Michael Stapleton); and *The Industrial
Muse* (Jeremy Warburg).

C1984 AMERICAN WEEK. *Reynold's News*, 5633, 21 September
1958:6. Review of *Selected Letters of Thomas Wolfe*;
The Log from the Sea of Cortez (John Steinbeck);
and *Expense Account* (Joe Morgan).

C1985   TOO FOND OF OKAY NAMES. *Reynold's News*, 5634, 28 September 1958:6. Review of *Culture and Society 1780-1950* (Raymond Williams); and *Madison Avenue USA* (Martin Mayer).

C1986   EAST AND WEST. *Reynold's News*, 5635, 5 October 1958: 6. Review of *Time of the Mango Flowers* (Roderick Cameron); *Flowering Lotus* (Harold Forster); *Temiar Jungle* (John Slimming); *Many Lagoons* (Ralph Varady); *The Yemen* (Hans Helfritz); *Give Me the World* (Leila Hadley); *I'm Wearing My Ninth Pair of Shoes* (Hans Gunther); *From Paris to Cadiz* (Alexander Dumas); *Go West Young Man* (Brian Magee); *London's Riverside* (Eric de Mare); and *Australian Accent* (John Pringle).

C1987   HIGH SPY COMEDY. *Reynold's News*, 5636, 12 October 1958:6. Review of *Our Man in Havana* (Graham Greene); and *Hide My Eyes* (Margery Allingham).

C1988   LADIES' DAY WINNERS. *Reynold's News*, 5637, 19 October 1958:6. Review of *Ask Me No More* (Pamela Frankau); *A Ripple from the Storm* (Doris Lessing); and *Ballerina* (Vicki Baum).

C1989   PRETTY GIRL AMONG THE RUSSIANS. *Reynold's News*, 5638, 26 October 1958:6. Review of *A Room in Moscow* (Sally Belfrage); and *The Russian Revolution* (Alan Moorehead).

C1990   ENGLISH AND AMERICAN HUMOUR. *Reynold's News*, 5639, 2 November 1958:6. Review of *Supermanship* (Stephen Potter); *More Caviare* (Art Buchwald); *Evelyn Waugh* (Frederick J. Stopp); and *Starke Parade* (Leslie Starke).

C1991   BUSHMEN AND OTHERS. *Reynold's News*, 5640, 9 November 1958:6. Review of *Lost World of the Kalahari* (Laurens van der Post); *American Moderns* (Maxwell Geismar); *The Observer Plays*; *Modern Verse in English 1900-50*; and *Sir Charles Dilke* (Roy Jenkins).

C1992   HOW WE LOST TITLE OF V.I.P.s. *Reynold's News*, 5641, 16 November 1958:6. Review of *Distinguished for Talent* (Woodrow Wyatt); *Elizabeth of the German Garden* (Leslie de Charmes); *Verlaine* (L. and E. Hanson); and *Chateaubriand* (Andre Maurois).

C1993 BIG FUTURE FOR A NEW ARRIVAL. *Reynold's News*, 5642,
23 November 1958:6. Review of *The Phantom Limb*
(Hamilton Johnson); *The Cautious Heart* (William
Sansom); *Position at Noon* (Eric Linklater); and
The Bell (Iris Murdoch).

C1994 PUBLISHING IN AMERICA. *Reynold's News*, 5644, 7 December 1958:6.

C1995 MORE FROM AMERICA. *Reynold's News*, 5645, 14 December
1958:6.

C1996 YOU THINK TOO MUCH OF CHILDREN. *Reynold's News*, 5646,
21 December 1958:6.

C1997 WHERE ARE THE BIG NAMES OF 1958? *Reynold's News*,
5647, 28 December 1958:4.

1959

C1998 THE MODERN POETS. *Reynold's News*, 5648, 4 January
1959:4.

C1999 A WINNER FROM WALES. *Reynold's News*, 5649, 11 January
1959:10. Review of *Rape of the Fair Country*
(Alexander Cordell).

C2000 I WOULD BE A POOR EXILE. *Reynold's News*, 5650, 18
January 1959:6. Review of *The Plague House* (Robert
Neumann).

C2001 TWO GREAT RUSSIANS. *Reynold's News*, 5651, 25 January
1959:6. Review of *Turgenev's Literary Reminiscences*;
Turgenev (David Magarshack); and *The Unknown
Chekhov*.

C2002 ON LITERATURE. *Punch*, CCXXXVI (6180), 21 January
1959:116-118.
Reprinted: *The New Book of Snobs by Various Hands*
(1959) (B99).

C2003 ROGUE MP RINGS TRUE. *Reynold's News*, 5652, 1 February 1959:6. Review of *No Love for Johnnie* (Wilfrid
Fienburgh).

C2004 THE ELUSIVE HAVELOCK ELLIS. *Reynold's News*, 5653, 8
       February 1959:6. Review of *An Artist of Life* (John
       Stewart Collis); and *Havelock Ellis* (Arthur Calder-
       Marshall).

C2005 JOYCE AS HE REALLY WAS. *Reynold's News*, 5654, 15 Feb-
       ruary 1959:6. Review of *Our Friend James Joyce*
       (Mary and Padraic Colum); *Frank Harris* (Vincent
       Brome); and *The Vet's Daughter* (Barbara Comyns).

C2006 PROTEST BY A POLE. *Reynold's News*, 5655, 22 February
       1959:6. Review of *The Eighth Day of the Week* (Marek
       Hlasko).

C2007 CRITICS WHO KICK THE THEATRE. *Reynold's News*, 5656,
       1 March 1959:6. Review of *Sights and Spectacles*
       (Mary McCarthy).

C2008 SOUTH - AND FARTHER SOUTH. *Reynold's News*, 5657, 8
       March 1959:6. Review of *Before Noon* (Ramon Sender);
       and *The Flame Trees of Thika* (Elspeth Huxley).

C2009 THE FATHER OF MOLE AND CO. *Reynold's News*, 5658, 15
       March 1959:6. Review of *Kenneth Grahame* (Peter
       Green); *A Mixture of Frailties* (Robertson Davies);
       and *Homer and the Aether* (John Cowper Powys).

C2010 THE DRINA AND DONS. *Reynold's News*, 5659, 22 March
       1959:6. Review of *The Bridge on the Drina* (Ivo
       Andric); *Paper Boats* (E.M. Butler); and *The Art
       of Living* (F.L. Lucas).

C2011 RAYMOND CHANDLER AND ALLEN. *Reynold's News*, 5661,
       5 April 1959:6. Review of *All in a Lifetime*
       (Walter Allen); and *Persephone* (D. Streatfield).

C2012 WINES AND LOW SPIRITS. *Reynold's News*, 5662, 12
       April 1959:6. Review of *I Am an Alcoholic* (Ray-
       mond Blackburn); *Katherine Mansfield* (John Middle-
       ton Murry); and *Wine of Life* (Charles Gorham).

C2013 MONSTER'S MOTHER. *Reynold's News*, 5663, 19 April
       1959:6. Review of *Life of Mary Shelley* (Eileen
       Bigland); *Supernatural in the English Short Story*
       (Pamela Search); and *The Day It Rained Forever*
       (Ray Bradbury).

C2014 THE LONELY IN LONDON. *Reynold's News*, 5665, 3 May
       1959:6. Review of *The True Voice* (Gerda Charles);
       and *The Admen* (Shepherd Mead).

C2015 FROM A POET TO PEERESS. *Reynold's News*, 5667, 17
       May 1959:6. Review of *An Essay in Autobiography*
       (Boris Pasternak); *Flight and Pursuit* (Stuart Hol-
       royd); and *The Light of Common Day* (Diana Cooper).

C2016 SHORT STORY RETURNS. *Reynold's News*, 5668, 24 May
       1959:6. Review of *The Hours after Noon* (Paul
       Bowles); *Native Ground* (Philip Callow); *Lover Man*
       (Alston Anderson); *A Little More Time* (Jean Boley);
       and *The Best Short Stories of Ring Lardner*.

C2017 BERTRAND RUSSELL HAS EARNED OUR GRATITUDE. *Reynold's
       News*, 5669, 31 May 1959:6. Review of *My Philosophi-
       cal Development* (Bertrand Russell); *Attorney for the
       Damned* (A. Weinburg); and *America in Doubt* (Alexan-
       der Werth).

C2018 NOVELISTS IN FAR PLACES. *Reynold's News*, 5670, 7 June
       1959:6. Review of *Henderson the Rain King* (Saul
       Bellow); *A Call on Kuprin* (Maurice Edelman); and
       The Slide Area (Gavin Lambert).

C2019 SCIENCE IN FICTION. *Reynold's News*, 5671, 14 June
       1959:6. Review of *Ossian's Ride* (Fred Hoyle);
       Night of the Big Heat (John Lymington); *Atom of
       Doubt* (Brian George); *The Fig Tree* (Aubrey Menen);
       and *A Change of Mind* (G.M. Glaskin).

C2020 TOLSTOY IN HIS OWN WORDS. *Reynold's News*, 5672, 21
       June 1959:6. Review of *By Deeds of Truth* (Modest
       Hoffman and Andre Pierre); and *The Masterpiece and
       the Man* (Monk Gibbon).

C2021 OUR THEME IS LOVE. *Reynold's News*, 5673, 28 June 1959:
       6. Review of *On Love* (Ortega y Gasset); *Love and
       the French* (Nina Epton); and *Love is a Fervent Fire*
       (Robin Jenkins).

C2022 IS THIS THE REAL AMERICA. *Reynold's News*, 5674, 5
       July 1959:4. Review of *Some Came Running* (James
       Jones); *The Travels of Jaimie McPheeters* (Robert
       Lewis Taylor); and *The Affair in Arcady* (James
       Wellard).

C2023 TRUTH ABOUT THE NEW YORKER. *Reynold's News*, 5675, 12
       July 1959:4. Review of *The Years with Ross* (James
       Thurber); and *Child of the Twenties* (Frances Donald-
       son).

C2024 TECS, MYSTERIES AND THRILLERS. *Reynold's News*, 5676,
       19 July 1959:4. Review of *The Visited* (Joan O'Dono-
       van); *Divided We Fall* (Eric Burgess); *Scandal at
       High Chimneys* (John Dickson Carr); *The Count of Nine*
       (A.A. Fair); *Crime and Again* (Rex Stout); *The Eighth
       Circle* (Stanley Ellin); and *Venetian Blind* (William
       Haggard).

C2025 THE BRADFORD SCHOOLMASTER. *The Listener*, LXII (1582),
       23 July 1959:129–130.

C2026 PLAYWRIGHT OF THE WESTERN WORLD. *Reynold's News*,
       5677, 26 July 1959:4. Review of *J.M. Synge* (D.H.
       Greene and E.M. Stevens); and *Coleridge the Vision-
       ary* (J.B. Beer).

C2027 STRANGE WORLD OF ESP AND PSI. *Reynold's News*, 5678,
       2 August 1959:4. Review of *The Sixth Sense* (Rosaline
       Heywood).

C2028 CONFESSIONS OF A BLONDE. *Reynold's News*, 5679, 9
       August 1959:4. Review of *Beloved Infidel* (Sheila
       Graham and Gerold Frank).

C2029 A GOOD BOOK AND BAD LAW. *Reynold's News*, 5680, 16
       August 1959:6. Review of *Odd Man Out* (Eustace
       Chesser).

C2030 NORMAN COLLINS IN BOND STREET. *Reynold's News*, 5681,
       23 August 1959:6. Review of *Bond Street Story*
       (Norman Collins); *A Tinkling in the Twilight* (Ed-
       gar Mittelholzer); and *An Affair with the Moon*
       (Terence de Vere White).

C2031 RADICAL TEMPER. *New Statesman*, LVIII (1485), 29
       August 1959:240, 242.

C2032 STRANGE WORLD OF TEENAGERS. *Reynold's News*, 5682,
       30 August 1959:6. Review of *Absolute Beginners*
       (Colin MacInnes); and *The Lopsider* (Leopold Louth).

C2033 PARTY LINE ON LEISURE. *New Statesman*, LVIII (1486),
       5 September 1959:266–267.

C2034 TOO LITTLE MIND BUT TOO MUCH INTELLECT. *Reynold's
       News*, 5683, 6 September 1959:6. Review of *The
       House of Intellect* (Jacques Barzun); and *Conscious-
       ness and Society* (H. Stuart Hughes).

C2035 THOUGHTS ON THE FAR EAST. *Reynold's News*, 5684, 13
September 1959:6. Review of *The Face of War* (Martha
Gellhorn); *Journey to the Beginning* (Edgar Snow);
and *Meeting with Japan* (Fosco Maraini).

C2036 BEST ANTI-BOMB STORY YET. *Reynold's News*, 5685, 20
September 1959:4. Review of *Level 7* (Mordecai
Roshwald); *The Flowers of Hiroshima* (Edita Morris);
and *The Listening Wells* (Margaret Millar).

C2037 THE TRUTH ABOUT PROUST. *Reynold's News*, 5686, 27 September 1959:4. Review of *Marcel Proust* (George D.
Painter).

C2038 LAWYERS WITH THE LID OFF. *Reynold's News*, 5687, 4
October 1959:4. Review of *Lawyer Heal Thyself*
(Bill Mortlock).

C2039 FORTY YEARS ON. *John O'London's*, 1 (1), 8 October
1959:1-2.
Reprinted: *John O'London's Anthology* (1961) (B102).

C2040 CONGRATULATORY LETTER. *John O'London's*, 1 (1), 8
October 1959:29.

C2041 FINDING ANOTHER MAGIC MOUNTAIN. *Reynold's News*,
5688, 11 October 1959:6. Review of *Mount Analogue*
(Rene Danmal); and *Concise Encyclopaedia of Living
Faiths*.

C2042 A PUBLISHER AND OTHERS. *Reynold's News*, 5689, 18 October 1959:6. Review of *An Occupation for Gentlemen* (Frederic Warburg); *The Spare Chancellor* (Alastair Buchan); *The Prof* (R.F. Harrod); and *Your
Obedient Servant* (Harold Scott).

C2043 NOT EXACTLY A GAY LIFE. *Reynold's News*, 5690, 25
October 1959:6. Review of *Streetwalker*; *Let No Man
Write My Epitaph* (Willard Motley); and *Two Persons
Singular* (Joyce Howard).

C2044 AMERICA AS ITS AUTHORS REVEAL IT. *Reynold's News*,
5692, 8 November 1959:4. Review of *Advise and Consent* (Allen Drury); *The Lotus Eaters* (Gerald Green);
For 2¢ Plain (Harry Golden); and *Act One* (Moss Hart).

C2045 BLITZ NIGHT, VILLAGE DAYS. *Reynold's News*, 5693, 15
November 1959:10. Review of *The City That Wouldn't*

Die (Richard Collier); and *Cider with Rosie* (Laurie Lee).

1960

C2046   FIRST DRAMA IN THE ROUND. *Reynold's News*, 5700, 3
        January 1960:10. Review of *Shakespeare's Wooden O*
        (Leslie Hotson).

C2047   AMONG THE BIRDS AND LAYABOUTS. *Reynold's News*, 5702,
        17 January 1960:12. Review of *Stand on Me* (Frank
        Norman); and *Barbara Greer* (Stephen Birmingham).

C2048   TROUBLE DOWN UNDER. *New Statesman*, LIX (1506), 23
        January 1960:95-96.

C2049   WAIST-HIGH CULTURE AND THE ADMASS. *Reynold's News*,
        5707, 21 February 1960:8.

C2050   I HAVE BEEN HERE BEFORE. *Radio Times*, 146 (1898),
        25 March 1960:7.

C2051   LABOUR AND THE BOMB. *Reynold's News*, 5713, 3 April
        1960:8.

C2052   FLIBBERTIGIBBET. *New Statesman*, LIX (1518), 16 April
        1960:562-563. Review of *Critic's London Diary*
        (Kingsley Martin).

C2053   TIBOR DERY AND FREEDOM FOR WRITERS. *The Listener*,
        LXIII (1621), 21 April 1960:693.

C2054   UNSOUND TO THE SUMMIT. *New Statesman*, LIX (1521), 7
        May 1960:662, 664-665.
        Reprinted as four-page folded leaflet (A125).

C2055   AFTER PARIS - letter. *The Times*, 54777, 21 May 1960:9.

C2056   PRIESTLEY IN AUSTRALIA - letter. *Encounter*, XIV (6),
        June 1960:90-91.

C2057   MORGAN IN A MIRROR. *New Statesman*, LX (1531), 16
        July 1960:92-93.
        Reprinted: *The Moments* (1966).

C2058   VISION, VISION, MR WOODCOCK. *New Statesman*, LX (1538),
          3 September 1960:298.

C2059   C.N.D'S FUTURE. *New Statesman*, LX (1544), 15 October
          1960:557, 560.

C2060   UNILATERALISM UNDER FIRE - letter. *New Statesman*, LX
          (1553), 17 December 1960:972.

                              1961

C2061   DAMN THE AUTHORS. *New Statesman*, LXI (1556), 6 Janu-
          ary 1961:6, 8.

C2062   WHAT HAPPENED TO FALSTAFF. *The Listener*, LXV (1660),
          19 January 1961:127-129.

C2063   WHAT HAPPENED TO FALSTAFF. *The Listener*, LXV (1661),
          26 January 1961:173-176.

C2064   KENNEDY'S AMERICA. *Sunday Telegraph*, 2, 12 February
          1961:5.

C2065   NOTES ON A BAD LAW. *Man and Society*, 1 (1), Spring
          1961:28-29.

C2066   I HAD THE TIME. *Sunday Times*, 7206, 25 June 1961:
          21-22. 'I wrote Part Three *I Had the Time*, after
          a talk over lunch with Mr. H.V. Hodson, then editor
          of the *Sunday Times*. We agreed that I should write
          some literary reminiscences that could be serialised
          in the paper. From the first, however, I saw these
          thirty thousand words or so not as Sunday journalism
          but as part of a book....' Preface to *Margin Re-
          leased* (A130).
          Reprinted: *Encore: The Sunday Times Book* (1962) (B110).

C2067   THE GREAT PANJANDRUMS. *Sunday Times*, 7207, 2 July
          1961:21-22.
          Reprinted: *Margin Released* (1962).

C2068   THE GOLDEN GUSHER. *Sunday Times*, 7208, 9 July 1961:
          22-23.
          Reprinted: *Margin Released* (1962).

C2069 FIFTY YEARS OF TOBACCO. *New Statesman*, LXII (1583),
14 July 1961:46, 48.
Reprinted: *The Moments* (1966).

C2070 A RISE OF CURTAINS. *Sunday Times*, 7209, 16 July 1961:
22-23.
Reprinted: *Margin Released* (1962).

C2071 THE BRIGHT EYES OF DANGER. *Sunday Times*, 7210, 23
July 1961:24-25.
Reprinted: *Margin Released* (1962).

C2072 THE MAGIC BEANSTALK. *Contrast*, 1 (1), Autumn 1961:
4-10.

C2073 SHAKESPEARE AND THE MODERN WORLD. *Texas Quarterly*,
IV (3), Autumn 1961:159-168.
Reprinted: *The Moments* (1966).

C2074 Item omitted.

1962

C2075 AMBIENCE OR AGENDA. *New Statesman*, LXIII (1612), 2
February 1962:156, 158.
Reprinted: *The Moments* (1966).

C2076 ONE MAN WENT TO WAR. THE SWAN ARCADIAN. *Sunday Times*,
7243, 11 March 1962:25-26.
Reprinted: *Margin Released* (1962).

C2077 CLOSE-UP OF CHANDLER. *New Statesman*, LXIII (1618),
16 March 1962:379-380. Review of *Raymond Chandler
Speaking* and *The Second Chandler Omnibus*.
Reprinted: *The Moments* (1966).

C2078 THE ROAD TO NO-MAN'S LAND. *Sunday Times*, 7244, 18
March 1962:25-26.
Reprinted: *Margin Released* (1962).

C2079 THE DAY THE WORLD BLEW UP. *Sunday Times*, 7245, 25
March 1962:28-29.
Reprinted: *Margin Released* (1962).

C2080 GOOD BAD BOOKS. *Punch*, CCXLII (6342), 28 March 1962:
498-500. Review of *The Incomparable Bellairs*
(Agnes and Egerton Castle).

C2081 TAKING THE LID OFF. *Twentieth Century*, 171 (1013), Spring 1962:29-33.

C2082 THE LAST MARCH HOME. *Sunday Times*, 7246, 1 April 1962:26.
Reprinted: *Margin Released* (1962).

C2083 BRAND IN SURPRISE PINK. *Punch*, CCXLIII (6358), 18 July 1962:76-78.

C2084 TOPSIDE SCHOOLS. *New Statesman*, LXIV (1636), 20 July 1962:77-78.

C2085 RIBBONS AND GARTERS. *New Statesman*, LXIV (1638), 3 August 1962:140,142.

C2086 WIGS AND ROBES. *New Statesman*, LXIV (1640), 17 August 1962:196-197.

C2087 MITRES AND GAITERS. *New Statesman*, LXIV (1642), 31 August 1962:251,253.

C2088 SOME TOTS AND SIPS. *The Wine Mine*, Autumn 1962:6-8.
Reprinted: *The Wine Mine* (1962).

C2089 THE OBLIGING NOBLESSE. *New Statesman*, LXIV (1644), 14 September 1962:317.

C2090 VOICE OF BRITAIN. *New Statesman*, LXIV (1646), 28 September 1962:398,400.

C2091 CROWN WITHOUT ANCHOR. *New Statesman*, LXIV (1648), 12 October 1962:485,487.

C2092 TOPSIDE STORY. *New Statesman*, LXIV (1650), 26 October 1962:564,566.

C2093 CHILDREN'S CLASSICS REVISITED. *Punch*, CCXLIII (6373), 31 October 1962:632-635. Review of *Five Children and It* and *The Story of the Amulet* (E. Nesbit).

C2094 MY FATHER. *Sunday Telegraph*, 95, 26 November 1962:4-5.

C2095 ROAD TO SAMARKAND. *Sunday Times*, 7281, 2 December 1962:25-26.
Reprinted: *Encore Second Year* (1963) (B112) and *The Moments* (1966).

C2096 PREFACE TO SECOND ISSUE. *Our Generation Against Nuclear War*, 2, Winter 1962:3.

1963

C2097   THE HAPPY INTROVERT. *Review of English Literature*,
        4 (1), January 1963:25-32.
        Reprinted: *The Moments* (1966).

C2098   QUIET PLEASE! A NEW YEAR'S PROPOSAL. *The Nation*, 196
        (1), 5 January 1963:4-6.
        Reprinted: *One Hundred Years of the Nation* (1965).

C2099   TAKE OFF YOUR LABELS. *Vogue*, 120 (4), 1921, March
        1963:85,138.

C2100   FIFTY YEARS OF THE ENGLISH. *New Statesman*, LXV (1675),
        19 April 1963:560, 562, 564, 566.
        Reprinted: *The Moments* (1966).

C2101   EROTICISM, SEX AND LOVE. *Saturday Evening Post*, 236,
        27 April 1963:10, 14.
        Note: There are at least two other printed versions
        of this essay: one reprinted in *The Moments* (1966)
        under this title and another as 'From Honest to
        Nasty', *Sunday Telegraph*, 2 June 1963 (C2102).

C2102   FROM HONEST TO NASTY. *Sunday Telegraph*, 122, 2 June
        1963:4.
        Note: A slightly different text to that of 'Eroticism,
        Sex and Love', *Saturday Evening Post*, 27 April 1963
        (C2101). Reprinted with yet other minor changes in
        The Moments (1966).

C2103   TODAY'S BIG DEBATE ON MORALS. *Today*, 7 (175), 29
        June 1963:4.

C2104   BOLD SELF-SCRUTINY OF A DREAMING GIANT. *Sunday Tele-
        graph*, 127, 7 July 1963:16. Review of *Memories,
        Dreams, Reflections* (C.G. Jung).

C2105   RANDOM REFLECTIONS ON SEX. *New Statesman*, LXVI
        (1693), 23 August 1963:222, 224.

C2106   THE BLUE YONDER BOYS. *New Statesman*, LXVI (1696),
        13 September 1963:314, 316.
        Reprinted: *The Moments* (1966).

C2107   DARK JUNCTION. *New Statesman*, LXVI (1699), 4 October
        1963:439, 441.
        Reprinted: *The Moments* (1966).

C2108 LOST LATHER. *New Statesman*, LXVI (1702), 25 October
1963:561–562.
Reprinted: *The Moments* (1966).

C2109 A RUPTURED PEACE MOVEMENT. *The Nation*, 197 (13),
26 October 1963:251–253.

C2110 CONJURING. *New Statesman*, LXVI (1707), 28 November
1963:777–778.
Reprinted: *The Moments* (1963).

C2111 MARGINS OF THE MIND: THE INITIAL SHOCK. *Punch*, CCXLV
(6430), 4 December 1963:800–802.

C2112 NOTES FOR 1964. *New Statesman*, LXVI (1711), 27 December
ber 1963:936–938.

1964

C2113 CHEERFUL REALIST – letter. *New Statesman*, LXVII
(1712), 3 January 1964:12.

C2114 THE MAD SAD WORLD. *New Statesman*, LXVII (1716), 31
January 1964:162–164.
Reprinted: *The Moments* (1966).

C2115 THE CHARACTER OF SHAKESPEARE. *Show*, February 1964.

C2116 THESE OUR REVELS. *Sunday Telegraph*, 169, 24 April
1964:5.
Reprinted: *The Moments* (1966).

C2117 WHAT IS WRONG WITH BRITAIN? *Today*, 9 (221), 16 May
1964:22–24.

C2118 ARE YOU ENJOYING LIFE? *Today*, 9 (223), 30 May 1964:
24–27.

C2119 COMEDY IN SHAKESPEARE. *The Listener*, LXXI (1838),
18 June 1964:985–988. Abridged from 'What Happened
to Falstaff' first printed in *The Listener*, 19
January and 26 January 1961 (C2062–C2063).

C2120 A HOPEFUL CHURCH. *Sunday Times*, 7374, 13 September
1964:33. Review of *The Voyage Home* (Richard Church).

C2121 LET'S STOP KIDDING OURSELVES. *Sunday Citizen*, 5948 (107), 4 October 1964:17.

C2122 A WALK IN THE PARK. *Sunday Times Magazine*, 4 October 1964:40-41, 43.

C2123 TIME OUT OF MIND. *The Observer*, 9043, 25 October 1964:21. Extract from *Man and Time*, 1964.

C2124 THE SAD MOOD OF NEW YORK ON THE EVE OF POLLING IN AMERICA. *The Observer*, 9044, 1 November 1964:11.

C2125 WHY PHYLLIS BENTLEY 'COULD NOT RETREAT'. *Yorkshire Post*, 36543, 19 November 1964:8.

C2126 WOMEN DON'T RUN THE COUNTRY. *Saturday Evening Post*, 237, 12 December 1964:8+.
Reprinted: *Essays of Five Decades* (1969).

C2127 WHERE HONOUR IS DUE. *The Author*, Winter 1964:1-3.

1965

C2128 Letter. *Books*, 358, March/April 1965:72.
Note: Refers to publication of *The Good Companions* and to Priestley's being employed as a publisher's reader in the 1920s.

C2129 GAY WITH THE ARTS? *New Statesman*, LXIX (1780), 23 April 1965:639.
Reprinted: *The Moments* (1966).

C2130 BUZZ AND BRUIT. *New Statesman*, LXIX (1784), 21 May 1965:797.
Reprinted: *The Moments* (1966).

C2131 B.B.C.'s DUTY TO SOCIETY. *The Listener*, LXXIV (1892), 1 July 1965:11-12.

C2132 THE MOMENTS. *New Statesman*, LXX (1791), 9 July 1965: 41.
Reprinted: *The Moments* (1966).

C2133 SENSE AND SENSIBILITY - letter. *New Statesman*, LXX (1793), 23 July 1965:118.

C2134 GIVING UP CONFERENCES. *Punch*, CCXLIX (6516), 28 July
1965:124-126.
Reprinted: *The Moments* (1966).

C2135 LABOUR'S FIRST YEAR. A REVIEW OF THE GOVERNMENT'S
RECORD. RADICALS AND COMMENT ON THE ANNIVERSARY.
New Statesman, LXX (1805), 15 October 1965:557.

C2136 DOUBTS ABOUT DYNAMISM. *New Statesman*, LXX (1807),
29 October 1965:641.
Reprinted: *The Moments* (1966).

C2137 STUDENT MOBS. *New Statesman*, LXX (1811), 26 November
1965:823.
Reprinted: *The Moments* (1966).

C2138 A CHILD'S GUIDE TO GENES: ENGLISH SOCIAL CLASSES.
Punch, CCXLIX (6535), 8 December 1965:826-828.

C2139 CENSOR AND STAGE. *New Statesman*, LXX (1814), 17 December 1965:967.
Reprinted: *The Moments* (1966).

C2140 MY MUSICAL LIFE. *The Wine Mine*, Winter 1965:10-12.

1966

C2141 THE MUSIC-HALLS. *New Statesman*, 71 (1820), 28 January
1966:117.
Reprinted: *The Moments* (1966).

C2142 WRONG ISM. *New Statesman*, 71 (1824), 25 February
1966:253.
Reprinted: *The Moments* (1966).

C2143 SIMPLE HOOLIGANISM? *Atlas*, March 1966.

C2144 HOW TO BE AN AUTHOR: READ GOOD AUTHORS - facsimile
letter. *Sunday Times Magazine*, 6 March 1966:43.

C2145 WUTHERING HEIGHTS TO ARCADIA IN A SHARP TWO-HOUR WALK.
Life, 7 March 1966:22-29.

C2146 ONE CLERK'S LIFE. *The Clerk*, 6 (4), April 1966:4.

C2147 WRITER AT WORK. *New Statesman*, 71 (1829), 1 April
    1966:461.
    Reprinted: *The Moments* (1966).

C2148 SIR ARTHUR BLISS - 75TH BIRTHDAY. *Composer*, 20, Summer
    1966:12-13.

C2149 GROWING OLD. *New Statesman*, 72 (1846), 29 July 1966:
    161.
    Reprinted: *Essays of Five Decades* (1969).

C2150 RADIO AND THE WRITER: THE BASIC PROBLEM. *The Author*,
    LXXVII (3), Autumn 1966:17-19.

C2151 THE LESSON OF GARFIELD SOBERS. *New Statesman*, 72
    (1852), 9 September 1966:347.

C2152 MRS DOROTHY WHIPPLE. *The Times*, 56742, 21 September
    1966:12.

C2153 DANDY DAYS. *New Statesman*, 72 (1860), 4 November
    1966:659.
    Reprinted: *Essays of Five Decades* (1969).

C2154 LIGHT IN A THOUSAND DARK PLACES. *Horizon*, VIII (1),
    Winter 1966:33-37.

1967

C2155 FACT OR FICTION? *New Statesman*, 73 (1869), 6 January
    1967:9.
    Reprinted: *Essays of Five Decades* (1969).

C2156 MOSTLY ABOUT NOTHING. *New Statesman*, 73 (1877), 3
    March 1967:289.

C2157 DISTURBING? *New Statesman*, 73 (1880), 24 March 1967:
    401.
    Reprinted: *Essays of Five Decades* (1969).

C2158 THE SKULL CINEMA. *New Statesman*, 73 (1886), 5 May
    1967:611.
    Reprinted: *Essays of Five Decades* (1969).

C2159 OFF-SHORE ISLAND MAN. *New Statesman*, 73 (1889), 26
    May 1967:715.
    Reprinted: *Essays of Five Decades* (1969).

C2160   AUTHOR'S CHOICE - UNCLE PHIL ON TV including insert
        WHY I CHOSE THIS STORY (initialled J.B.P.).
        Argosy, XXVIII (7), July 1967:34-53.

C2161   A HOLIDAY IN GOUACHE. *Envoy*, August 1967:24-29.

C2162   MESSAGE FROM J.B. PRIESTLEY. *Anglo-Soviet Journal*,
        28 (1), October 1967:4. On fiftieth anniversary of
        the Russian Revolution 1917-1967.

C2163   AUTHORS TAKE SIDES ON VIETNAM. *Envoy*, September 1967:
        14-15.
        Reprinted: *Authors Take Sides on Vietnam* edited by
        Cecil Woolf and John Bagguley (1967) (B125).

                            1968

C2164   THE MYTHS. *New Statesman*, 75 (1922), 12 January 1968:
        37.

C2165   HOME THOUGHTS FROM HOME. *New Statesman*, 75 (1946),
        28 June 1968:865.

C2166   PRIESTLEY'S BRADFORD. *Telegraph and Argus Centenary
        Supplement 1868-1968*, 16 July 1968:3.

C2167   WHO'S BARMY? *New Statesman*, 76 (1952), 8 August
        1968:165.

C2168   BUT MAKING WHAT? *Sunday Times*, 7579, 1 September
        1968:27. Review of *Making It* (Norman Podhoretz).

C2169   ANYONE FOR TENNIS? *Radio Times*, 180 (2341), 19 Sep-
        tember 1968:40.

                            1969

C2170   OTHER WRITERS ON SIMENON: J.B. PRIESTLEY. *Adam
        International Review*, Nos 328-330, Thirty-fourth
        year 1969:50.

C2171   ON CIVILISATION. *Sunday Times*, 7617, 25 May 1969:12.
        1969:51. Initialled J.B.P.

C2172   GEORGE BERNARD SHAW. *Sunday Times Magazine*, 14 September 1969:51.   Initialled J.B.P.

C2173   A TIME FOR BEAU BRUMMEL. *Daily Telegraph Magazine*, 261, 10 October 1969:554, 556.

C2174   AT THE REMBRANDT SHOW. *New Statesman*, 78 (2018), 14 November 1969:684.   The second half of this account is reprinted in *Outcries and Asides* (1974).

C2175   LIFE CLASS. *Sunday Times*, 7643, 23 November 1969:51.

C2176   STOP THIS MAD, BAD, NOISY WORLD - IT'S TIME TO GET OFF. *T.V. Times*, 58 (65), 11 December 1969:18.

C2177   AMERICA: DREAM AND SCENE. *New Statesman*, 78 (2022), 12 December 1969:852-853.   Excerpts published in *Atlas*, March 1970 under title of IS AMERICA COMING OF AGE?

C2178   AND I PREFER THE OLD STYLE. *T.V. Times*, 58 (66), 18 December 1969:19.

1970

C2179   ISN'T IT BETTER TO BE A SQUARE THAN A SHORT BROKEN LINE? *T.V. Times*, 58 (1), 1 January 1970:20.

C2180   WE'RE RUSHING HEADLONG INTO CAPITAL MURDER. *T.V. Times*, 58 (2), 8 January 1970:13.

C2181   IS AMERICA COMING OF AGE? *Atlas*, March 1970. Reprinted from *New Statesman*, 12 December 1969 (C2177).

C2182   CONIFERS IN YORKSHIRE DALES - letter. *The Times*, 57809, 3 March 1970:11.

C2183   LET'S RAISE HELL. *Daily Mail*, 22967, 7 March 1970:10.

C2184   THE TRUTH ABOUT THE ENGLISH (AND THEIR BLOODY-MINDED-NESS). *Sunday Times*, 7686, 20 September 1970:12.

C2185   PRIESTLEY BOOKS A BOX AT THEATRE - letter quoted at length. *Yorkshire Post*, 38384, 28 October 1970:6.

C2186　GOOD OLD TEDDIE. *The Observer Magazine*, 1 November 1970:14-22, 25-26, 28, 31 . Extract from *The Edwardians* (1970) (A153).

C2187　THE GOLDEN AGE WITH THE GILT OFF. *The Observer Magazine*, 8 November 1970:32-35, 37-39, 41-42. Extract from *The Edwardians* (1970) (A153).

C2188　DEAN OF STAGECRAFT. *Sunday Times*, 7694, 15 November 1970:29. Review of *An Autobiography 1888-1927* (Basil Dean).

C2189　FALLING BACKWARD DOWN AN ESCALATOR. *New Statesman*, 80 (2075), 25 December 1970:860.

1971

C2190　THINKING ABOUT BEETHOVEN. *Adam International Review*, Nos 346-348, Thirty-fifth year, 1971:10.

C2191　MY FRIEND BLISS. *Musical Times*, 112 (1542), August 1971:740-741.

C2192　TO MARKET, TO MARKET? *New Statesman*, 82 (2108), 13 August 1971:205.

C2193　THE MEANING OF BROWN EGGS. *New Statesman*, 82 (2125), 10 December 1971:815. Excerpts from this essay were reprinted in the *New York Times*, 17 December 1971, where it prompted intermittent correspondence until the beginning of February. It was later included in amended form in *Outcries and Asides* (1974) (A159).

C2194　CURSE THE CAR. *New Statesman*, 82 (2126), 17 December 1971:857.

C2195　FASHION HATER. *New Statesman*, 82 (2127), 24 December 1971:886.
Reprinted in amended form: *Outcries and Asides* (1974).

C2196　DRINKING TIME. *New Statesman*, 82 (2128), 31 December 1971:921.
Reprinted in amended form: *Outcries and Asides* (1974).

1972

C2197   SHOWBIZ. *New Statesman*, 83 (2129), 6 January 1972:11.
      Reprinted in amended form: *Outcries and Asides* (1974).

C2198   AFTER WHITAKER. *New Statesman*, 83 (2130), 14 January
      1972:43.
      Reprinted in amended form: *Outcries and Asides* (1974).

C2199   BEGGING TO DIFFER. *New Statesman*, 83 (2131), 21
      January 1972:78.

C2200   RUNNING DOWN. *New Statesman*, 83 (2132), 28 January
      1972:110.

C2201   THE SELVES. *New Statesman*, 83 (2133), 4 February
      1972:142.

C2202   TOUCH OF FROST. *New Statesman*, 83 (2134), 11 February
      1972:175.
      Reprinted in amended form: *Outcries and Asides* (1974).

C2203   A NOTE ON THE THEATRE. *New Statesman*, 83 (2135), 18
      February 1972:207.
      Reprinted in amended form: *Outcries and Asides* (1974).

C2204   LOLLY AND HARD CASH. *New Statesman*, 83 (2136), 25
      February 1972:239-240.
      Reprinted in amended form: *Outcries and Asides* (1974).

C2205   LETTER FROM LOS ANGELES. *New Statesman*, 84 (2137), 3
      March 1972:274-275.

C2206   NO FOUNDATION? *New Statesman*, 84 (2138), 10 March
      1972:309.

C2207   CLASS. *New Statesman*, 84 (2139), 17 March 1972:344.

C2208   AT SCHOOL. *New Statesman*, 84 (2140), 24 March 1972:
      390.

C2209   WHAT SHOULD WE DO ABOUT POLLUTION? *The Countryman*,
      77 (1), Spring 1972:29.

C2210   BRIEF THANKSGIVING. *New Statesman*, 84 (2142), 7
      April 1972:455.

C2211   THE GOLDEN DAYS OF QUEEN VICTORIA. *The Observer Magazine*, 9 April 1972:16-19, 22-23, 25-26. Extract from *Victoria's Heyday* (1972).

C2212   LOST GRANVILLE. *New Statesman*, 84 (2143), 14 April 1972:489.

C2213   PLEASURES AND PALACES. *The Observer Magazine*, 16 April 1972:36-39, 41-42, 44, 46, 49. Extract from *Victoria's Heyday* (1972).

C2214   STOP FEELING GHOUL. *New Statesman*, 84 (2144), 21 April 1972:526.
Reprinted in amended form: *Outcries and Asides* (1974).

C2215   HIGHER EDUCATION. *New Statesman*, 84 (2145), 28 April 1972:561.
Reprinted in amended form: *Outcries and Asides* (1974).

C2216   REVIEW of *The Pick of Punch* edited by William Davis. *Punch*, 263 (6889), 20 September 1972:384.

C2217   PRIESTLEY'S SENTIMENTAL JOURNEY. *The Observer Magazine*, 1 October 1972:20-22, 25-26.

C2218   TIME AND THE LENS. *Sunday Times Magazine*, 15 October 1972:59, 61, 63.

C2219   IF ONLY TALLULAH HAD MARRIED THE ONE MAN SHE LOVED. *Daily Mail*, 23784, 9 November 1972:7. Review of *Tallulah - Darling of the Gods* (Kieran Tunney).

C2220   THE MEMORABLE YEAR OF 1942. *Woman*, 71 (1854), 30 December 1972:28.

1973

C2221   Letter. *Yorkshire Arts Association: April in Yorkshire*, April 1973. Wishing success to Ilkley Literature Festival (Extra insert).

C2222   BRADFORD THAT I KNEW BEST. *Telegraph and Argus*, 32734, 7 September 1973:6.

C2223   Item omitted.

C2224 PARADISE WITH PREMONITIONS OF HELL. *The Observer Magazine*, 9 September 1973:36–37, 39, 41, 43.

1974

C2225 FRIDAY NIGHT IS HALLE NIGHT. *Halle Magazine*, 2 (2), Spring 1974:3.

C2226 ALISTAIR COOKE'S AMERICA AND MINE. *Books and Bookmen*, 19 (7), 223, April 1974:17–18.

C2227 THOUGH OFTEN QUITE SUCCESSFUL I WAS NEVER A FASHIONABLE PLAYWRIGHT. *The Guardian*, 39711, 5 April 1974:10.

C2228 ALISTAIR COOKE'S AMERICA AND MINE. *Books and Bookmen*, 19 (8), 224, May 1974:21–22.

C2229 A MAN OF HIS WORD. *The Observer*, 4535, 28 April 1974: 12.

C2230 AND WHAT PRIESTLEY THINKS OF HIMSELF. *The Listener*, 92 (2372), 12 September 1974:336–338.

C2231 IN THE LIMELIGHT. *Sunday Times*, 7898, 27 October 1974:31. Review of *My Life in Pictures* (Charles Chaplin).

C2232 SUPPRESSION TURNS A BELIEVER INTO A FANATIC. *The Times*, 59264, 7 December 1974:16.

C2233 LET'S PRETEND WE'RE ALL IN ALBANIA. *Sunday Times*, 7906, 22 December 1974:12.

C2234 UNSOCIAL HOURS. *Sunday Times*, 7907, 29 December 1974:9.

C2235 UNDERGROUND. *Illustrated London News*, Christmas 1974: 28–30.
Reprinted: *The Carfitt Crisis* (1975).

1975

C2236 LET THE PEOPLE SING. *Books and Bookmen*, 20 (5), 233,
February 1975. Review of *A Touch of the Times:
Songs of Social Change* (Roy Palmer).

C2237 LET THE PEOPLE SING 2. *Books and Bookmen*, 20 (6),
234, March 1975:35-37.

C2238 SIR NEVILLE CARDUS. *The Guardian*, 39989, 1 March
1975:8.
Reprinted: *The Bedside 'Guardian'*, 24 (1975) (B146).

C2239 MIDDLE CLASS AWAKENING. *Sunday Times*, 7918, 16 March
1975:16.

C2240 MR HEALEY SHOULD HEAR THE SQUEAK OF PIPS. *Sunday
Times*, 7921, 6 April 1975:17.

C2241 J.B. PRIESTLEY ON THE HEYDAY OF THE ROYALS. *The Observer Magazine*, 20 April 1975:25-26, 29.

C2242 THE ENGLISH DISEASE. *Sunday Times*, 7931, 15 June
1975:17.

C2243 DECADE OF DREAMERS. *Books and Bookmen*, 20 (10), 238,
July 1975:26-27. Review of *The Thirties* (Julian
Symons).

C2244 GODS SEEN FROM THE STALLS. *Daily Telegraph Magazine*,
564, 19 September 1975:39-40, 42, 44, 46. Extract
from *Particular Pleasures* (1975) (A161).

C2245 SIX CLOWNS. *Illustrated London News*, 263 (6927),
October 1975:46-47, 49. Extracts from *Particular
Pleasures* (1975).

C2246 LIBERTY BUT NOT EQUALITY SHOULD BE THE U.K. WATCHWORD.
Sunday Telegraph, 766, 2 November 1975:23.
Reprinted: *What's Wrong with Britain?* (1978) (B152).

C2247 A WARM SNOWMAN. *Books and Bookmen*, 21 (8), 243,
December 1975:28-29. Review of *Trollope* (C.P.
Snow).

C2248 PERSONAL CHOICE 1975. *The Listener*, 94 (2438), 25
December 1975 and 1 January 1976:870.

1976

C2249 CRABBED OLD AGE. *The Times* (Saturday Review section),
       59836, 16 October 1976:6. Extract from *Instead
       of the Trees* (1977) (A165).

C2250 TO HELL WITH GOOD INTENT. *Sunday Telegraph Magazine*,
       7, 24 October 1976:7.

1977

C2251 PHILOSOPHER OF FILM. *Books and Bookmen*, 22 (5), 257,
       February 1977:44. Review of *Jacques Tati* (Penelope
       Gilliatt).

C2252 FAULTY WINKS. *Sunday Times Magazine*, 25 September
       1977:12. Short paragraph in reply to question on
       how he coped with insomnia.

1978

C2253 CACTUS COUNTRY. *The Observer Magazine*, 1 January
       1978:20.

C2254 POETS' ISLAND. *The Observer Magazine*, 27 August
       1978:30-31.

C2255 A LIFE IN THE DAY OF. *Sunday Times Magazine*, 1
       October 1978:126.

1979

C2256 JOURNEY INTO DAYLIGHT. *The Listener*, 101 (2594), 18
       January 1979:108, 110. First printed *The Listener*,
       17 May 1946 (C1406).

C2257 A DALESMAN'S DIARY (includes message from J.B. Priest-
       ley). *The Dalesman*, 40 (12), March 1979:991.
       Note: refers to message in first issue of *Yorkshire
       Dalesman*, April 1939 (C1143).

ADDENDA

C2258   THREE EPIGRAMS: THE AUTHOR OF THE SHROPSHIRE LAD; THE
         POETRY OF W.B. YEATS; AE. *Cambridge Review*, XLIII
         (1058), 25 November 1921:114.
         Reprinted: *Brief Diversions* (1922) (A2).

C2259   FOUR EPIGRAMS: COLERIDGE, TO PROFESSOR G.B. SAINTS-
         BURY. A VERY OLD MAN. TO THE PRODUCER OF A RECENT
         LIGHT ENTERTAINMENT. *Cambridge Review*, XLIII
         (1060), 20 January 1922:152.
         Reprinted: *Brief Diversions* (1922).

C2260   MR LUBBOCK AND THE CRAFT OF FICTION. *Cambridge Re-
         view*, XLIII (1067), 10 March 1922:282. Review of
         The Craft of Fiction (Percy Lubbock).

C2261   AUDACITY IN LITERATURE. *The Challenge*, n.s. 1 (5),
         27 October 1922:89-90. Initialled J.B.P.
         Reprinted: *Papers from Lilliput* (1922) (A3) under the
         title of 'Audacity in Authorship'.

C2262   A DEFENCE OF COMFORT. *The Challenge*, n.s. II (27),
         28 September 1923:530-532.

C2263   CHILDREN ARE A NUISANCE, BUT. *Daily Mirror*, 7664, 7
         June 1928:6.

C2264   WHY SHOULD WE BE DULL? *Daily Mirror*, 7678, 23 June
         1928:13.

C2265   A FRESH GLANCE AT OUR SEASIDE RESORTS. *Daily Mirror*,
         7690, 7 July 1928:9.

C2266   WHY FOOTBALL IS SO POPULAR. *Daily Mirror*, 7732, 25
         August 1928:13.

C2267   WHY WOMEN LIKE THRILLERS. *Daily Mirror*, 7742, 6 Sep-
         tember 1928:13.

C2268   DO WE ALL SMOKE TOO MUCH? *Daily Mirror*, 7764, 2 Oc-
         tober 1928:13.

C2269   WHAT I THINK OF THE WAR NOW. *Daily Mirror*, 7799,
         12 November 1928:13.

C2270   WHY ARE WE SO GLOOMY? *Daily Mirror*, 7813, 28 November
         1928:11.

C2271   HOW MANY DAYS TO CHRISTMAS? *Daily Mirror*, 7827, 14
        December 1928:11.

C2272   ENTER NINETEEN TWENTYNINE. *Daily Mirror*, 7840, 1
        January 1929:4.

C2273   THESE BORED COSMOPOLITES. *Daily Mirror*, 7869, 4 Feb-
        ruary 1929:13.

C2274   C.E. MONTAGUE. *Everyman*, 2 (38), 17 October 1929:
        283-284.

C2275   MY FAVOURITE QUOTATION. *John O'London's*, XXVI (659),
        Christmas 1931:335.

C2276   HERE AND NOW. *Week-End Review*, VII (156), 4 March
        1933:245-246.

C2277   WHY DOES BRITAIN STAND IT? *Sunday Chronicle*, 2520,
        10 December 1933:9.

C2278   THE WICKEDEST TAX IN THE WORLD. *Sunday Chronicle*,
        2523, 31 December 1933:7.

C2279   A JUBILEE GATHERING. *Dent's Almanack*, No. 1, 1938:
        4-5. Extract from speech at dinner to celebrate
        the 50th Anniversary of the publishing house of
        J.M. Dent.

C2280   LUXURY ON TAP. *News Chronicle*, 29056, 19 June 1939:10.

C2281   PRIESTLEY ON BRITISH FILMS. *The Era*, 102 (5257),
        6 July 1939:1.
        Note: In the form of an interview with R.B. Marriott
        but almost exclusively in Priestley's own words.

C2282   TRUTH ABOUT EVACUATION. *News Chronicle*, 29141, 26
        September 1939:3.

C2283   THE MILITARY MOUSTACHE IS BEGINNING TO SPROUT AGAIN.
        News Chronicle, 29162, 20 October 1939:3.

C2284   BRITAIN SPEAKS. *The Listener*, XXIII (598), 27 June
        1940:1187-1188.
        Reprinted: *Britain Speaks* (1940) (A57).

C2285   OUT WITH THE PARASHOTS. *Answers*, CV (2721), 27 July
        1940:3.
        Reprinted: *Postscripts* (1940) (A56).

C2286 THAT'S THE STUFF TO GIVE 'EM! *Answers,* CV (2724), 17
       August 1940:3.
       Reprinted: *Postscripts* (1940) (A56).

C2287 DON'T LET THE WAR GET YOU DOWN. *Answers,* CV (2730),
       28 September 1940:3.
       Reprinted: *Postscripts* (1940) (A56).

C2288 HERE IN THE NORTH THEY SAY. *Sunday Express,* 1135,
       29 September 1940:2.

C2289 THE TRIUMPH OF THE WOMEN. *Answers,* CV (2734), 26
       October 1940:3.
       Reprinted: *Postscripts* (1940) (A56).

C2290 THE PIE THEY COULDN'T BOMB. *Answers,* CV (2735), 2
       November 1940:3.
       Reprinted: *Postscripts* (1940) (A56).

C2291 I'M NOT BLAMING ANYBODY, BUT. *Answers,* CVI (2736), 9
       November 1940:3.
       Reprinted: *Postscripts* (1940) (A56).

C2292 RIBBENTROP SHOULD HAVE MET 'MA'. *Answers,* CVI (2737),
       16 November 1940:3.
       Reprinted: *Postscripts* (1940) (A56).

C2293 MY LAST POSTSCRIPT. *Answers,* CVI (2738), 23 November
       1940:3.
       Reprinted: *Postscripts* (1940) (A56).

C2294 DUNKIRK - EXCURSION TO HELL! *Answers,* CVI (2739),
       30 November 1940:3.
       Reprinted: *Postscripts* (1940) (A56).

C2295 PLAIN WORDS ABOUT PLAYS. *Tribune,* 350, 10 September
       1943:12.

C2296 THE MODERN THEATRE. *John O'London's,* XLIX (1216),
       24 September 1943:243. Review of *Theatre in
       Soviet Russia* (Andre van Gyseghem).

C2297 REFRIGERATORS OR SQUARE MEALS? *Reynold's News,* 4892,
       4 June 1944:2.

C2298 MR PRIESTLEY EXPLAINS THE ENGLISH. *Maclure's Maga-
       zine,* 15 June 1944:5-6, 41-44.

C2299 YOUR RADIO LICENCE SHOULD COST MORE. *Reynold's News,*
       4911, 15 October 1944:2.

C2300   GREATEST EVENT IN A THOUSAND YEARS. *Reynold's News*,
        4950, 15 July 1945:4.

C2301   POLITICAL AND SOCIAL DEMOCRACY. *Oxford Mail*, 5686,
        19 March 1947:2.

C2302   HENRY WALLACE REPRESENTS THE TRUE USA. *Oxford Mail*,
        5715, 23 April 1947:2.

C2303   HARVEST HOME. *Daily Herald*, 9849, 25 September
        1947:2.

C2304   LETTERS FROM TWO ISLANDS. *New Statesman*, XXXVIII
        (966), 10 September 1949:269-270.

C2305   LETTERS FROM TWO ISLANDS. *New Statesman*, XXXVIII
        (967), 17 September 1949:297.

C2306   A PLEA FOR THE TRAVELLER. *The Listener*, XLII (1078),
        22 September 1949:508.

C2307   LETTERS FROM TWO ISLANDS. *New Statesman*, XXXVIII
        (968), 24 September 1949:324.

C2308   DANNY KAYE'S SECRET. *News Chronicle*, 32761, 2 June
        1951:2.

C2309   A STRANGE GIRL. *Collier's Magazine*, 131, 9 May 1953:
        16-17.
        Reprinted: *The Other Place* (1953) (A108).

C2310   REVIEW of *Autobiography* (David Low). *New York Times
        Book Review*, 7 April 1957:1.

C2311   THIS IS WHERE THE MASS MEDIA FAIL. *Oxford Mail*, 9121,
        15 April 1958:4.

C2312   A WIFE WHO KEPT A DIARY. *Reynold's News*, 5643, 30
        November 1958:6. Review of *A Prison, A Paradise*
        (Loran Hurnscot); *A Painter of Our Time* (John
        Berger); and *Under Six Reigns* (G.P. Gooch).

C2313   THE TWO NOVELISTS. *Reynold's News*, 5660, 29 March
        1959:6. Review of *World of Henry Orient* (Nora
        Johnson); and *The Following Seasons* (Donald Ford).

C2314   WESTERN AND MID-EASTERN. *Reynold's News*, 5666, 10
        May 1959:6. Review of *Warlock* (Oakley Hall); and
        The Romance of the Rubaiyat (A.J. Arberry).

C2315 GOOD NOVEL - BUT WHERE'S THE BOMB. *Reynold's News*,
        5691, 1 November 1959:4. Review of *The Humbler
        Creation* (Pamela Hansford Johnson); *Everybody Is a
        God* (Raymond Postgate); *The Light Infantry Ball*
        (Hamilton Basso); *The Big Company Look* (J.H. Howells);
        and *Love on a Branch Line* (John Hadfield).

C2316 THE FADING IMAGE. *New Statesman*, LXI (1575), 19 May
        1961:784-786.

C2317 A CERTAIN PIETY. *New Statesman*, 84 (2141), 31 March
        1972:422.

C2318 WHY THE WRITTEN WORD STILL MATTERS. *Now!* No. 1, 14
        September 1979:114.

D. THEATRE PROGRAMMES

Only those programmes which contain specially written notes by J.B. Priestley, or are otherwise of particular interest, are recorded here. Most of them are accessible for reference in the Enthoven Theatre Collection, Department of Prints and Drawings, Victoria and Albert Museum, South Kensington, London SW7.

D1 AUTHOR'S NOTE. *How Are They at Home?* Apollo Theatre (London), 1944.

D2 NOTES ON THE PLAY and UNDER THE BEACON AGAIN. *An Inspector Calls*, Malvern Festival Theatre, 1965.

D3 MR KETTLE AND MRS MOON. *The Scandalous Affair of Mr Kettle and Mrs Moon*, Malvern Festival Theatre, 1965.

D4 SOME NOTES ON THE PLAY. *When We Are Married*, Nottingham Playhouse, 1965.

D5 J.B. PRIESTLEY. *When We Are Married*, Leeds Grand Theatre and Opera House, 1970. Unsigned.

Note: This item consists of two paragraphs: the first, giving the usual brief biographical information, is in the third person, and is followed, without warning or indication, by Priestley's own comments.

D6 'Untitled Introduction' to *J.B. Priestley's Open House*, Phoenix Theatre (Leicester), 1972.

Note: 'An evening's entertainment consisting of excerpts from my plays, novels and essays'.

D7 PROGRAMME NOTE. *An Inspector Calls*, Mermaid Theatre (London), 1973.

Note: Also includes 'Priestley on Theatre', an excerpt from *Margin Released* (A130).

D8   AUTHOR'S PROGRAMME NOTE. *Time and the Conways*, 69
     Theatre Company at the Royal Exchange, Manchester,
     1973.

D9   'Untitled Reflections'. *I Have Been Here Before*, Welsh
     Drama Company – Theatre y wern, Aberystwyth; Theatr
     Gwynedd, Bangor; and Sherman Theatre, University
     College, Cardiff, 1974.

D10 EDWARDIAN THEATREGOING, excerpt from *The Edwardians*
     (A153), and RAGTIME, excerpt from *Margin Released*
     (A130). *Eden End*, The National Theatre (London), 1974.

     Note: Also includes 'J.B. Priestley and Eden End' by
     Gareth Lloyd Evans.

E. ADVERTISEMENTS

A number of diverse items are collected here because their
only common characteristic is that they were all, in one form
or another, advertisements.

E1   SOME OPINIONS ON EVERYMAN'S ENCYCLOPAEDIA. The reverse
     side of a bookmark, *Everyman's Encyclopaedia*, measuring
     approximately 17cm x 6 cm. Priestley was one of five who
     offered an opinion on the encyclopaedia; the others were
     Sir Austen Chamberlain, Sir Josiah Stamp, Sir Arthur
     Keith, and Ethel, Viscountess Snowden. Copies have been
     found printed on light green, cream, and bright blue
     coloured paper.

E2   MR J.B. PRIESTLEY WRITES in support of The Cancer Hospi-
     tal (Free), Fulham Road, London SW3. A letter accompanied
     by a photograph placed in various periodicals. Noted in
     Theatre World, April 1935.

E3   THE NEW LONELINESS.
     London and New York, Reader's Digest Association Limited,
        1938.

     Note: A mail-order-advertising leaflet, 15cm x 8½cm, ex-
     tolling the merits of *The Reader's Digest* in alleviating
     the loneliness of modern city life, illustrated by a head
     and shoulders drawing of Priestley. More than one version
     exists: the text remains the same but with a different
     drawing.

E4   In 1940 Lever Brothers, Port Sunlight Ltd, evolved a scheme
     whereby popular personalities were commissioned to write a
     short series of short up-lift articles which were inserted
     weekly in the national press under the title 'Through the
     Sunlight Window'. The first series was written by J.B.
     Priestley as follows:

                  WAR-TIME OPPORTUNITY   May 1940
                  A LITTLE IMAGINATION   May 1940

TAKE THE RAILINGS AWAY   May 1940
I ENJOY SPLITTING LOGS   June 1940
TAKE YOUR OWN TOWEL   June 1940
THE REASON FOR PRAYER   June 1940

It is not possible to give a more exact date as they did
not appear on the same day in all the national newspapers.
WAR-TIME OPPORTUNITY, for example, was printed in *Daily
Mail*, 6 May 1940 and in *News Chronicle*, 9 May 1940.

E5 J.B. PRIESTLEY WRITES FOR OXFAM.
    Leaflet 22½cm x 9½cm, 1966.
    On reverse side a letter explains why he donated *The
    Moments* (A138) to Oxfam. At the foot is a printed
    order form.

F. NON-PRINT PUBLICATIONS

Stage Plays

F1 THE REBELS

Note: A thirty-minute one-act play performed by Bradford
Civic Playhouse, October 1938. The scene is a North-
country household where the head of the house is accus-
tomed to spend his evenings listening to the radio. One
evening the radio tells him a few home truths.... It is
tempting to discern here the germ of 'Uncle Phil on TV'
(A108).

F2 THE BAD SAMARITAN

Note: Produced at the Liverpool Playhouse in 1937. 'Mr
Priestley's charlatan hero ... is a young doctor. An il-
legal operation performed to oblige a friend has finished
his career with a term in gaol. Free once more, he finds
as a travelling mystic a profession in which his clinical
experience is of use, for it enables him to 'Divine' the
medical history of his clients. In Brassdale he meets a
woman who figured in a brief but vividly remembered epi-
sode of his early life. From that moment his caution drops
off and he is imbroiled in a bitter feud with the foremost
(and also most disreputable) manipulators of Brassdale's
affairs' ('New Priestley Play', *Manchester Guardian*, 25
March 1937). In *Rain upon Godshill* Priestley remarks: 'I
was so much dissatisfied with it that not only did I not
bring it to London but I did not even have it printed.'

F3 JENNY VILLIERS

Note: Produced in Bristol 1946 and published as a novel
in 1947 (A84).

F4 THE WHITE COUNTESS by J.B. Priestley and Jacquetta Hawkes

Note: Produced at the Gaiety Theatre, Dublin, February

1974 and at the Saville Theatre, London, March 1974
where it was withdrawn after only five performances.

F5   THESE OUR ACTORS

Note: Produced in Glasgow 1956. Originally intended for
publication as a novel dealing with a period of ten years
in the life of an actor. The unfinished typescript is
now at the Humanities Research Center, The University of
Texas.

F6   THE THIRTY FIRST OF JUNE

Note: Produced in the Old Theatre, London School of
Economics, February 1957. Published as a novel in 1961
(A127).

F7   TAKE THE FOOL AWAY

Note: First staged at the Burg Theatre, Vienna, December
1955. Its British premiere was at the Nottingham Playhouse, September 1959. 'The story ... is contained in a
nightmare, which transports a music hall clown out of
Victorian London on the eve of the twentieth century in a
cloud of gin fumes into the horrid future of 1984 and All
That - in this case, a colony of human automata called
The Project' (W.L.W.: 'Nightmare Journey with Priestley
into the Future', *Manchester Guardian*, 30 September 1959).

F8   THE PAVILION OF MASKS

Note: Produced in Germany 1961, it was first seen on the
British stage at the Little Theatre, Bristol, 1963. Published in novella form in *The Carfitt Crisis*, 1975 (A160).

F9   TIME IS TIME WAS

Note: This two-act play, with fourteen characters, was
reported to be completed in *Yorkshire Post*, 24 August
1974.

F10 THE WHITE COCKATOO

Note: Not yet published or performed.

Radio Plays

F11 THE RETURN OF MR OAKROYD

Note: 'Since 'Priestley's Notebook' had to end, how could
it end better than by his conjuring up some of the characters he created so superbly in 'The Good Companions'?
We shall hear what some of them have been doing since the
story finished. Jess Oakroyd, back from Canada to help
the war effort, talks to Sam Oglethorpe. He has a surprise and meets one or two of the old troupe' ('Priestley's Notebook', *Radio Times*, 19 December 1941). Broadcast 27 December 1941.

F12 THE GOLDEN ENTRY

Note: Broadcast 30 November 1955 in the BBC Light
Programme J.B. Priestley Festival. 'Why I Wrote a Play
about an Art Dealer', *Radio Times*, 25 November 1955
(C1824) and 'The Golden Entry', *BBC Light Programme
J.B. Priestley Festival*, 1955 (A114) refer.

F13 END GAME AT THE DOLPHIN

Note: Broadcast in Saturday Night Theatre, BBC Home
Service, 4 August 1956. Frederick Law's 'Priestley
Premiere', *Radio Times*, 27 July 1956 refers.

Television Plays

F14 THE ROSE AND CROWN. BBC 1946

Note: Specifically written for television. Published in
an acting edition 1947 (A86).

F15 TREASURE ON PELICAN ISLAND. BBC 1951

Note: Published in an acting edition as *Treasure on
Pelican* (A109), 1953. Lionel Hale discusses the play in
Radio Times, 31 August 1951.

F16 NOW LET HIM GO. ABC Television 1957

Note: 'Old Simon Kendall, eyes afire, lay in the frowsty
hotel bedroom, and with his last strength plotted the
disposal of his pictures, while below relatives haggled,
reporters waited, and a trombone wailed 'Oh my saviour

lifted'. Not until everything was right did he give up
his grip on life...' (Philip Purser, 'Big Exciting
Priestley Bulges out of the Set', *Daily Mail*, 16 September 1957).

F17   THE STONE FACES. BBC 1957

Note: 'Set in La Venta, a remote spot in Mexico, where
a single hotel accommodates oil-men there on business,
as well as tourists and archaeologists who have come to
see the huge, bodiless, prehistoric, carved stone faces
which stand at the edge of the jungle, and which lend
to the play's title a symbolism that becomes clear in
the course of the action...' ('Writing for Television',
Radio Times, 1 December 1957). In this article J.B.
Priestley discusses in an interview with Peter Forster
the increasing opportunities of the medium, and his own
attitude towards it. Priestley's article 'My T.V. Play -
And How the Critics Failed', *Reynold's News*, 15 December
1957) (C1930) should be consulted.

F18   DOOMSDAY FOR DYSON. Granada Television 1958

Note: 'The satire was distributed freely all round the
clock, with Russian and American Air Force generals making
almost equally wooden appearances. The crucial incident
turned out to have been the error of a Soviet signaller
in reporting an accidental nuclear explosion as an attack.
But Dyson was the real criminal for his little man's com-
placency. The end, when he woke from his dream and de-
cided to go with his wife and daughters to a Priestley
protest meeting, was a rather odd example of the technique
of the advertising commercial as applied to the apoca-
lypse' (Maurice Richardson: 'Didactic Missile', *The Observer*, 16 March 1958).

F19   THE RACK   1958

F20   THE FORTROSE INCIDENT   1959

Note: Based on *Home Is Tomorrow*, published in 1949 (A95).

F21   LEVEL SEVEN   1966

Note: Adapted from the novel of the same name by Mordecai
Roshwald.

F22   ANYONE FOR TENNIS? BBC 1968

Note: 'My leading character, Garry Brendon, has committed
suicide, preferring extinction to disgrace and imprison-

ment. We've only one life to live, haven't we? - as so
many people say. And this play replies No' ('Anyone for
Tennis?', *Radio Times*, 19 September 1968).

F23 LINDA AT PULTENEY'S. BBC 1969

Note: 'Linda Carfield was on a night plane from New York
that crashed at London Airport and she lost all consciousness in the terror of the disaster. She had planned to
stay at Pulteney's Hotel, and when she recovers some kind
of consciousness apparently there she is, in a bedroom
of the hotel...' (Programme Note, *Radio Times*, 2 January
1969).

Films - Original Screenplays

F24 SING AS WE GO
Gaumont British 1934

F25 LOOK UP AND LAUGH
Gaumont British 1935

F26 WE LIVE IN TWO WORLDS
G.P.O. Film Unit 1937

Note: 'John Grierson, then head of the G.P.O. Film Unit
and the great white chief of British documentary films,
came to me and said that after doing a short film for the
Swiss Post Office they had a mass of good stuff left over
- lovely shots of the Swiss peasants in the fields, and
so on - and perhaps I could see my way into turning this
stuff into a good lecture film. They could add a certain
amount of new material for me, but it would all have to
be done very economically. So on the basis of the list
of shots supplied to me, I concocted a little talk about
nationalism and the new internationalism of transport and
communications, blandly took Switzerland as an example of
both ... and thanks to a very able director, Alberto
Cavalcanti, we ended with an excellent little documentary
film, which has, I believe, been quite popular' (*Rain
upon Godshill*).

F27 JAMAICA INN
Gaumont British 1939

Note: 'I was able to do a little job of film work, cre-
ating for Charles Laughton the outline of the crazy squire
in *Jamaica Inn*...' (*Rain upon Godshill*).

F28   OUR RUSSIAN ALLIES
      1941

F29   BRITAIN AT BAY
      G.P.O. Film Unit 1940

      Note: A five-minute documentary produced by Ministry of
      Information and G.P.O. Film Unit.

F30   PRIESTLEY'S POSTSCRIPT
      1941

      Note: A screen short in technicolor inspired by that
      memorable broadcast, 'The Hour of Greatness', written and
      commentated by Priestley and adapted for the screen by
      E.M. Delafield. The film depicted the fight for freedom,
      the ideals of democracy, and the hope for the future,
      against a background of English landscape and life.

F31   THE FOREMAN WENT TO FRANCE
      Gaumont British 1941

F32   LAST HOLIDAY
      Gaumont British 1950

                    Filmed Books and Plays

F33   THE OLD DARK HOUSE (A13)
      Universal 1932
      British Lion 1963

F34   THE GOOD COMPANIONS (A18)
      Fox 1933
      Associated British 1957

F35   DANGEROUS CORNER (A23)
      RKO 1934

F36   LABURNUM GROVE (A30)
      ATP 1941

F37   LET THE PEOPLE SING (A54)
      British National 1942

F38   WHEN WE ARE MARRIED (A51)
      British National 1943

F39   THEY CAME TO A CITY (A68)
      Ealing 1945

Note: 'Managers of West End cinemas refused to show it, saying that they felt a film without a plot taking place in the confines of one set would have no appeal. They insisted that Priestley's arguments as expounded in the film had nothing to do with this decision. So, despite the fact that the film had exactly the same cast as the West End show notching up one of the longest-running productions of a serious work during the whole war, and that the same jeremiad forecasts had been levelled at the play as were now levelled at the film, its distribution was severely limited. It did, however, play in many suburban cinemas' (William Harrington and Peter Jones: *The 1945 Revolution*, 1978).

F40 AN INSPECTOR CALLS (A83)
British Lion 1954

F41 MR KETTLE AND MRS MOON (A117)
A German film version

Radio and Television Programmes

Mr Priestley has made frequent appearances on both radio and television. Most of his radio talks for the British Broadcasting Corporation were printed in *The Listener* and are entered under Section C of this bibliography. His famous 1940 postscripts to the main Sunday evening nine o'clock news programme were published in *Postscripts* (A56); those delivered in the B.B.C.'s North American broadcasts were printed in *London Calling*, a few in *The Listener*, and published in *Britain Speaks* (A57). Only those programmes actually written by Priestley which have not appeared in print are recorded here.

Radio

F42 A NEW ENGLISH JOURNEY 'A programme for St. George's Day, telling the story of life in England today'

Note: 'Priestley has just retraced his steps, and in a St. George's Day programme that he is presenting in collaboration with D.G. Bridson ... he will tell of the changes brought about by the war' (*Radio Times*, 19 April 1940). Broadcast 23 April 1940.

F43   LISTEN TO MY NOTEBOOK

Note: 'Priestley's New Series', *Radio Times*, 10 October
1941 refers.   Broadcast weekly 16 October 1941 - 27 December 1941.   See also Grace Wyndham Goldie's 'Priestley
Pioneers Again', *The Listener*, XXVI (667), 23 October
1941:576.

Television

F44   YOU KNOW WHAT PEOPLE ARE.   BBC 1955

Note: 'I have called this series You Know What People Are
because this familiar phrase expresses the mood of the
programmes.   They are about people, that is, about all of
us - how we talk and behave to one another, how we are
influenced by our sex or by our professions, how we imag-
ine one thing and then actually experience something
quite different.   As I talk informally along these lines,
the points I want to make will be dramatically illustrated
by monologues, duologues, little sketches I have written
for my little team of players - two actors, two actresses'
('You Know What People Are', *Radio Times*, 27 May 1955).
Televised every Wednesday evening 1 June 1955 - 6 July 1955.

F45   LOST CITY.   BBC 1958

Note: 'Much of the time Priestley was talking with a girl
reporter or, rather, feeding her with questions to which
he could give knock-down answers.   I preferred his
straight-forward narration, spoken in that slow, deep,
ruminative voice that always sounds as though it has hit
on the right word spontaneously.   Here was some more ex-
ploration of the possibilities of the television essay
in which careful writing and pictures back each other up'
('Teleview', *Daily Mail*, 27 October 1958).

F46   THE ENGLISH NOVEL.   Associated Television 1965

Note: A series of nine programmes broadcast on succes-
sive Sundays beginning 25 April 1965.   They were 'A Late
Arrival'; 'Sentiment and Vigour: The Eighteenth Century';
'The Age of Scott and Jane Austen'; 'Charles Dickens';
'Dickens' Contemporaries'; 'The Later Victorians'; 'The
Edwardians'; 'Between the Wars'; and 'Since the War'.   A
booklet, *The English Novel*, a list of one hundred books,
intended primarily as a bibliography for those following

the programmes, was prepared by the National Book League in conjunction with Associated Television.

F47   1940 A REMINISCENCE IN FIVE PARTS. BBC 1965

Note: '... almost inevitably, the author and narrator of this immensely long programme is J.B. Priestley, whose pen and voice in 1940 were more famous than any but Churchill's' (Tony Essex: '1940', *Radio Times*, 9 September 1965).

Musical Shows and Recordings

F48   THE GOOD COMPANIONS A play by J.B. Priestley with music by Richard Addinsell, lyrics by Harry Graham and Frank Eyton. His Majesty's Theatre 14 May 1931.

Contents: Adele Dixon: GOING HOME (with John Gielgud, Lawrence Bascomb and Deering Wells) / SLIPPING AROUND THE CORNER (with John Gielgud). HMV C2288. 1931.

F49   THE GOOD COMPANIONS The musical of the novel by J.B. Priestley. Book by Ronald Harwood, Music by Andre Previn. Lyrics by Johnny Mercer. His Majesty's Theatre 11 July 1974.

Note: Score published as:

J.B. PRIESTLEY'S THE GOOD COMPANIONS
London, Chappell, 1976.
vi, 78p, 26cm.
Cover title: *Good Companions: The Musical of the Novel by J.B. Priestley*

THE GOOD COMPANIONS
EMI EMC-3042. 1974.

Contents: Camaraderie (The Dinky Doos); The Pools (John Mills); Footloose (John Mills, Judi Dench, Christopher Gable); The Pleasure of Your Company (Malcolm Rennie, Christopher Gable); Stage Struck (Marti Webb); Dance of Life (Judi Dench); Slippin' around the Corner (Ray C. Davis); Good Companions (Christopher Gable, Malcolm Rennie); A Little Travelling Music (The Company); And Points Beyond (John Mills); Darkest Before the Dawn (Judi Dench); Susy for Everybody (Marti Webb, Christopher Gable); Ta Luv (John Mills); I'll Tell the World (Marti Webb, Chris-

topher Gable, Ray C. Davis); Stage Door John (Marti Webb);
Ta Luv (John Mills, Marti Webb); Good Companions (The
Company).

Other Recordings

F50   J.B. PRIESTLEY: PRELUDE TO PEARL HARBOUR: DUNKIRK (1940)
      Decca AD3001.   1940.

F51   J.B. PRIESTLEY: WOMEN AND THE WAR (an appreciation). A
         Postscript to the Nine O'Clock News Broadcast 22 Sep-
         tember 1940.
      HMV C3190.   1940.

F52   ESSAYS FROM DELIGHT READ BY THE AUTHOR
      Argo RC 159 (A Spoken Arts Recording).   1958.

      Contents: Side 1: Introduction; Fantasies; Orchestral
      Conductor; A Smell of Tahiti; Smoking in a Hot Bath;
      Not Going; Blossom Wood. *Side 2:* No School Report; Long
      Trousers; Pleasure and Gratitude of Children; Mineral
      Water; Orchestra Tuning Up; The Delight That Never Was;
      But This Is Where We Came In.

      Note: An appreciation by Harvey J. Usill is printed on
      the sleeve.

G. PRIESTLEY THE PAINTER

G1 Priestley's own account of when, why, and how he started
    painting may be read in Chapter VII, *Instead of the Trees*,
    1977 (A165).

G2 Frank Dowling's 'Priestley the Painter', *Leisure Painter*,
    Summer 1967, is in the form of an interview and includes
    black-and-white reproductions of an early oil painting of
    the West Wight, a very rapid water colour sketch of Mrs
    Priestley reading a newspaper in the bedroom of a San
    Francisco hotel, a gouache of the Peak District, Derby-
    shire, and a pen and gouache of the market place in
    Chiche Castenango, Guatemala.

G3 'J.B. Priestley Vividly Portrays an Old Love The York-
    shire Dales' preceding his 'Wuthering Heights to Arcadia
    in a Sharp Two-Hour Walk', *Life Magazine*, 7 March 1966
    (C2145) has four gouaches in colour: 'Ingleborough', 'Tan
    Hill Inn', 'Littondale', and 'Penyghent'.

G4 'A Holiday in Gouache', *Envoy*, August 1967 (C2161) repro-
    duces seven Irish sea- and landscapes in colour.

G5 'A Holiday Painter', *Saturday Book 29*, 1969 (B132) is
    illustrated with a full-page colour reproduction of 'Mayan
    Temple in the Jungle at Texal, Northern Guatemala'; half-
    page black-and-white reproductions of 'Golden Canyon in
    Death Valley, California', 'Ingleborough in the Yorkshire
    Dales', 'A Vine-Growing Valley in Georgia, Soviet Union',
    and 'Stormy Afternoon in Breconshire'; and half-page
    colour reproductions of 'The Meteora in Thessaly' and
    'Road in Kerry'.

G6 *A Visit to New Zealand*, 1974 (A158) includes full-colour
    reproductions of a sketch of the late-afternoon scene from
    the viewpoint high above Waitomo, North Island (presented
    to Mr Norman Kirk, the Prime Minister); a distant view

of Wellington, North Island; a view along the road not
far from the Dalgety homestead, South Island; an early
morning impression of one of Mount Cook's smaller companions, South Island; a distant view of Queenstown,
South Island; a landscape near Queenstown; late afternoon
on a road near Queenstown; a coastal scene near Dunedin,
South Island; the steam at Wairakei, North Island; and
Lake Taupo, North Island.

G7   Two newspaper black-and-white reproductions of a peasant-
     pilgrim camp in Georgia and Lake Sevan headed the text of
     'The Road to Samarkand', *Sunday Times*, 2 December 1962
     (C2095).

G8   'A quick angry sketch ... afterwards furiously transformed
     into an impressionistic, angry gouache' of a Polish scene,
     in colour, 'Priestley's Sentimental Journey', *Observer
     Magazine*, 1 October 1972 (C2217).

H. STUDIES OF PRIESTLEY

Bibliography

H1   I. Alun Jones: 'The First Editions of J.B. Priestley',
The Bookman, 31 April 1931.

H2   J.T.W.: 'Et Tu Priestley?' *The Bookman* (US), 25 November
1933.

     Note: Describes suppression of *A Chapman of Rhymes* (A1).

H3   *Contemporary British Literature: A Critical Survey and
232 Author-Bibliographies* by Fred B. Millett. 3rd revised and enlarged edition, based on the 2nd revised and
enlarged edition by John M. Manly and Edith Rickett.
Harrap, 1935.

H4   J.B. PRIESTLEY: AN EXHIBITION OF MANUSCRIPTS AND BOOKS.
Austin (Texas), The Humanities Research Center: The
University of Texas, 1963.
32p. frontis (port), illus, facsims. 25cm. sd.

     Contents: 156 items arranged under the headings: Beginnings;
Familiar Essays; Criticism; Novels and Short Stories; The
Theatre; The War Years; and Retrospect. Lucetta Teagarden
contributes an introduction.

     Note: The cover title is *A Writer's Life.*

H5   Lucetta J. Teagarden: 'The J.B. Priestley Collection',
The Library Chronicles of the University of Texas,
Summer 1963.

H6   Alan Edwin Day: 'J.B. Priestley: A Checklist', *Bulletin
of Bibliography*, April-June 1971.

Monograph Studies

H7   J.B. PRIESTLEY AND THE THEATRE by Rex Pogson
      Clevedon (Somerset), Triangle Press, 1947.
      55p. 18cm. sd.

H8   J.B. PRIESTLEY by Ivor Brown
      London, Longmans, Green & Co. for the British Council and
         the National Book League, 1957.
      39p. frontis (port). bibliog. 22cm. sd.
      (Writers and Their Work No 84)

      Note: Replaced by *J.B. Priestley* (Kenneth Young) (H12).

H9   J.B. PRIESTLEY An Informal Study of His Work by David
         Hughes
      London, Rupert Hart-Davis, 1958.
      226p. frontis. bibliog. 22cm.

H10   J.B. PRIESTLEY – THE DRAMATIST   by Gareth Lloyd Evans
      London, Heinemann, 1964.
      ix, 230p. 22cm.

H11   J.B. PRIESTLEY Portrait of an Author by Susan Cooper
      London, Heinemann, 1970.
      240p. frontis (port). bibliog. 22cm.

H12   J.B. PRIESTLEY by Kenneth Young
      London, Longman Group for the British Council, 1977.
      56p. frontis (port). bibliog. 22cm. sd.
      (Writers and Their Work No 257)

      Note: Replaced *J.B. Priestley* (Ivor Brown) (H8).

H12a J.B. PRIESTLEY by John Braine
      London, Weidenfeld and Nicolson, 1979.
      163p. illus (inc frontis). bibliog. 24cm.

Parodies

H13   Maurice L. Richardson: *The Bad Companions*, John Miles,
      1936.

H14   A.G. MacDonnell: 'Eden Weekend (After You Mr J.B. Pr++st-
      ley)' in *Parody Party* edited by Leonard Russell,
      Hutchinson, 1936.

H15 K. Waterhouse and Willis Hall: 'Time and Mr Priestley'
     in *That Was the Week That Was* edited by David Frost
     and Ned Sherrin, W.H. Allen, 1963.

                         General Studies
             (Literary, Dramatic and Political)

H16 'J.B. Priestley Author of The Good Companions', *Wilson
     Library Bulletin*, February 1930.

H17 Oliver Warner: 'The Significance of Mr Priestley',
     Everyman, 9 October 1930.

H18 Dorothea Lawrence Mann: 'J.B. Priestley: Servant of the
     Comic Spirit', *The Bookman* (US), May 1931.

H19 F.L. Stevens: 'J.B. Priestley. A Yorkshireman at Large',
     Everyman, 27 August 1931.

H20 Gilbert Armitage: 'An Examination of J.B. Priestley's
     "Best-Sellers"', *The Bookman*, November 1931.

H21 Edward Shanks: 'How J.B. Priestley Found Success',
     Evening Standard, 2 December 1931.

H22 Edward Shanks: 'Mr Priestley's Novels', *London Mercury*,
     July 1932.

H23 Frank Swinnerton: 'Some Later Novelists', Chap XVII,
     The Georgian Literary Scene, Heinemann, 1935.

H24 Vernon Fane: 'The Case of Mr J.B. Priestley. An Examina-
     tion of a Notable Novelist', *The Sphere*, 8 August 1936.

H25 Sydney W. Carroll: 'Mr Priestley Again: A Writer with
     Ideas', *Daily Telegraph*, 7 October 1937.

H26 Morton Eustis: 'On Time and Theatre', *Theatre Arts
     Monthly*, January 1938.

H27 John T. Frederick: 'J.B. Priestley All-Round Man of
     Letters on the 18th-Century Plan', *English Journal*,
     May 1938.

H28 Richard Prentis: 'Pantomime and Mr Priestley', *John
     O'London's*, 6 January 1939.

Note: Occasioned by 'A Grumble about Pantomime', *News Chronicle*, 27 December 1938 (C1122).

H29 'The Men Who Speak for Britain. 1. J.B. Priestley', *London Calling*, 43, 4 July 1940.

H30 Robert W. Reid: 'When Priestley Talks to America', *Radio Times*, 18 October 1940.

H31 Dennis Stoll: 'Priestley - An Appreciation', *London Phil-harmonic Post*, January 1941.

H32 R.W. Whidden: 'Priestley and His Novels', *Queen's Quarterly*, Vol. XLVIII, 1941.

H33 Johannes Steel: *Men Behind the War*, Sheridan House, 1943: 58-64.

H34 Donald Brook: 'J.B. Priestley', *Writers' Gallery: Biographical Sketches of Prominent British Writers, and Their Views on Reconstruction*, Rockliff Publishing Corporation, 1944.

H35 Simon Drieden: 'Priestley on the Russian Stage', *Theatre World*, October 1945.

H36 Peter Noble: 'Profile of J.B. Priestley', *Theatre*, Spring 1946.

H37 'Yorkshire's Don Quixote', *John Bull*, 11 May 1946.

H38 Jack Lindsay: 'J.B. Priestley', Chap 6, *Writers of Today* edited by Denys Val Baker, Sidgwick and Jackson, 1946.

H39 H.V. Routh: 'The Last Phase', Chap XI, *English Literature in the Twentieth Century*, Methuen, 1946.

H40 Collin Brooks: 'Two Novelists', Chap 15, *Devil's Decade: Portraits of the Nineteen-Thirties*, Macdonald, 1947.

H41 D. Waldo Clarke: 'J.B. Priestley', Chap XI, *Modern English Writers*, Longmans Green, 1947.

H42 Richard Church: *British Authors: A Twentieth Century Gallery*, Longmans Green for the British Council, 1948: 130-132.

H43   Michael Foot: 'The Futility of Mr Priestley', *Tribune*,
      28 January 1949.

H44   A.K. Hudson: 'J.B. Priestley: The Butt of the Intellec-
      tuals', *The School Librarian*, March 1950.

H45   Ivor Montagu: 'Peace and Mr Priestley', *Labour Monthly*,
      June 1950.

H46   Ivor Brown: Introduction to *The Priestley Companion*,
      1951 (A102).

H47   'Plays in the Home', *The Times*, 11 September 1951.

      Note: Discusses the methods of Priestley and Terence
      Rattigan in dealing with drama on television.

H48   Audrey Williamson: 'A Priestley Progression', Chap 5,
      Theatre of Two Decades, Rockliff, 1951.

H49   J.C. Trewin: 'Priestley and Bridie', *Drama 1945-1950*,
      Longmans Green for the British Council, 1951.

H50   Ernest Short: 'The Disillusioned 'Twenties and the
      Anxious 'Thirties', Chap 18, *Sixty Years of Theatre*,
      Eyre & Spottiswoode, 1951.

H51   Clifford Bax: 'Contemporary British Dramatists No 2.
      J.B. Priestley', *Drama*, Winter 1952.

H52   Harold Hobson: 'A Burst of Life', Chap 8, *Verdict at
      Midnight: Sixty Years of Dramatic Criticism*, Long-
      mans Green, 1952.

H53   J.C. Trewin: 'Bradford Enchanted', Chap 10, *Dramatists
      of Today*, Staples Press, 1953.

H54   A BOOK OF BRITISH PROFILES compiled from *The Observer*
      by Sebastian Haffner, Heinemann, 1954:27-30.

      Note: First printed in *The Observer*, 22 October 1949.

H55   Richard Church: 'An Appreciation', *BBC Light Programme
      Festival*, 1955 (A114).

H56   David Millwood: 'Magnificent Grumbler', *Books and Book-
      men*, October 1955.

      Note: Priestley responded to points made in this article
      in 'Two Failures', a letter printed in *Books and Book-
      men*, November 1955 (C1821).

H57 Richard Church: 'The Priestley I Know', *TV Monthly*,
     February 1956.

H58 Eric Gillett: 'Introduction' to *All About Ourselves*,
     1956 (A116).

H59 Harvey Breit: 'J.B. Priestley', *The Writer Observed*,
     New York, World Publishing Co, 1956; London, Alvin
     Redman, 1957.

     Note: This appreciation first appeared in *New York Times
     Book Review*.

H60 Grover Smith: 'Time Alive: J.W. Dunne and J.B. Priest-
     ley', *South Atlantic Quarterly*, April 1957.

H61 Evelyn Waugh: 'Anything Wrong with Priestley?' *The Spec-
     tator*, 13 September 1957.

     Note: Provoked by 'Pinfold', *New Statesman*, 31 August
     1957 (C1905).

H62 'J.B. Priestley: Plain Man's Plain Man', *Books and
     Bookmen*, November 1957.

H63 George W. Bishop: 'Somerset Maugham. Priestley. Walpole',
     Chap 10, *My Betters*, Heinemann, 1957.

H64 Henry Fairlie: 'I Won't Go with the Sentimental Three',
     Daily Mail, 6 March 1958.

     Note: A letter, 'Is Fairlie Wrong about the Bomb?' signed
     by L. John Collins, J.B. Priestley, and Earl Russell,
     appeared in *Daily Mail*, 8 March 1958.

H65 Kenneth Allsop: 'I've Had Enough of This Do-Gooder
     Priestley Hamming It Up', *Daily Mail*, 13 March 1958.

H66 John Braine: 'Lunch with J.B. Priestley. Two Gentlemen
     from Bradford', *Encounter*, June 1958.

H67 Alick West: *The Mountain in the Sunlight: Studies in
     Conflict and Unity*, Lawrence & Wishart, 1958:153-183.

H68 Gareth Lloyd Evans: 'Implacable Northern Man', *Manchester
     Guardian*, 11 August 1960.

H69 'Storytelling Plus Ideas', J.B. Priestley discusses his
     books with the editor. *Books and Bookmen*, July 1961.

H70   Marie Hartley and Joan Ingilby: *Yorkshire Portraits*,
      Dent, 1961:224-228.

H71   John Pearson: 'Priestley Celebrates 40 Years as a
      Writer', *Sunday Times*, 23 September 1962.

H72   Ernest Bradbury: 'Priestley as Music Critic', *Yorkshire
      Post*, 24 November 1964.

H73   Irene Hentschel: 'Producing for Shaw and Priestley',
      Drama, Winter 1964.

H74   Priestley, J(ohn) B(oynton): *Contemporary Authors   A Bio-
      Bibliographical Guide to Current Authors and Their Work
      Vol 9-10*, Detroit, Gale Research Company, 1964.

      Note: Writings listed under novels, essays and other
      books; plays; edited; booklets; introductions. Biblio-
      graphical sources are indicated.

H75   Donald G. MacRae: 'Introduction', *The World of J.B.
      Priestley*, 1967 (A140).

H76   Ivor Brown: 'J.B. Priestley' i.e. General Introduction
      to Heron Books' The Collected Masterpieces of J.B.
      Priestley, *Angel Pavement*, 1967, Pp VII-XVIII (A169).

H77   Ivor A. Rogers: 'The Time Plays of J.B. Priestley', *Ex-
      trapolation*, December 1968.

H78   A.E. Day: 'J.B. Priestley: Man of Letters', *Library Re-
      view*, Summer 1969.

H79   S.M.C.: 'John Boynton Priestley', Makers of the Twen-
      tieth Century Part 12, *Sunday Times Magazine*, 31 August
      1969.

H80   Asa Briggs: *The History of Broadcasting in the United
      Kingdom   Vol III   The War of Words*, 1970:210-213,
      320-323, 598-599, 619-621.

      Note: A thoroughly documented examination of the furor
      caused by Priestley's second series of 'Postscripts',
      broadcast after the nine o'clock news on Sundays in
      the spring of 1941. A high-level decision was taken
      to replace Priestley, who believes that it was Winston
      Churchill himself who made this decision. See p50
      Radio Times 50th Anniversary Souvenir 1923-1973
      (B144).

H81   Robert Skloot: 'The Time Plays of J.B. Priestley', *Quarterly Journal of Speech*, December 1970.

H82   Frederick Lumley: 'The State of the Drama in Britain', Chap 18, *New Trends in Twentieth Century Drama*, Barrie & Jenkins, 4e 1972.

H83   M. Billington: 'Big Daddy', *The Guardian*, 24 August 1973.

H84   Alec Baron: 'Priestley at 80', *January in Yorkshire 1974*.

H85   David Wright: 'Priestley and the Art of the Dramatist', *Drama*, Spring 1974.

H86   Richard Eder: 'J.B. Priestley, at 80, Chuffs but Works On', *New York Times*, 6 April 1974:2.

H87   S.S. Dale: 'Priestley as Music Critic', *Musical Opinion*, July 1974.

H88   Gareth Lloyd Evans: 'Open Letter to J.B. Priestley', *The Guardian*, 27 October 1975.

H89   Frederick Bowers: untitled appreciation, *Contemporary Novelists*, London, St. James Press / New York, St. Martin's Press, 2e 1976.

      Note: Entry for J.B. Priestley lists his publications arranged by literary form, i.e., novels; short stories; plays (including screenplays, radio plays and TV plays); verse; and other.

H90   Lawrence Kitchin: untitled appreciation, *Contemporary Dramatists*, London, St. James Press / New York, St. Martin's Press, 2e 1977.

      Note: Entry for J.B. Priestley lists his publications arranged by literary form, i.e., plays (including screenplays, radio plays and TV plays); novels; short stories; verse; and other.

H91   Priestley, J(ohn) B(oynton), *Current Biography Yearbook 1976*. New York: H.W. Wilson, 1977.

Birthday Tributes and Assessments

H92   'Priestley on the Brink of 70', *Sunday Telegraph*, 6
      September 1964.

H93   Jacquetta Hawkes: 'Jack's All Right!' *TV Times*, 11
      September 1964.

H94   Kingsley Martin: 'Birthday Letter', *New Statesman*, 11
      September 1964.

H95   Gareth Lloyd Evans: 'J.B. Priestley at 70', *Manchester
      Guardian*, 12 September 1964.

H96   'The Disappearing All Rounder', *The Times*, 14 September
      1964 (fourth leader).

H97   R.B. Marriott: 'J.B. Priestley', *The Stage*, 17 September
      1964.

H98   Susan Cooper: 'That's J.B. Priestley for You', *Sunday
      Times Magazine*, 7 September 1969.

H99   Gareth Lloyd Evans: 'They're All Wrong about Priestley',
      The Guardian, 11 September 1969.

H100 Anne Chisholm: 'The 75th Birthday of the Glowering
      Pudding', *Radio Times*, 11 September 1969.

H101 Paul Johnson: 'A Birthday Letter', *New Statesman*, 11
      September 1969.

H102 John Gale: 'A Touch of Magic in Mr Priestley's World',
      The Observer, 14 September 1969.

H103 Ian Cotton: 'J.B. Priestley the Remarkably Good Com-
      panion', *TV Times*, 29 August 1974.

H104 David Pryce-Jones: 'My Strongest Point Is My Great
      Feeling for Life', *Radio Times*, 5 September 1974.

H105 Paul Bailey: 'Priestley: One Hell of a Lot of Talent ...
      a Birthday Portrait', *The Listener*, 12 September
      1974.

H106 Phyllis Bentley: 'There Is Never Anything Mean, or Pet-
      ty, or Scruffy in His Writing', *Yorkshire Post*, 12
      September 1974.

H107   Ray Gosling: 'The Good Companion', *The Times*, 12 September 1974.

H108   David Hughes: 'Union Jack', *The Guardian*, 14 September 1974.

H109   Stanley Reynolds: 'The Accepted Anachronism ... the Jolly Uncle to a Whole Nation', *The Guardian*, 14 September 1974.

H110   'A Time for Celebration', *Sunday Times*, 8 September 1974.

H111   Peter Dews: 'Coming Again, Like Parkin. A Look at J.B. Priestley as Dramatist on His Eightieth Birthday', *Drama*, Winter 1974.

H112   Evelyn Ames: 'J.B. Priestley at 80', *New York Times Book Review*, 18 June 1975.

Family

H113   'The Best of Good Companions. My Husband by His Wife No. 5. J.B. Priestley', *Daily Express*, 19 October 1934.

H114   Mrs Priestley, as told to Winifred Loraine: 'We Are Such Good Companions', *Daily Mail*, 9 November 1938.

H115   David Mills: 'If You Were Mrs J.B. Priestley', *Good Housekeeping*, November 1944.

H116   Jacquetta Hawkes: 'Jack's All Right!', *TV Times*, 11 September 1964.

H117   Mary Priestley: 'A Famous Father', *Homes and Gardens*, March 1968.

Homes and Gardens

H118   'J.B. Priestley at Home', *The Queen*, 22 June 1932.

H119   'Where Coleridge Lived in J.B. Priestley's Home. The Famous Man of Letters Talks to John Gliddon', *Modern Home*, January 1933.

H120 'Other Peoples' Homes No 17. Mr J.B. Priestley at Home', *Publishers Circular*, 17 February 1934.

H121 Joan Woollcombe: 'Inside Albany', *Homes and Gardens*, July 1970.

H122 'A Day Off with J.B. Priestley', *Weekly Illustrated*, 1 September 1934.

> *Note:* This item is appended here because no alternative place for it easily suggests itself.

Horoscope

H123 Joan Revill: 'j.b. priestley the Man in the Time Machine', *Prediction*, November 1970.

I. PRIESTLEIANA

The items listed here add nothing to our enjoyment of Priestley's books and plays, or to our knowledge and understanding
of his place in English literature or the social history of
our times; only avid enthusiasts or slightly nor' nor' west
collectors will place any value on them.

I1 *Famous British Authors. A Series of 40. No 27 J.B. Priest-
    ley.* A cigarette card issued by W.D. & H.O. Wills c.
    1935-1936. A blue and sepia autographed head and shoulder
    portrait. Brief career details are printed on back.

I2 Bronze medallion of bust of J.B. Priestley, four centi-
    metres in diameter, specially struck for subscribers to
    Heron Books' *Collected Masterpieces of J.B. Priestley*
    (A169) who replied within five days of the initial adver-
    tisement.

    Note: 'The medallion shows Mr Priestley (thought to be
    when he was 60) and bears his name. But he knows nothing
    about its origin. If it was struck in his honour, he says
    it is the first he has heard about it. An elderly woman
    took it into a Bradford coin expert's shop recently to
    sell but neither the expert, the old lady, nor Mr Priest-
    ley have been able to discover when, where and why it was
    made', 'A Puzzle for J.B. Priestley', *Yorkshire Post*, 19
    July 1973.

I3 ADMISSION OF JOHN BOYNTON PRIESTLEY MA (Cantab) LL.D
        (St Andrews) D.Litt (Universities of Colorado, Birmingham,
        Bradford) TO THE ROLL OF HONORARY FREEMEN OF THE CITY
        OF BRADFORD. Saturday 8th September 1973.
    Bradford, City of Bradford, 1973.
    12p. port, illus. 30cm x 21cm. sd.

    Contents: Order of proceedings; J.B. Priestley, Esq will
    swear an oath as follows; A copy of the text of the scroll;
    Portrait; and Biographical notes.

14   David Hockney: Portrait of J.B. Priestley, an ink draw-
       ing.
      Bradford, Bradford Art Galleries and Museums, 1976.
      Postcard 14.7cm. x 10.5cm.

      Note: The original was presented by the artist in 1973
      and hangs in the Cartwright Museum, Bradford.

15   James P. Barraclough: Portrait of J.B. Priestley 1932.
       Oil on canvas.
      Bradford, Bradford Art Galleries and Museums, 1974.
      Postcard 14.8cm. x 10.3cm.

That Quarter C813
That Was the Week That Was
  H15
That's the Stuff to Give 'Em!
  C2286
Theatre (Bradford) C1410,
  C1731
Theatre and Stage B27
Theatre and World C1518
The Theatre and You C1123
Theatre Arts Monthly (New
  York) C779
Theatre Conference C1557-1558
Theatre Conference Makes a
  Start - The Opening Address
  C1556
Theatre Curtains A96
Theatre Leadership C1578
Theatre Newsletter C1441,
  C1470, C1548, C1556, C1564,
  C1577
Theatre 1954-55 B90
Theatre of Two Decades (Audrey
  Williamson) H48
Theatre Outlook A82
Theatre Today C1452
Then and Now C1443
There Must Be No Going Back
  C1225
These Bored Cosmopolites
  C2273
These Cockney Boys Have Made
  a Home Happier C1195
These Diversions Series A9
These Novels C783
These Our Actors (1929) A25,
  A145, C710
These Our Actors (1956) F5
These Our Revels A138, C2116
They Are Called Pobs B131
They Came to a City A64, A68-
  69, F39
They Can't Agree with Me More
  C1627
They Come from Inner Space
  A119, C1747
They Made It a Sin to Drink
  C937
They Make the Guns We Need
  C1272

They Plan to Steal Your
  Spare Time Now C944
They Play Halma, But It's a
  Real War Game C1194
They Say C781
They Take My Money C1021
They Walk in the City A43,
  A169
They've Slighted Britain
  C941
Thick Notebooks A15, C565
Things Are Making Slaves of
  Us C1791
Things to Come and As They
  Are C1057
Thinking about Beethoven
  C2190
The Thirty First of June
  A127, A169, F6
This Air-Raid Life of Ours
  C1236
This Astonishing City C2223
This Banned Book Nonsense
  C967
This Education Business
  C1105
This England at Zero Hour
  C1349
This Fateful Day C1372
This Insubstantial Pageant
  A4, A8, A116, C218
This Is May Day C1027
This Is Our Duty C1938
This Is Where the Mass Media
  Fail C2311
This Jew Business C1037
This Land of Ours B55
This New Religion C956
This Nonsense of Passports
  C987
This Nuclear Madness C1952
This Problem of Coal C1274
This Quarter (Paris) C813
This Small World A96
This Strange Country Shows
  Us Our Future C1019
This Talk about Liberty
  C1402
This World of Fear C1103

INDEX OF BOOKS
REVIEWED BY J.B. PRIESTLEY

Abercrombie, Lascelles: *Essay Towards a Theory of Art*   C192;
    Idea of Great Poetry   C387; *Romanticism*   C192
Ableman, Paul: *I Hear Voices*   C1954
Ackerley, J.R.: *Hindoo Holiday*   C865
Acland, Alice: *Caroline Norton*   C1565
Acland, Dyke: *Sticky Fingers*   C888
Acton, Harold: *Humdrum*   C609; *Lost Medici*   C861
Adams, Samuel Hopkins: *Alexander Woollcott*   C1449
Adventures of Ralph Rashleigh   C693, C705
Agate, James: *Brief Chronicles*   C1354; *English Dramatic*
    Critics 1660-1932   C903; *Fantasies and Impromptus*   C305,
    C308; *First Nights*   C982; *Innocent Toys*   C1400
Aiken, Conrad: *Costumes by Eros*   C668
Alain-Fournier: *The Wanderer*   C678, C683
Aldington, Richard: *Death of a Hero*   C736; *Soft Answers*   C866;
    Voltaire   C419
Allen, H. Warner: *Celestina*   C313
Allen, Frederick Lewis: *Only Yesterday*   C854
Allen, Hervey: *Anthony Adverse*   C962
Allen, Walter: *All in a Lifetime*   C2011
Allingham, Margery: *Hide My Eyes*   C1987
Allsop, Kenneth: *The Angry Decade*   C1967
Amis, Kingsley: *Lucky Jim*   C1777
Anderson, Alston: *Lover Man*   C2016
Anderson, Sherwood: *Many Marriages*   C286
Anderton, Basil: *Sketches from a Library Window*   C183
Andric, Ivo: *The Bridge on the Drina*   C2010
Anstey, Fred: *Humour and Fantasy*   C817; *The Last Road*   C401
Anthell, George: *Bad Boy of Music*   C1523
An Anthology of Nineties Verse   C621
Arberry, A.J.: *Romance of the Rubaiyat*   C2314
Arlen, Michael: *Lily Christine*   C643; *Man's Immortality*   C913
Armstrong, Martin: *The Bazaar*   C328; *The Sleeping Fury*   C708
Ashley, Kenneth: *Death of a Curate*   C862
Ashmun, Margaret: *The Lovely Lake*   C368

Drew, Elizabeth: *The Modern Novel* C452
Drinkwater, John: *Collected Plays* C396; *Discovery* C896; *The Eighteen Sixties* C875
Drummond, Anthony: *The Scented Death* C349
Drury, Allen: *Advise and Consent* C2044, C2047
Duffus, R.L.: *Tomorrow and Tomorrow* C724
Duffy, Hans: *In England Now* C854
Duhamel, Georges: *Light on My Days* C1571
Dumas, Alexander: *From Paris to Cadiz* C1986
Du Maurier, Daphne: *Gerald: A Portrait* C986; *I'll Never Be Young Again* C869
Dunne, J.W.: *Experiment with Time* C646, C966, C1109
Dunsany, Lord: *The King of Elfland's Daughter* C346
Dyke, Watson: *Cousin Matthew* C668

Eckersley, Arthur: *Odds and Ends of a Learned Clerk* C183
Edelman, Maurice: *A Call on Kuprin* C2018
Edwards, Charman: *Big Strong Man* C296
Ehrenburg, Ilya: *The Thaw* C1798
Eldershaw, M. Bernard: *A House Is Built* C705
Eliat, Helen: *Sheba Visits Solomon* C881
Eliot, T.S.: *Selected Essays* C894
Ellin, Stanley: *The Eighth Circle* C2024
Ellis, Havelock: *The Dance of Life* C280
Elwin, Malcolm: *Landor* C1970; *Thackeray* C894
Epton, Nina: *Love and the French* C2021
Erskine, Laurie York: *The Confidence Man* C381
Ervine, St. John: *Some Impressions of My Elders* C231
Essays by Divers Hands C174, C344
Everton, Francis: *The Young Vanish* C869
Everymans Dictionary of Literary Biography C1946
'Evoe': *These Liberties* C202
Ewald, Carl: *The Old Pest* C165
Eyles, Leonora: *Hidden Lives* C194

Fabricius, Johan: *The Girl in a Blue Hat* C863
Fair, A.A.: *The Count at Nine* C2024; *Some Women Won't Wait* C1971
Fairley, Barker: *Goethe* C861
Falls, Cyril: *The Critic's Armoury* C369
Famous Plays of 1932 C903
The Farington Diary 1802-1804 C275
Farrell, M.J.: *Convention Piece* C906
Fast, Howard: *The Naked God* C1977
Faulkner, William: *The Town* C1945
Faure, Gabriel: *Sicily* C879
Fausset, Agatha: *The Naked Face of Genius* C1980
Fausset, Hugh L'Anson: *John Donne* C358; *Studies in Idealism* C309

Greene, Graham: *Loser Takes All* C1795; *The Man Within* C708;
  Our Man in Havana C1987; *Stamboul Train* C910
Greene, H. Plunket: *Where the Bright Waters Meet* C355
Greig, J.Y.T.: *The Psychology of Laughter* C238
Gretton, R.H.: *A Modern History of the English People 1880-
  1922* C789
Grierson, H.J.C.: *The Background of English Literature* C414
Guedalla, Philip: *The Two Marshalls* C1334
A Guide to Russian Literature C183
Guilbert, Yvette: *Song of My Life* C699
Gunther, Hans: *I'm Wearing My Ninth Pair of Shoes* C1986
Gunther, John: *The Golden Fleece* C683
Guthrie, Ramon: *Parachute* C665
Guthrie, Tyrone: *Theatre Prospect* C903
Gyseghem, Andre van: *Theatre in Soviet Russia* C1354, C2296

Hackett, Francis: *Henry VIII* C717
Hackney, Alan: *Private Life* C1970; *Private's Progress* C1779
Hadfield, John: *Love on a Branch Line* C2315
Hadley, Leila: *Give Me the World* C1986
Haggard, William: *Venetian Blind* C2024
Haldane, J.B.S.: *The Inequality of Man* C903
Hall, D.J.: *Enchanted Sand* C871
Hall, Oakley: *Warlock* C2314
Hamilton, A.C.: *This Smoking World* C579
Hamilton, Patrick: *Midnight Bell* C708; *Siege of Pleasure*
  C857; *Slaves of Solitude* C1495
Hammett, Dashiell: *Modern Tales of Horror* C883
Hanley, James: *Ebb and Flood* C891
Hanson, L. and E.: *Verlaine* C1992
Hardwicke, Cedric: *Let's Pretend* C863
Hardy, Mrs.: *Early Life of Thomas Hardy* C610
Hardy, Thomas: *Short Stories* C620, *Winter Words* C602
Hare, Martin: *Butler's Gift* C890
Harris, Frank: *Bernard Shaw* C841
Harrison, Frederic: *De Senectute* C245, C250
Harrison, Michael: *Reported Safe Arrival* C1354
Harrod, R.F.: *The Prof* C2042
Harsch, Joseph C.: *Pattern of Conquest* C1295
Hart, Moss: *Act One* C2044
Hartley, L.P.: *Night Fears* C346
Harvey, C.P.: *The Advocate's Devil* C1953
Harwood, H.C.: *Judgement Eve* C328
Haslip, Joan: *Grandfather's Steps* C868
Hawk, John: *Murder of a Mystery Writer* C661
Hayes, Annie: *The Crime at Tattenham Corner* C661
Haynes, E.S.P.: *The Enemies of Liberty* C282
Hazlitt, William: *New Writings* C378